BLOOD
BROTHERHOODS

BLOOD BROTHERHOODS

THE RISE OF THE ITALIAN MAFIAS

JOHN DICKIE

SCEPTRE

7278350

First published in Great Britain in 2011 by Sceptre
An imprint of Hodder & Stoughton
An Hachette UK company

1

Copyright © John Dickie 2011

Maps by Neil Gower

The right of John Dickie to be identified as the Author of the Work has been asserted
by him in accordance with the Copyright, Designs and Patents Act 1988.

A CIP catalogue record for this title is available from the British Library

Hardback ISBN 978 0 340 96392 0
Trade Paperback ISBN 978 0 340 96393 7
eBook ISBN 978 1 444 73430 0

Typeset in Sabon MT by Palimpsest Book Production Ltd, Falkirk, Stirlingshire

Printed and bound by CPI Mackays, Chatham ME5 8TD

Hodder & Stoughton policy is to use papers that are natural, renewable and recyclable products
and made from wood grown in sustainable forests. The logging and manufacturing processes
are expected to conform to the environmental regulations of the country of origin.

Hodder & Stoughton Ltd
338 Euston Road
London NW1 3BH

www.hodder.co.uk

'The blackest despair that can take
hold of any society is the fear
that living honestly is futile.'

Corrado Alvaro

Contents

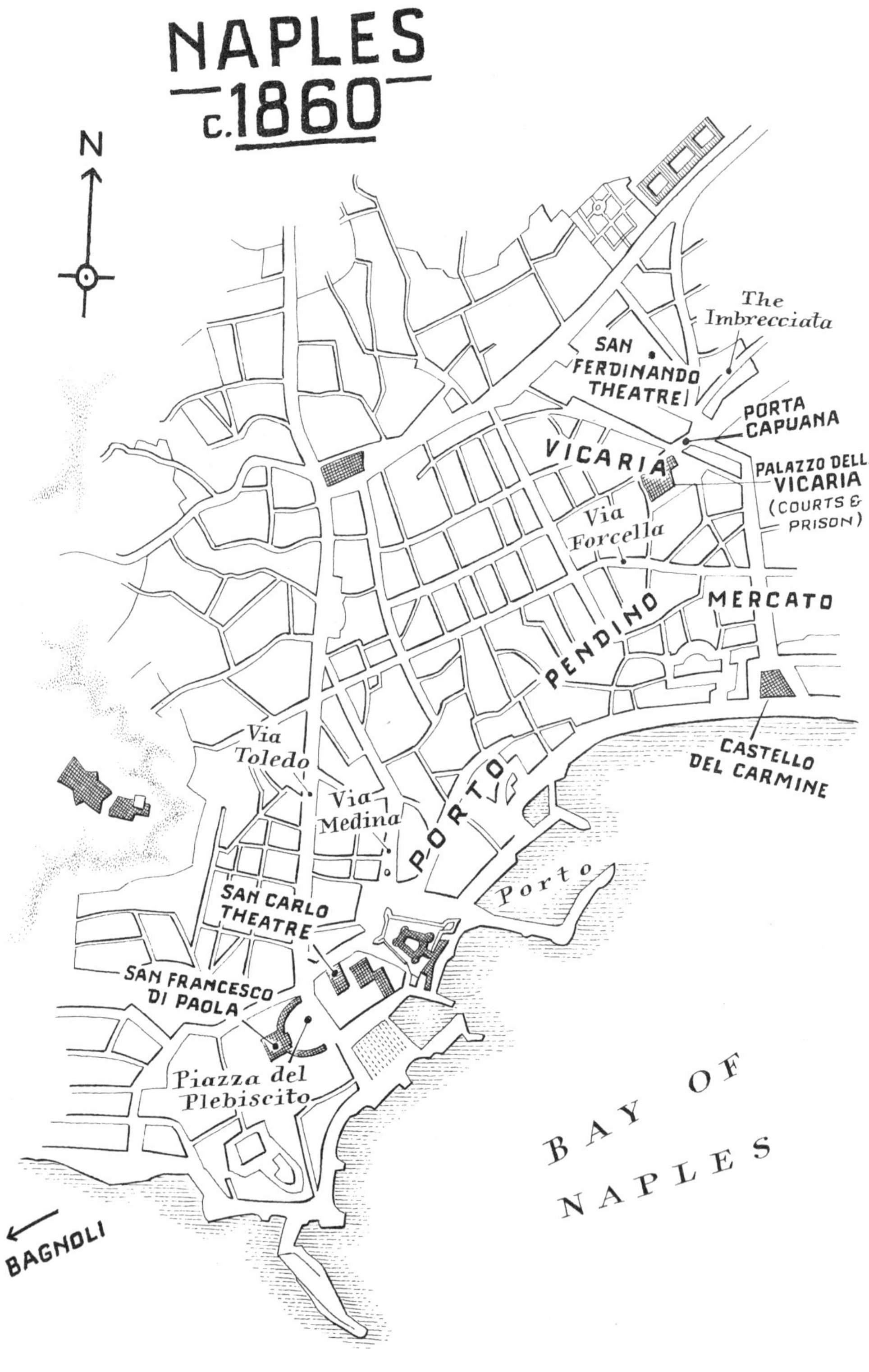

NAPLES
c.1860

N

The Imbrecciata

SAN
FERDINANDO
THEATRE

PORTA
CAPUANA

VICARIA

PALAZZO DELLA
VICARIA
(COURTS &
PRISON)

Via
Forcella

MERCATO

PENDINO

PORTO

CASTELLO
DEL CARMINE

Via
Toledo

Via
Medina

Porto

SAN CARLO
THEATRE

SAN FRANCESCO
DI PAOLA

Piazza del
Plebiscito

BAY OF

NAPLES

BAGNOLI

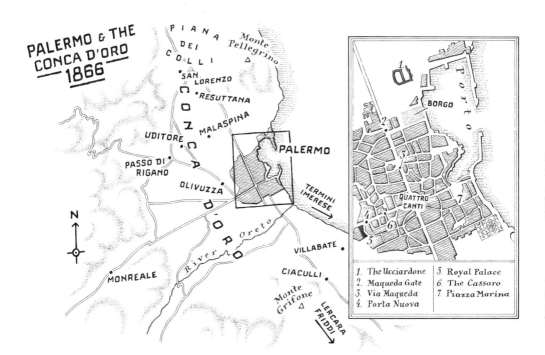

PALERMO & THE
CONCA D'ORO
1866

PIANA
DEI
COLLI

Monte
Pellegrino
△

SAN
LORENZO

RESUTTANA

C
O
N
C
A

MALASPINA

UDITORE

PASSO DI
RIGANO

OLIVUZZA

D'ORO

River   Oreto

MONREALE

N

PALERMO

TERMINI
IMERESE

VILLABATE

CIACULLI

Monte
Grifone
△

LERCARA
FRIDDI

Porto

BORGO

QUATTRO
CANTI

1. The Ucciardone   5. Royal Palace
2. Maqueda Gate   6. The Cassaro
3. Via Maqueda   7. Piazza Marina
4. Porta Nuova

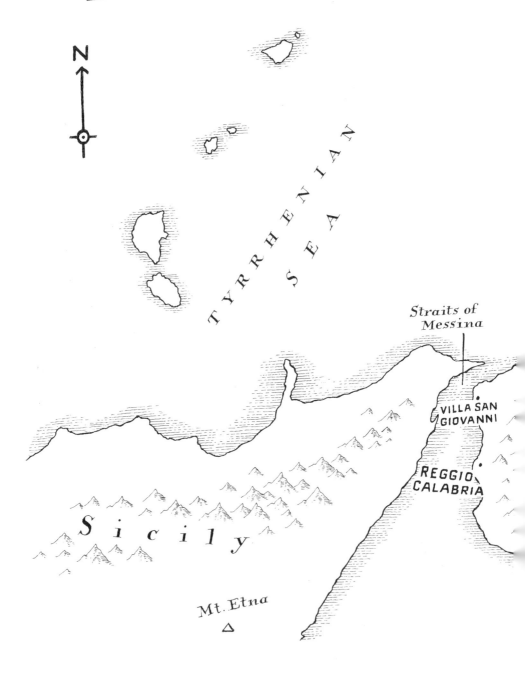

THE 'NDRANGHETA HEARTLANDS

N

TYRRHENIAN SEA

Straits of Messina

VILLA SAN GIOVANNI

REGGIO CALABRIA

Sicily

Mt. Etna

NICASTRO

Miles 0—15

Kilometres 0—25

VIBO VALENTIA

Calabria

NICOTERA

ROSARNO

GIOIA TAURO

POLISTENA

TAURIANOVA *

CITTANOVA

GROTTERIA

PALMI

ANTONIMINA

GERACE

SIDERNO

CIRELLA

LOCRI

PLATI

PORTGLIOLA

SANTO STEFANO

ARDORE

Aspromonte

+

Sanctuary of the Madonna of Polsi

SAN LUCA

BOVALINO

AFRICO

ROCCAFORTE DEL GRECO

ROGHUDI

BOVA

STAITI

IONIAN SEA

*TAURIANOVA CAME INTO BEING IN 1928
WHEN RADICENA AND IATRÌNOLI MERGED

Preface

Once upon a time, three Spanish knights landed on the island of Favignana, just off the westernmost tip of Sicily. They were called Osso, Mastrosso and Carcagnosso and they were fugitives. One of their sisters had been raped by an arrogant nobleman and the three knights had fled Spain after washing the crime in blood.

Somewhere among Favignana's many caves and grottoes, Osso, Mastrosso and Carcagnosso found sanctuary. But they also found a place where they could channel their sense of injustice into creating a new code of conduct, a new form of brotherhood. Over the next twenty-nine years, they dreamed up and refined the rules of the Honoured Society. Then, at last, they took their mission out into the world.

Osso dedicated himself to Saint George, and crossed into nearby Sicily where he founded the branch of the Honoured Society that would become known as the mafia.

Mastrosso chose the Madonna as his sponsor, and sailed to Naples where he founded another branch: the camorra.

Carcagnosso became a devotee of the Archangel Michael, and crossed the straits between Sicily and the Italian mainland to reach Calabria. There, he founded the 'ndrangheta.

Blood Brotherhoods is a history of the origins and early development of Italy's three most feared criminal organisations, or mafias. But no historian can claim to be the first person drawn toward the mystery of how the Sicilian mafia, the Neapolitan camorra and the Calabrian 'ndrangheta began. *Mafiosi* got there first. Each of Italy's major underworld fraternities has its own foundation myth. For example, the story of Osso, Mastrosso and Carcagnosso (names that mean something like 'Bone', 'Masterbone', and 'Heelbone' in English) is the 'ndrangheta's official account of its own birth: it is a tale told to Calabrian recruits when they prepare to join the local clan and embark on a life of murder, extortion and trafficking.

As history, the three Spanish knights have about as much substance as the three bears. Their story is tosh. But it is serious, sacramental tosh all the same. The study of nationalism has given us fair warning: any number of savage iniquities can be committed in the name of fables about the past.

The very fact that the mafias value their own history so highly betrays the outrageous scale of their ambition. Ordinary gangsters, by contrast, have no such pretensions. Over the course of the last 150 years, the criminal brotherhoods have frequently occluded the truth by imposing their own narrative on events: all too often the official version of history turns out to be the mafias' version.

The story of the mafias is filled with many other outrages. The leading bosses in Sicily, Naples and Calabria enjoy wealth, status, and influence. They are also men of nonchalant violence – and have been since the outset. But they are also much, much more than brutal criminals. The real outrage of Italy's mafias is not the countless lives that have been cruelly curtailed – including, very frequently, the lives of the *mafiosi* themselves. Nor is it the livelihoods stunted, the resources wasted, the priceless landscapes defiled. The real outrage is that these murderers constitute a parallel ruling class in southern Italy. They infiltrate the police, the judiciary, local councils, national ministries, and the economy.

They also have a measure of public support. Since Italy was first created in the middle of the 1800s, organised crime has occupied ever more of the territory that the Italian state, in theory, claims as its own. Such outrages demand a historical explanation rooted squarely in the facts.

Writing mafia history is a young field of scholarship: it is a child of the unprecedented mafia savagery of the 1980s and early 1990s, when Italian researchers began to channel their own sense of outrage into patient and rigorous study. Overwhelmingly, those historians, whose numbers have grown steadily, hail from the same regions of southern Italy that are worst afflicted by Italy's permanent crime emergency – regions where mafia history is still being made. Some researchers are lucky enough to hold university positions. Others are magistrates and officers of the law. Some are just ordinary citizens. But all of them are bent on pitting hard evidence and open debate against mafia lies and myth-making, which are a great deal more insidious than the hokum about the Spanish knights might initially suggest. There can be few other branches of history in which the discipline of under-standing the past can make such a direct contribution to building a better future. To defeat the mafias, one has to know what they are; and they are what their history shows us, no more and no less. Thanks to the labours of a number of historians, we can now shine lights into the obscurity of Italian organised crime's early years, revealing a narrative that is both disturbing and disturbingly relevant to the present.

Blood Brotherhoods springs from my belief that the findings of this growing body of research are too important to be kept among specialists. It draws together the known documentation and the best research to create a 'choral' work, as the Italians might say: a book in which many voices tell a single tale. My own voice is one of those in the chorus, in that *Blood Brother-hoods* also incorporates substantial new findings that comple-ment and correct the story that has emerged from the exciting work being done in Italy.

In 2004 I published *Cosa Nostra: A History of the Sicilian Mafia*, in which I brought together the best Italian research on the most notorious of Italy's criminal fraternities. *Blood Brotherhoods* is not a sequel to *Cosa Nostra*: it will stand or fall on its own terms. But readers of *Cosa Nostra* may recognise my retelling of one or two episodes from that earlier book, so they deserve to know before starting why the Sicilian mafia is integral to my concerns here. There are two reasons: first, because even in the last three or four years new discoveries have radically changed our view of key moments in the history of organised crime in Sicily; second, because there is also much to learn about the Sicilian mafia by comparing it with the camorra and the 'ndrangheta. One thing that the comparison teaches us is that the sinister fame enjoyed by Sicilian *mafiosi* is amply deserved.

Sicily gave the world the term 'mafia', and the fact that that term has entered daily use not just in Italy but across the world is itself a symptom of Sicilian organised crime's pervasive influence. In the dialect of Palermo, the island's capital, 'mafia' denoted beauty and self-confidence: 'cool' comes about as close as English can to its original meaning. In the 1860s, just after the troubled island of Sicily became part of the newly united state of Italy, 'mafia' began to serve as a label for an organisation whose shape briefly became visible through a fog of violence and corruption. The mafia (which would soon disappear into the fog once more) had existed for some time by then, and it had already reached a level of power and wealth that delinquents on the mainland could only aspire to. That power and wealth explains why the Sicilian word 'mafia' became an umbrella term for all of Italy's underworld brotherhoods, including the camorra and 'ndrangheta. Over the course of a century or so – the arc of time covered in these pages – we can chart the fortunes of the peninsula's other two mafias against the heights that the Sicilians reached from the outset.

These days the Sicilian mafia is usually known as Cosa Nostra ('our thing'), a moniker that *mafiosi* in both the United States and Sicily adopted in the 1960s. The name 'ndrangheta stuck to the Calabrian mafia in the mid-1950s. (It means 'manliness' or 'courage'.) In both cases, the new names coalesced because post-war public opinion and law enforcement were becoming more searching, bringing into focus a picture that had been blurred by a century of muddle, negligence and downright collusion. So *Blood Brotherhoods*, which concludes with the fall of Fascism and the Allied Liberation of Italy, is a history of underworld regimes that were as yet, if not nameless, then certainly ignored or mysterious, surrounded either by silence (in the case of the 'ndrangheta), or by endless, inconclusive dispute (in the case of the Sicilian mafia).

The camorra has had a different relationship to its name. While structured criminal power has waxed and waned through Neapolitan history, the camorra has always been called the camorra. The Honoured Society of Naples may have been a sworn, occult sect of gangsters, but it had strangely few secrets. *Everyone* in Naples knew all about it. Which is one reason why its history has a dramatically different trajectory to the Honoured Societies of Sicily and Calabria.

Comparative research into the history of the mafias is still very rare. Perhaps that is understandable. In the early days, the criminal fraternities of Sicily, Naples and Calabria differed more than the catch-all tag 'mafia' might lead us to assume. Each evolved to fit the characteristic features of the territory it fed off. Yet studying Italy's underworld organisations in isolation, for all their individual peculiarities, can sometimes seem like trying to figure out the dynamics of natural selection by staring at beetles impaled on pins in a dusty display case. Italy does not have solitary, static criminal organisms; rather it has a rich underworld ecosystem that continues to generate new life forms to this day.

The mafias have never existed in isolation. What they share is just as important as the many things that distinguish them. Throughout their history, all three have communicated and learned from one another. The traces of that common history are visible in a shared language. *Omertà* is one example – or *umiltà* (humility) to give its original form. Across southern Italy and Sicily, *omertà-umiltà* has denoted a code of silence and submission to criminal authority. 'Honour' is another instance: all three associations invoked a code of honour, and called themselves the Honoured Society.

But the links between these Honoured Societies go far beyond words, and are one of the reasons for the mafias' success and longevity. So the virtues of comparison, and of reading the histories of the mafia, the camorra and the 'ndrangheta in parallel, are perhaps the only lessons in historical method that the fable of Osso, Mastrosso and Carcagnosso has to teach us. (The 'ndrangheta's foundation myth does contain one other speck of veracity, as will become clear: Favignana, the island where the fable is set, was once a penal colony and as such, was indeed one of the places where the Honoured Societies were hatched.)

By taking a comparative approach, *Blood Brotherhoods* will offer answers to some insistent questions. How did Italy's secret criminal societies begin? How were they first discovered? Why did they not only survive being discovered, but grow in power? The worst answers to these questions recycle baseless legends that blame Arab invaders in Sicily and Spanish rulers in Naples. Such stories are close to the yarns spun by the Honoured Societies themselves – suspiciously close. Scarcely any better are the answers that evoke abstractions like 'the culture', 'the mentality', or 'the southern Italian family'.

Many university textbooks give responses that sound more sophisticated: they talk about the fragile legitimacy of the state, the citizens' lack of trust in the government institutions, the prevalence of clientelism and patronage in politics and administration, and so on. As a professor of Italian history, I myself have recited phrases like this in the past. So I know only too well that they rarely leave anyone much wiser. Nonetheless there is one crucial nugget of truth underneath all this jargon: the history of organised crime in Italy is as much about Italy's weakness as it is about the mafias' strength. *Omertà* leads us to the heart of the issue: it is often portrayed as being an iron code of silence, a stark choice between collusion and death. In some cases, it certainly is just as harsh a law as its reputation suggests. Yet the historical sources also show that, under the right kind of pressure, *omertà* has broken again and again. That is one reason why so many of the underworld's darkest secrets are still there in the archives for us to unearth. And one reason why mafia history is often more about misinformation and intrigue than it is about violence and death.

The best way to divulge those secrets, to reconstruct those intrigues, and in doing so to provide more satisfying answers to the questions surrounding the mafias' origins, is to begin by simply telling stories. Documented stories that feature real men and women, real choices made in specific times and places, real crimes. The best historians of organised crime in Italy reconstruct those stories from fragmentary archival sources, and from the accounts of people (notably criminals) who often have very good reasons to distort what they say. It is not banal to compare this kind of historical research to detective work. Detectives labour to create a coherent prosecution case by matching the material evidence to what witnesses and suspects tell them. In both tasks – the historian's and the detective's – the truth emerges as much from the gaps and inconsistencies in the available testimonies, as it does from the facts those testimonies contain.

But the question that drives research into Italy's long and fraught relationship to these sinister fraternities is not just who committed which crimes. The question is also who knew what. Over the last century and a half, police, magistrates, politicians, opinion formers and even the general public have had access to a surprising amount of information about the mafia problem, thanks in part to the fragility of *omertà*. Italians have also, repeatedly, been shocked and angered by mafia violence, and by the way some of its police, judiciary and politicians have colluded with crime bosses. As a result, the mafia drama has frequently

been played out very visibly: as high-profile political confrontation, as media event. Yet Italy has also proved positively ingenious
in finding reasons to look the other way. So the story of Italy's
mafias is not just a *whodunit?* It is also a *whoknewit?* and, most
importantly, a *whyonearthdidn'theydosomethingaboutit?*

INTRODUCTION: **Blood brothers**

In the early hours of 15 August 2007, in the German steel town of Duisburg, six young men of Italian origin climbed into a car and a van, a few metres away from the Da Bruno restaurant where they had been celebrating a birthday. One of them was just eighteen (it was his party), and another was only sixteen. Like the rest of the group, these two boys died very quickly, where they sat. Two killers fired fifty-four shots, even taking the time to reload their 9mm pistols and administer a *coup de grâce* to each of the six in turn.

This was the worst ever mafia bloodbath outside Italy and the United States – northern Europe's equivalent to the St Valentine's Day massacre in Chicago in 1929. As the background to the murders emerged – a long-running blood feud in a little known region of southern Italy – journalists across the globe began struggling with what the *New York Times* called an 'unpronounceable name': 'ndrangheta.

For the record, the name is pronounced as follows: *en-drang-get-ah*. The 'ndrangheta hails from Calabria (the 'toe' of the Italian boot), and it is oldest and strongest in the province of Reggio Calabria where the peninsula almost touches Sicily. Calabria is Italy's poorest region, but its mafia has now become the country's richest and most powerful. In the 1990s, *'ndranghetisti* (as Calabrian Men of Honour are called) earned themselves a leading position within the European cocaine market by dealing directly with South American producer cartels. The Calabrians have the strongest regime of *omertà* – of silence and secrecy. Very few informants ever abandon the organisation's ranks and give evidence to the state. In recent years, the Calabrian mafia has also been the most successful of the three major criminal organisations at establishing cells outside of its home territory. It has branches in the centre and north of Italy, and also abroad: the existence of 'ndrangheta colonies has been confirmed in six different German cities, as well as in Switzerland, Canada and Australia. According to a recent report from Italy's Parliamentary Commission of Inquiry into mafia crime, the 'ndrangheta also has a presence in Belgium, Holland, Great Britain, Portugal, Spain, Argentina, Brazil, Chile, Colombia, Morocco, Turkey, Venezuela and the USA. Of all southern Italy's mafias, the 'ndrangheta is the youngest and has come the furthest to find its recent success and notoriety; over the course of time, it has learned more than any other Italian criminal group. My research suggests that it absorbed its most important lessons long before the world was even aware that it existed.

The Duisburg massacre demonstrated with appalling clarity that Italy, and the many parts of the world where there are mafia colonies, still lives with the consequences of the story to be told here. So before delving into the past it is essential to introduce its protagonists in the present, to sketch three profiles that show succinctly what mafia history is a history *of*. Because, even after Duisburg, the world is still getting used to the idea that Italy has more than one mafia. There is only a hazy public understanding of how the camorra and the 'ndrangheta, in particular, are organised.

Blood seeps through the pages of mafia history. In all its many meanings, blood can also serve to introduce the obscure world of Italian organised crime today. Blood is perhaps humanity's oldest and most elemental symbol, and *mafiosi* still exploit its every facet. Blood as violence. Blood as both birth and death. Blood as a sign of manhood and courage. Blood as kinship and family. Each of the three mafias belongs to its own category – its own blood group, as it were – that is distinct but related to the other two in both its rituals and its organisation.

Rituals first: by taking blood oaths, becoming blood brothers, Italian gangsters establish a bond between themselves, a bond forged in and for violence that is loosened only when life ends. That bond is almost always exclusively between men. Yet the act of marriage – symbolised by the shedding of virginal blood – is also a key ritual in mafia life. For that reason, one of the many recurring themes in this book will be women, and how *mafiosi* have learned to manage them.

And then organisation: each of the mafias has evolved its own structure. The primary aim of structure is to impose discipline, because discipline can be a huge competitive advantage in the turmoil of the underworld. But structure also serves other purposes, notably that of exploiting the loyalties within blood-lines, within families.

One thing that the 'ndrangheta in particular has understood from the beginning of its history is the magic of ritual. And ritual often comes into play at the beginning of an *'ndranghet-ista*'s life, as we know from one of the very few autobiographies written by a member of the Calabria mafia (a multiple murderer) who has turned state's evidence (after developing a phobia about blood so acute that he could not even face a rare steak).

Antonio Zagari's career in organised crime started two minutes into January 1, 1954. It began, that is, the very moment he issued from his mother's womb. He was a firstborn son, so his arrival was greeted with particular joy: his father Giacomo grabbed a wartime heavy machine gun and pumped a stream of bullets toward the stars over the gulf of Gioia Tauro. The barrage just gave the midwife time to dab the blood from the baby's tiny body, before he was taken by his father and presented to the members of the clan who were assembled in the house. The baby was gently laid down before them, and a knife and a large key were set near his feebly flailing arms. His destiny would be decided by which he touched first. If it were the key, symbol of confinement, he would become a *sbirro* – a cop, a slave of the law. But if it were the knife, he would live and die by the code of honour.

It was the knife, much to everyone's approval. (Although, truth be told, a helpful adult finger had nudged the blade under the tiny hand.)

Delighted by his son's bold career choice, Giacomo Zagari hoisted the baby in the air, parted his tiny buttocks, and spat noisily on his arsehole for luck. He would be christened Antonio. The name came from his grandfather, a brutal criminal who looked approvingly on at the scene from above a walrus moustache turned a graveolent yellow by the cigar that jutted permanently from between his teeth. Baby Antonio was now 'half in and half out', as the men of the Honoured Society termed it. He was not yet a full member – he would have to be trained, tested and observed before that happened. But his path towards a more than usually gruesome life of crime had been marked out.

Zagari grew up not in Calabria, but near Varese by Italy's border with Switzerland, where his father led the local 'ndrangheta cell. As a youth, during his father's occasional jail stints, Antonio was sent back south to work with his uncles who were citrus fruit dealers in the rich agricultural plain of Gioia Tauro on Calabria's Tyrrhenian Sea coast. He came to admire his father's relatives and friends for the respect they commanded locally, and even for the delicacy of their speech. Before uttering a vaguely vulgar word like 'feet', 'toilet', or 'underpants', they would crave forgiveness: 'Speaking with all due respect . . .' 'Excuse the phrase . . .' And when they had no alternative but to utter genuine profanities such as 'policeman', 'magistrate', or 'courtroom', their sentences would topple over themselves with pre-emptive apologies.

> I have to say that – for the sake of preserving all those present, and the fine and honoured faces of all our good friends, speaking with all due respect, and excusing the phrase – when the *Carabinieri* [military police] . . .

As the son of a boss, Antonio Zagari's criminal apprenticeship was a short one. He took a few secret messages into prison, hid

4

DELLA SOCIETA? PERCHE ERA PIU GROSSO
E MALANDRINO D'EGLIALTRI?
R. NO NON ERA NE PIU GROSSO NE PIU
MALANDRINO POICHE IN QUEL MOMENTO
AVEVA DUE CARICHE SPECIALI E INVIOLABILI
CHE ERA STATA ACLETTA DI TUTTI NOI
CAMORRISTI COME A UN PADRE IN UNA FAMIGLIA
D. DOVE VI ANNO BATTEZZATO?
R. SOPRA A UN MONTE DOVE VI E RA UN
GIARDINO DI ROSE E FIORE E CERANO
I NOSTRI 3 FRATELLI E CAVALIERI
SPAGNOLI OSSO MASTROSSO E SCARCAGNOSSO
CONVENZIONATI PER LA MIA CONSACRAZIONE.
D. COME SONO VESTITI I CAMORRISTI
A SOCIETA FORMATA?
R. I CAMORRISTI A SOCIETA FORMATA
DEVONO ESSERE VESTITI DI VERDE DI
ROSSO E DI BIACO.
D. PERCHE DEVONO ESSERE VESTITI DI VERDE
DI ROSSO E DI BIANCO?
R. PERCHE RAPPRESENTONO IL SIMBOLO
DELLA SOCIETA.

The 'social rules'. One of many pages of instructions for 'ndrangheta initiation rituals that were found in June 1987 in the hideout of Giuseppe Chilà. Osso, Mastrosso and Carcagnosso, the three Spanish knights who (according to criminal legend) were the founders of the mafia, camorra and 'ndrangheta, are mentioned.

a few weapons, and soon, at age seventeen, he was ready to make the passage into full membership.

One day his 'friends', as he termed them, copied out a few pages of the *Rules and Social Prescriptions* he was required to learn by heart before being inducted. It was all, he later recalled, like the catechism children have to memorise before Confirmation and First Communion.

The 'catechism' also included lessons in 'ndrangheta history. And having committed the deeds of Osso, Mastrosso and Carcagnosso to memory, Zagari was deemed ready to undergo the most elaborate initiation rite used by any mafia. He was shown into an isolated, darkened room and introduced to the senior members present, who were all arrayed in a circle. For the time being, he had to remain silent, excluded from the group.

> 'Are you comfortable my dear comrades?', the boss began.
> *'Very comfortable. On what?'*
> 'On the social rules.'
> *'Very comfortable.'*
> 'Then, in the name of the organised and faithful society, I baptise this place as our ancestors Osso, Mastrosso and Carcagnosso baptised it, who baptised it with iron and chains.

The boss then passed round the room, relieving each *'ndranghetista* of the tools of his trade, and pronouncing the same formula at each stop.

> In the name of our most severe Saint Michael the Archangel, who carried a set of scales in one hand and a sword in the other, I confiscate your weaponry.

The scene was now set, and the Chief Cudgel could intone his preamble to the ceremony proper.

The society is a ball that goes wandering around the world, as cold as ice, as hot as fire, and as fine as silk. Let us swear, handsome comrades, that anyone who betrays the society will pay with five or six dagger thrusts to the chest, as the social rules prescribe. Silver chalice, consecrated host, with words of humility I form the society.

Another 'thank you' was sounded, as the *'ndranghetisti* moved closer together and linked arms.

Three times the boss then asked his comrades whether Zagari was ready for acceptance into the Honoured Society. When he had received the same affirmative reply three times, the circle opened, and a space was made for the newcomer immediately to the boss's right. The boss then took a knife, and cut a cross into the initiate's left thumb so that blood from the wound could drip onto a playing card sized picture of the Archangel Michael. The boss then ripped off the Archangel's head and burned the rest in a candle flame, symbolising the utter annihilation of all traitors.

Only then could Zagari open his mouth to take the 'ndrangheta oath.

I swear before the organised and faithful society, represented by our honoured and wise boss and by all the members, to carry out all the duties for which I am responsible and all those that are imposed on me – if necessary even with my blood.

The boss then kissed the new member on both cheeks and set out for him the rules of honour. There followed another surreal incantation to wind the ceremony up.

Oh, beautiful humility! You who have covered me in roses and flowers and carried me to the island of Favignana, there to teach me the first steps. Italy, Germany and Sicily once waged a great war. Much blood was shed for the

> honour of the society. And this blood, gathered in a ball,
> goes wandering round the world, as cold as ice, as hot
> as fire, and as fine as silk.

The *'ndranghetisti* could at last take up arms again – in the name
of Osso, Mastrosso, Carcagnosso, and the Archangel Michael
– and resume their day-to-day criminal activity.

These solemn ravings make the 'ndrangheta seem like a version
of the Scouts invented by the boys from *The Lord of the Flies*
based on a passing encounter with *Monty Python and the Holy
Grail*. It would all verge on the comic if the result were not so
much death and misery. Yet there is no incompatibility between
the creepy fantasy world of 'ndrangheta ritual, and the brutal
reality of killings and cocaine deals.

Initiation rituals are even more important to the 'ndrangheta
than the story of Osso, Mastrosso and Carcagnosso that helps
give it an ancient and noble aura. At whatever stage in life they
are performed, mafia rites of affiliation are a *baptism*, to use
Antonio Zagari's word. Like a baptism, such ceremonies dramatise a change in identity; they draw a line in blood between one
state of being and another. No wonder, then, that because of
the rituals they undergo, *'ndranghetisti* consider themselves a
breed apart. A Calabrian *mafioso*'s initiation is a special day
indeed.

15 August 2007, in Duisburg, was one such special day. The
morning after the massacre, German police searched the victims'
mutilated corpses for clues. They found a partly burned image
of the Archangel Michael in the pocket of the eighteen-year-old
boy who had just been celebrating his birthday.

The mafia of Sicily, now known as Cosa Nostra, also has its
myths and ceremonies. For example, many *mafiosi* hold (or at
least held until recently) the deluded belief that their organisation
began as a medieval brotherhood of caped avengers called the
Beati Paoli. The Sicilian mafia uses an initiation ritual that deploys
the symbolism of blood in a similar but simpler fashion to the

'ndrangheta. The same darkened room. The same assembly of members, who typically sit round a table with a gun and a knife at its centre. The aspirant's 'godfather' explains the rules to him, and then pricks his trigger finger and sheds a little of his blood on a holy image – usually the Madonna of the Annunciation. The image is burned in the neophyte's hands as the oath is taken: 'If I betray Cosa Nostra, may my flesh burn like this holy woman.' Blood once shed can never be restored. Matter once burned can never be repaired. When one enters the Sicilian mafia, one enters for life.

As well as being a vital part of the internal life of the Calabrian and Sicilian mafias, initiation rites are very important historical evidence. The earliest references to the 'ndrangheta ritual date from the late nineteenth century. The Sicilian mafia's version is older: the first documentary evidence emerged in 1876. The rituals surface from the documentation again and again thereafter, leaving bloody fingerprints through history, exposing Italian organised crime's DNA. They also tell us very clearly what happened to that evidence once it came into the hands of the Italian authorities: it was repeatedly ignored, undervalued and suppressed.

Rituals are evidence of historical change, too. The oldest admission ceremony of all belonged to the Neapolitan camorra. Once upon a time, the camorra also signalled a young member's new status with the shedding of blood. In the 1850s, a recruit usually took an oath over crossed knives, and then had to have a dagger fight, either with a *camorrista* or with another aspiring member. Often the blade would be wrapped tightly in rags or string, leaving only the point exposed: too much blood, and the duel might stop being a symbolic exercise in male bonding, and start being a battle. When the first hit was registered, the fight was declared over, and the new affiliate received both the embraces of the other *camorristi*, and the most junior rank in the Honoured Society's organisational hierarchy.

Today's camorra bosses do not put their recruits through

formal initiation ceremonies or oaths. The traditions have disappeared. The Neapolitan camorra is no longer a sworn sect, an Honoured Society. In fact, as we shall see later, the Honoured Society of Naples died out in 1912 in bizarre and utterly Neapolitan circumstances.

The camorra that has emerged since 1912 is not a single association. Instead it is a vast pullulating world of gangs. They form, split, descend into vicious feuds, and re-emerge in new alliances only to then be annihilated in some new internecine war or police roundup. The Neapolitan underworld is frighteningly unstable. Whereas a Sicilian *capo* has a decent chance of seeing his grandchildren set out on their criminal careers, a senior *camorrista* is lucky if he lives to forty.

The camorra's lack of formal structure and ritual has not stopped its most successful clans from controlling vast swathes of Campanian territory, from turning entire city blocks into fortified police no-go zones and drug hypermarkets, from making millions from the trade in bootleg DVDs and designer handbags. It has not stopped them devastating the landscape of Campania with their lucrative trade in fly-tipped waste. Or from infiltrating the national construction industry and dealing internationally in narcotics and weapons.

Camorra clans are nonetheless organised: together they form 'the System', as those on the inside call it. At the centre of the System in each area of the city and its hinterland is a charismatic boss: protector and punisher. Below him there are ranks, and specialised roles — like zone chiefs, assassins, drug wholesalers — who are all chosen and nominated by the boss, and who will almost invariably live and die with him. Like the other mafias, the camorra clans redistribute some of the profits of their crimes, often pay wages to their troops, and set aside funds for those in prison.

Blood, in the sense of kinship, is now the glue that holds the most fearsome camorra clans together. But the individual clans tend not to be led by a Grand Old Man. The core of any camorra group is usually a cluster of relatives – brothers, cousins, in-laws – all roughly the same age. Around them there are friends, neighbours, and more relatives.

So, Neapolitan organised crime has seen a great deal of change since the days when the camorra was an Honoured Society. Yet the veins of tradition have never been entirely severed. For one thing, *camorristi* have an enduring weakness for gangster bling. Gold accessories and expensive shirts have been in evidence since the nineteenth century. Now there are also showy cars and motorbikes. The Neapolitan boss's bike of choice was until recently the Honda Dominator. The point of all this conspicuous consumption, then and now, is to advertise power: to proclaim territorial dominion, and to be a walking symbol of success to hangers-on.

Cosa Nostra's bosses are generally dowdy compared to the camorra chiefs of Naples, and they spend much more of their time on the kind of organisational formalities that can have a lethal significance in their world.

Each boss (or, strictly speaking, 'representative') of the Sicilian mafia presides over a cell known as a Family. By no means everyone in a Family is related. Indeed, Cosa Nostra often invokes a rule designed to prevent clusters of relatives from becoming too influential within a Family: no more than two brothers may become members at any one time, so that the boss can't pack the clan with his own kin.

The structure of each Family is simple. The representative is flanked by an underboss and a *consigliere* or adviser. The ordinary members, known as soldiers, are organised into groups of ten. Each of these groups reports to a *capodecina* – a 'boss of ten' – who in turn reports to the boss.

Above its base in the Families, Cosa Nostra is shaped like a pyramid. Three mafia Families in adjoining territories form another tier of the organisation's structure, the *mandamento* (precinct), presided over by a *capomandamento* (precinct boss). This precinct boss has a seat on the Commission, which combines

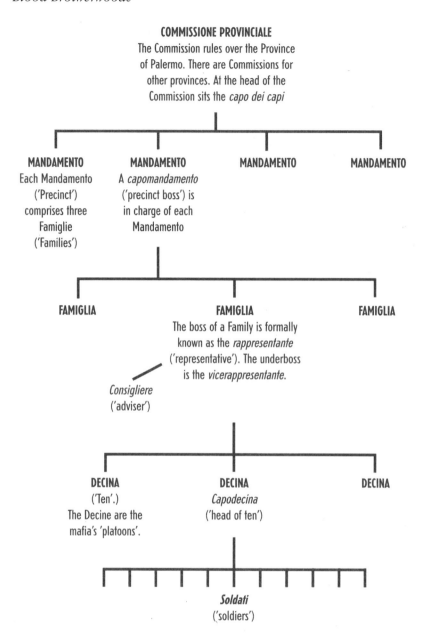

COMMISSIONE PROVINCIALE
The Commission rules over the Province of Palermo. There are Commissions for other provinces. At the head of the Commission sits the *capo dei capi*

MANDAMENTO
Each Mandamento ('Precinct') comprises three Famiglie ('Families')

MANDAMENTO
A *capomandamento* ('precinct boss') is in charge of each Mandamento

MANDAMENTO

MANDAMENTO

FAMIGLIA

FAMIGLIA
The boss of a Family is formally known as the *rappresentante* ('representative'). The underboss is the *vicerappresentante*.

FAMIGLIA

Consigliere ('adviser')

DECINA
('Ten'.)
The Decine are the mafia's 'platoons'.

DECINA
Capodecina ('head of ten')

DECINA

Soldati ('soldiers')

THE STRUCTURE OF COSA NOSTRA
As first described by Tommaso Buscetta in 1984

the functions of a parliament, a high court, and a chamber of commerce for Cosa Nostra in each of Sicily's four most mafia-infested provinces. Presiding over them all, at the very apex of the mafia pyramid, there is a *capo di tutti i capi* – the 'boss of all bosses'. The *capo di tutti i capi* is invariably from the province of Palermo, the island's capital, because about half of Cosa Nostra's manpower, and about half of its Families, are based in the Palermo area.

So much for the diagram. But in the underworld, more even than in the upper world inhabited by law-abiding citizens, power is invested in people, and not in the nameplates on office doors. Comparisons between a mafia boss and the managing director of a capitalist enterprise are not only trite, they completely fail to capture the acutely cagey and political world in which *mafiosi* operate.

Cosa Nostra has gone through phases of greater and lesser coordination; different bosses have had different styles of leadership, and have had all manner of external limits placed on their power. Confusion, double-dealing, mutual suspicion, and civil war have been constants in the mafia from the get-go. The cast of character-types is vast. There are certainly party leaders, policy-makers, reformers and legislative tinkerers. But also a good many rebels, grey eminences, impatient tycoons, young Turks, and isolationists. And of course *everyone* in the mafia is also both a conspirator, and a near-paranoid conspiracy theorist. All of these characters may choose to twist the mafia's precedents, traditions and rules; they may even trample and deride them. But no boss, however powerful, can do so without calculating the political price.

One of the big issues in the history of the Sicilian mafia is just how old the organisation's pyramidal structure is. Some of the most disquieting recent research has shown that it is a lot older than we thought until only a couple of years ago. The mafia would not be the mafia without its inborn drive to formalise and coordinate its activities. As I write, to the best of our knowledge, the Palermo Commission of Cosa Nostra has not met since 1993, a fact that is symptomatic of the worst crisis in the organisation's century and a half of history. Quite whether today's crisis turns into a terminal decline depends, in part, on how well Italy absorbs the lessons of the mafia's history, lessons that spell out the Sicilian mafia's astonishing power to regenerate itself.

In Calabria, just as in Sicily, there is a fraught relationship between the gangland rulebook and the expediency determined by the sheer chaos of criminal life.

When I began writing this book, there was a consensus in both the law courts and the criminology textbooks that the 'ndrangheta's structure was very different to Cosa Nostra's. The 'ndrangheta is a *federal* organisation, it was said, a loose fellowship of local gangs.

Then in July 2010 the police and *Carabinieri* arrested more than three hundred men, including the eighty-year-old Domenico Oppedisano, who investigators claim, was elected to the 'ndrangheta's highest office in August 2009. Since their arrest, Oppedisano and most of his fellows have availed themselves of the right to remain silent. So we cannot know what defence they will mount against the charges. Nor can we know whether the courts will decide that those charges have substance. Operation Crime, as the investigation is called, is at its very early stages. Yet whatever its final result, it constitutes a lesson in humility for anyone trying to write about the secret world of Italian gangsterism. At any moment, historical certainties can be overturned by new police-work, or by discoveries in the many unexplored archives.

The magistrates directing Operation Crime allege that Oppedisano's official title is *capocrimine*, or 'chief of the crime'. The 'Crime' or 'Great Crime', which *'ndranghetisti* also refer to as the 'Province', is thought to be the 'ndrangheta's supreme coordinating body. It is sub-divided into three *mandamenti*, or precincts, covering the three zones of the province of Reggio Calabria.

22

Many newspapers in Italy and abroad that covered Operation Crime portrayed the Great Crime as the 'ndrangheta version of the Sicilian mafia Commission, and Domenico Oppedisano as a Calabrian *capo di tutti i capi*: the peak of the 'ndrangheta pyramid, as it were. But that image does not correspond to what the magistrates are claiming. Instead they paint a picture of Oppedisano as a master of ceremonies, the speaker of an assembly, a wise old judge whose job is to interpret the rules. The head of crime's responsibilities relate to procedure and politics, not to business.

But then procedure and politics can easily have fatal consequences in Italian gangland. The Great Crime has real power: it may be based in the province of Reggio Calabria, but *'ndranghetisti* across the world are answerable to it, according to the investigating magistrates. In the spring of 2008, the boss, or 'general master', of the 'ndrangheta's colonies in the Lombardy region (the northern heart of the Italian economy) decided to declare independence from the Great Crime. In July of that year, the police bugged a conversation in which one senior boss reported to his men that the Great Crime had decided to 'sack' the insubordinate general master. A few days later the sacking took effect, when two men in motorbike jackets shot the Lombardy boss four times just as he was getting up from his usual table at a bar in a small town near Milan. Shortly afterwards, the *Carabinieri* secretly filmed a meeting at which the Lombardy chiefs raised their hands in unanimous approval of their new general master; needless to say, he was the Great Crime's nominee.

It seems that the textbooks on the 'ndrangheta may have to be rewritten. And historians will have to take up a new prompt for research. My own findings suggest that the links – procedural, political *and* business links – between the 'ndrangheta's local cells have been there right from the beginning.

Despite all the new information about the Great Crime, much of what we knew about the lower reaches of the 'ndrangheta's

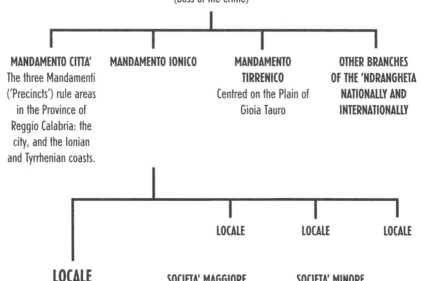

LA PROVINCIA / IL CRIMINE
The Province (aka Crime or Great Crime) is a supervisory body headed by the *capocrimine* (boss of the crime)

MANDAMENTO CITTA'
The three Mandamenti ('Precincts') rule areas in the Province of Reggio Calabria: the city, and the Ionian and Tyrrhenian coasts.

MANDAMENTO IONICO

MANDAMENTO TIRRENICO
Centred on the Plain of Gioia Tauro

OTHER BRANCHES OF THE 'NDRANGHETA NATIONALLY AND INTERNATIONALLY

LOCALE   **LOCALE**   **LOCALE**

LOCALE
The 'Locals' into which each Mandamento is divided govern territory. For reasons of secrecy, each Locale is sub-divided into two compartments:

SOCIETA' MAGGIORE
The 'Major Society' is run by officers such as:
Capolocale (boss of the local)
Contabile (bookkeeper)
Capocrimine (head of crime)

SOCIETA' MINORE
The 'Minor Society', the more junior compartment of the Locale, also has its officers.

'NDRINA

'NDRINA
The 'ndrine are the cells of the 'ndrangheta organization. They are based around families, and dominated by a patriarch.

THE STRUCTURE OF THE 'NDRANGHETA

(Source: 'Operazione Crimine', summer 2010.)

DOTI The 'gifts' (i.e. ranks) that mark the status of an *'ndranghetista*. They are also known as FIORI ('flowers').	*Padrino* ('godfather')	Members of the 'ndrangheta have to attain these 'flowers' to be eligible for the most senior positions.
	Quartino	
	Trequartino	
	Vangelista ('gospelist')	*'Ndranghetisti* have to reach these doti to become officials in the Major Society
	Santista ('saintist')	
	Camorrista di sgarro ('*camorrista* who is up for a fight', a.k.a. *sgarrista*)	*'Ndranghetisti* with these ranks belong to the Minor Society
	Camorrista	
	Picciotto ('lad')	
	Giovane d'onore ('honoured youth')	*Giovani d'onore* are being prepared to enter the organisation.

structure remains valid. The 'ndrangheta of today is built around family, in that a kinship group forms the backbone of each unit, or *'ndrina*. (The term *'ndrina* may well originate from the word *malandrina*, which used to refer to the special cell in prison reserved for gangsters.) The boss of an *'ndrina*, often called a *capobastone* ('chief cudgel'), is typically a father with a good number of male children. Unlike his peers in Cosa Nostra, the chief cudgel can bring as many boys into the 'ndrangheta as he is able to sire. Clustered around the boss and his kin are other families, often bound in by blood and/or marriage. Accordingly, each *'ndrina* takes its name from the surname(s) of its leading dynasty or dynasties, such as the Pelle-Vottari and the Strangio-Nirta – respectively the victims and perpetrators of the massacre in Duisburg.

One or more *'ndrine* report up to a *locale* or 'Local', whose boss is known as the *capolocale*, and who is assisted by two other senior officers. The *contabile* ('bookkeeper') handles the gang's common fund, or what *'ndranghetisti* rather quaintly call the *valigetta* ('valise'). The *capo crimine* ('head of crime') is in charge of surveillance and day-to-day criminal activity. When the time comes, the head of crime also acts as the clan's Minister of War. For extra security the Local is divided into two compartments, insulated from one another: the lower ranking *'ndranghetisti* are grouped in the Minor Society, and the higher ones in the Major Society.

So far, so (relatively) straightforward. But at this point the 'ndrangheta's peculiar fondness for arcane rules and procedures takes over again. In Cosa Nostra, holding office is the only official measure of a Man of Honour's status. In the 'ndrangheta, if a member is to hold one of the official positions of power in a Local, a Precinct or in the Great Crime, then he has to have reached a certain degree of seniority. Seniority is measured in *doti*, meaning 'qualities' or 'gifts', which are the ranks in the organisation's membership hierarchy. Sometimes, more poetically, the ranks are called *fiori* – 'flowers'. The offices in the Local are temporary appointments, whereas the flowers are permanent marks of status. As he steals, extorts and kills, an *'ndranghetista* wins new flowers. Every new flower means yet another protracted induction ceremony, and after it a greater share of power and secrets. The young initiate starts at the bottom as a *picciotto d'onore* ('honoured lad') and ascends through a series of other flowers like *camorrista* and *camorrista di sgarro* (which means something like 'camorrist who is up for a fight') and then on to the more senior flowers, such as *santista*, *vangelista* and *padrino* (or saintist, gospelist, and godfather).

As if this were not complicated enough, *'ndranghetisti* disagree about how many flowers there are, and what rights and responsibilities they bring with them. There also seems to have been floral inflation in recent years: inventing new badges of status is a cheap way to resolve disputes. For instance *gospelist* (so called because the initiation ritual for this flower involves swearing on a bible) seems to have been created recently.

None of this is harmless etiquette. The rituals and organisational structures are a liturgical apparatus that is intended to turn young men into professional delinquents, and transform a mere life of crime into a calling in savagery. A calling that, despite the antique origins its members boast, is only a century and a half old. Only as old, that is, as Italy itself.

VIVA LA PATRIA! THE CAMORRA,

1851–61

How to extract gold from fleas

Sigismondo Castromediano, Duke of Morciano, Marquis of Caballino, lord of seven baronies, sat on the ground with his right calf resting on an anvil. Rangy and blue-eyed, he seemed like an entirely distinct order of being from the Neapolitan jailers who stood before him under a lean-to roof, toying with their ironmongery. Next to the Duke, his fellow patriot Nicola Schiavoni sat in the same undignified position, with the same look of dread on his face.

One of the jailers grabbed the Duke's foot and slipped a stirrup-shaped metal shackle over it. He then enclosed the ankle entirely by pushing a rivet through the small holes at each end of the shackle; sandwiched between them was the last link of a heavy chain. Laughing and singing, the jailer smashed the rivet flat with blows that could have splintered bones.

The Duke flinched repeatedly, and was assailed by the jailers' mocking cheers: 'Give 'em some more! They're enemies of the king. They wanted to get their hands on our women and our property.'

Ordered to stand, Castromediano and Schiavoni lifted their fetters for the first time: some ten kilos of chain in three and a half metres of oblong links. For both of them, this moment marked the beginning of a prison sentence of thirty years in irons for conspiring against the government of the Kingdom of Naples, one of the many states into which the Italian peninsula was divided. The two prisoners embraced before mustering a show of their undaunted belief in the sacred cause of Italy: 'we kissed those chains tenderly', the Duke wrote, 'as if they were our brides'.

The guards were briefly taken aback. But they soon got on with the rituals that marked admission to the Castello del Carmine, one of the worst prisons in the Kingdom of Naples. Civilian clothes were replaced by uniforms comprising brown breeches and a red tunic, both in the same rough wool. Heads were scraped bald and bloody with a sickle-shaped razor. Into each pair of hands were thrust a rag-stuffed palliasse, a donkey-hair blanket, and a bowl.

It was sunset by the time the Duke and his companion were led across the prison yard and shoved through the door of the dungeon.

What they saw inside, Castromediano recalled, was a sight fit to 'annihilate the most generous soul, the most steadfast heart'. It could have been a sewer: a long room with a low ceiling, its floor set with sharp stones, its tiny windows high and heavily barred, its air sick and clammy. A stench like rotting meat emanated from the filth smeared everywhere, and from the figures of misery skulking in the half-light.

As the new arrivals were nervously looking for a place to lay their mattresses, another shackled pair approached from among the crowd. One was tall and handsome, with a swagger in his walk. He was dressed in black plush trousers, with polished buttons at the haunches, and a brightly coloured belt; his matching waistcoat displayed a watch and chain. With elaborate civility, he addressed the two patriots.

> Well, well, gentlemen! Fortune has smiled on you. All of us here have been waiting to honour you. Long live Italy! Long live Liberty! We *camorristi*, who share your sad and honourable fate, hereby exempt you from any camorra obligation . . . Gentlemen, take heart! I swear by God that no one in this place will touch a hair on your head. I am the boss of the camorra here, and so I'm the only one in charge. Absolutely everyone is at my beck and call, including the commander and his jailers.

Within an hour the new prisoners learned two stark lessons: that the camorra boss had made no hollow boasts about his power; and that his promise to exempt them from any 'camorra obligation' was utterly worthless. The *camorrista* did get them back their purses, which had been confiscated on arrival at the prison. But that courtesy was a self-interested one: it meant that he could cajole the bewildered Duke into paying an exorbitant sum for revolting food.

That first exaction was crushing. Castromediano visualised his future as an endless ordeal by protection racket, and found himself contemplating suicide.

The Duke of Castromediano was clapped in irons on 4 June, 1851. The scene is true but also irresistibly metaphorical for it was in prison, in the mid-1800s, that Italy was first chained to the hoodlums that have hampered its every step, ever since.

The camorra was born in prison. By the time the Duke of Castromediano entered the Castello del Carmine, gang rule behind bars had been a fact of life in southern Italy for centuries. Under the *ancien régime* it was easier and cheaper to devolve day-to-day control of the prisons to the toughest inmates. Then in the 1800s the prison extortionists turned themselves into a sworn secret society and gained a foothold in the world beyond the dungeons. The story of how that happened is thick with intrigue, but in essence it involves picking out every nuance and irony in the opening encounter between Duke Castromediano and the *camorrista*. For now, that story can be summarised in one word: Italy.

In 1851, what we now call Italy was still only a 'geographical expression' rather than a state; it was divided between one foreign power (Austria), two Dukedoms, a Grand Dukedom, two Kingdoms, and one Papal State. The biggest of those territories was also the southernmost: the Kingdom of Naples, or the Kingdom of the Two Sicilies, to use its official name.

From the Kingdom's capital, Naples, a King born of the Bourbon dynasty reigned over the southern Italian mainland and the island of Sicily. Like most princes in Italy, the Bourbons of Naples were haunted by the memory of what had happened to them in the years following the French Revolution of 1789. In 1805 Napoleon deposed the Bourbons and put his own nominees on the throne. French rule brought a whole series of innovations in the way the Kingdom was run. Out went feudalism, and in came private property. Out went a messy assemblage of local customs, baronial and church jurisdictions, and public ordinances: in came a new code of civil law and the beginnings of a police force. The southern part of the Italian peninsula began to resemble a modern, centralised state.

In 1815 Napoleon was finally vanquished. When the Bourbons returned to power, they caught on to the big advantages that the French-style reforms could have for securing their own authority. But the theory and the practice of modern administration were hard to reconcile. The throne of the Kingdom of the Two Sicilies was still shaky. There was widespread opposition to the new, more centralised system. Moreover, the French Revolution had not only introduced continental Europe to new ways of administering a state, it had also spread volatile ideas about constitutional government, the nation, and even democracy.

Duke Castromediano was one of a generation of young men who dedicated themselves to building an Italian *Patria*, a Fatherland that would embody the values of constitutional government, liberty, and the rule of law. After trying and failing to turn those values into a political reality during the revolts of 1848–49, many patriots like Castromediano paid for their beliefs by being hurled into the dungeon realm of the *camorristi*.

Such treatment of political prisoners, of *gentlemen* prisoners, soon became a scandal. In 1850 a highly strung Member of the British Parliament, William Ewart Gladstone – the future Grand Old Man – began a long sojourn in Naples for the sake of his daughter's health. Gladstone was drawn into local issues by the plight of men like Castromediano. Early in 1851 the authorities in Naples unwisely allowed Gladstone to visit some of the city's jails. He was horrified by the 'beastly filth' he witnessed. Here political detainees and common criminals of the worst kind mingled indiscriminately, and without any kind of supervision. The prisoners ran the place themselves.

> They are a self-governed community, the main authority being that of the *gamorristi*, the men of most celebrity among them for audacious crime.

Gladstone's unfamiliar spelling did not change the truth of what he wrote. Or indeed the polemical force of his argument: no sooner had he emerged from the Neapolitan prisons than he unleashed two open letters condemning the rule of the Bourbon King as 'the negation of God, erected into a system of Government'. *Camorristi* were now a diplomatic stick with which to beat the Bourbons. Any government that farmed out the management of its prisons to violent thugs surely did not deserve to stand. Courtesy of Gladstone, Italy's organised criminal gangs became what they have never ceased to be since: a detonator of political controversy.

The international sympathy aroused by the jailed patriot martyrs came to play an important role in the almost miraculous sequence of events that finally turned Italy into a *Patria*, or something like it. In 1858 the Prime Minister of the northern Italian Kingdom of Piedmont-Sardinia struck a secret deal with France to drive Austria out of northern Italy by force. The following year, after appalling bloodshed at the battles of Magenta and Solferino, Piedmont-Sardinia absorbed the former Austrian domain of Lombardy. Piedmont's military success triggered uprisings further south, in the various central Dukedoms, as well as in part of the Pope's territory. Much of the north of the peninsula had now become Italy. Europe held its breath and awaited the next move.

Then in May 1860 Giuseppe Garibaldi launched one of

idealism's greatest ever feats when he landed at Marsala, at Sicily's furthest western shore, with just over 1,000 red-shirted patriotic volunteers. After his first touch-and-go victories, the momentum of revolution began to build behind Garibaldi's expedition. He soon conquered the Sicilian capital Palermo, and then turned his growing army eastwards to invade the Italian mainland. In early September, he entered Naples. Italy would henceforth, for the first time in history, be one country.

With Italy unified, the patriotic prisoners of the Kingdom of the Two Sicilies could now convert their long sufferings into political credibility. They travelled north, to the Piedmontese capital of Turin at the foot of the Alps, and joined the new country's first national elite.

The tale of the *Risorgimento*, of how Italy was unified, has been told countless times. Much less well-known is its sinister subplot: the emergence of the camorra. Most of the multiple threads of that subplot were set in motion in the dungeons where the patriots met the *camorristi*. So the patriotic prisoners are our most important witnesses to the camorra's early history. Not only that: some of them stepped bodily into the historical fray, as both heroes and villains.

A united Italy was still a formless dream when Duke Sigismondo Castromediano was clapped in irons in 1851. But as his traumatic first hours in prison turned into days, months, and years, he found sources of resilience to add to his political dreams: the companionship of his fellows in degradation; but also a determination to understand his enemy. For the Duke of Castromediano, making sense of the camorra was a matter of life and death.

His discoveries should be ours, since they still hold good today. In prison, Castromediano was able to observe the early camorra in laboratory conditions as it perfected a criminal methodology destined to infiltrate and subvert the very nation that Duke Castromediano suffered so much to create.

Castromediano began his study of the camorra in the most down to earth way: he followed the money. And the thing that most struck him about what he called the camorra's 'taxes' was that they were levied on absolutely every aspect of a prisoner's life, down to the last crust of bread and the most miserable shred of clothing.

At one end of most dungeons in the Kingdom was a tiny altar to the Madonna. The first tax extracted from a newly arrived prisoner was often claimed as a payment for 'oil for the Madonna's lamp' – a lamp that rarely, if ever, burned. Prisoners even had to rent the patch of ground where they slept. In prison slang, this sleeping place was called a *pizzo*. Perhaps not coincidentally, the same word today means a bribe or a protection payment. Anyone reluctant to pay the *pizzo* was treated to punishments that ranged from insults, through beatings and razor slashes, to murder.

Duke Castromediano witnessed one episode that illustrates how the camorra's prison funding system involved something far more profound than brute robbery – and something much more sinister than taxation. On one occasion a *camorrista*, who had just eaten 'a succulent soup and a nice hunk of roast', threw a turnip into the face of a man whose meagre ration of bread and broth he had confiscated in lieu of a bribe. Insults were hurled along with the vegetable.

> Here you go, a turnip! That should be enough to keep you alive – at least for today. Tomorrow the Devil will take care of you.

The camorra turned the needs and rights of their fellow prisoners (like their bread or their *pizzo*) into favours. Favours that had to be paid for, one way or another. The camorra system was based on the power to grant those favours and to take them away.

Presidente di tribunale . . . .

Giudice . . . .

Ispettore di p. s. . . . . .

Pubblico ministero . . . .

Carabiniere . . . . . .

Questurino . . . . . .

Furto . . . .

Questore . . . . . .

Caposocietà . . . . .

Capintrito . . . . .

Camorrista . . . . .

Contajuolo . . . . .

Picciuotto . . . . .

Giovinotto onorato . . . .

Palo . . . . . .

A
B
C
D
E
F
G
H
I
L
M
N
O
P
Q
R
S
T
U
V
X
Z

Camorra code book. Reportedly confiscated from a prison *camorrista* who kept it secreted in his anus, this secret table explains the symbols *camorristi* used in messages they smuggled in and out of prison. From a nineteenth century study of the Honoured Society of Naples.

Or even to throw them in people's faces. The real cruelty of the turnip-throwing episode is that the *camorrista* was bestowing a favour that he could just as easily have withheld.

Duke Castromediano had an acute eye for episodes that drama-tised the underlying structures of camorra power in the prisons. He once overheard two prisoners arguing about a debt. There were only a few pennies at stake. But before long, a *camorrista* intervened. 'What right have you got to have an argument, unless the camorra has given you permission?' With that, he seized the disputed coins.

Any prisoner who asserted a basic right – like having an argu-ment or breathing air – was insulting the camorra's authority. And any prisoner who tried to appeal for justice to an authority beyond the prison was committing treason. The Duke met one man who had had his hands plunged into boiling water for daring to write to the government about prison conditions.

Much of what Castromediano learned about the camorra came from his time in a prison on Procida, one of the islands that, like its beautiful sisters Capri and Ischia, is posted at the mouth of the Bay of Naples. When he later looked back at his time on Procida, the Duke unleashed an undigested anger.

> The biggest jail in the southern provinces. The queen of jails, the camorra's honey pot, and the fattest feeding trough for the guard commanders and anyone else who has a hand in supporting the camorra; the great latrine where, by force of nature, society's most abominable scum percolates.

It was in Procida prison's own latrine, which fed straight into the sea, that the Duke came across another crucial facet of the camorra system. One day he noticed two human figures sketched in coal on the wall. The first had wide, goggling eyes and a silent howl of rage issuing from his twisted mouth. With his right hand he was thrusting a dagger into the belly of the second, who was writhing in excruciating pain as he keeled over. Each figure had his initials on the wall above his head. Below the scene was written, 'Judged by the Society', followed by the very date on which the Duke had come across it.

Castromediano already knew that the Society or Honoured Society was the name that the camorra gave itself. But the doodle on the wall was obscure. 'What does that mean?' he asked, with his usual candour, of the first person he came across.

> It means that today is a day of justice against a traitor. Either the victim drawn there is already in the chapel, breathing his last. Or within a few hours the penal colony on Procida will have one less inmate, and hell will have one more.

The prisoner explained how the Society had reached a decision, how its bosses had made a ruling, and how all members except for the victim had been informed of what was about to happen. No one, of course, had divulged this open secret.

Then, just as he was warning the Duke to keep quiet, from the next corridor there came a loud curse, followed by a long and anguished cry that was gradually smothered, followed in turn by a clinking of chains and the sound of hurried footsteps.

'The murder has happened,' was all that the other prisoner said.

In a panic, the Duke bolted for his own cell. But he had hardly turned the first corner when he stumbled upon the victim, three stab wounds to his heart. The only other person there was the man the victim was chained to. The man's attitude would remain seared into Castromediano's memory. Perhaps he was the killer. At the very least he was an eyewitness. Yet he gazed down at the corpse with 'an indescribable combination of stupidity and ferocity' as he waited calmly for the guards to bring the hammer and anvil they needed to separate him from his dead companion.

Castromediano called what he had witnessed a 'simulacrum' of justice; this was murder in the borrowed clothes of capital punishment. The camorra not only killed the traitor. More importantly, it sought to make that killing legitimate, 'legal'. There was a trial with a judge, witnesses, and advocates for the prosecution and the defence. The verdict and sentence that issued from the trial were made public – albeit on the walls of a latrine rather than in a court proclamation. The camorra also sought a twisted form of democratic approval for its judicial decisions, by making sure that everyone bar the victim knew what was about to take place.

The camorra courts did not reach their decisions in the name of justice. Rather, their lodestar value was *honour*. Honour, in the sense that the Society understood it (a sense that Castromediano called an 'aberration of the human mind'), meant that an affiliate had to protect his fellows at all costs, and share his fortunes with them. Disputes had to be resolved in the approved fashion, usually by a dagger duel; oaths and pacts had to be respected, orders obeyed, and punishment accepted when it was due.

Despite all the talk of honour, the reality of camorra life was far from harmonious, as Castromediano recalled.

> Relations between those accursed men seethed with arguments, hatred, and envy. Sudden murders and horrible acts of vengeance were perpetrated every day.

A murder committed as a vendetta was a murder to defend one's personal honour, and as such it could easily be sanctioned by the camorra's shadow judicial system. Quite whether a vendetta was legitimate or not depended partly on the Society's rules and legal precedents, which were transmitted orally from one generation of criminals to the next. More importantly, it depended on whether the vendetta was committed by a *camorrista* fearsome enough to impose his will. In the prison camorra, even more than anywhere else, the rules were the tool of the rich and powerful. Honour was law for those who placed themselves above the law.

Camorra 'taxation'. Camorra 'justice'. Castromediano also talks of the camorra's 'jurisdiction', its 'badges of office', and its 'administration'. His terminology is striking, consistent and apt: it is the vocabulary of state power. What he is describing is a system of criminal authority that apes the workings of a modern state – even within a dungeon's sepulchral gloom.

If the camorra of the prisons was a kind of shadow state, it had a very interventionist idea of how the state should behave. Duke Castromediano saw that *camorristi* fostered gambling and drinking in the full knowledge that these activities could be taxed. (Indeed the practice of taking bribes from gamers was so closely associated with gangsters that it generated a popular theory about how the camorra got its name. *Morra* was a game, and the *capo della morra* was the man who watched over the players. It was said that this title was shortened at some stage to *ca-morra*. The theory is probably apocryphal: in Naples, *camorra* meant 'bribe' or 'extortion' long before anyone thought of applying the term to a secret society.)

Card games and bottles of wine generated other moneymaking opportunities: the camorra provided the only source of credit for unlucky gamblers, and it controlled the prison's own stinking, rat-infested tavern. Moreover, every object that the camorra confiscated from a prisoner unable to afford his interest payments, his bottle, or his bribe, could be sold on at an eye-watering markup. The dungeons echoed to the cries of pedlars selling greasy rags and bits of stale bread. A whole squalid economy sprouted from exploiting the prisoners at every turn. As an old saying within the camorra would have it, '*Facimmo caccia' l'oro de' piducchie*': 'We extract gold from fleas.'

The camorra system also reached up into the prisons' supposed command. Naturally, many guards were on the payroll. This corruption not only gave the camorra the freedom it needed to operate, it also put even more favours into circulation. For a price, prisoners could wear their own clothes, sleep in separate cells, eat better food, and have access to medicine, letters, books and candles. By managing the traffic in goods that came in and out of prison, the camorra both invented and monopolised a whole market in contraband items.

So the prison camorra had a dual business model designed to extract gold from fleas: extortion 'taxes' on the one hand and contraband commerce on the other. The camorra of today works on exactly the same principles. All that has changed is that the 'fleas' have become bigger. Bribes once taken on a place to lay a palliasse are now cuts taken on huge public works contracts. Candles and food smuggled into prison are now consignments of narcotics smuggled into the country.

Duke Castromediano's years as a political prisoner were spent in several jails but everywhere he went he found the camorra in charge. So his story is not just about the origins of what today is called the *Neapolitan* camorra. Prisoners from different regions mingled in jails across the southern part of the Italian peninsula, on Sicily, and on many small islands. They all referred to themselves as *camorristi*.

The Duke did however notice distinctions in the dress code adopted by *camorristi* from different regions. Sicilians tended to opt for the black plush look. (The *camorrista* who introduced himself to the Duke on his first day in the Castello del Carmine was Sicilian.) Not long before, Neapolitans had dressed in the same way. But for some time now they had preferred to signal their status with clothes that could come in any colour, as long as it was of good quality and accessorised in gold: gold watch and chain; gold earrings; chunky gold finger rings; all topped off with a fez decorated with lots of braid, embroidery and a golden tassel.

There were strong loyalties and rivalries between *camorristi* from different regions. In Duke Castromediano's experience, the Neapolitans nurtured an 'inveterate antipathy' towards the

Calabrians. When this antipathy exploded into open hostilities, *camorristi* from elsewhere tended to take sides in a familiar formation: with the Neapolitans would stand the men from the countryside near Naples and from Puglia; everyone else would side with the Calabrians. The Sicilians 'loved to keep themselves to themselves', said Castromediano. 'But if they came down in favour of one side or the other, oh! the savage vendettas!' In the worst cases, 'tens of dead bodies took their places in the prison cemetery'.

For all their vicious rivalries and their many distinctive qualities, Sicilian *mafiosi*, like Neapolitan *camorristi* and Calabrian *'ndranghetisti*, have all referred to themselves as members of the 'Honoured Society'. Their shared vocabulary is a sign of shared origins in the prison system of the Kingdom of the Two Sicilies. In fact, everything Castromediano discovered in prison about the camorra not only still holds good – it still holds good for the Sicilian mafia and the Calabrian 'ndrangheta too. Italy's criminal organisations both engage in illegal commerce and act as a shadow state that combines extortion 'taxes' and alternative judicial and political systems. If they had their way, Italy's Honoured Societies would turn the whole world into a giant prison, run by their simple but brutally effective rules.

Seven and a half years after Sigismondo Castromediano was admitted to the Castello del Carmine, the diplomatic pressure on the Bourbon government finally paid off for the patriotic prisoners; like others, the Duke had his sentence commuted to permanent exile. By then his hair had turned completely white. One of the last things he did before being freed was to bribe a jailor to let him keep two mournful souvenirs: his shackles and his red tunic. The humiliations of his prison years would remain with him for the rest of his life.

The Duke spent just over a year in exile. Then came Garibaldi:

the Bourbon state collapsed and its territory became part of Italy. In Turin, on 17 March 1861, Castromediano was in parliament to see Victor Emmanuel, the King of Piedmont-Sardinia, pronounced hereditary monarch of the new Kingdom. The ideal for which he had suffered so long was now an official reality.

But Castromediano soon lost the parliamentary position his prison martyrdom had earned. He returned to his ancestral seat in Puglia, the region that forms the heel of the Italian boot. While he was in jail his castle near the city of Lecce had fallen into serious disrepair. But he had been leeched to near penury by the camorra and would never have the money to renovate. The Duke's occasional visitors over the years found the castle a fitting setting for a man who had endured so much in the national cause: it became a semi-ruin like those in the romantic novels that had so fired the Duke's patriotism when he was young. In one corner of the castle chapel, on permanent display, were what he called his 'decorations': the prison chain and tunic. The camorra had seeped into the Duke's soul, infecting him with a recurring melancholy: 'the spawn of hell', he called it. 'One of the most immoral and disastrous sects that human infamy has ever invented.'

The Duke began writing a memoir of his captivity only days after he was released; yet it remained unfinished when he died in his castle thirty-six years later. Castromediano's *Political Prisons and Jails* reads like the work of a man still struggling to come to terms with his past. The Duke's narrative is occasionally jumbled and repetitive but at its best, it is a vivid first-hand account of where Italy's mafias began.

What Castromediano could not appreciate while in jail was that the camorra had already made its first steps out from the dungeon and into the streets.

Co-managing crime

Naples teemed. There were just under half a million inhabitants in the 1850s, making the capital of the Kingdom of the Two Sicilies the biggest city in Italy. With the highest population density in Europe, it packed more misery into each square metre than any other town on the continent. Every grotto and cellar, every nook and doorway had its ragged and emaciated inhabitants.

The quarters of Porto, Pendino, Mercato and Vicaria held the most notorious concentrations of indigence; they made up the so-called 'low city'. Some of the alleyways were so narrow it was impossible to open an umbrella. Many of the low city's poorest lived in tenements known as *fondaci* ('depositories') where whole families and their animals were crammed into single, windowless rooms. Vermin were rife and the stench unholy: sewage overflowed the ancient cesspits and ran through the alleys. In the 1840s close to 30 per cent of infants in the low city died before their first birthday. None of these four quarters had a life expectancy above twenty-five years.

But unlike London, Naples did not hide its poor away. Under the southern sun, in every street and piazza, tradesmen and pedlars of all conceivable varieties put on daily performances. Slum-dwellers scraped their living picking rags, weaving straw or singing stories; they hawked snails and pizza slices, collected cigar butts, or portered the occasional box.

Nowhere was the variety of this starveling economy more apparent than in the via Toledo, the city's main thoroughfare and 'the noisiest street in Europe'. Here, each morning, the city's life would seep from the hovels and palazzi, spill through the side streets and converge to form a roiling flood of people. Poor and wealthy, the scuttling urchin and the promenading bourgeois, all dodged the carriages on via Toledo. The din of haggling was immense. And to add to it, everyone from the sausage vendors with their braziers to the sellers of ice water in their grandly decorated pagodas, had a distinctive, sonorous cry.

There was also a less picturesque side to the industry of the Neapolitan poor. Tourists were most vexed by the crowds of beggars who thrust their maimed limbs at anyone likely to surrender a coin. Veteran travellers considered that the child pickpockets of Naples set an international standard for dexterity. Theft, swindling and prostitution were crucial survival strategies for many of the poor. The low city, in particular, lived almost entirely outside the law.

Not even the world's most zealous and honest constabulary could have imposed order on this swarm. So in Naples, the nineteenth-century's proud new science of policing quickly became a modest routine of minimising the nuisance caused by the plebs. Because Naples was so vast and so poor, the police learned that the best way to contain that nuisance was to collaborate with the hardest plebeian thugs.

In 1857 Antonio Scialoja wrote a pamphlet that continued the patriotic propaganda offensive against the Kingdom of the Two Sicilies. Scialoja was a brilliant Neapolitan economist living in political exile in Turin. Because he was himself a veteran of the Bourbon jails, the prison camorra was a centrepiece of his polemic. He claimed that 'the Society of *camorristi*' was so powerful that it could carry out death sentences in any prison in the Kingdom. The Society made other prisoners pay for everything, Scialoja reported, even for escaping what he delicately referred to as the 'turpitudes' of their fellow detainees: he meant rape.

But Scialoja's diagnosis of the malaise in Naples went far beyond the prison walls. Using his accounting skills, he identified a slush fund that did not appear in the official police budget. He then showed how some of this cash was spent hiring ruffians and spies. Nor did the corruption stop there. For decades the Bourbons had recruited their police from among the city's most feared criminals. The ordinary people of Naples referred to them as the *feroci*, the 'ferocious ones'. There were 181 *feroci* at the time Scialoja was writing. Although they were paid their meagre wages out of the official police budget, they nonetheless habitually supplemented their income with bribes.

Italian has a useful piece of jargon to describe this kind of arrangement: it is called 'co-managing' crime. And if the *feroci* who co-managed crime with the police are beginning to look rather like the *camorristi* who co-managed the prison system with the warders, that is because they were sometimes one and the same thing. But policing the streets with the cooperation of the toughest delinquents was always a messy affair. Some *camorristi* proved to be more loyal to their criminal comrades than they were to their police paymasters, while others provoked intense suspicion and hatred in the underworld. Nevertheless, thanks to co-management, the bosses who had been left in charge of the dungeons for centuries now held a government licence to be a power on the streets. By the early 1850s, *camorristi* decked out in the latest gangster uniform of slicked hair, velvet jacket and flared trousers were as conspicuous a part of the life of Naples as pizza-pedlars and strolling players.

Once the camorra of the prisons had been given its foothold in the outside world, it began doing what it was best at: extracting gold from fleas. Just as in prison, extortion was the basis of the camorra's power. Illegal or semi-illegal activities were particularly vulnerable. *Camorristi* would demand a cut of any thief's takings and they came to occupy a dominant position in prostitution. Gambling was another lucrative racket.

Large sections of the *legal* economy also came to be subject to extortion rackets. Outsiders would often encounter *camorristi* in action without really understanding what they were seeing.

As the visitor stepped from a hired boat, his oarsman would be approached by a gaudily dressed man, often wearing lots of jewellery, who would silently expect and receive an offering. As the visitor arrived at his hotel, his porter would discreetly slip a coin into the hand of a stocky stranger. And as the visitor stepped into a hackney carriage, the driver would pay up to yet another waiting heavy.

Camorristi demanded their taxes at the pressure points of the urban economy: at the quays where cargo, fish, and passengers were landed; at the city gates where produce arrived from the countryside; at the markets where it was distributed. Boatmen and stevedores, customs officers and cart-drivers, wholesalers and hawkers: all were forced to pay in the same way that had long been familiar for prison inmates.

The heart of the camorra's Naples became the Vicaria quarter, located at what was then the city's eastern boundary. The slums of the Vicaria were where every criminal sphere of influence overlapped, as if at the intersection of a Venn diagram. The quarter took its name from the Palazzo della Vicaria, a medieval block that housed the courtrooms and, in its basement, a notorious dungeon. The walls of the Vicaria prison looked solid enough but in reality they were a membrane through which messages, food and weapons constantly slipped into and out of the surrounding slums.

Near the prison was the Porta Capuana, a stone archway adorned with friezes and frescos through which much of the produce from the hinterland arrived ready to be 'taxed'. But the criminal epicentre of the Vicaria was what is now a stretch of via Martiri d'Otranto that, with the alleys running off it, was known as the Imbrecciata. The Imbrecciata was a kasbah of cheap carnal pleasures; its inhabitants were almost all involved in prostitution and live sex shows. The area was so notorious that the authorities tried several times to cordon it off by building walls at its exits.

With all these opportunities for illegal income close to hand

in the Vicaria, it is not surprising that first supreme bosses of
the Honoured Society in the outside world came from here.

The 'co-management' of crime in Naples was indeed scandalous.
But the exiled economist Antonio Scialoja was particularly
angered by the way the Bourbon authorities gave their spies,
feroci and *camorristi* a free rein to harass and blackmail liberal
patriots. In fact these rough and ready cops were no respecters
of political affiliation: even Bourbon royalists had to cough up
to avoid what the *feroci* smilingly called 'judicial complications'.
In this way, amid the uncertainties of the 1850s, with the Bourbon
monarchy vulnerable and wary, the camorra was given its first
chance to meddle in politics.

Scialoja concluded his pamphlet with an exemplary tale drawn
from his own memories of life as a political prisoner in the early
1850s. He recalled that the common criminals in jail referred to
the captive patriots simply as 'the gentlemen', because their
leaders were educated men of property like him. But by no means
everyone who got mixed up in liberal politics was a gentleman.
Some were tough artisans. A case in point was one Giuseppe
D'Alessandro, known as *Peppe l'aversano* – 'Aversa Joe' (Aversa
being a agricultural settlement not far north of Naples). Aversa
Joe was sent to jail for his part in the revolutionary events of
1848. When he encountered the camorra, he quickly decided that
joining the ranks of the extortionists was preferable to suffering
alongside the gentlemen martyrs. He was initiated into the
Honoured Society and was soon swaggering along the corridors
in his flares.

In the spring of 1851, at about the time when Gladstone was
thundering about the *gamorristi* to his British readers, one
particularly zealous branch of the Neapolitan police conceived
a plan to kill off some of the incarcerated patriots. But not even
the police could carry out such a scheme without help from the

prison management – the camorra. In Aversa Joe they found the perfect man for the job; in fact they didn't even have to pay him since he was still under sentence of death for treason and was glad simply to be spared his date with the executioner.

Aversa Joe twice attempted to carry out his mission, with a scrum of *camorristi* ready to answer his call to attack. But both times the gentlemen managed to stick together and face down their would-be killers.

The political prisoners then wrote to the police authorities to remind them of the diplomatic scandal that would ensue if they were torn to pieces by a mob. The reminder worked. Aversa Joe was transferred elsewhere, then released, and finally given the chance to swap his velvet jacket for a police uniform: he had completed the transformation from treasonable patriot, to *camorrista*, to policeman in the space of a couple of years.

For Scialoja, the Aversa Joe story typified everything that was bad about Bourbon rule, with its habit of co-managing crime with mobsters. The Italian *Patria* would stand in shining contrast to such sleaze. The new nation of Italy, whenever it came, would finally bring good government to the benighted metropolis in the shadow of Mount Vesuvius.

But Naples being Naples, forming the *Patria* turned out to be a much stranger and murkier business than anyone could have expected.

The redemption of the camorra

The summer of 1860 was the summer of Garibaldi's expedition, when marvels of patriotic heroism finally turned the Kingdom of the Two Sicilies into part of the Kingdom of Italy. In Naples, history was being made at such a gallop that journalists scarcely had time to dwell on what they saw and heard. This was a moment when the incredible seemed possible, and thus a time for narrative. Explanation would have to wait.

There was consternation in Naples when news broke that Garibaldi and his Thousand redshirted Italian patriots had invaded Sicily. On 11 May 1860 the official newspaper announced that what it called Garibaldi's 'freebooters' had landed in Marsala. By the end of the month it was confirmed that the insurgent forces had gained control of the Sicilian capital, Palermo.

The ineffectual young king, Francesco II, was scarcely a year into his reign. As the *garibaldini* consolidated their grip on Sicily and prepared to invade the Italian mainland and march north, Francesco dithered in Naples and his ministers argued and schemed.

Only on 26 June did Neapolitans find out how the Bourbon monarchy planned to respond to the crisis. Early that morning, posters were plastered along the major streets proclaiming a 'Sovereign Act'. King Francesco decreed that the Kingdom of the Two Sicilies was to cease being an absolute monarchy and embrace constitutional politics. A government comprising liberal patriots had already been formed. There would also be an amnesty for all political prisoners. And the flag would henceforth comprise the Italian tricolour of red, white and green, surmounted by the Bourbon dynasty's coat of arms.

The early risers who came across the Sovereign Act on the morning of 26 June were afraid to be seen reading it: there was always the chance that it was a provocation intended to force liberals out into the open, and make them easy targets for the *feroci*. But within hours Neapolitans had absorbed what the posters really meant: the Sovereign Act was a feeble and desperate attempt to cling onto power. The gathering momentum of Garibaldi's expedition had put Francesco in a hopeless position, and the Bourbon state was tottering.

The day the Sovereign Act was published was a bad day to be a policeman in Naples. For years the police had been feared and despised as corrupt instruments of repression. Now they were left politically exposed when there was almost certain to be a battle for control of the streets.

The evening of the day that the Sovereign Act posters appeared, clusters of people from the poorest alleyways came down onto via Toledo to jeer and whistle at the police. Shopkeepers pulled down their shutters and expected the worst. They had good reason to be afraid. Mass disorder visited Naples with what seemed like seasonal regularity, and pillaging inevitably accompanied it.

Serious trouble began the following afternoon. Two rival proletarian crowds were looking for a confrontation: the royalists yelling 'long live the King', and the patriots marching to the call of 'viva Garibaldi'. One colourful character, difficult to miss in the mêlée, was Marianna De Crescenzo, who went by the nickname of *la Sangiovannara*. One report described her as being 'decked out like a brigand', festooned in ribbons and flags. Responding to her yelled commands was a gang of similarly attired women brandishing knives and pistols. Loyalists to the Bourbon cause suspected that *la Sangiovannara* had stoked up the trouble by handing out cheap booze from her tavern, as well as large measures of subversive Italian propaganda.

On via Toledo, two police patrols found themselves caught between the factions. When an inspector gave the unenforceable order to disarm the crowd, fighting broke out. Some onlookers heard shots. After a running battle, the police were forced to withdraw. Only the arrival of a cavalry unit prevented the situation degenerating even further.

There were two notable casualties of the clash. The first was the French ambassador, who was passing along via Toledo in his carriage when he was accosted and coshed. Although he survived, no one ever discovered who was responsible for the attack.

The second victim was Aversa Joe, the patriot, turned prison *camorrista*, turned Bourbon assassin, turned policeman. He was stabbed at the demonstration and then hacked to death while he was being carried to hospital on a stretcher. The murder was clearly planned in advance, although again the culprits remained unknown.

Everyone thought that this was only the overture to the coming terror. Fearing the worst, many policemen ran for their lives. There was no one left to resist the mob. Organised gangs armed with muskets, sword-sticks, daggers and pistols visited each of the city's twelve police stations in turn; they broke down the doors, tossed files and furniture out of the windows, and lit great bonfires in the street.

The Neapolitan police force had ceased to exist.

But by the afternoon, a peculiar calm had descended. The *Times* correspondent felt safe enough to go and see the ruined police station in the Montecalvario quarter and found the words 'DEATH TO THE COPS!' and 'CLOSED DUE TO DEATH!' scrawled on either side of the entrance. These bloodcurdling slogans did not match what had actually happened, though. Witness after witness related how unexpectedly peaceful, ordered and even playful the scenes of destruction were. The mob did rough up the few cops they caught. But instead of lynching their uniformed captives, they handed them over to the army. The *London Daily News*'s man at the scene wrote that, although rumours suggested that many policemen had been murdered, he had been unable to verify a single fatality. Around the

ATTO SOVRANO

Desiderando di dare ai Nostri amatissimi sudditi un attestato della Nostra Sovrana benevolenza, Ci siamo determinati di concedere gli Ordini costituzionali e rappsesentativi nel Regno in armonia co' principii italiani e nazionali in modo da garentire la sicurezza e prosperità in avvenire e da stringere sempre più i legami che Ci uniscono a'popoli che la Provvidenza Ci ha chiamati a governare.

A quest'oggetto siamo venuti nelle seguenti determinazioni:

1. Accordiamo una generale amnistia per tutt' i reati politici fine a questo giorno.

2 Abbiamo incaricato il Commendatore D. Antonio Sbinelli della formazione d' un nuovo Ministro, il quale compilerà nel più breve termine possibile gli articoli dello Statuto sulle base delle istituzioni rappresentativi' italiane e nazionali.

3. Sarà stabilito con S. M. il Re di Sardegna un accordo per gl' interessi comuni delle due Corone in Italia.

4. La Nostra bandiera sarà d'ora innanzi fregiata de'colori Nazionali Italiani in tre fasce verticali, conservando sempre nel mezzo le Armi della Nostra Dinastia.

5. In quanto alla Sicilia, accorderemo analoghe istituzioni rappresentative che possono soddisfare i bisogni dell' Isola ; ed uno de' Principi della Nostra Real Casa ne sarà il nostro Vicerè.

Portici 25 Giugno 1860.

FRANCESCO.

The Neapolitan camorra's cue to take to the streets. In desperation, on 25 June 1860, Francesco II of the Kingdom of the Two Sicilies issued the *Atto Sovrano* (Sovereign Act).

bonfires of police paraphernalia there was cheering, laughing and dancing; street urchins cut up police uniforms and handed the pieces out as souvenirs. This was less a riot than a piece of street theatre.

The most unexpected part of it all was that there was no stealing. On every previous occasion when political upheaval had come to Naples, a predatory mob had risen from the low city. Yet this time, outlandishly, rioters from the same slums even handed over any cash and valuables they found to army officers or parish priests. Moving through the streets from one target to the next, they shouted reassurance to the traders cowering behind their shutters. 'Why close up your shops? We aren't going to rob you. We only wanted to drive off the cops.' According to the *Times* correspondent, one man took several watches from the wreckage of a police station. But instead of pocketing them, he threw them on the bonfire burning outside. 'No one shall say that I stole them', he proclaimed.

These were strange days, and they were about to get even stranger. The evening before the police stations were attacked in such carnivalesque style, King Francesco II appointed a new Prefect of Police, a lawyer by the name of Liborio Romano.

Like Duke Sigismondo Castromediano and economist Antonio Scialoja, Liborio Romano was sent to jail in the early 1850s for his liberal, patriotic beliefs. But he was already nearing sixty and suffered from excruciating gout so he was released early in 1852; and in 1854 he was allowed to return to Naples after signing an oath of loyalty to the throne. Romano thus owed the Bourbon monarchy a debt of honour. In June 1860 when King Francesco was looking for tame patriots to take up positions in the liberal cabinet announced by the Sovereign Act, Romano's obligation seemed to make him the perfect candidate. So he was put in charge of the police – the toughest job of them all.

Within hours of taking office Romano launched one of the boldest initiatives in the history of policing: he offered the camorra the chance to 'rehabilitate itself' (his words) by replacing the police. The Honoured Society's bosses accepted the offer with alacrity, and soon *camorristi* sporting cockades in the red, white and green of the Italian flag were on patrol. Naples remained calm as a result, and Liborio Romano became a hero. The Piedmontese ambassador gushed that he 'is deeply loved by the public and has very Italian feelings'. *The Times* called Romano a statesman 'who has gained the confidence of all by his ability and firmness', and said that, but for him, the city would be in chaos. On 23 July his saint's day was marked with public illuminations and a lantern-lit parade. Indeed, so successful was Romano's policy that many *camorristi* were subsequently recruited into a new National Guard. The risky summer between a crumbling Bourbon regime and the arrival of Garibaldi passed more peacefully than anyone could ever have hoped.

The camorra's extraordinary role in the Naples drama made news in Turin, the new Italy's capital city. One magazine even marked the occasion by publishing flattering pictures of three leading camorra bosses. One of them, Salvatore De Crescenzo, is worth looking at closely.

In the 1860 engraving, De Crescenzo is shown sporting a tricolour rosette, his right hand resting Napoleonically inside his waistcoat, his hair parted neatly and his earnest expression framed by a fuzzy, chin-strap beard. De Crescenzo's police files allow us to add some facts to these impressions. They tell us that he was a shoemaker by trade, probably born in 1822. He was manifestly a violent man, first jailed in 1849 for seriously wounding a sailor, and strongly suspected of killing a fellow inmate later the same year. He spent the 1850s in and out of prison, and the last arrest before his picture appeared in the press was in November 1859. Despite this frightening CV, the Turin magazine declared that De Crescenzo and the other *camorristi* were now 'honest men who were held in high regard by both the national party and the people'.

In the south, Garibaldi was performing miracles, conquering

a whole Kingdom with a handful of volunteers. In Naples, it seemed to some observers, there was a miracle before Garibaldi even arrived. The camorra had been redeemed, converted in the sacred name of the *Patria*.

But in the shadows where politics, mob violence and organised crime overlap, there had been no miracle, and no redemption of the camorra. The truth – or at least fragments of it – would only emerge later. Many of those fragments were in the possession of one of the more sympathetic characters in the history of Italian organised crime, a myopic, bearded Swiss hotelier called Marc Monnier.

Monnier never spent time in jail, and never held political office. Yet he knew the camorra as well as anyone in Naples thanks to his job: he ran the Hôtel de Genève, which stood amid the hubbub of via Medina. The hotel catered mainly for commercial travellers; Herman Melville, author of *Moby Dick*, was one of its few notable guests. The family business put Monnier in daily contact with the camorra's territorial control: with the porters, carriage drivers, greengrocers and butchers who paid kickbacks to the mob. From the very windows of the Hôtel de Genève, Monnier could watch hoodlums taking their 10 per cent cut on street card games.

The hotel business gave Marc Monnier a priceless knowledge of how the city worked, as well as a reliable source of income. Reliable, but dreary. Monnier's real passion was writing, particularly drama. In the mid-1850s he was converted to the patriotic cause and thereby acquired a journalistic mission: to explain Italy to the rest of the world. The unfolding story of Italy's unification was by turns inspiring and confusing to foreign onlookers – not to mention to Italians themselves. Being both an insider and an outsider, Monnier had a perspective that Italians and foreigners alike could trust.

Monnier's *The Camorra* was published in 1862. As a guide to the Neapolitan Honoured Society of the nineteenth century, it has never been surpassed. One of the key testimonies in *The*

Camorra is from a patriot, one of a number who had returned
to Naples to conspire in secret for the overthrow of the Bourbon
monarchy. Many of these conspirators joined an underground
group called the 'Committee of Order' (a name chosen so as
to disguise the revolutionaries' real intentions). Monnier knew
the conspirators well because the Committee of Order used to
hold some of its meetings in the Hôtel de Genève. And what
Monnier learned from his contacts in the Committee of Order
was that there was a secret pact between the movement for
Italian unification and the camorra that dated back to the
mid-1950s.

Here, then, is our first lesson in Neapolitan politics: while
some patriots were being persecuted by the camorra in jail and
others were decrying it as the worst product of the Bourbons'
sordid despotism from exile, back in Naples still others were
trying to strike a deal with the gangland leaders.

But why on earth would the Committee of Order want to
befriend the gangsters of the camorra? Because they knew the
lessons of Neapolitan history. Time and time again the Bourbon
monarchy had enlisted the urban poor to defend itself from
change: rabble-rousers were plied with cash and told to direct
the mob at political enemies. Any political revolution would fail
if it could not control the streets. The camorra was organised,
violent and rooted in the very alleyways that generated the
notorious mobs. With the camorra on its side – or at least a
substantial faction within the camorra – Italy could win Naples
and thus the whole of the south. The Committee of Order was
set to compete with the Bourbon police for the camorra's
friendship.

Not all of the patriotic leaders agreed with this Machiavellian
tactic. And by no means all *camorristi* went along with it. But
the prospect of a deal between patriots and hoodlums raised
genuine fears for the Bourbon authorities. In October 1853 the
police (themselves of course riddled with *camorristi*) reported
that 'the liberals are trying to recruit from among a pernicious

class of individuals from the plebs, who go by the name of *camorristi*.' Among the list of politically suspect *camorristi* was Salvatore De Crescenzo: the boss whose 'redemption' would make headlines seven years later.

Marc Monnier learned about the pact between the Committee of Order and the Honoured Society from a source he referred to only as the 'Neopolitan gentleman'. The Neapolitan gentleman told Monnier that at some time in the mid-1850s, he himself had arranged to meet leading *camorristi* on the northern outskirts of the city. He watched them arrive, one by one, each with a hat pulled down low, each announcing himself with the same signal: a noise made with the lips that sounded like a kiss.

The Neapolitan gentleman reported that his first meeting with the leaders of the Honoured Society started badly and very quickly got much worse. The *camorristi* began by berating him: he and his well-dressed and well-educated friends had ignored the needs of the poor. The 'holy rabble', they said, had no intention of letting people like him, who were already rich, glean all the fruits of revolution. After this opening verbal assault, the *camorristi* got down to business. It would take money to provoke a patriotic revolt against the Bourbon monarchy. A lot of money. To start with, they demanded a bounty of 10,000 ducats each. In 2010 values, by a very rough calculation, the bosses were demanding a bung of €125,000 or £105,000 per head to help bring down the Bourbon state.

The Neapolitan gentleman splutteringly pleaded with the *camorristi* to take a less materialistic view of things, but his protest was in vain. The patriots agreed to pay the camorra. Thereafter, each underworld chief received regular sums according to the number of men he commanded.

As it turned out, the camorra's preparations for the coming revolution were less than wholehearted. They gave their followers ranks, as if they were in an army, and emblazoned large parchment signs with the patriots' watchword: ORDER. Yet somehow they never quite made the leap from preparing for a revolt to actually starting one. In fact, they were more interested in blackmailing the patriotic conspirators by threatening to tell the Bourbon police everything unless they were given more money.

Things were looking very bleak for the patriots of Naples, when suddenly in 1859 the situation changed, with the completion of the first stage of Italian unification in the north. In the south, the Kingdom of the Two Sicilies suddenly looked very vulnerable. The relationship between the Bourbon police and street thugs broke down in the new climate of fear. In November 1859, the government ordered a big roundup of *camorristi* and many of them, including Salvatore De Crescenzo, were transported to prison islands off the Italian coast.

The camorra bosses – some of them at least – realised that an alliance with the Committee of Order might actually prove useful, rather than merely lucrative.

Garibaldi's invasion of Sicily in May of the following year, and the Bourbon government's desperate lurch towards constitutional politics, brought the situation to a climax. The police chief who had masterminded the November roundup of gangsters was sacked. Political prisoners were released, as were many *camorristi* – all of them spitting bile about the Bourbon police. Then the government issued the Sovereign Act, and the street theatre began.

The reason why the armed crowd that attacked the police stations showed such remarkable self-discipline was that many of them were *camorristi* allied with the patriots, who wanted to take the Bourbon police out of the game, but did not want the city to descend into anarchy. Marianna De Crescenzo, the tavern owner known as *la Sangiovannara* who festooned herself with ribbons and flags to lead the patriotic mob, was a key figure here. She was rumoured to have helped patriotic prisoners smuggle messages out of Bourbon jails. More importantly, she was camorra boss Salvatore De Crescenzo's cousin. As our Swiss hotelier Marc Monnier said of her

Without being affiliated to the Society, she knew all of its members and brought them together at her house for highly risky secret parleys.

The parleys between the patriots and the camorra entered a new phase once the Neapolitan police force melted away, and Liborio Romano took control of enforcing order in the city. Why did Romano ask the camorra to police Naples? Several different theories circulated in the aftermath. Marc Monnier, generous soul that he was, gave a very charitable explanation. Romano, like his father before him, was a Freemason, as were some other patriotic leaders, as indeed was Garibaldi himself. The typical Masonic cocktail of fellowship, high ideals and ritualistic mumbo-jumbo fitted very well with the seemingly far-fetched project of creating a common *Patria* out of Italy's disjointed parts. Garibaldi's conquest of the Kingdom of the Two Sicilies seemed to be turning those ideals into a reality. Perhaps, argued Monnier, Liborio Romano saw the Honoured Society as a primitive version of his own sect, and hoped it could be turned to the same humanitarian ends. Perhaps.

Less generous and much more realistic commentators said simply that the camorra threatened Romano that they would unleash anarchy on the streets unless they were recruited into the police. It was also claimed that the camorra threatened to kill Romano himself. Other voices – bitter Bourbon supporters it must be said – claimed that Romano was not threatened at all, and that he and some other patriots were the camorra's willing partners all along.

For several years Romano squirmed silently as others tried to make sense of what he had done. Over time, his public image as the saviour of Naples was upended. Most opinion-formers came to regard him as cynical, corrupt and vain; the consensus was that Romano had colluded with the camorra all along. Finally, several years later, Romano made his bid to tell his side of the story and to magnify his history-making role in the turbulent summer of 1860. But his memoir, with its mixture of self-dramatisation and evasive bluster, only served to fuel the worst suspicions, showing that at the very least he was a man with a great deal to hide.

Romano's explanation of how he persuaded the camorra to replace the Bourbon police is so wooden and devious as to be almost comic. He tells us that he asked the most famous *capo* of the Honoured Society to meet him in his office at the Prefecture. Face-to-face with the notorious crook, Romano began with a stirring speech. He explained that the previous government had denied all routes to self-improvement for hardworking people with no property. (The *camorrista* could be forgiven a blush of recognition as it sank in that this meant him.) Romano pressed on: the men of the Honoured Society should be given a chance to draw a veil over their shady past and 'rehabilitate themselves'. The best of them were to be recruited into a refounded police force that would no longer be manned by 'nasty thugs and vile stoolpigeons, but by honest people'.

Romano tells us that the mob boss was moved to tears by this vision of a new dawn. Camorra legend has it that he was none other than Salvatore De Crescenzo.

The tale is far-fetched enough to be a scene from an opera. Indeed the whole memoir is best read in precisely that way: as an adaptation, written to impose a unity of time, place and action – not to mention a sentimental gloss – on the more sinister reality of the role that both Liborio Romano and the camorra played in the birth of a united Italian nation. The likelihood is that Romano and the Honoured Society were hand in glove from the outset.

Ultimately the precise details of the accord that was undoubtedly struck between gangsters and patriots do not matter. As events in Naples would soon prove, a pact with the devil is a pact with the devil, whatever the small print says.

Uncle Peppe's stuff:
The camorra cashes in

The last Bourbon King of Naples abandoned his capital on 6 September 1860.

The following morning, the city's population poured into the streets and converged on the station to hail the arrival of Giuseppe Garibaldi. Bands played, banners fluttered. Ladies of the highest rank mixed with the rankest plebs, and everyone shouted 'viva Garibaldi!' until they could do little more than croak. Marc Monnier left his hotel early to join the throng. 'I didn't believe that national enthusiasm could ever make so much noise', he recorded. Through a gap in the rejoicing multitude he glimpsed Garibaldi from close enough to make out the smile of tired happiness on his face. He did not have to peer to see *la Sangiovannara*, with her large following of armed women. Or indeed the *camorristi* who stood above the crowd in their carriages, waving weapons in the air.

Liborio Romano shared Garibaldi's glory. The camorra's great friend had been the first to shake Garibaldi's hand on the platform at Naples station; the two of them later climbed into the same carriage and rode together through the rejoicing crowds.

Garibaldi's Neapolitan triumph was also the cue for 'redeemed' camorra bosses like Salvatore De Crescenzo to cash in on the power they had won, and to turn their tricolour cockades into a licence to extort. After Garibaldi arrived in Naples a temporary authority was set up to rule in his name while the south's incorporation into the Kingdom of Italy was arranged. The short period of Garibaldian rule saw the camorra reveal its true, unredeemed self. As Marc Monnier wryly noted

> When they were made into policemen they stopped
> being *camorristi* for a while. Now they went back to
> being *camorristi* but did not stop being policemen.

The *camorristi* now found extortion and smuggling easier and more profitable than ever. Maritime contraband was a particular speciality of Salvatore De Crescenzo's – he was the 'the sailors' *generalissimo*', according to Monnier. While his armed gangs intimidated customs officials, he is said to have imported enough duty-free clothes to dress the whole city. A less well-known but no less powerful *camorrista*, Pasquale Merolle, came to dominate illegal commerce from the city's agricultural hinterland. As any cartload of wine, meat or milk approached the customs office, Merolle's men would form a scrum around it, shouting '*È roba d' o si Peppe*'. 'This is Uncle Peppe's stuff. Let it through'. Uncle Peppe being Giuseppe Garibaldi. The camorra established a grip on commercial traffic with frightening rapidity; the government's customs revenue crashed. On one day only 25 *soldi* were collected: enough to buy a few pizzas.

The camorra also found entirely new places to exert its influence. Hard on the public celebrations for Garibaldi's arrival there followed widespread feelings of insecurity. Naples was not just a metropolis of plebeian squalor. It was also a city of place-seekers and hangers-on, of underemployed lawyers and of pen-pushers who owed their jobs to favours dished out by the powerful. Much of Naples' precarious livelihood depended heavily on the spin-offs from the Bourbon court and the government. If Naples lost its status as a capital it would also forfeit much of its economic *raison d'être*. People soon began wondering whether their jobs would be safe. A purge, or just a wave of carpet-baggers eager to give jobs to their friends could bring unemployment for thousands. But if no job seemed safe, then no job seemed beyond reach either. The sensible thing to do was to make as much fuss as possible and to constantly harass anyone in authority. That way you were less likely to be forgotten and shunted aside when it came to allocating jobs, contracts and pensions.

In the weeks following Garibaldi's triumphant entry the ministers and administrators trying to run the city on his behalf had to fight their way through crowds of supplicants to get into their offices. *Camorristi* were often waiting at the head of the queue. Antonio Scialoja, the economist who had written such an incisive analysis of the camorra back in 1857, returned to Naples in 1860 and witnessed the mess created under Garibaldi's brief rule.

> The current government has descended into the mire, and is now smeared with it. All the ministers have dished out jobs hand over fist to anyone who pleads loudly enough. Some ministers have reduced themselves to holding court surrounded by those scoundrel chieftains of the people that are referred to here as *camorristi*.

'Some ministers' undoubtedly included Liborio Romano. Not even under the discredited Bourbons had *camorristi* had such opportunities to turn the screws of influence and profit.

Spanishry: **The first battle against the camorra**

On 21 October 1860, an autumn Sunday blessed with joyous sunshine and a clear blue sky, almost every man in Naples voted to enter the Kingdom of Italy. The scenes in the city's biggest piazza – later to be re-baptised Piazza del Plebiscito (Plebiscite Square) in memory of that day – were unforgettable. The basilica of San Francesco di Paola seemed to stretch its vast semi-circular colonnade out to embrace the crowds. Under the portico, a banner reading 'People's assemblies' was stretched between the columns. Beneath there were two huge baskets labelled 'Yes' and 'No'.

In incalculable numbers, yet with patience and good humour, the poorest Neapolitans waited their turn to climb the marble steps and vote. Ragged old men too infirm to walk were carried, weeping with joy, to deposit their ballot in the 'Yes' basket. The tavern-owner, patriotic enforcer and camorra agent known as *la Sangiovannara* was again much in evidence. She was even allowed to vote – the only woman given such an honour – because of her services to the national cause. Etchings of her strong features were published in the press: she was 'the model of Greco-Neapolitan beauty' according to one observer.

Shortly after the plebiscite Garibaldi relinquished his temporary dictatorship and handed over the appalling mess that Liborio Romano had created to the interim authority managing the integration of Naples into the Kingdom of Italy. Over the coming months the camorra would face the first determined drive to break its stranglehold. Naples was set for a struggle to decide who really controlled the streets.

The man given the job of tackling the policing crisis in Naples was another southern Italian patriot, another veteran of the Bourbon jails: Silvio Spaventa. But Spaventa was a very different politician to his predecessor Liborio Romano. A squat man with a black beard suspended below his flabby cheeks, Spaventa applied moral standards as rigidly to his own behaviour as he did to other people's. Where Romano pandered to the crowd, Spaventa was a model of self-containment with an acute aversion to self-display. On one occasion back in 1848 he had attended a political banquet held in a theatre. The climax of the evening came when he was supposed to parade across the stage. Annoyed and flustered, he failed to notice the prompter's box and fell straight into it.

Spaventa responded to the hardships of prison by forcing himself to pore over the philosophies of Hegel and Spinoza. Like the Duke of Castromediano, he was only freed in 1859. When the King of Naples issued the Sovereign Act he returned to Naples to work with the underground Committee of Order. But the incorruptible Spaventa would have nothing to do with any deal with *camorristi*. To avoid the Bourbon police he slept in a different bed every night; the Hôtel de Genève, owned by his friend Marc Monnier, was one of his refuges. Then the fall of the Kingdom of the Two Sicilies gave him the long-awaited chance to implement the lofty conception of the state's ethical role that he had learned from his prison studies. Spaventa was not just a formidable intellect, he was also an adept networker who knew how much personal loyalty could count in building a power base. But Spaventa's character, his principles and his networking skills would all be tested to breaking point when he became the first Italian politician to face down the camorra. Where Liborio Romano had made himself the most loved politician in Naples by cosying up to organised crime, Silvio Spaventa's crackdown earned him nothing but revulsion.

It did not take Spaventa long to realise how hard his task was going to be. On 28 October 1860 he wrote to his brother.

The stench and the rotting mess here are polluting my senses. You just can't imagine what is happening, what they are up to. Everywhere you turn there are people begging and grasping for as much as they can. Everywhere there is wheeler-dealing, intrigue and theft. I see no earthly way this country can return to some reasonable state of affairs. It seems like the moral order has been torn off its hinges . . . The Kingdom is full of murders, robberies and all kinds of disorder.

Southern Italy was sliding towards anarchy. Prices began to rise steeply as new free-market policies were implemented. The economic downturn sharpened latent conflicts between peasants and landowners. The remains of two armies – Garibaldi's and King Francesco II's – were roaming the countryside. Many *garibaldini* gravitated towards Naples, creating another source of trouble. The bulk of Garibaldi's army resented the fact that they had conquered southern Italy only to lose it to sly political manoeuvres directed by a conservative government in far-off Turin. Mingling with them were hangers-on who hoped that putting on a red shirt might help them get a job or just beg a few coins. The new Italian government tried to create jobs in public works to soak up some of the pool of hungry labour. But as the value of government bonds fell, it proved impossible to raise the funds needed.

Given this daunting disarray, Silvio Spaventa deserves great credit for fighting the camorra with such brio. The first mass arrests came on 16 November 1860. Large quantities of arms and police uniforms were recovered. Salvatore De Crescenzo, the 'redeemed' camorra chieftain and *generalissimo* of maritime contraband, was returned to jail. There he would continue his rise to the top. Nearly two years later, on the morning of 3 October 1862 at the very threshold of the Vicaria jail, De Crescenzo would have his main rival in the Honoured Society stabbed to death. In so doing, he became the first supreme *capo* of the Society who did not come from the Vicaria quarter.

But even with De Crescenzo in prison the camorra was not about to buckle under Spaventa's assault. On the night of 21 November 1860 *camorristi* attacked the Prefecture in the hope of liberating their bosses from the cells.

Spaventa pressed on into the New Year, purging the police and sacking many of the corrupt old turnkeys in the prisons. His rigour rapidly made him the focus for Neapolitans' frustration. Although he was a southerner, he seemed like just the kind of haughty northern politician they had feared would be imposed on them from Turin. *The Times* reported that he was widely regarded as 'obnoxious'. In January 1861 there was a street demonstration against him. Many of those shouting 'Down with Spaventa!' were *camorristi* in National Guard uniforms. There followed a petition with several thousand signatures calling for him to be sacked. Oblivious to his own unpopularity, Spaventa responded with more arrests.

In April 1861, in the heat of the battle between the new Italian state and the Neapolitan camorra, Silvio Spaventa received the order from Turin to conduct an investigation into how the camorra operated. Everyone knew it had begun in the prisons but there were still many questions. How did it come to be a secret society, a sect? When was it founded? In search of answers, Spaventa's civil servants began to rummage in the Neapolitan archives and speak to a number of confidential sources.

All of this research produced two outstanding short reports: the Italian government's first ever identikit of the camorra. Keen to generate publicity for his battle, Spaventa later passed on many of the documents he gathered to Marc Monnier. Monnier added his own material by interviewing everyone he could, including Liborio Romano and several *camorristi*.

Spaventa discovered that the camorra in Naples had different chapters, one for each of the city's twelve quarters. Its power, nevertheless, was heavily concentrated in the four quarters of the low city. The *capo camorrista* of each chapter was elected by his peers. Holding office at the *capo*'s side was a *contarulo* or book-keeper, who was charged with the highly sensitive task of gathering and redistributing the Society's money.

Anyone who aspired to become a member of the camorra had to show that he met the Society's criteria: there was a ban on passive homosexuals, for example, and on any man whose wife or sister was a prostitute. (Although this, more even than other clauses in the underworld's rulebook, was honoured almost entirely in the breaking.) Candidates for membership also had to be put to the test and observed by their superiors in the Society. They might be required to commit a murder or administer a disfiguring razor slash to the face of one of the Society's enemies. These razor slashes were used as a form of punishment both for outsiders and members who had broken the rules. They became a horribly visible trademark of the camorra's power in the slums of Naples.

Once a new affiliate was deemed ready, he had to swear an oath over crossed knives and fight a duel by dagger against a *camorrista* who was chosen by lot. If the new recruit proved his courage he became a *picciotto di sgarro* (meaning either 'lad who is up for a fight' or 'lad who rubs you up the wrong way').

Knife fights were so important to the Society that its members spent a great deal of time practising their skills; some *camorristi* even became specialised teachers of the art. Duelling to the death was relatively rare. More often the fight had a ceremonial function, so the participants would be told to aim only for the arms. A dagger fencing contest also marked each criminal's elevation to the Society's more senior rank: *camorrista* proper. Becoming a *camorrista* meant gaining access to decision-making power within the Society, and to a greater share of the profits of crime.

Marc Monnier added some very important riders to this organisational sketch. He explained that the various ranks were inherently flexible.

> The members of the sect do not know how to read, and therefore do not have written laws. They hand down their customs and regulations orally, modifying them according to the time and place, and according to the bosses' will and the decisions taken by their meetings.

Underlying the hierarchies within the camorra there was nevertheless a single principle: exploitation. The *camorristi* pitilessly exploited their juniors, the *picciotti di sgarro*. Monnier describes the life of a 'lad who is up for a fight' as a blend of 'toil, humiliation and danger', all endured in the hope of being promoted to *camorrista* at some point. One common test of a *picciotto di sgarro*'s mettle was to take the blame for a felony committed by a senior member of the Society. Ten years of prison was a price worth paying for the chance to become a *camorrista* in your own right.

What about the sect's origins? The civil servants burrowed further into the archives, but found nothing. Spaventa was puzzled.

> Neapolitan police took action against *camorristi* on many occasions. Yet it is strange but true that they did not leave a single important document that might be useful in deducing the origins of this social plague.

Spaventa did not know that in 1857, for unknown reasons, the Bourbon authorities had burned the police archives that would have told him, and us, a great deal more about how the 'social plague' came into being. The holes in the historical record left space only for suspicion. And suspicion, for Spaventa and his civil servants, centred on Spain.

Monnier and Spaventa together assembled a theory that the camorra arrived in Naples at some point during the sixteenth or seventeenth centuries when the Kingdom of Naples, including Sicily, was part of the Spanish empire, ruled by Viceroys appointed in Madrid. The same theory has been in circulation ever since. The evidence Monnier and Spaventa found to support it is very thin, and comes down to four points that scarcely withstand scrutiny.

First, that *camorra* is a Spanish word, meaning 'quarrel' or 'fight' – which it certainly is, and certainly does. But the origins of the Spanish word are Italian anyway, putting us back where we started: in Naples.

Second, that Miguel de Cervantes, the author of *Don Quixote*, published a short story entitled 'Rinconete and Cortadillo' in 1613 that is set in Seville and concerns a criminal confraternity that looks very like the camorra. The obvious problem here is that Cervantes's story is a fiction, and even if it were based on reality, that hardly constitutes proof of any relationship with the camorra two centuries later.

Third, that there was a secret criminal society in Spain called the *Garduña*, which emerged in the early 1400s. But recent research has shown that the *Garduña* was a fiction too, an intellectual con trick. There is no reference to the supposedly medieval sect before 1845, when it appears from nowhere in a very successful French pulp novel about the terrors of the Spanish Inquisition. The novel was translated into Italian in 1847. Its author seems to have got the idea from Cervantes's 'Rinconete and Cortadillo'.

And last, that Spanish rule was proverbially corrupt, which is the weakest point of all. For our tastes, Spanish rule in Italy may well have been arrogant, ostentatious and devious. In fact, Spain became a byword for a government that showed a haughty contempt for the people it ruled. *Spagnolismo* ('Spanishry') was an Italian political insult that evoked lavish displays of power coupled with deadly manoeuvres behind the scenes. But Spain surrendered control of Naples in 1707. There is absolutely no trace of the camorra before the nineteenth century – well over a hundred years later. Spanish influence would have to be very, very devious indeed to have generated the camorra.

The story of the camorra's Spanish origins is nonsense. Indeed in all probability it is nonsense from the jailbird school of history, a story first put about by the *camorristi* themselves. Rather like the tale of the Spanish knights Osso, Mastrosso and Carcagnosso that we have already encountered in the 'ndrangheta's official account of its own roots, the tale of the *Garduña* and all that is a criminal foundation myth which was likely cobbled together in the mid-nineteenth century at precisely the time that the camorra was asserting itself outside the prison system.

If the story of the camorra's Spanish origins is indeed a foundation myth, how come intelligent people like Silvio Spaventa, Marc Monnier and many others after them were fooled by it? It may be that Spaventa simply lowered his formidable intellectual guard, and this piece of hooey sneaked through unanalysed. But there is an alternative theory: all the talk of Spain was a convenient cover story, and the real origins of the camorra were a little too close for comfort for Italian patriots.

As a historical witness, the Swiss hotelier Marc Monnier had the advantage of his outsider's capacity to be amazed by what he saw, while still being able to get close to many of the leading players. Nevertheless, there are moments when he gets too close to be entirely dispassionate. Monnier was Spaventa's mouthpiece, and as such he dutifully repeated and elaborated what he had learned from the official reports about the camorra's Spanish beginnings. To his credit he also hints at a much more convincing and rather more disturbing theory. As if he knows the truth unconsciously, but cannot quite allow himself to utter it, Monnier compares some camorra rituals to a 'pseudo Masonic fantasmagoria' without elaborating on his point. This is more than an idle comparison: the rules and rituals of the Honoured Society were almost certainly derived not from the mythical *Garduña* but from Freemasonry and other Masonic-style sects.

Masonic organisations were integral to the way politics was done in the early nineteenth century. When the French were in charge in Naples they tried to recruit their elite administrators into the Freemasons as a way of flattering and controlling them. But Masonic groups subsequently became a centre of resistance to French rule and were banned in 1813. The Bourbons were highly suspicious of the secret societies when they were restored to the throne – and with good reason. A Masonic sect of patriots called the *Carbonari* ('Charcoal Burners') infiltrated the army and instigated an unsuccessful revolution in Naples in 1820. When the revolution collapsed, many Charcoal Burners ended up in jail where they came into contact with *camorristi*. Interestingly, Liborio Romano was once a Charcoal Burner.

So, while we will never know *exactly* when and how the camorra of the prison system came to ape the patriotic secret sects of the *Risorgimento*, it seems certain that they did. In short Italy, and Italy's chronic problem with organised crime, were profoundly intertwined from the nation's birth. In 1860 the precise moment when the camorra adopted Masonic-style rituals was still recent enough for the truth to bleed through the words still used by *camorristi*. The camorra's local chapters were sometimes called 'lodges', for example, and *camorristi* referred to the members of their Society as the *Patria*: in other words, the camorra saw itself as a 'nation' of elite criminals.

Even by the 1850s, this criminal *Patria* had its own national anthem, a song summarising the spirit in which the Society viewed the whole business of Italian Unification. It goes something like this:

> The Charcoal Burners are a travesty;
> The Bourbon party's a farce.
> We are the *camorristi*!
> And we take them both up the arse.

Camorristi connived with the Bourbons against the patriots, and then with the patriots against the Bourbons. In doing so, they played a key role in making Naples into part of the new Italy. But through all those murky dealings, *camorristi* held true to the methods that Duke Sigismondo Castromediano had observed in jail. Their aim was to extort and smuggle, to 'extract gold from fleas'. Politics – even the inspiring politics of the *Risorgimento* and Garibaldi's heroism – were only a means to that sordid end.

While his civil servants were researching the secrets of the camorra's past, the incorruptible Silvio Spaventa continued his efforts to curtail its present power. One measure he adopted annoyed *camorristi* more than anything else: he stopped National Guardsmen wearing their uniforms when they were not on duty. For the hoodlums who had infiltrated the National Guard, this ban meant that they could not use the uniform as a cover for extortion operations.

Revenge followed swiftly. On 26 April 1861 an angry mob comprising many *camorristi* invaded the ministry building. This time, the cry was not 'Down with Spaventa!' but 'Death to Spaventa!' They forced their way past the guards and into his office but his loyal secretaries managed to buy time while he escaped down a secret staircase. The mob then followed him to his house and smashed its way in. Spectators in the street looked up to see a man appear on the balcony; he waved a long knife and cried, 'Here's the blade I killed him with, and here is his blood!'

In reality, Spaventa had escaped once more. But the attack was so shocking as to make him overcome his deep-seated abhorrence of public attention. The following day he put on a show of courage by going to lunch at the Caffè d'Europa. That evening he sat in a second tier box on the first night of a new production of Bellini's *Norma* at the Teatro San Carlo – the theatre where the rulers of Naples had traditionally made themselves visible to the public that counted. Spaventa even left by the main staircase, under the eyes of a stupefied crowd. He had learned the hard way that Naples could not be governed without a little Spanishry, a little ostentation.

Three months later it became clear that he had learned some other lessons too. In July 1861, in a busy street a short walk from Spaventa's house, a senior police officer called Ferdinando Mele was stabbed behind the ear in broad daylight; he was dead within hours. Mele embodied all the contradictions of the time and place: a *camorrista* who had allied himself with the patriots, he was one of the chief suspects in the murder of Aversa Joe; he was then recruited into the police by Liborio Romano in June 1860 and put in charge of law and order in a whole city quarter.

Mele's killer was soon caught and dragged through the streets into custody. His name was De Mata; he had killed Mele out of revenge because Mele had arrested his equally thuggish brother. De Mata also embodied some very strange contradictions. Although he was not a member of the Honoured Society, he was still an extortionist who had escaped from prison. Yet somehow, thanks to a powerful friend, this dangerous man had found a no-show job at the Post Office.

That powerful friend, it turned out, was Silvio Spaventa. Both De Mata brothers were members of Spaventa's personal bodyguard. There were rumours that Spaventa used the De Matas and their gang to close down politically dangerous newspapers and beat up uncooperative journalists. So it seems that even the incorruptible Spaventa had ended up 'co-managing' Naples with criminals.

Spaventa resigned in the wake of the scandal – although the government spun out a cover story to conceal the real reason why he had stepped down. *The Times* commented glumly on the whole affair for its perplexed readers back in London.

> Nothing will bear examination in Naples. Under the fairest aspects you will find nothing but rottenness; and

any man who expects order and tranquillity in this province during the next generation must be very slightly acquainted with the country and the people.

Spaventa's story did indeed foreshadow a sombre future for law and order in Naples. Although the authorities would never again ask the camorra to keep order as Liborio Romano had done, there would be the same dreary swings of the policing pendulum for years to come: first towards repression, with mass arrests accompanied by loud anti-camorra rhetoric; then back towards 'co-management', as the bosses reasserted their hold over the low city. Italian unification in Naples had been a chaotic and unpredictable affair, but it had nonetheless set a simple and lasting pattern for the future history of the camorra.

The events of 1860–61 also heralded the future in ways that were still more worrying. Marc Monnier, our Swiss hotelier, saw the evidence with his own eyes during Spaventa's crackdown.

I can tell all: every *camorrista* that was arrested could call on influential protectors who issued certificates of good conduct for him. The moment a member of the sect was led to the Vicaria prison, the Chief of Police was sure to receive twenty letters defending the 'poor man'; the letters were all signed by respectable people!

Politicians were prominent among these 'respectable people' who had befriended the camorra.

During elections the *camorristi* stopped some candidates from standing; and if any voter objected to this on grounds of conscience or religion, they would appease him with their cudgels. What is more, the *camorristi* were not content to send a deputy to Parliament, and then just watch over his behaviour from a distance. They kept a beady eye on what he did, and had his speeches read aloud to them – since they could not read themselves. If they were not happy with what they heard, they would greet their Member of Parliament on his return from Turin with a bestial chorus of whistling and shouting that would burst out suddenly under the windows of his house.

Clearly the Honoured Society had learned an important lesson from everything that had happened during the crisis of the Bourbon regime and the foundation of a united Italy: a lesson in wedding its own opportunism to the opportunism of the more unscrupulous politicians.

Where once the camorra had lurked, cockroach-like, in the seamiest corners of the Kingdom of the Two Sicilies, now it had begun to climb up through the cracks in the social structure and infest the representative institutions of the Kingdom of Italy. At the end of all the intrigues of Italian Unification, the camorra was no longer just a problem that lay where the state could not reach: it was a problem within the state itself.

In 1864, Marc Monnier, who had done so much to explain the camorra to readers across Italy, was awarded honorary citizenship following a recommendation by a friend and patriotic hero, Gennaro Sambiase Sanseverino, Duke of San Donato. San Donato had known prison and exile during the 1850s. He became a Colonel in the National Guard under Liborio Romano in 1860. After the plebiscite, during Silvio Spaventa's campaign against the camorra, San Donato was given charge of the city's theatres; in the course of his duties, a *camorrista* stabbed him in the back outside the Teatro San Carlo. We do not know why the camorra tried to kill San Donato, but we can guess, because we have met the Duke already: he was the 'Neapolitan gentleman' and patriotic conspirator who told Monnier about his secret meeting with the camorra bosses in the 1850s. He was one of the minds behind the patriots' deal with the Honoured Society. San Donato would go on to be mayor of Naples from 1876 to 1878, and was a key figure in the city's sleazy machine politics until the end of the century. The camorra was part of his patronage network. San Donato became what the camorra's redeemer, Liborio Romano, might have become had he not died in 1867.

Marc Monnier had passed through the intrigues of the 1850s and early 1860s with the serenity of an inert particle in a raging chemical reaction. After receiving his honorary citizenship there was little left for him to write about in Italy, so he sold the Hôtel de Genève and moved his young family to Switzerland. He could now finally realise his ambition to be a Genevan author rather than a Neapolitan hotelier. He went on to write a great deal more journalism (for money) and tens of plays (for literary immortality). None of his works has enjoyed anything like the lasting success of his book on the camorra.

Italy was governed between 1860 and 1876 by a loose coalition known as the Right. The Right's leaders were typically land-owning, conservative free-marketeers; they favoured rigour in finance and in the application of the law; they admired Britain and believed that the vote was not a right for all but a respon-sibility that came in a package with property ownership. (Accord-ingly, until 1882, only around 2 per cent of the Italian population was entitled to vote.)

The men of the Right were also predominantly from the north. The problem they faced in the south throughout their time in power was that there were all too few southerners like Silvio Spaventa. Too few men, in other words, who shared the Right's underlying values.

The Right's fight against the Neapolitan camorra did not end with Spaventa's undignified exit from the city in the summer of 1861. There were more big roundups of *camorristi* in 1862. Late in the same year Spaventa himself became deputy to the Interior Minister in Turin, and began once more to gather information on the Honoured Society. While the publication of Marc

Monnier's *The Camorra* kept the issue in the public mind, Spaventa made sure that the camorra was included within the terms of reference of a new Parliamentary Commission of Inquiry into the so-called 'Great Brigandage', a wave of peasant unrest and banditry that had engulfed much of the southern Italian countryside. The outcome of the Commission's work was a notoriously draconian law passed in August 1863 – a law that heralds the most enduring historical irony of Silvio Spaventa's personal crusade against organised crime, and of the Right's time in power. The name for that irony is 'enforced residence'.

The new law of August 1863 gave small panels of government functionaries and magistrates the power to punish certain categories of suspects without a trial. The punishment they could hand down was enforced residence – meaning internal exile to a penal colony on some rocky island off the Italian coast. Thanks to Spaventa, *camorristi* were included in the list of people who could be arbitrarily deprived of their liberty in this way.

Enforced residence was designed to deal with *camorristi* because they were difficult to prosecute by normal means, not least because they were so good at intimidating witnesses and could call on protectors among the elite of Neapolitan society. But once on their penal islands, *camorristi* had every opportunity to go about their usual business and also to turn younger inmates into hardened delinquents. In 1876 an army doctor spent three months working in a typical penal colony in the Adriatic Sea.

> Among the enforced residents there are men who demand respect and unlimited veneration from the rest. Every day they buy, sell and meddle without provoking hatred or rivalry. Their word is usually law, and their every gesture a command. They are called *camorristi*. They have their statutes, their rites, their bosses. They win promotion according to the wickedness of their deeds. Each of them has a primary duty to keep silent about any crime, and to respond to orders from above with blind obedience.

Enforced residence became the police's main weapon against suspected gangsters. But far from being a solution to Italy's organised crime emergency as Silvio Spaventa hoped, it would turn out to be a way of perpetuating it.

In 1865, before these ironies had time to unfold, rumours of another criminal sect began to reach the Right's administrators – 'the so-called Maffia' of Sicily. The mafia would soon penetrate Italy's new governing institutions far more thoroughly than did the camorra in Naples. So thoroughly as to make it impossible to tell where the sect ended and the state began.

2

GETTING TO KNOW THE MAFIA

1865–1877

Rebels in corduroy

Like the camorra, the Sicilian mafia precipitated out from the dirty politics of Italian unification.

Before Garibaldi conquered Sicily in 1860 and handed it over to the new Kingdom of Italy, the island was ruled from Naples as part of the Kingdom of the Two Sicilies. In Sicily, as in Naples, the prisons of the early nineteenth century were filthy, overcrowded, badly managed, and run from within by *camorristi*. Educated revolutionaries joined secret Masonic sects like the Charcoal Burners. When the sect members were jailed they built relationships with the prison gangsters and recruited them as insurrectionary muscle. Soon those gangsters learned the benefits of organising along Masonic lines and, sure enough, the Bourbon authorities found it hard to govern without coming to terms with the thugs. In Sicily, just as in Naples, Italian patriots would overthrow the old regime only to find themselves repeating some of its nefarious dealings with organised crime.

But the Sicilian mafia was, from the outset, far more powerful than the Neapolitan camorra, far more profoundly enmeshed with political power, far more ferocious in its grip on the economy. Why? The short answer is that the mafia developed on an island that was not just lawless: it was a giant research institute for perfecting criminal business models.

The problems began before Italian unification, when Sicily belonged to the Kingdom of the Two Sicilies. The authority of the Bourbon state was more fragile in Sicily than anywhere else. The island had an entirely justified reputation as a crucible of revolution. In addition to half a dozen minor revolts there were major insurrections in 1820, 1848, and of course in May 1860, when Giuseppe Garibaldi's redshirted invasion triggered the overthrow of Bourbon rule on the island. Sicily lurched between revolution and the restoration of order.

Under the Bourbons, Naples completely failed to impose order on the Sicilians, and the Sicilians proved too politically divided to impose order on themselves. Once upon a time, before the invention of policing, private militias beholden to great landowners kept the peace on much of the island. In the early nineteenth century, despite the attempt to introduce a centralised, modern police force, the situation began to degenerate. All too often, rather than being impartial enforcers of the law, the new policemen were merely one more competing source of power among many – racketeers in uniform. Alongside the cops were private armies, groups of bandits, armed bands of fathers and sons, local political factions, cattle rustlers: all of them murdered, stole, extorted and twisted the law in their own interests.

To make matters worse, Sicily was also going through the turmoil brought about by the transition from a feudal to a capitalist system of land ownership. No longer would property only be handed down from noble father to noble firstborn son. It could now be bought and sold on the open market. Wealth was becoming more mobile than it had ever been. In the west of Sicily there were fewer great landowners than in the east and the market for buying land, and particularly for renting and managing it, was more fluid. Here becoming a man of means was easier – as long as you were good with a gun and could buy good friends in the law and politics.

By the 1830s there were already signs of which criminal business model would eventually emerge victorious. In Naples the members of patriotic sects made a covenant with the street toughs of the camorra. But in lawless Sicily, scattered documentary records tell us that the revolutionary sects themselves sometimes turned to crime. One official report from 1830 tells of a Charcoal Burner sect that was muscling its way into local government contracts. In 1838 a Bourbon investigating magistrate sent a report from Trapani with news of what he called 'Unions or brotherhoods, sects of a kind': these Unions formed 'little governments within the government'; they were an ongoing conspiracy against the efficient administration of state business. Were these Unions the mafia, or at least forerunners of the mafia? They may have been. But the documentary record is just too fragmentary and biased for us to be sure.

The condition of Sicily only seemed to worsen after it became part of Italy in 1860. The Right governments faced even graver problems imposing order here than they did in the rest of the south. A good proportion of Sicily's political class favoured autonomy within the Kingdom of Italy. But the Right was highly reluctant to grant that autonomy. How could Sicily govern its own affairs, the Right reasoned, when the political landscape was filled with a parade of folk demons? A reactionary clergy who were nostalgic for the Bourbon kings; revolutionaries who wanted a republic and were prepared to ally themselves with outlaws in order to achieve it; local political cliques who stole, murdered and kidnapped their way to power. However, the Right's only alternative to autonomy was military law. The Right ruled Sicily with both an iron fist and a wagging finger. In doing so, it made itself hated.

In 1865 came the first news of 'the so-called Maffia or criminal association'. The Maffia was powerful, and powerfully enmeshed in Sicilian politics, or so one government envoy reported. Whatever this new word 'Maffia' or 'mafia' meant (and the uncertainty in the spelling was symptomatic of all manner of deeper mysteries), it provided a very good excuse for yet another crackdown: mass roundups of deserters, draft dodgers and suspected *maffiosi* duly followed.

Then, on Sunday 16 September 1866, the Right paid the price for the hatred it inspired in Sicily. On that morning, Italy – and history – got its first clear look at what is now the world's most notorious criminal band.

Palermo in 1866. Almost the entire city was sliced into four quarters by two rectilinear streets, each lined with grimy-grand palaces and churches, each perhaps fifteen minutes' walk from one gated end to the other. At the city's centre, the meeting point of its two axes, was the piazza known as the Quattro Canti. The via Maqueda pointed north-west from here, aiming towards the only gap in the surrounding ring of mountains. Palermo's one true suburb, the Borgo, ran along the north shore from near the Maqueda gate. The Borgo connected the city to its port and to the looming, bastioned walls of the Ucciardone – the great prison.

Palermo's other principal thoroughfare, the Cassaro, ran directly inland from near the bay, across the Quattro Canti, and left the city at its south-western entrance adjacent to the massive bulk of the Royal Palace. In the middle distance it climbed the flank of Monte Caputo to Monreale, a city famed for its cathedral's golden, mosaic-encrusted vault which is dominated by the figure of Christ 'Pantocrator' – the ruler of the universe, in all his kindly omnipotence.

The magnificent view inside Monreale cathedral was matched by the one outside: from this height the eye scanned the expanse of countryside that separated Palermo from the mountains. Framed by the blue of the bay, the glossy green of orange groves was dappled with the grey of the olives; one-storey cottages threw out their white angles among the foliage, and water towers pointed at the sky. This was the Conca d'Oro ('golden hollow' or 'golden shell').

More than any other aspect of Palermo's beautiful setting, it was the Conca d'Oro that earned the city the nickname *la felice* – 'the happy', or 'the lucky'. Yet any outsider unwise enough to wander along the lanes of the Conca d'Oro would have soon detected that there was something seriously wrong behind the Edenic façade. At many points along the walls surrounding the orange groves a sculpted crucifix accompanied by a crude inscription proclaimed the point where someone had been murdered for reporting a crime to the authorities. The Conca d'Oro was the most lawless place in the lawless island of Sicily; it was the birthplace of the Sicilian mafia.

So no one was surprised that when trouble entered Palermo on the morning of 16 September 1866, it came from the Conca d'Oro. Specifically, it came down the long, straight, dusty road from Monreale, through the citrus gardens, and past the Royal Palace. The vanguard of the revolt was a squad from Monreale itself; it comprised some 300 men, most of them armed with hunting guns and wearing the corduroy and fustian that were habitual for farmers and agricultural labourers. Similar squads marched on Palermo from the satellite villages of the Conca d'Oro and from the small towns in the mountains behind. Some sported caps, scarves and flags in republican red, or carried banners with the image of the city's patron, Saint Rosalia.

By seven o'clock even the heaviest sleepers in the furthest corners of Palermo had been woken by the sound of musketry and shouting. There was confusion. But the urban masses quickly grabbed the chance to vent their frustrations.

Seven and a half days passed before troops restored order. Seven and a half days when barricades went up in the streets, when arms depots and official buildings were ransacked, when police stations and law courts were raided and criminal records burned, when respectable citizens were robbed at gunpoint in their homes, or forced to make contributions to support the insurrection.

The revolt of September 1866 came at a terrible time for Italian national morale. One of the reasons for the rebels' initial success was that Palermo was lightly garrisoned. All available military forces had been sent to the north-eastern frontier where the Austrians inflicted humiliation by both land and sea at the battles of Custoza and Lissa. The anarchy down in western Sicily was a stab in the back.

Things could easily have been much worse. One of the revolt's primary targets was the Ucciardone, housing two and a half thousand prisoners; many of them would have swollen the ranks of the squads. The rebels surrounded the jail and tried to blow a breach in the walls. But just in time, on the morning of 18 September, the steam corvette *Tancredi* arrived to shower the besiegers with grapeshot and grenades. One of the first men to be hit in this bombardment, his legs grotesquely mangled by shrapnel, was Turi Miceli, the fifty-three-year-old leader of the Monreale crew that had spearheaded the rebellion; he took hours to die of his injuries, and did so without uttering the slightest murmur of complaint.

Turi Miceli was a *mafioso*. He was a tall, imposing figure with a distinctive large scar on his face. Violence was his livelihood. The very sight of him, with his arquebus over his shoulder, had struck terror into the countryside around Palermo. Yet by the time Miceli died he was also a man of money and property, one of the wealthiest people in Monreale.

The camorra was, in its origins, a proletarian criminal association, incubated among the scum of the Neapolitan jails and slums. *Mafiosi* like Turi Miceli were, by contrast, 'middle-class villains' – as one early mafia expert would term them. In much of the rest of western Europe this would have sounded like a contradiction in terms: 'it seemed to subvert every single principle of political economy and social science', as one bewildered observer noted. Men of property had a stake in maintaining the law – that much was surely a self-evident truth. Yet in Palermo's environs, landowners had become criminals and accomplices. In western Sicily, violence was a profession for the upwardly mobile.

So before we retrace the path of *mafioso* Turi Miceli's rise up the social ranks, it is worth highlighting the other striking contrasts between him and someone like Salvatore De Crescenzo, the 'redeemed' camorra boss. Early *camorristi* like De Crescenzo almost invariably had a long stretch inside on their underworld *curriculum vitae*. Yet prison does not appear in the documentary records that Turi Miceli left in his wake. As far as we know, Miceli did not spend a single day in jail, and the same can be said of many of the other bosses we will meet. Sicily certainly had its prison *camorristi*, and the mafia's leaders willingly recruited such men. But some of the most important bosses perfected their skills elsewhere.

The first secret of Turi Miceli's upward mobility lay in the business he was involved in. The land around Miceli's hometown of Monreale was typical of the Conca d'Oro. It was divided up into smallholdings and the dominant crops were olives, vines and particularly oranges and lemons. Citrus fruit trees certainly appealed to the aesthetic senses of visitors, but they also furnished Sicily's most important export business. From Palermo the lemons were mainly shipped across the Atlantic to the burgeoning market of the United States. There was serious money in citrus fruit: in 1860 it was calculated that Palermo's lemon plantations were the most profitable agricultural land in Europe.

The big profits attracted big investment. To create an orange or lemon garden from nothing involved far more than just sticking a few trees in the ground; it was an expensive, long-term project. High walls had to be built to protect the plants from cold. There were roads to lay, storage facilities to construct and irrigation channels to dig. In fact, sophisticated irrigation was vital because if they were watered correctly, citrus fruit trees could crop twice a year instead of once. Yet after all this groundwork was done, it still took around eight years for the trees to start to produce fruit, and several more before the investment turned a profit.

In the Conca d'Oro, as everywhere else in the world, investment and profit came with a third indispensible ingredient of capitalism: risk. But in the Conca d'Oro, risk came dressed in corduroy.

The *mafiosi* of the Palermo hinterland learned the art of the protection racket by vandalising fruit groves, or threatening to vandalise them. Rather than extracting gold from fleas, they squeezed it from lemons. The options were many and varied: they could cut down trees, intimidate farmhands, starve irrigation channels of water at crucial moments of the season, kidnap landowners and their families, threaten wholesalers and cart drivers, and so on. So *mafiosi* wore many hats: they were the men who controlled the sluices of the precious irrigation channels; the guards who protected the groves at night; they were the brokers who took the lemons to market; the contractors who managed the groves on behalf of landowners; and they were also the bandits who kidnapped farmers and stole their highly valuable crops. By creating risk with one hand, and proffering protection with the other, *mafiosi* could infiltrate and manipulate the citrus fruit business in myriad ways. Some of them, like Turi Miceli, could even vandalise and murder their way to ownership of a lemon grove.

Turi Miceli the *mafioso* was both a criminal and a market gardener. But, as the events of September 1866 showed, he was a revolutionary too – as were the other early mafia bosses. Sicily's revolutions provided the other crucial propellant for the mafia's ascent.

For when revolution came along, as it regularly did, it proved good for criminal business. The typical *mafioso* understood that fact better even than the typical *camorrista*. The inevitable confusion of revolution offered men like Turi Miceli the chance to open prisons, burn police records, kill off cops and informers and rob and blackmail wealthy people associated with the fallen regime. Then, once the bloodletting had passed, new revolutionary governments whose leaders needed enforcers would grant amnesties to powerful men 'persecuted' under the old order. In Sicily, much more than in Naples, revolution was the test bed of organised crime, and the launch pad for many a mobster's rise up the social scale.

Turi Miceli's rebel opportunism during the *Risorgimento* was breathtaking. When revolution against the Bourbons broke out in January 1848, Miceli was a known bandit – meaning that he indulged in cattle rustling and armed robbery. But he grasped the chance offered by the revolt with impressive daring: his squad, mostly comprising market gardeners, captured the Bourbon garrison in Monreale before trooping down the hill to Palermo.

There, Miceli was celebrated by local poets and lauded in official dispatches for defeating a Bourbon cavalry unit near the Royal Palace. Despite disturbing reports of crimes committed by his men, Miceli was awarded the rank of Colonel by the new revolutionary government, partly because his goons packed the meeting at which the officers were elected. The Monreale bandit had 'remade his virginity', as the Sicilian saying goes.

The following year, when the revolution began to fall apart and Bourbon troops were advancing on Palermo, Miceli promptly swapped sides: he toured the main streets and defensive entrenchments persuading the populace not to offer any resistance. His reward from the restored Bourbon authorities was yet another virginity: he was amnestied and given the chance to stuff his pockets. First he was made customs officer, paid 30 ducats a month to pick his own band of men and patrol a long stretch of coastline in eastern Sicily, presumably confiscating contraband and taking hefty bribes at the same time. Not long after that he won the tax-collecting franchise in Lercara Friddi, a sulphur-mining town not too far from Palermo. A senior government official gave him a job reference that said – in blatant contradiction of the facts – that Miceli played no part whatsoever in the 1848 revolution.

In 1860 Miceli nonchalantly changed sides once more and supported Garibaldi's fight against the Bourbons. Naturally, he was then recruited into the National Guard. Under Miceli's control, the National Guard in Monreale was described in an official report of July 1862 as being made up of 'robbers, *cammoristi* [sic], Bourbon royalists and corrupt men'.

Miceli did not have the same success in building his career under the Italian government as he had done under the Bourbons. And like everyone else, he could see how detested Italian government authority in Sicily was. So in September 1866, Miceli staked his fortunes on revolution for what turned out to be the last time. The revolt's aims were confused: Bourbon restoration, or a republic – no one was very sure. That did not matter to Turi

Miceli. Politics, of whatever stripe, was just a way to convert ferocity into influence, position and money.

In September 1866, for the first and last time, Turi Miceli backed the wrong side and found an agonising death. The revolt was crushed. There were to be no more revolutions in Sicily. For good or ill, Italy was in the island to stay. Other mafia bosses understood that better than Miceli. Instead of forming squads and leading the revolt, they formed what were called 'counter-squads' and defended the Italian status quo. Their strategy echoed the moves made by 'redeemed' camorra boss of Naples, Salvatore De Crescenzo: like De Crescenzo, most top *mafiosi* calculated that supporting the cause of Italy was now the surest way to guarantee their criminal fortunes. September 1866 was to be a crucial transitional moment in the history of the mafia.

The benign mafia

In nineteenth-century Naples, nobody ever questioned whether the camorra existed. Of course there was occasional reticence about the contacts between the early camorra and the Masonic societies of the *Risorgimento*. But nobody ever tried to pretend that 'camorra' meant anything other than what it really was: a secret criminal sect.

Yet for most of the Sicilian mafia's history, most people did not believe it was a sworn criminal fraternity, a Freemasonry of delinquents. 'Mafia', or better, 'mafiosity' – it was said – was a characteristic Sicilian mentality, an island syndrome. If you were *mafioso* you suffered from a swelling of the ego that made you reluctant to settle your disputes through official channels. The symptoms of this strange malady were probably inherited from Sicily's ninth-century Arab invaders.

Late-twentieth-century sociologists had their own versions of the same theory. *Mafiosi* were affiliates of self-help groups in poor, isolated villages – who just happened to kill people occasionally. Or they were local problem solvers and mediators, judges whose courtroom was the piazza and whose law book was an ancient, unwritten code of honour. Meadow Soprano, daughter of TV mafia boss Tony, summed up the theory nicely when she said that the mafia was 'an informal method of conflict resolution in Mediterranean societies'.

As we shall see, this tangle of mystifications was deliberately spun by the mafia and its allies in the Sicilian ruling class. One of the main reasons why the Sicilian mafia was for so long Italy's most powerful criminal organisation was because of its ability to perpetuate the illusion that it did not even exist. The illusion was first created in the years following the Palermo revolt of 1866.

From the Right government's point of view, the miserable story of the 1866 revolt did at least have a hero in Antonio Starabba, Marquis of Rudinì, and Mayor of Palermo. Like all mayors at this time, he was appointed directly by the king rather than being elected by the local people. Rudinì got the Palermo job because despite being a Sicilian, indeed one of the island's biggest land-owners, he was a man of the Right. His rectitude and courage amid the mayhem did honour to the Italian flag, and drew the admiration of the European press.

When the squads descended on the city Rudinì mustered the members of his administration to defend the town hall from the rebels. His house at the Quattro Canti was ransacked; his father died from shock as a result; and his wife only just escaped by clambering through a window with their baby in her arms. When the town hall became indefensible, Rudinì led its occupants to the safer surroundings of the Royal Palace. There, with other beleaguered government loyalists, he survived for the rest of the week on horse meat, and shot back at the insurgents with musket balls made from melted down gas pipes. Tall, blonde and hand-some, with an easy authority to his manner, Rudinì was not yet thirty years old but his political career was set on a steep, upward trajectory. He was now a poster boy for the Right's project to civilise Sicily. Soon after the revolt he was promoted from Mayor to Prefect. In other words, he was the eyes and ears of central government in the provinces, an official with access to high-level police intelligence. When it came to the problems of Sicily, nobody could command the attention of central government more than him.

Marquis Rudinì was given a platform for his opinions eight months after the Palermo revolt of September 1866, when a parliamentary commission of inquiry came to Sicily to learn the lessons. The commissioners assembled in the comfort of the Hotel Trinacria set back from the marina, its doors protected by a picket of troops. They heard Rudinì give a testimony that addressed the mafia issue with shocking clarity.

> The Mafia is powerful – perhaps even more powerful than people believe. Uncovering it and punishing it is very often impossible, because there is no proof, either of the crimes, or of who is to blame . . . We've never been able to pull together enough evidence to prepare a trial and bring it to a successful conclusion.
>
> Only people who have the Mafia's protection can move around freely in the countryside . . . The lack of security has brought about the following situation: anyone who wants to go into the countryside and live there has to become a brigand. There is no alternative. To defend yourself and your property, you have to obtain protection from the criminals, and tie yourself to them in some way.
>
> The Ucciardone – the Palermo prison – is a kind of government. That's where rules, orders, etc. are issued. In the Ucciardone they know everything. So that might lead us to believe that the Mafia has formally recognised bosses.
>
> In the countryside around Palermo criminal gangs are very widespread, and there are many different bosses. But they often act in agreement with one another and look to the Ucciardone for leadership.
>
> Their aim is to get rich in the disorder and bump off their enemies. Robbery and vendetta, in short.

Rudinì was right. Or at least he was as right as he could feasibly be at this early stage in the mafia's history. Granted, talking about the mafia was politically convenient for the young Marquis. For one thing, it saved his having to address his own share of the blame for the revolt. His high-handed policies as mayor had made him as loathed in Palermo as Silvio Spaventa was in Naples.

Nevertheless, we can now appreciate just how far towards a

full understanding of the mafia Rudinì had advanced. He was particularly astute in identifying how the property owners of the area had to 'tie themselves' to the mafia. The threats and promises that won the mafia such a big slice of the citrus fruit business also won them freedom from the law and friends in high places. Here lay the genuine shock effect of Rudinì's words: the land-owners who had become 'brigands' were also the ruling class of the province of Palermo, its political leadership.

The self-assured young Marquis Rudinì did not have all the answers, of course. He was sensible enough to acknowledge as much: he confessed that he could not tell how many bosses and affiliates the mafia had, for instance. 'To really appreciate the Mafia's power and influence, we would need to get to know this mysterious organisation better.'

A decade later, another parliamentary inquiry squinted into the murk of Sicilian affairs. In March 1876, this time in Rome (which had become the capital city in 1870), Marquis Rudinì was called to demonstrate whether he had indeed managed to get to know the mysterious mafia organisation any better.

Rudinì's political career had made further progress in the mean-time: he became Minister of the Interior for a while in 1869. Yet the years seemed to have eroded his confidence. His views on the mafia were now hesitant, slippery, and confusing.

He began by saying that, in Sicily, public opinion had been 'led astray' in such a way that criminals had become 'likeable' to the local population. Perhaps sensing that these words might not play well in Sicily, he tried to claim that the same thing 'happens in every country in the world'. Ignoring the puzzled frowns of the commission members sitting before him, he blundered on.

> Now when public opinion and indeed the very moral sense of any population is led astray in the way I have described, the result is the maffia. The famous maffia! But what is this maffia? Let me say first of all that there

is a benign maffia. The benign maffia is a sort of bravado. It is a strange inclination not to allow yourself to be bullied; instead, you bully others. It's about striking an attitude – the attitude of the *farceur*, or practical joker, as the French would say. Thus I myself could be a benign *maffioso*. Not that I am one. But, in a nutshell, anyone who respects himself, who has a dash of exaggerated haughtiness, could be one.

Rudinì's waffling testimony then moved onto what he called the 'malign maffia', which was, he asserted, the unfortunate result of the 'atmosphere' created by the benign maffia. As if he had not already done enough to baffle his listeners, he further divided the malign mafia into two distinct and apparently unconnected types. First there was the prison mafia – but that had all but disappeared anyway; then there was what he called a 'high mafia'. Unlike the prison mafia, the high mafia was not a genuine criminal association. Instead, it was what he termed a 'solidarity in crime'.

It was all about as clear as a glass of black Sicilian wine. No mention of an organisation. No mention of bosses or links between the prisons and criminals on the outside. No reference to landowners who become 'brigands' or to protection rackets. No mention of lemon groves, witnesses being intimidated, or robbery and vendetta. Not even a suggestion that there might be more to learn.

Between 1867 and 1876, Marquis Rudinì's views on the mafia had retreated from clarity into muddle, from forthright condemnation into woolly apologia.

Rudinì was not the only witness to spin out such verbiage in 1876. Some flatly denied that the mafia even existed. Many others talked about a 'good mafia' and a 'bad mafia', about the islanders' proud way of taking the law into their own hands, and so on. If the mafia did exist, it was something shapeless and hard to explain to an outsider, something that Sicilians felt in their bones. Nobody could ever hope to get to know the mafia better.

Rudinì had very good reasons for being flustered when he came before the 1876 commission of inquiry. The commission itself had been instituted in the aftermath of a scandal involving the Chief of Police of Palermo, a man called Giuseppe Albanese. In 1871 Albanese went on the run to avoid being arrested for arranging several murders in concert with the mafia chief of Monreale, who was presumably Turi Miceli's successor as boss of the town. While in hiding, Police Chief Albanese was received in Rome by no less than the Prime Minister, who promised him the government's protection. Not surprisingly there was an outcry in Sicily when Albanese was acquitted for lack of evidence some months later. Then in June 1875 further scandalous details about the Police Chief emerged. His favourite underworld informer led a gang of criminals who had perpetrated a series of burglaries from aristocratic palaces, from the offices of the Court of Appeal, from a pawnbroker's, and even from the city museum. The loot was recovered in the house of a policeman who worked in Albanese's office.

Rudinì was profoundly implicated in the scandal since he had appointed Albanese in the first place. Rudinì had also been Interior Minister, with direct responsibility for law and order policy, when Albanese was employing the mafia to murder people in Monreale. (Albanese's aim, once more, was to co-manage crime with the underworld elite.)

Rudinì also had political reasons for unlearning what he knew about the mafia. As Member of Parliament for a Sicilian constituency, he was one of only a small handful of Right MPs that the island had sent to Rome in the last general election. The Right had bludgeoned Sicily to get rid of the mafia, but then hired the mafia to help in its repressive work. Now it was paying the political price for its hypocrisy and double-dealing. Rudinì was trying desperately to fit in with the new mood, but his efforts proved futile. Eight days after Rudinì's testimony, on 18 March 1876, the Right coalition government split over the issue of railway nationalisation and the Left entered government for the first time. Rudinì was destined for a long spell in the political wilderness.

Like the Right, the Left was a very loose coalition: its unifying themes were the desire to extend democracy and to invest more money in the country's backward infrastructure. The Left was also more southern than the Right, and in particular more Sicilian. With the advent of the Left, Sicilian politicians gained access to power, and the Italian state finally won consent for its authority on the island. Yet among the politicians who now represented Sicily in a Left-dominated chamber were the 'brigands' that Rudinì had spoken of in 1867 – landowners who, willingly or not, had struck a deal with the *mafiosi* to protect and manage their land. The mafia was now able to offer other services to its patrons: election management, for one. Once the Left was in power, the mafia's political sponsors enjoyed purchase with central government.

After the Bourbons, the Right. After the Right, the Left. Whether in times of revolution or in times of peace, no government could control Sicily without going through *mafiosi*.

A sect with a life of its own:
The mafia's rituals discovered

On 29 February 1876, eleven days before Marquis Rudinì put forward his abstruse theories about the 'benign mafia', the Italian government discovered the most important piece of evidence in the entire history of Sicilian organised crime. The Palermo Police Chief wrote to the Minister of the Interior to describe, for the first time, the initiation ritual used by *mafiosi* in a settlement in the Conca d'Oro called Uditore.

Uditore was a suburban village, a *borgata*, of only 700–800 souls, but there had been no less than thirty-four murders there in 1874, as rival mafia factions fought for a monopoly over the lucrative business of 'protecting' the market gardens. The local boss was don Antonino Giammona, described by the Chief of Police as 'almost completely lacking in education, but with a natural intelligence'. Another witness described him as 'taciturn, puffed up, and wary'. Giammona even fancied himself as something of a poet and wrote verse in Sicilian dialect.

He also made each of his gang's members-to-be undergo a kind of baptism into a new, more exalted life of crime, the Chief of Police explained. The aspiring *mafioso* was taken to a secluded spot and shown into the company of Giammona and his underbosses. The recruit offered his finger or arm to be punctured with a dagger, and then dripped blood onto a small picture of a saint. The picture was then burned and its ashes scattered to signify the total obliteration of traitors, while the recruit swore eternal loyalty to the sect.

The Police Chief of Palermo was in no doubt about how

significant this find was: it utterly discredited all the waffle about the 'benign mafia', the mafia as an inborn Sicilian egotism.

> It shows that the maffia is not only an individual mani-
> festation of an instinctive tendency to bully people, but
> is instead a sect with a life of its own, which operates in
> the shadows.

The same ritual recurs throughout the history of the mafia in Sicily and North America. But the rules by which individual mafia gangs or *cosche* (pronounced *kos-keh*) live are very rarely written down. So, because they are transmitted by word of mouth, they are susceptible to minor local variations: in the wording of the oath taken by the initiate, for example. Sometimes the bottom lip was pierced, more often the trigger finger. Most *cosche* use a pin to draw blood, some use the thorn from a Seville orange-tree. Different figures appeared on the sacred image that was consumed by the flames, although the Madonna of the Annun-ciation is by far the most frequent. There is nevertheless a strong family resemblance between all the variants. That family resem-blance is the clearest possible demonstration that the mafia is not just a haughty attitude or some vague 'solidarity in crime', as Marquis Rudinì would try to claim. It is an organisation. And that organisation has a history – a single line of continuity that runs from the lemon groves of the Palermo hinterland to the streets of New York and beyond.

In the months following the first unearthing of the initiation rite, news of very similar oaths arrived from elsewhere in the province of Palermo and even across the island in the province of Agrigento. Curiously, one of the *cosche* using these rites was discovered in the town of Canicattì, where Marquis Rudinì had his constituency.

The resemblances between the different mafia gangs were striking. Like the Giammona crew in Uditore, the other *cosche* also used a coded dialogue so that *mafiosi* who did not know one another personally could recognise one another as brothers in crime. The dialogue began when one *mafioso* complained about a toothache and pointed to one of the canines in his upper jaw. The second *mafioso* would reply that he too had a toothache. The two would proceed to tell one another where they were when the tooth began to hurt, who was present, and so on. The 'toothache' signified membership of the mafia; and the references to the time and place the toothache began recalled the moment when the *mafioso* was initiated.

All of this evidence arrived at a politically sensitive time. The Left was consolidating itself in power and discovering that the mafia was something rather more menacing than a peculiar Sicilian form of bravado. Then in November 1876 the state of law and order in Sicily became an international embarrassment when the English manager of a sulphur company was kidnapped in the province of Palermo; there were strong suspicions of mafia involvement.

The Left's new Prefect of Palermo, Antonio Malusardi, became convinced that there was a link, or as he termed it 'a real correspondence' between the various mafia cells. On 30 January 1877 the Prefect wrote to the Chief Prosecutor, the man in charge of the whole judicial system in Palermo, and urged him to unify the different mafia investigations so that the connections between the different *cosche* could be explored. In short, the Prefect of Palermo was asking the Chief Prosecutor to answer a simple but crucial question. Were there many criminal sects in Sicily, or was there just one single Freemasonry of delinquency? One Sicilian mafia, or many?

No Sicilian old enough to remember the 1980s can read Prefect Malusardi's words without a shiver of recognition. For only in 1983, amid a terrifying upsurge in mafia violence, did Palermo investigators finally begin to base their strategy on the 'real correspondences' between the mafia gangs across western Sicily. To trace and document those correspondences, they formed an anti-mafia 'pool' of four specialised prosecutors.

In the summer of the following year, a leading Man of Honour called Tommaso Buscetta, who had lost many of his relatives in the ongoing slaughter, turned state's witness. Buscetta, who was known as the 'boss of the two worlds' because of his transatlantic influence, gave the pool of investigators a deeper insight into the mafia than they had ever had. Among the many vital revelations provided by Buscetta was the initiation ritual that he, like every other Man of Honour, had undergone. In 1992, a verdict from the Court of Cassation, Italy's highest court, finally accepted the boss of two worlds' testimony; it confirmed for *the first time in history* that the mafia was not a loose ensemble of local gangs but a single organisation, bound by an oath of loyalty until death. There was only one Sicilian mafia.

Two of Italy's most courageous and able men would soon pay for this truth with their lives. Within weeks of the Court of Cassation's ruling, the leading members of the anti-mafia pool, Giovanni Falcone and Paolo Borsellino, were both blown up. Tragically, Prefect Malusardi's hunch had finally been proven incontrovertibly – more than a century of bloodshed later. New research tells us that Italy could and should have answered Malusardi's question shortly after he asked it.

The Chief Prosecutor's reply to Prefect Malusardi's letter about the mafia's rituals took more than a month to arrive – a strange delay given the importance of the matter. Its conclusions were absolutely categorical.

> Doubtless there are groups or associations of criminals of various sizes here and there in Sicily. But they are *not* confederated or bound to one another by links of mutual complicity.

The Chief Prosecutor was very hostile to the suggestion that there should be large-scale mafia prosecutions – Italians today call them 'maxi-trials'. Such trials would trample on the autonomy of the magistracy, he protested, and open the way for politically motivated abuses of the law by the government. This argument won the day. In courts across Sicily over the following six years, *mafiosi* were put on trial, many of them for the first time. But they were tried as members of separate, locally based criminal organisations.

The Chief Prosecutor's letter has often been cited by historians sceptical about the existence of a unified criminal network called 'the mafia'. Falcone and Borsellino may have demonstrated beyond doubt the existence of the organisation known as Cosa Nostra, they argue, but it is naïve to project that finding back into the past. In 1877 the far-fetched theory that there was only one mafia suited the government's purposes all too well, it has been claimed. There are few better pretexts for an authoritarian crackdown than the fantasy of a mysterious clandestine sect of murderers with links right across western Sicily. The Chief Prosecutor had access to all the available police evidence on the early mafia, much of which has since been lost. So if someone as knowledgeable as him thought that the different gangs were not 'confederated', who are we, at more than a century's distance, to cast doubt on his conclusions?

Yet on closer inspection, the Chief Prosecutor's letter is hardly a shining example of forensic logic. The different associations could not be linked, he argued, because fighting often broke out between them. The toothache dialogue was not a recent discovery, he added: tough guys across the island had been using the same formulaic exchange for a while to check whether the people they met shared a similar mindset; they had started doing it in the prison in Milazzo, and had probably copied the idea from a story about a noble bandit written by Alexandre Dumas, author of *The Three Musketeers*. The Chief Prosecutor concluded by conceding that on one occasion, and one only, the different gangs had indeed shown a sense of shared purpose: in the revolt of September 1866, when they united in the cause of overthrowing what they called the 'despicable government'.

Quite why these points make for a decisive rebuttal of the

theory that there was a single, unified mafia network is not entirely clear.

Mafiosi killed one another before 1877, and they have done so ever since. But that does not stop them being members of the same brotherhood.

The fact that the toothache routine may have been invented in prison does nothing to diminish the suspicions that surround it – quite the contrary. Nor indeed does the fact that it may have been copied from a novel, an opera, or whatever. As we know from the fable of the camorra's Spanish origins, Italian criminal organisations like to create a rich mythology for themselves; we can hardly be surprised if they are unscrupulous enough to do it by plagiarising bits and pieces from the culture around them.

Last but not least, if many of the gangs were able to coordinate sufficiently well to rise up in simultaneous revolt in September 1866, did that not provide deeply worrying evidence of the links between them?

It is time we met the Chief Prosecutor who put his name to these shaky arguments. He was Carlo Morena, a highly respected magistrate who had been given many decorations during his distinguished career. He came from a place immune to Sicily's 'exaggerated haughtiness', its proudly truculent attitude to official legality: he was born in 1821 in a village in the north, not far from the Ligurian coastal town of Savona.

In March 1876, just after being appointed to the most senior judicial position in Sicily, Morena was interviewed by a Parliamentary inquiry about the state of justice in the Palermo area. His replies were frank – as befitted a magistrate who clearly believed in upholding the rule of law. Sicilian magistrates were weak or corrupt, Morena said; there was a wall of *omertà* among witnesses and even victims; and the courts handed out feeble punishments for violent crimes that undermined the authority of the state.

But by the time he came to reply to Prefect Malusardi ten months later, Carlo Morena was a *mafioso*. He did not have a 'toothache', and was not part of the sworn criminal fraternity. Nor was he necessarily even a willing aide to the gangsters. But he was nonetheless a 'friend of the friends', as the Sicilian expression has it.

Quite what the mafia did to win Morena over in 1876 is not known. He may have been subjected to any mixture of threats, bribery, blackmail, and political pressure. As with the landowners that Marquis Rudinì labelled 'brigands', or indeed with Rudinì himself, many different scenarios are possible. But we can at least be sure that Chief Prosecutor Morena was working for the Honoured Society of Sicily. To find out why, we need to move much, much deeper into the world of the mafia – deeper than was ever possible before the discovery in 2009 of a quite exceptionally revealing document. That document is in the neat handwriting of the first genuine hero in the history of Italian organised crime, a man whose long and eventful career we will follow from now on.

If there is one thing that the mafia fears, it is good police. Despite all the co-management of crime in Naples and Palermo, nineteenth-century Italy did produce some very good police. Among the best of them was a blonde, square-jawed officer called Ermanno Sangiorgi. Sangiorgi's bulky personal file is kept among the endless Ministry of the Interior papers in Rome's Central State Archive. It covers a career that lasted nearly five decades. Sangiorgi retired in 1907, by which time he was the country's most experienced and decorated mafia-fighter. Sangiorgi embodies all the tribulations of the fight against the mafia after Italian unification.

For very good personal and professional reasons, Sangiorgi had no doubts about what the mafia was: a clandestine sect of murderers with links right across western Sicily. For one thing, it was Sangiorgi who led the inquiry into the Uditore mafia whose boss was the dialect poet, don Antonino Giammona, and Sangiorgi who first discovered the initiation ritual and the 'toothache' dialogue.

What follows in the next chapter is the story of a previously unknown investigation that ran in parallel to the case of the Uditore mob. The mafia did not lightly forgive Ermanno Sangiorgi for exposing its initiation ritual. As the mafia's vengeance played itself out, Sangiorgi was to discover just how subtle and ramified was its authority, and just how wrong Carlo Morena was to deny the existence of a unified criminal brotherhood in western Sicily.

Sangiorgi's investigation also reveals the sinister manoeuvrings during the early years of the Left, which saw the mafia put on trial for the first time, but which also saw Sicilian politicians, among them the mafia's friends, step onto the national political stage.

There is one background political issue that is worth keeping in mind from the outset of this story: discontinuity. The problem has bedevilled Italy's response to organised crime for much of the last century and a half. After 1860, whether under the Right or the Left, the Italian system generated one fragile coalition government after another, and therefore a dizzying turnover of officials and policies.

Policing policy is a prime example. The short chain of command that concerns us here descends as follows: from the Prime Minister and then the Interior Minister in Rome, down to the Prefect of Palermo and then through the city's Chief of Police to his officers on the ground. The following story is set over three and a half years, from November 1874 to June 1878. It was a bad period for policy discontinuity, but not unrepresentative: there were three Prime Ministers, four Interior Ministers, six Prefects of Palermo and three Chiefs of Police. Some of them barely had time to hang their jackets up before they were transferred. All the time, at every level, policy swung unpredictably between repressing the mafia and cultivating it. For front-line policemen like Ermanno Sangiorgi, these rapid changes in the political weather could have terrifying consequences.

Double vendetta

Like most Italian policemen, Ermanno Sangiorgi badly wanted to win the favour of the civil servants who controlled his destiny and monitored every detail of his private life. Pay was poor. Conditions were tough. The Public Security Service had a national career structure and a habit of moving its officers rapidly between postings, so that even the rank and file could spend their entire careers in wandering exile among alien communities where the locals spoke incomprehensible dialects and regarded the cops with contempt.

Sangiorgi was from the centre-north of the country; he was born in 1840 in the Romagnol spa town of Riolo. He knew only too well how a police career could play havoc with family life. His first wife died, probably in childbirth, leaving him with a son, Achille, to care for on his own when he was not yet out of his teens. He got married for a second time in 1861, to Enrica Ricci, a girl from a respectable lower-middle-class Faenza family, and the couple gave their children the patriotic names of Italo and Italia. After 1863, much of Sangiorgi's service was spent fighting brigand bands in the south. Posted to primitive mountain communities, he and his wife could not keep Achille with them much of the time. Promotion was the only path to a less arduous life, yet every step up the career ladder had to be twisted from the grasp of politicians and bureaucrats by means of strenuous hard work, string pulling, and sob stories. Sangiorgi had a high sense of his own worth and was dogged in the pursuit of his ambition. As a Prefect would later write of him, 'he seeks out every possible means of getting himself noticed'.

In December 1874 Sangiorgi tried to get himself noticed by the Minister of the Interior, no less. For nine months he had been acting Inspector in Trapani, on the westernmost tip of Sicily, he wrote. The permanent promotion to Inspector that he had been promised had not yet materialised. Of course he had absolute confidence that this promise would be kept – so much so that he had not hesitated to dip into his own pocket to supplement his police pay. After all, he had a wife and three children to support. But his 'intense desire' was to show his gratitude to the minister with further services, and 'to make himself ever more worthy of the Royal Government's consideration'. Would it be possible, therefore, for him to be transferred 'to a place where the conditions of law and order leave more to be desired'?

Sangiorgi was looking for action, and he got all the action he could ever have hoped for. In March 1875 he took charge of the biggest, most heavily populated, and most mafia-infested police district in Sicily: Castel Molo, covering the northern part of the Conca d'Oro. Within its administrative boundaries lay the Piana dei Colli – a fertile plain bounded on one side by the small mountains to Palermo's north-west, and on the other by Monte Pellegrino, an isolated mass of rock that surges from the shore just to the city's north. The Piana dei Colli was dotted with the villas and gardens of the wealthy. Yet, like the rest of the Conca d'Oro, its settlements had a fearsome reputation for lawlessness. A little further to the west, Castel Molo cops also policed the lemon groves of Passo di Rigano and Uditore. These satellite villages were, in Sangiorgi's words, 'sadly renowned for criminal associations and bloody crimes'. Sangiorgi diagnosed the cause of the bloodshed in Castel Molo with incisive calm.

> The mafia dominated the situation, and it had even managed to infect the police station. In fact the main mafia bosses had all been granted gun licences. When murders and other serious crimes happened in the Castel Molo district, as they did frequently, the police chose its informers from among these men . . . They turned to the most notorious *mafiosi* for confidential information on

who was guilty, with the frequent result that poor, honest families were sacrificed, criminals went unpunished, and the general public was disheartened and distrustful.

Clearly the policy of co-managing crime with the mafia was still fully operative. One of the most egregious cases of this policy concerned Sangiorgi's immediate predecessor in charge of the Castel Molo police station, Inspector Matteo Ferro. Ferro had a close friendship with the *mafioso* who was to occupy a central role in Sangiorgi's story: Giovanni Cusimano, known as *il nero* ('Darky') because of his complexion.

Inspector Ferro had already done a great deal to obstruct investigations into the Uditore mafia before Sangiorgi arrived; he had also gone on record to defend Darky, denying that he was a *capomafia*, calling him instead 'an upright man, an individual who is completely devoted to law and order'. This despite the fact that Darky, among many other crimes, had recently terrorised one landowner into granting him a lease on a villa worth 200,000 *Lire* for the derisory annual fee of one hundred litres of olive oil. (A rent which, needless to say, Darky did not even deign to pay.) Once installed in the villa, Darky regularly received visits not only from the friendly local police Inspector, Matteo Ferro, but also from a sergeant in the *Carabinieri*, and the editor of the local newspaper, *L'Amico del Popolo* (*The People's Friend*). Everyone with any influence in the Piana dei Colli was a friend of Darky's.

Soon after establishing himself in Castel Molo police station, Sangiorgi acted.

> I quickly grasped that I needed to adopt a method diametrically opposed to the one that the police had used thus far. So at once I started openly fighting the mafia.

An open fight against the mafia. The simplicity of these words should not mislead as to just how difficult the task really was.

When Sangiorgi revoked the mafia bosses' gun licences and handed out police cautions to them all, he had to overcome opposition on a scale that the police fighting the camorra in Naples had never encountered: Sangiorgi referred to 'the intervention of Senators, MPs, senior magistrates and other notables' in defence of the crime bosses. In other words, the mafia was already part of a network that reached up towards the higher echelons of Italy's governing institutions. Sangiorgi's story is a parable of just how difficult an open fight against that network can be.

At first, Sangiorgi achieved excellent results. 'The mafia went into its shell', he later recalled, 'there was a positive reawakening of public morale, and a marked reduction in the number of crimes.'

Then in November 1875, eight months after Sangiorgi arrived in Palermo, a crippled old man, leaning heavily on a lawyer's arm, was shown into his office. His name was Calogero Gambino, and he was the owner of a lemon grove in the Piana dei Colli, near the *borgata* of San Lorenzo. He began by saying that he had heard of Sangiorgi's reputation as an honest and energetic cop, and so was now turning to him to obtain justice against the mafia.

Gambino had two sons, Antonino and Salvatore. Some eighteen months earlier, on 18 June 1874, Antonino had been ambushed and killed – shot in the back from behind the wall of a lemon grove as he was on his way to spray the family's vines with sulphur. Gambino's other son Salvatore was about to stand trial for his brother's murder. But this 'fratricide' was nothing of the sort, old man Gambino explained. The mafia, in the shape of Darky Cusimano, had killed one son and framed the other: this was its last, cunning act of vengeance against his family.

Without needing to be told, Sangiorgi understood why Gambino had come to see him now: Giovanni 'Darky' Cusimano was dead, a recent victim of the semi-permanent mafia war to control the lemon groves. The bloody end to Cusimano's reign in the Piana dei Colli left Calogero Gambino free to tell his extraordinary story.

A story that was a stick of political dynamite with a fizzing fuse. For old man Gambino also claimed that the police had helped the mafia arrange the fake fratricide. The national scandal surrounding former Chief of Police Albanese had reached its peak only a few months earlier. If what Gambino said was true, it would prove that the corruption had not ended with Albanese; it would prove that the mafia's infiltration of the police in Palermo was still well-nigh systematic.

The 'fratricide' plot against Gambino's surviving son was only the climactic moment of a campaign of vengeance that stretched back over fourteen years, to the time when Garibaldi's expedition to Sicily made the island part of a unified Italian kingdom. The old man said that the mafia had originally targeted him because he was a well-to-do outsider who was not born in San Lorenzo. His son-in-law, Giuseppe Biundi, was the original source of his troubles; Biundi was the nephew of Darky's underboss. In 1860 Biundi kidnapped and raped Gambino's daughter to force a marriage. A few months after the wedding, Gambino's new son-in-law stole several thousand *Lire* from his house. The young man's family connections made old man Gambino too afraid to report the burglary to the authorities, he said.

Then, in 1863, Giuseppe Biundi kidnapped and murdered Gambino's own brother. The old man could no longer keep quiet: following his tip-off to the police, Biundi and his accomplice were caught and sentenced to fifteen years' hard labour.

Sitting in Sangiorgi's office eleven years later, Gambino explained the dread consequences of his actions.

> First the mafia persecuted me for vile reasons of economic speculation. But after what I revealed to the police, there

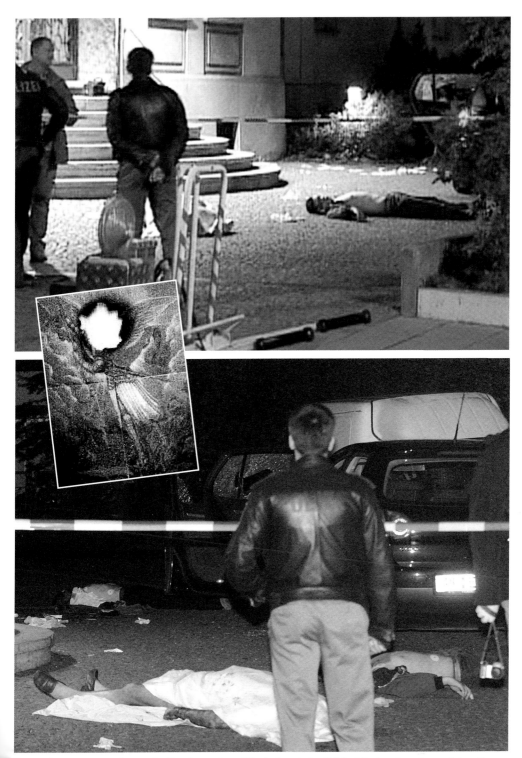

The Duisburg massacre. Europe finally takes notice of the 'ndrangheta, Italy's richest and most powerful mafia, on 15 August 2007. One of the six victims, Tommaso Venturi, had just celebrated both his eighteenth birthday and his admission into the Honoured Society of Calabria. The partially burned image of the Archangel Michael (inset top), used during the 'ndrangheta initiation ritual, was found in his pocket.

Camorristi settle their differences over a card game; gambling was one of the Honoured Society's primary rackets.

The flashy dress and strutting posture of a *guappo*, or street-corner boss. By the 1850s, when these illustrations were published, the camorra was already a highly visible presence on the streets of Naples.

Duke Sigismondo Castromediano who analysed the camorra's methods while in prison in the 1850s. He called it 'one of the most immoral and disastrous sects that human infamy has ever invented.'

Miracle worker. Liborio Romano, who kept order in Naples after June 1860 by recruiting the camorra to replace the police.

Anarchy in Naples! A mob orchestrated by the camorra ransacks the city's police stations in June 1860.

The pivotal figure in the murky Neapolitan intrigues of 1860. At age 30, Marianna De Crescenzo a.k.a. *la Sangiovannara*, became famous for her charismatic leadership of a patriotic mob. A prosperous tavern owner, she also led the celebrations when Garibaldi entered the city (below with flag).

A French journalist found *la Sangiovannara* hard to pin down: 'a young woman's innocent smile alternates on her face with a wolfish cackle'. He described her tavern, adorned with patriotic flags and religious icons, as being a hang-out for thugs. He did not know that she was a powerful figure in the Neapolitan underworld.

Salvatore De Crescienzo, camorrista.

The redemption of the camorra. Crime bosses become patriotic heroes and have flattering portraits printed in the press. Among them is Salvatore De Crescenzo (left), the most notorious *camorrista* of the era.

Michele il piazziere, camorrista.

Silvio Spaventa, who led the first crackdown on the Honoured Society and the first investigations into its mysterious origins.

Mastro Tredici, camorrista.

Two more redeemed *camorristi*: Michele 'the Town Crier' and 'Master Thirteen'.

Palermo 1860: freed prisoners parade their warder through the streets before shooting him. The Sicilian mafia was incubated in the political violence of the early-to-mid-1800s.

The play that gave the Sicilian mafia its name. A poster advertising *The Mafiosi of Vicaria Prison* (1863). Set in the 1850s, it tells the story of an honourable sect of prison extortionists who are recruited to the cause of a unified Italy.

Day-to-day criminal business in Naples.

A *camorrista*, in typical flared trousers, takes protection money from a cab driver (1880s).

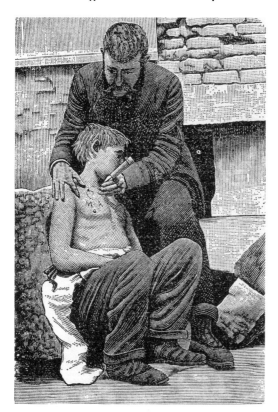

A youngster gets his first criminal insignia. A street tattooist at work in Naples.

The camorra takes to the streets again. A mob battles with police during the hackney cab drivers' strike of August 1893.

The Honoured Society of Naples conducts its first ever initiation ritual. A scene from Edoardo Minichini's highly successful play, *The Foundation of the Camorra*, from 1899.

came another, much more serious reason for turning the
screw on me: personal vendetta.

But vendetta did not arrive immediately: Giovanni 'Darky' Cusimano had to wait three years, until the revolt of September 1866.

At the outbreak of the revolt, Gambino was confidentially
warned that he was in grave danger, and had to leave San Lorenzo
immediately. His sons threw the family's cash, clothes, linen,
cooking implements and chickens onto a mule cart, and set off
to take refuge at another farm managed by a friend of theirs.
On the way, they were attacked by a party of seventeen *mafiosi*.
A fierce gun battle followed; Salvatore Gambino was wounded
in the left thigh. But both brothers knew the area well, and
managed to escape over the wall of a nearby estate, abandoning
the family's possessions to be ransacked by their tormentors.

The Palermo countryside was by then almost completely in
the hands of the rebellious squads. Fearing that their chosen
place of safety no longer offered sufficient protection, the
Gambino family went to Resuttana, the village next to San
Lorenzo in the Piana dei Colli. There they were taken in by one
Salvatore Licata. It was in Salvatore Licata's house, the following
day, that the Gambinos took delivery of a package from Giovanni
'Darky' Cusimano: it contained a hunk of meat from their own
mare. As a mafia message, the horse flesh may not have had
the cinematic flair of the decapitated stallion deployed in *The
Godfather*, but its meaning was very similar all the same: Darky
had not yet concluded his business with the Gambino family.

Inspector Sangiorgi does not tell us what his thoughts were as
he listened to old man Gambino – he was far too savvy a
policeman to write those thoughts down. Yet to appreciate the
full drama of what Sangiorgi was hearing, and the intrigue that
he was being drawn into, we have no choice but to figure out
how his mind began to work when he learned who had offered
sanctuary to the beleaguered Gambinos in Resuttana in September
1866. Sangiorgi was an outsider to Sicily, a northerner. But he

had been in Palermo long enough to know the baleful power of the Licatas. The very mention of the Licata name told him, more clearly than any other detail, that Gambino was hiding a crucial part of the truth.

Salvatore Licata, aged sixty-one at the time he took in the Gambinos, was one of the most venerable and best-connected *mafiosi* in the Conca d'Oro.

Like many important mafia bosses, including Turi Miceli from Monreale, Darky Cusimano from San Lorenzo, and don Antonino Giammona from Uditore, Licata had led a revolutionary squad into Palermo in 1848 and 1860. But during the 1866 revolt Licata mobilised his heavies to oppose the insurgents. They formed a 'counter-squad', as such gangs were termed at the time. Licata, in other words, was one of the smart *mafiosi* who realised that he had more to lose than to gain by rebelling.

His son Andrea was an officer in the Horse Militia, a notoriously corrupt mounted police force. His three other sons were armed robbers and extortionists who were guaranteed impunity by the family's connections.

Like the Licatas, and like don Antonino Giammona who was a pillar of the National Guard, many Palermo bosses broke their remaining links with revolutionary politics during the revolt of 1866.

Old man Gambino's friendship with the fearsome Licata clan raises the very strong suspicion that Gambino and his sons were also *mafiosi*. Several aspects of his story stretched credulity too far. He was asking Inspector Sangiorgi to believe that he was entirely an innocent victim. Fear alone, according to Gambino, had kept him from going to the law when persecuted by Darky, even though that persecution had been going on for nearly a decade and a half. The way he described his murdered son Antonino was also suspicious.

> My son Antonino was a young man who was full of courage. He had too much respect for himself to lose his composure and allow his enemies, and his family's

enemies, to assume too much familiarity with him. That is why Darky and his allies were constantly worried, afraid that my son had in mind to take out his revenge against them.

A man of bravado and self-respect who would not stand for being bullied. A 'benign maffioso', to use Marquis Rudinì's term. This is how the mafia likes to represent itself to the outside world.

The conclusion forming in Sangiorgi's mind was inexorable: old man Gambino and his two sons were not being persecuted *by* the mafia, they were participants in a struggle for power *within* the mafia. It was only when they faced final defeat in that struggle that old man Gambino got his lawyer to take him to the police. Sangiorgi was to be his instrument of revenge against his former comrades; turning to the state was a vendetta of last resort.

Fear must have honed Sangiorgi's concentration as he listened to the rest of the story.

Once again, after sending the hunk of horse-flesh to old man Gambino, Darky Cusimano was forced to postpone his campaign against the Gambino family. When the revolt of September 1866 was subdued there was a brutal crackdown by the authorities. Fearing that they had exposed themselves with their open assault on the Gambinos, Cusimano's people made peace overtures. Emissaries approached Gambino, who was still living with 'counter-squad' leader Salvatore Licata, to propose what Darky termed a 'spiritual kinship': two of his lieutenants were to become godfathers to Gambino's grandchildren.

Reluctantly – according to his own very selective narrative of events – old man Gambino agreed to the proposal, and decided not to report the attack he had suffered to the authorities. Much more likely, the 'spiritual kinship' was in reality an alliance between mafia bloodlines.

In Sicily, and in much of the southern Italian mainland, a godfather is called a *compare*, literally a 'co-father'. *Comparatico* ('co-fatherhood') was a way of cementing a family's important friendships, of extending the blood bond further out into society. Often a poor peasant would ask a wealthy and powerful man to become 'co-father' to his child as a sign of deference and loyalty. But ever since the days of old man Gambino and 'Darky' Cusimano, *mafiosi* too have taken advantage of *comparatico*: senior bosses establish 'spiritual kinships' as a way of building their following within the sect.

The Gambino family's enforced stay with Salvatore Licata during the 1866 revolt produced another intriguing development: old man Gambino's son Salvatore married one of Licata's daughters.

Naturally Gambino did not say as much to Sangiorgi, but this marriage was in all probability as political as the 'spiritual kinship' with Darky Cusimano: it bound the Gambinos firmly into the Licata clan. Mafia bosses in more recent and better documented times have used marriages in exactly the same way that the crowned heads of Europe did for centuries: to end or prevent wars, to forge military alliances, to earn money and prestige, and to secure their power and wealth down the generations.

Sangiorgi was learning that, through 'co-fatherhood' and marriage, the bosses of the Conca d'Oro were developing a *dynastic* strategy. Although they were profoundly immersed in short-term mafia politics, in the bloodletting and alliance building that are a constant in the mafia's world, they were also thinking for the long term, trying to project their power into the future. Mafia patriarchs shaped their families to meet the peculiar needs of their business in a way that made their behaviour very distinct from other Sicilians. (Contrary to a widespread stereotype, in Sicily at this time the nuclear family was dominant, rather than the extended family.)

Calogero Gambino's story tells us that, where women and marriage were concerned, the difference between early *camorristi* and early *mafiosi* was striking and very important. *Mafiosi* used their wives and daughters as political pawns and by doing so built their illicit gains into patrimonies. *Camorristi*, by contrast, consorted with prostitutes and spent money as soon as they had stolen it.

Marc Monnier (as always the Swiss hotelier is one of the most insightful sources on the Honoured Society of Naples) tells us that the average *camorrista*'s wife was 'a power in her own right' who had the authority to collect protection racket payments.

> Even the toughest among the common people would tremble before the petticoats of these female hoods. Everyone knew that one day their husbands would leave prison and, cudgel in hand, visit reluctant payers to demand an explanation for the outstanding debts.

Such *camorriste* also ensured that their children 'made themselves respected right from the cradle'. So the camorra was trying to use its women and to think to the future too. But they were not as strategic, either in their use of marriage as a dynasty-building tool, or in their preservation of family life from the potentially destabilising effects of contact with prostitution.

The early crime bosses of Naples almost invariably had pimping on their criminal records, whereas profiting from the sex trade was notably *absent* from the biographies of the Sicilian mafia's first bosses. Palermo certainly had its pimps, known by the revolting nickname of *ricottari* – literally 'ricotta cheese makers'. But Turi Miceli, don Antonino Giammona and the other mafia chieftains of the 1860s and 1870s never had anything to do with the *ricottari*. In the city of Palermo, just as in Naples, many prostitutes and their pimps could be seen wearing the serpentine facial scars that were the sex trade's ugly signature. But just outside Palermo, among the lemon groves where the mafia dominated, the *sfregio*, or disfiguring razor slash, was all but unknown.

Cosa Nostra today forbids its members to profit from prostitution because, as murdered anti-mafia magistrate Giovanni Falcone explained, they have to ensure that their womenfolk 'are not humiliated in their own social environment'. A disaffected woman, as the bearer of gruesome family secrets, is a great danger to the organisation.

It seems that it was always thus: the Sicilian mafia of the 1860s may have brutalised and used women domestically but it did not humiliate them publicly – as any involvement with prostitution would have done – because it needed them; it needed them to keep quiet, breed sons and educate those sons in the ways of honour.

It is noticeable that no female personality in Sicily earned the upper world fame or underworld status that surrounded some of the women in the early camorra's orbit: like *la Sangiovannara* and her armed female band, or the brothel keepers who won the title of *matrona annurrata* – 'honoured madam'. It seems that the mafia's women wielded less overt power because, in their domestic role, they were *more* important to the organisation. The mafia's iron strategic control over women is a vital secret of its extraordinary resilience over time. A resilience that the Honoured Society of Naples, with its persistent weakness for the short-term profits of pimping, would ultimately prove unable to match.

Old man Gambino's tale was moving towards its conclusion. The 'spiritual kinship' between the Gambinos and Darky Cusimano held for six years. Then, on 17 December 1872, the Gambino brothers were once more ambushed in the Piana dei Colli. Following an initial volley of shots, they fought the six assailants hand-to-hand. Again the brothers escaped through the lemon groves. Despite receiving a head wound, Antonino Gambino managed to wrestle a rifle away from one of the attackers.

The Gambinos knew who had waylaid them: they recognised all six attackers. Predictably, five of them were Darky's men. Less predictably, and much more worryingly, a *mafioso* called Giuseppe 'Thanks be to God' Riccobono was also part of the firing party. Riccobono was son-in-law to Antonino Giammona, the poet-*capo* of Uditore. What this meant to old man Gambino was that his family now faced the combined wrath of *two* mafia factions based in different *borgate*: their old enemies the Cusimano group from San Lorenzo; but now also the Giammona group from Uditore. Gambino referred to these factions as 'parties' or 'associations'. Today we would refer to them as mafia Families.

Yet at the same time that the attack revealed a worrying new alliance ranged against the Gambinos, it also offered them a potentially devastating weapon against their enemies: the rifle that Antonino Gambino had captured. Here was concrete proof of the attackers' identity – as long as the Gambinos could find the right person in law enforcement to offer that proof to.

Still pretending to Sangiorgi that he was an innocent victim of mafia persecution, old man Gambino explained that he turned to the Licatas, his dynastic allies, to make the best use of the rifle captured from Darky Cusimano's men.

But what seemed like a smart move only exposed the Gambinos' isolation even more cruelly. The senior police connected to the Licatas ignored the rifle. Much worse than that, they made moves that suggested to old man Gambino that they were going to try and frame him for stealing it.

The Gambinos were now being targeted by the three most powerful mafia *cosche* in the Piana dei Colli. Their protection, the web of 'spiritual kinships' and marriage pacts, had been torn apart, isolating the family completely. Eighteen months later, at dawn on 18 June 1874, the lethal consequences of that isolation hit home, when Antonino Gambino was shot dead.

As Sangiorgi listened, the old man described his response to his son's death in tones that were both genuinely moving and creepily manipulative. When news of the murder reached him, grimly certain that Giovanni 'Darky' Cusimano had accomplished his vendetta, Gambino hobbled as fast as he could to embrace the bleeding corpse. He then sat holding his son for hours.

After a while, Darky himself appeared. Leaning over the corpse, he roughly pushed back an eyelid, turned to the distraught father and told him that there was nothing more to be done.

Some time later the police arrived in the person of Inspector Matteo Ferro, Sangiorgi's predecessor as Inspector in the Castel Molo district, and the very man who had defined Darky as 'an individual completely devoted to law and order'.

By this time, Gambino was 'crying out as if he was obsessed'. He heard Inspector Ferro tell him to pull himself together, and felt Darky's hands try to tug him to his feet. Gambino scrambled away from them, yelling 'Get back! Don't touch me!' He then listened, in rage and despair, as Inspector Ferro asked him if he could 'shed any light' on the murder. Of course, with the *mafioso* who ordered the killing looking on, he could say nothing in reply.

Inspector Ferro left old man Gambino to his grief and went to the nearby villa that was 'rented' by Giovanni 'Darky' Cusimano. He was joined by the sergeant of the local *Carabinieri* who, as we know, was also a regular guest of Darky's.

At that point, Calogero Gambino's other son Salvatore also came to weep for the murdered Antonino. Word of Salvatore's arrival quickly reached the *mafiosi* and police in Darky's villa. At which point, the *Carabiniere* sergeant came out and promptly arrested Salvatore for killing his own brother. The mafia's fratricide plot had been set in motion – a 'double vendetta', the old man called it.

Many times, through forty-eight years of service to the cause of law and order, Sangiorgi would make pleas for promotion. Many times, his superiors would give him glowing references: brave, able and tactful, they called him. These were precisely the attributes that he had to call on during his first months as a mafia-fighter when Calogero Gambino hobbled into his office on his lawyer's arm.

Brave. Sangiorgi knew that, even though Giovanni 'Darky' Cusimano was now dead, the investigation implicated many other violent and well-connected *mafiosi*.

GIURO DI ESSERE FEDELE "A COSA NOSTRA" SE DOVESSI TRADIRE LE MIE CARNI DEVONO BRUCIARE - COME BRUCIA QUESTA IMMAGINE.

DIVIETI E DOVERI.

NON CI SI PUO' PRESENTARE DA SOLI AD UN'ALTRO AMICO NOSTRO - SE NON E' UN TERZO A FARLO.

NON SI GUARDANO MOGLI DI AMICI NOSTRI.

NON SI FANNO COMPARATI CON GLI SBIRRI.

NON SI FREQUENTANO NE'TAVERNE E NE'CIRCOLI.

SI E' IL DOVERE IN QUALSIASI MOMENTO DI ESSERE DISPONIBILE A COSA NOSTRA.ANCHE SE CE LA MOGLIE CHE STA PER PARTORIRE.

SI RISPETTANO IN MANIERA CATEGORICA GLI APPUNTAMENTI.

SI CI DEVE PORTARE RISPETTO ALLA MOGLIE.

QUANDO SI E' CHIAMATI A SAPERE QUALCOSA SI DOVRA' DIRE LA VERITA'.

NON CI SI PUO' APPROPRIARE DI SOLDI CHE SONO DI ALTRI E.DI ALTRE FAMIGLIE.

CHI NON PUO' ENTRARE A FAR PARTE DI COSA NOSTRA.

CHI HA UN PARENTE STRETTO NELLE VARIE FORZE DELL'ORDINE.

CHI HA TRADIMENTI SENTIMENTALI IN FAMIGLIA.

CHI HA UN COMPORTAMENTO PESSIMO - E CHE NON TIENE AI VALORI MORALI.

SAN MAURO CASTELVERDE.
TRABIA. I PAESI DI APPARTENENZA:CACCAMO,VICARI,ROCCA PALUMBA E ALTRI
BAGHERIA. " " " VILLABATE,CASTELDACCIA,MILICIA,
BELMONTE MEZZAGNO. " " " MISILMERI,
BRANCACCIO. " " " CORSO DEI MILLE,ROCCELLA,CIACULLI.
SANTA MARIA DI GESU'. " " " VILLA GRAZIA DI PALERMO.
PALERMO CENTRO. " " " PORTA NUOVA,BORGO VECCHIO.
RESUTTANA " " " ACQUASANTA,ARENELLA.
PAGLIARELLI." " " MOLARA,CORSO CALATAFIMI,
VILLAGRAZIA DI FALCO." " " UDITORE,TORRETTA.
TOMMASO NATALE." " " SAN LOR,PARTANN,CAPACI,CARINI,CINISI,TERRASINI.
CRUILLAS. " " " NOCE,ALTARELLO.
PARTINICO. " " " BORGETTO,BALESTRADE,MONTELEPRE?
SAN GIUSEPPE JATO." " " MORREALE,ALTOFONTE,SAN CIPIRELLO
CORLEONE. " " " PRIZZI,FICUZZA,

Mafia morality. A very rare Cosa Nostra rulebook from 2007. Among the regulations crammed onto a single, badly typed page are: 'Respect your wife' and 'The following people cannot become part of Cosa Nostra: Anyone who has a close relative in the police. Anyone who has emotional infidelities in their family. Anyone who behaves very badly or does not keep to moral values.'

Able. Sangiorgi needed all his investigative skills to verify what old man Gambino had told him. He quickly ascertained that the old man's story tallied perfectly with the facts.

And, most of all, tactful. The case took Sangiorgi deeper and deeper into the sinister nexus between the state and the criminal sect that had brought death to the lemon groves of the Conca d'Oro.

Sangiorgi found damning evidence about the *Carabiniere* sergeant who emerged directly from Darky's villa to arrest Salvatore Gambino. His source within the *Carabinieri* explained how the mafia had entrapped the sergeant by using a two-pronged strategy it deployed frequently against law enforcement. Cusimano and other mafia bosses first buttered the sergeant up: they took him out into the countryside on what Sangiorgi referred to as 'frequent *tavulidde*'. The Inspector had evidently picked up some Sicilian dialect during his time on the island. A *tavulidda* was (and is) a languorous al fresco lunch at which men bond over roast goat, artichokes, *macco* (broad bean purée), and wine as dark as treacle. The mafia was introducing the sergeant to a bit of local culture.

The second prong involved the mafia's womenfolk, who sidled up to the sergeant's wife and told her

> In the Piana dei Colli, any woman who likes to keep out
> of all sorts of bother needs to stay close to her husband.

An oblique threat, but a blood-freezingly clear one all the same. Over a century and a half this form of wheedling intimidation has done more to protect the mafia than any other form of corruption in its wide repertoire. There is no better way to incapacitate the state than to nullify the effectiveness of its operatives on the ground.

Sangiorgi's investigations then concentrated on the key prosecution witness in the fratricide case. Standing guard not far from the point where Antonino Gambino was murdered was a soldier who heard the shots and ran to the scene. When he arrived, he saw two men standing over the victim, who was still emitting his dying groans. The two men took to their heels. But the soldier got a good view of one of them, who was wearing a straw hat with a black ribbon round it. Later he picked Salvatore Gambino out of an identity parade and said that he was the man in the straw hat.

Old man Gambino told Sangiorgi that the witness was lying, and that the identity parade was fixed. Sangiorgi soon found evidence to back up the old man's accusations. He discovered that, when Darky Cusimano was shot dead, a receipt for a 200 *Lire* loan was found on his body. The beneficiary of the loan was the commander of an army platoon stationed in San Lorenzo – the same platoon that the key witness came from. The loan made the framing of Salvatore Gambino look very much like one token in a murky exchange of favours between the mafia boss and the platoon commander. Sangiorgi could add the army to the long list of organisations that had been infiltrated by the mafia of the Conca d'Oro.

Tact, indeed.

Inspector Sangiorgi now faced the delicate task of telling the magistrates what he knew. If he exposed the Gambino case as a mafia plot, he risked trampling on some very important toes inside the Palace of Justice, because the 'fratricide' prosecution was already scheduled to come before the Court of Assizes.

When Sangiorgi approached the magistrates he received a reassuring response: they told him he was right to let them know, and asked him to submit a full report. In the meantime, the fratricide case kept being adjourned because the soldier who was supposed to have recognised Salvatore Gambino in the straw hat twice failed to appear as a witness.

During this delay, there was a change in the political weather.

In March 1876 the Right fell from government, and the first Left administration, including Sicilian politicians, took office in Rome. A new Prefect was sent to Palermo, and the Right's senior personnel were rapidly purged, irrespective of their competence and honesty. The Chief of Police under whom Sangiorgi had worked was sent to Tuscany.

Sangiorgi was now exposed: he, more than any officer in Sicily, had been in the front line of the struggle against the mafia; he had even discovered the mafia's secret initiation ritual. Without the backing of his superiors, his career, and possibly his life, were in danger. The corrupt elements within the Palermo police were already lobbying against him, pouring poison in the new Prefect's ear. In July 1876 the Prefect sent an urgent telegram to the Minister of the Interior.

> Above all, I beg you, get rid of young Sangiorgi for me. He is able, but a schemer and gossiper who boasts that he has protectors in the Ministry and in Parliament. I prefer timewasters to cops like him.

Sangiorgi put in a transfer request which was quickly granted: in August 1876 he took up a posting in Syracuse, the least crime-ridden province of Sicily, in the opposite corner of the island to Palermo. The mafia was both very well informed of this development and delighted by it: even before confirmation of the transfer came through, the news was trumpeted to the Piana dei Colli by *L'Amico del Popolo*, whose editor had been spotted consorting with Darky in his 'rented' villa. The mafia's rumour mill spread the falsehood that Sangiorgi had been moved for disciplinary reasons.

While Sangiorgi was in Syracuse the Gambino case dragged on in perfunctory hearings, through 1876 and into 1877. Old man Gambino got the chance to tell his story directly to the magistrates. But the new atmosphere in Palermo began to turn the case against Sangiorgi. Some of the witnesses he had interviewed lost confidence and changed their stories. Nothing was done to verify whether the soldier had really seen Salvatore Gambino in a straw hat at the murder scene. Corrupt cops, whom

Sangiorgi had removed for incompetence or collusion with the mafia, seemed to get their fingers into the case again. As Sangiorgi noted wistfully

> If I were fatalistic, I would regrettably have to admit that an evil spirit, an arcane and pernicious influence overcame all the procedures I went through to investigate the deductions I had based on old man Gambino's evidence.

Inspector Sangiorgi had yet to experience just how pernicious that 'evil spirit' could be.

A few more months passed and once again the political weather around Sangiorgi changed. The Left found that it was not as easy to enforce the law in Sicily as it had been led to believe during fifteen years of noisy Sicilian protests against the hated Right's repressive measures. The kidnap of the English sulphur-mining company manager in November 1876 meant that something had to be done. So early in 1877 the Left reversed its policy and sent yet another new Prefect to Palermo to crack the whip. Across Sicily, a vast new anti-mafia campaign – as big as anything under the Right – was set in motion.

Given this transformation in the Left's official attitude to organised crime in Sicily, Inspector Sangiorgi was too valuable an asset to be parked in peaceful Syracuse. Early in 1877 he was re-assigned to the province of Agrigento, home turf of yet another recently discovered mafia sect. He was given a pay rise and recommended for a decoration. Sangiorgi was back in the front line, and soon renewed his 'open fight against the mafia' – and against one *mafioso* in particular: Pietro De Michele, the boss of the town of Burgio, near Agrigento, where Sangiorgi was now stationed. De Michele insisted on being called 'Baron', although he seems to have had no real claim on the title. His CV displayed the *mafioso's* typical combination of crime and opportunistic political thuggery. More than that, it showed that the province of Palermo was not the only place where Men of

Honour had used sexual violence as a short-cut to wealth and position, and indeed that there were close business links between *mafiosi* from different provinces.

In 1847 De Michele kidnapped and raped the daughter of a rich landowner who had refused his advances. But the rape backfired. De Michele's reputation was so bad that the girl's family refused to repair the damage to her honour by conceding a wedding: family disgrace was far better than a marriage to a known hood. But De Michele would not accept defeat. In 1848, he allied himself to the revolution of that year, and took advantage of it to take back the girl, forcibly marry her and rob her family of a large dowry. He served a short time in jail after the authority of the Bourbon state was restored; and he was suspected of many murders after being released.

The 'Baron' joined the revolution again in 1860 when Garibaldi invaded. At some point during the upheaval, all the town's police and judicial documents were burned.

When Sicily became part of Italy, De Michele went on to manage the cattle rustlers and bandits who operated between the provinces of Palermo, Agrigento and Trapani in the 1860s and 1870s. He armed them, fed them and hid them from the authorities. Most importantly, he used his mafia connections to sell their stolen cattle in far distant cities: animals robbed near Palermo would end up butchered in Trapani, where they could never be traced.

This was an exceptionally lucrative traffic. By the time Sangiorgi caught up with De Michele, he was the richest landowner in town and completely controlled the local council. The fearless Inspector showed no deference to De Michele. Sangiorgi took away his firearms licence, placed him under police surveillance, and ordered his arrest when he went on the run. Baron or not, the boss of Burgio was to be subject to the law like everyone else.

The bad news about the Gambino fratricide case arrived soon after 28 August 1877. In Agrigento, Inspector Sangiorgi read the report on the long-delayed trial in the *Gazzetta di Palermo*. It is not hard to imagine his emotions as he did so. Disappointment first: the court had not believed old man Gambino's story; Salvatore Gambino was found guilty of murdering his brother and sentenced to hard labour for life. Then resignation: the outcome was not a surprise.

Sangiorgi's eyes then moved down the page to read the *Gazzetta di Palermo*'s admiring paraphrase of the prosecution's summing up. As they did, his heart began to thump with shock.

> The honourable magistrate then had extremely grave things to say about the behaviour of a Police Inspector, a certain Ermanno Sangiorgi. Because he wanted to take advantage of the position that he still undeservedly holds, Sangiorgi tried to throw justice off its course by denying that Salvatore Gambino had committed the crime, and claiming instead that the culprit was someone or other called Darky Cusimano.
>
> This is not the first case that shows us that there are police officers who have become the maffia's protectors. They make a big show of wanting to strike at some other, hypothetical maffia; and to do so they contrive investigations that have no basis in fact.
>
> Then the prosecuting magistrate said that Sangiorgi had deceived, mystified and duped justice by trying to find a way to give someone else the blame. On the eve of the first hearings Sangiorgi haughtily sent a report to the Chief Prosecutor's Office that made out that Gambino was not guilty of his brother's murder.
>
> Sangiorgi's dishonest conduct (the word is the prosecutor's) was motivated by his desire to pay back the dirty services that Calogero Gambino had provided to the police.

Thus, in effect, the prosecuting magistrate's eloquent speech to the court was making two separate accusations: the first against Salvatore Gambino, and the second against Ermanno Sangiorgi who has made himself into the maffia's protector. He signs off gun licences for people who have police cautions hanging over them and he releases dangerous criminals from police surveillance.

Any policing system that is represented by men like Sangiorgi is absolutely pitiful. This is government banditry – no more and no less. It is the police maffia that has imposed itself on the law.

The presiding judge used the prosecutor's own solemn words to bring his highly fluent précis of the case to a conclusion: 'If the jury award the accused a verdict of not guilty, it will amount to a crown of plaudits awarded to this corrupt police officer for the dirty services performed by Calogero Gambino.'

Dishonest. Corrupt. Deceiver of justice. Broker of dirty services. Protector of the maffia. There was an unnervingly symmetrical irony to the charges against Sangiorgi, as if the judicial system and the *Gazzetta di Palermo* were mocking his 'open fight' against the mafia. It was alleged that he had indulged in precisely the kind of shady policing that he had overturned when he first came to the Castel Molo district. That he was precisely the kind of double-dealing cop that he had expelled from among his subordinates.

Police like Albanese and Ferro had used *mafiosi* by siding with the winners in the underworld's internal power struggles; they had co-managed crime with the victorious mafia bosses. What Sangiorgi had done with old man Gambino was very different: he had sought to adopt the mafia's losers so as to attack the very basis of the sect's authority. The difference between these two approaches was as clear as the difference between wrong and right.

Yet together, the judiciary and the *Gazzetta di Palermo* had obliterated any distinction. The new villain of the story, Inspector Sangiorgi, came out as just another scheming northern cop. Meanwhile, the real mafia, the mafia of Darky Cusimano, of the poet-boss Giammona, of Salvatore Licata and his sons, the mafia whose blood-spattered victims Sangiorgi had seen lying among the lemon trees, was dismissed as a 'hypothetical maffia', a mere pretext, a fiction dreamed up by a policeman in the cynical pursuit of power and influence.

Inspector Ermanno Sangiorgi was in very serious trouble.

The mortifying allegations made against Inspector Sangiorgi in the Palermo Court of Assizes were bound to reach the ears of his superiors. Dispatches were duly sent, reports were requested and collated: the Gambino case became the Sangiorgi case. The Minister of the Interior asked the Minister of Justice to make inquiries. On 12 October 1877 the Minister of Justice gave his verdict: 'the accusations against Inspector Sangiorgi are, alas, true'. Sangiorgi now faced disgrace, dismissal and possibly jail.

The principal witness against him, the man who investigated the case on behalf of the Minister of Justice, was also the magistrate to whom Sangiorgi had turned when Calogero Gambino's testimony first raised such grave doubts about the 'fratricide': Chief Prosecutor Carlo Morena – the same Carlo Morena who just a few months earlier had dismissed the theory that there could be any kind of 'confederation' between the different mafia cells across Sicily. Carlo Morena, a man with responsibility for supervising the justice system across the whole of Sicily, was exacting a vendetta on behalf of the mafia against Ermanno Sangiorgi.

On behalf of one *mafioso* in particular: 'Baron' Pietro De Michele, the Burgio boss. Chief Prosecutor Morena knew all about the Baron's past, but spent his credibility in spadefuls to defend him from Sangiorgi. De Michele had made a few mistakes in the past, Morena reported. But now he was a friend of the law and the government, who had become a victim of political persecution. To accuse the Baron of raping his future wife back in 1847 was unfair: the families had made peace afterwards. So the accusation of rape was based on an ignorance of Sicilian customs, Morena argued.

> Kidnap and rape of this kind constitute a primitive phenomenon that occasionally crops up even in the most civilised societies. Sometimes there are no bad consequences arising from it. Indeed sometimes the very family who were supposedly harmed by the rape actually approve of it by agreeing to a subsequent marriage. Society readily approves of such arrangements. When that happens, the state should forget about the whole affair.

Morena went on to explain that the mafia was a local tradition of the same kind as kidnapping and raping young girls, albeit a much vaguer one.

> The word mafia is such an ill-defined concept, which is spoken much more often than its meaning is understood.

Thanks to Chief Prosecutor Morena, the order to arrest *capomafia* 'Baron' De Michele was rescinded.

Of course Morena knew perfectly well that the mafia was no 'ill-defined concept'. It was a secret criminal organisation whose influence stretched right across western Sicily. At the lowest level, the network linking the local mafia gangs was held together by the long-distance business of banditry and cattle rustling. Sangiorgi discovered that the same cattle rustlers who were sheltered by De Michele were also friends with Palermo *mafiosi* like don Antonino Giammona, the Licatas, and Darky Cusimano. At an intermediate level, the mafia sought to control the market for buying and renting land, which had its hub in

Palermo. At the highest level, the mafia network's strength came from the favours it could call in from 'friends of the friends' in politics and the legal system. Favours like persecuting policemen who had the temerity to mount an open fight against organised crime and the foolish courage to discover the Honoured Society's secret initiation ceremony.

There was only one Sicilian mafia.

On 18 October 1877, the Minister of the Interior wrote to Sangiorgi's boss, the Prefect of Agrigento, relaying the details of the case exactly as it had been set out in the *Gazzetta di Palermo*. Sangiorgi could and perhaps should have been prosecuted, the Minister explained. But he was still an important witness in some outstanding cases. Did the Prefect consider that a severe reprimand was sufficient punishment for his behaviour?

Only then did Sangiorgi's luck change. The Prefect of Agrigento urged the Minister to hear the other side of the story. Sangiorgi rapidly put together a long and precise account of the 'fratricide' affair. This is the documentation I have drawn on to tell his story here.

The Prefect backed up Sangiorgi's report by telling the Minister that Sangiorgi was one of his most intelligent and energetic officers, one who had gone beyond the call of duty to fight organised crime and to bring order to the province of Agrigento. He even recommended the supposed 'protector of the mafia' for a promotion.

Meanwhile the Minister of the Interior also received alarming reports on Chief Prosecutor Carlo Morena. In addition to defending the mafia boss De Michele, Morena had been sending urgent memos to magistrates around western Sicily, digging up every technicality possible to secure the release of *mafiosi* subject to police surveillance and 'enforced residence'. The Minister pronounced himself 'profoundly shocked' by Morena's behaviour.

The Interior Ministry now held a compelling body of evidence.

The saga of Sangiorgi's dealings with old man Gambino exposed gangland infiltration not only of the police, but also of the magistrature; it provided new evidence that the different *cosche* that used the same rituals were actually part of *one* criminal brotherhood; it made for the most vivid picture of the mafia yet assembled by any police investigation. For a moment, it seemed that someone in power in Rome was going to take notice.

But nothing happened. The Minister of the Interior who was 'profoundly shocked' by Morena was soon toppled, and his successor had other priorities.

There was no inquiry into the systematic mafia infiltration of the police and magistrature that Sangiorgi had uncovered. No one took the time to make the connection between the whole 'fratricide' affair and the crucial role that Chief Prosecutor Carlo Morena had played in blocking any attempt to treat the mafia as a single criminal brotherhood. Morena kept his job, but for unknown reasons he volunteered for early retirement in 1879, at age fifty-eight. He was granted all the honours his prestigious legal career had earned.

Old man Gambino was left to the tender mercies of the Piana dei Colli mafia; it is not known what happened to him. His son Salvatore, aged thirty-four when he was wrongly convicted of murdering his own brother, broke rocks for the rest of his life.

The two *mafiosi* that Sangiorgi believed were the real culprits in the Antonino Gambino murder were not investigated; neither were the people responsible for framing his brother, Salvatore.

'Baron' De Michele became mayor of Burgio in 1878; his son would become a Member of Parliament.

Then there were the unspoken victims of the tragedy. Victims on whom not even Sangiorgi wastes enough ink for the historian to be able to cite their names: the women. We have no resource but the imagination to reconstruct their hellish fate. First, in Palermo, there was the Gambino daughter forced to marry the *mafioso* who raped her – a *mafioso* who was part of the same Cusimano clan that would end up murdering both her uncle and her brother. Then there was the Licata girl given in expedient marriage to a Gambino son who was destined to be framed for fratricide. Finally, in Burgio, there was the wife of 'Baron' De Michele: kidnapped, disgraced, kidnapped again, and forcibly married to the man who robbed her family. We can only presume that all of these women spent the rest of their lives performing their marital duties – duties which, as Sangiorgi had learned, included issuing smiling threats to the wives of policemen.

It is a sad truth that Inspector Sangiorgi himself bears some of the responsibility for the fact that the 'fratricide' affair went nowhere but the archives. Responsibility, but not blame. It was a question of tact. It seems certain that Sangiorgi believed that the Gambinos were *mafiosi*. But he was hardly stupid enough to say so in his report to the Minister of the Interior, when his career was on the line. For that would have given ammunition to those who accused him of being a protector of the mafia. He pitched his report with the utmost care, making it clear that he knew that the Gambinos were no angels, or no 'saint's shin-bones', as the Italian phrase has it. But he had to stop short of drawing the obvious conclusion that they were deeply immersed in the mafia world.

Inspector Sangiorgi's tact helped preserve his career. It may, just may, have helped preserve his life too. An obvious question that arises from the 'fratricide' affair is why the mafia did not just kill Sangiorgi. The answer is probably a cost-benefit calculation: killing a prominent cop would probably have brought more trouble than rewards for the Honoured Society. Far better to just discredit him. But then, for the mafia, discrediting someone is often only a prelude to killing them. Shamed murder victims are not mourned and not remembered.

As it was, the police authorities gave Sangiorgi the very mildest of warnings about his future conduct but turned him down for a promotion on the grounds that he was not old enough. In 1878, he had to defend himself again when the same accusations of colluding with the mafia turned up once more in the press.

It turned out that 'Baron' De Michele was the author of the defamatory pieces. But Sangiorgi had much graver worries at this point: his life was thrown into turmoil when his wife died; he was a single parent once more. But he did not stop fighting the mafia. In 1883 he dismantled a *cosca* known as the Brotherhood of Favara, which controlled the infernal sulphur mines of the Agrigento area by using the same tactics the *mafiosi* of the Conca d'Oro used in the lemon groves. Hereafter, Sangiorgi's unfolding career will lead us through another twenty-five years of mafia history.

The Left's 1877 crackdown did not destroy the mafia, far from it. Granted, most of the bandits who roamed the Sicilian countryside were shot down or betrayed to the authorities. But the *mafiosi* who protected them – men like 'Baron' De Michele – were left unmolested. With a relative calm now restored in Sicily, the political agenda could move on. The Left's great law and order campaign was to be the last for two decades. As in the low city of Naples, in Sicily it proved easier to govern with organised crime than against it. *Mafiosi* learned to keep their violence within levels that were suited to the new political environment. With the Left in power, Sicilian politicians could exercise their elbows in jostling for a share of the funds now being spent on roads, railways, sewers, and the like. With the help of their friends in the mafia, they could convert those funds from *Lire* into the south's real currency: the Favour.

Meanwhile the trials that had been triggered by Sangiorgi's discovery of the mafia initiation ritual went ahead, with very mixed results. Many juries were profoundly and understandably suspicious of the police and were reluctant to issue guilty verdicts. As a rule, only the losers in mafia wars were successfully prosecuted. Losers like the Gambinos: *mafiosi* who had spent all their favours, who had lost their 'friends of friends', whose 'spiritual kinships' and marriage alliances had broken down, and whose enemies within the mafia proved shrewder, more violent and better connected than them. And above all, thanks to Chief Prosecutor Carlo Morena, the trials treated the mafia as an unconnected and temporary ensemble of local gangs.

The country had been on a long journey between the Palermo revolt of 1866 and the anti-mafia campaign of 1877. Two parliamentary commissions of inquiry and countless police and judicial investigations had tried to define the mafia. But despite all the compelling evidence that had surfaced, the mafia was destined to remain what Carlo Morena had called it: 'an ill-defined concept'. Within a few years, the Honoured Society's initiation ritual would slip from Italy's institutional memory. *Il tempo è galantuomo*, as they say in Italy: 'Time heals all wounds' or, more literally, 'Time is a gentleman'. Perhaps it would be better to say that, in Sicily, time is a Man of Honour.

3

THE NEW CRIMINAL NORMALITY

1877–1900

Born delinquents: **Science and the mob**

In both Naples and Palermo, the late 1870s inaugurated a quiet period in the history of organised crime. Successive Left governments seemed to find an accommodation with the camorra and mafia. The underlying problems that had made the new state such a welcoming host to the underworld sects became endemic: political instability and malpractice; police co-management of delinquency with gangsters; criminal rule within the prison system. But the issue of underworld sects did not disappear from public debate. Indeed *mafiosi* and *camorristi* loomed large in Italian culture during the 1880s and 1890s. Their deeds, their habits, and above all their faces were displayed for all to see – whether on the page or on stage. Italians were often fascinated and horrified by what they saw. But they deluded themselves that the spectacle was merely a primitive hangover, a monument to old evils that was about to crumble into the dust of history. Thus, while Italy could not eradicate the gangs, it could at least change the way it thought about them: the organised crime issue became a matter of perceptions. Unfortunately, illegal Italy showed itself to be even more adept at perception management than legal Italy. This was the new criminal normality. A normality that, with all its ironies, was set to welcome a third criminal brotherhood into its midst.

The Right had viewed criminal organisations, understandably enough, as something much more threatening than mere crime. The camorra and the mafia (at least to those prepared to accept that the mafia was something more than an 'ill-defined concept') constituted a challenge to the state's very right to rule its own territory; they were a kind of state within the state that no modern society could tolerate.

This view had always faced opposition, not least from lawyers who thought that the fight against the 'anti-state' did not give the government the right to trample over individual rights. One piece of legislation, passed in 1861, made lawyers particularly nervous: it targeted 'associations of wrongdoers'. This was the law used in the anti-mafia trials of the late 1870s and early 1880s. It stipulated that any group of five or more people who came together to break the law were now deemed to be committing an extra crime – that of forming an 'association of wrongdoers'. The government's tendency to use this law as a catch-all for clamping down on groups of political dissidents helped increase the lawyers' anxiety.

The law was revised in 1889, and rephrased as a measure against 'associating for delinquency'. But some fundamental legal dilemmas survived the rewrite. What exactly was an 'association for delinquency'? How could it be proved, beyond reasonable doubt, that one existed? Rivers of legal ink were spilt in the search for a solution. The crime of 'associating for delinquency' only attracted quite minor penalties in any case – a couple of extra years in prison. So it was much easier to forget the elaborate business of dragging the mafia and camorra before a judge. Better to fall back on 'enforced residence', and send any conspicuous offenders off to a penal colony without a trial. Put another way, organised crime was to be pruned, and not uprooted.

The nitpicking legalistic approach to the mafia and camorra was a dead end. From the late 1870s until the end of the century, sociology seemed to have far greater purchase on the problem. And at that time, sociology largely meant *positivist* sociology – positivism being a school of thought that dreamed of applying science to society. From a properly scientific perspective, the positivists reasoned, lawbreakers were creatures of flesh and blood; they were human animals to be observed, prodded, weighed, measured, photographed, and catalogued. If only science could identify these 'born delinquents' *physically*, then it could defend society against them – irrespective of what the legal quibblers said.

The most optimistic, and most notorious, attempt to identify a 'delinquent man' and a 'delinquent woman' by their physical appearance was articulated by the Turinese doctor Cesare Lombroso. He claimed to have identified certain anomalies in criminal bodies, like sticky-out ears or a bulky jaw. These 'stigmata', as he termed them, revealed that criminals actually belonged to an earlier era of human development, somewhere between apes and negroes on the evolutionary ladder. Lombroso made a great career out of his theory and defended it doggedly, even when some other sociologists demonstrated what claptrap it was.

Lombroso was not the only academic who thought science could unlock the crime issue. Others sought the key in factors like diet, overcrowding, the weather, and of course race. Southern Italians and Sicilians seemed to be made of different stuff from other Europeans, if not physically, then at least psychologically. In 1898 one celebrated young sociologist, Alfredo Niceforo, gave a derogatory twist to the mafia's own propaganda when he argued that the Sicilian psyche and the mafia were one and the same thing.

> In many respects the Sicilian is a true Arab: proud, often cruel, vigorous, inflexible. Hence the fact that the individual Sicilian does not allow others to give him orders. Hence also the fact that Saracen pride, conjoined with the feudal hankering after power, turned the Sicilian into a man who always has rebellion and the unbounded passion of his own ego in his bloodstream. The *mafioso* in a nutshell.

Neapolitans emerged in just as unflattering a light from Niceforo's research: they were 'frivolous, fickle and restless' – just like women, in fact. But the camorra was distinct from the Neapolitan 'woman-people' among which it lived. After all, there was wide agreement that the camorra, unlike the mafia, was a secret society. The camorra's weird rituals, its duels and the elaborate symbolic language with which *picciotti* addressed their *capo-camorrista* showed that the camorra was nothing less than a savage clan, identical to the tribes of central Africa as described by Livingstone or Stanley.

Camorra tattoos particularly fascinated 'scientists' like Lombroso and Niceforo. As far as anyone knew, *camorristi* had always adorned their skin with the names of the prostitutes they protected, the vendettas they had sworn to perform and the badges of their criminal rank. Tattoos served a double purpose: they were a sign of loyalty to the Honoured Society that also helped intimidate its victims. Like the flashy clothes early *camorristi* wore, tattoos tell us a great deal about the nature and limits of camorra power. At a time when the Society was rooted in places where the state scarcely bothered to extend its reach – in prison, or among the plebeian labyrinth of central Naples – it mattered little that these bodily pictographs could also be deciphered by the prison authorities and the police. However, needless to say, these subtleties escaped the criminologists, who just took tattoos to be one more bodily symptom of degeneracy.

Positivist criminology became a fashion; in the name of scientific inquiry it pandered to the public's fascination for secret societies and gruesome misdemeanours. A hungry readership was fed with titles like: *The Maffia in its Factors and Manifestations: a Study of Sicily's Dangerous Classes* (1886); *The Camorra Duel* (1893); *Habits and Customs of Camorristi* (1897); and *Hereditary and Psychical Tattoos in Neapolitan Camorristi* (1898). Naples had a particularly avid market for guides to the structure and special vocabulary of the camorra. It was as if these were textbooks, part of an informal curriculum on the Honoured Society

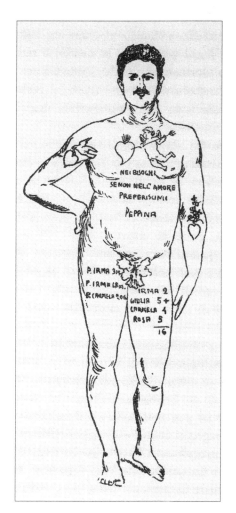

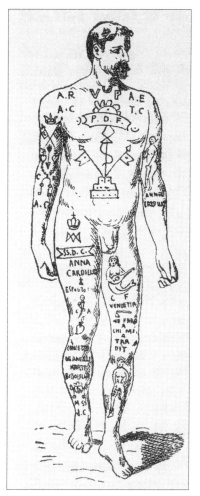

'Camorra pimp', with signature body adornments. Taken from one of many prurient studies of gangland tattooing published in the late nineteenth century.

'Bloodthirsty camorrista.'

that the locals had to digest before they could lay claim to knowing Naples, to being truly Neapolitan.

Some of the authors of these guides were police officers and lawyers who brought a great deal of hard evidence to the debate about organised crime. For instance, it was shown that for reasons of secrecy, affiliates of the Honoured Society were actually grouped into two separate compartments: the junior *picciotti* belonged to the 'Minor Society' and the more senior *camorristi* formed the 'Major Society'. Yet the same authors who relayed insights such as this also blithely threw in recycled folklore (about the camorra's Spanish origins, for example), pseudo-scientific speculation, and plain old titillation. Many of the books carried garish illustrations of delinquent ears, prostitutes disfigured by horrendous scars, or torsos tattooed with arcane gang motifs. Underlying it all was the simplistic but seductive belief that seeing and knowing are the same thing. As one police officer-cum-sociologist wrote

> The majority of *camorristi* have a dark complexion with pale tones, and abundant frizzy hair. Most have dark, sparkling, darting eyes, although a few have clear, frosty eyes. Their facial hair is sparse. Apart from a few harmonious physiognomies (which are in any case often spoiled by long scars), one can observe many noses that are misshapen, large or snubbed. There are also many low or bulbous foreheads, large cheekbones and jaws, ears that are either enormous or tiny, and finally rotten or crooked teeth.

Positivist criminology treated crime as if it were no more complicated than a smear on the bottom of a Petri dish. Yet *mafiosi* and *camorristi*, just like the rest of us, are capable of rational, strategic planning. And, more even than the rest of us, they have every reason to be fascinated by tales of secret societies and gruesome misdemeanours . . .

An audience of hoods

Among the more intriguing items held in the National Library in Naples is a photograph, no less, of the moment when the camorra was founded. Or at least, that is what it appears to be. With remarkable clarity it shows the camorra's founding members – all nine of them – arranged in a semi-circle in a large prison cell. They are evidently taking an oath by swearing on the sacred objects that lie on the floor before them: a crucifix with crossed daggers arranged at its foot. The new members have their gaze fixed on the man who seems to be leading the ceremony. He is a confident figure with a brimmed hat pushed to the back of his head, who is shown pointing at the dagger and crucifix and placing a reassuring hand on the shoulder of one nervous looking novice.

The photograph was taken during rehearsals for *The Foundation of the Camorra*, a play first performed on the evening of 18 October 1899. It may well have been a publicity shot. If so, it certainly did the trick. Interest in the play was such that tickets for the second night sold out by midday and the *Carabinieri* had to be called in to calm the scrum of frustrated theatregoers.

The script for *The Foundation of the Camorra* is lost, alas. But the reviews give us some idea of why it generated such excitement.

The audience was intensely interested in the episodes that led to the establishment among us of the evil sect. Returned travellers came here to transplant it from Spain, and chose the Vicaria prison as the place to found what someone, perhaps ironically, once called the 'Dishonoured

147

Society'. In any case, the Vicaria was for some time after that the seat of its supreme command and its tribunal.

The drama reproduces the affiliates' first feats, their first oaths, their first acts of extortion, their first ritualised knife fights, and their fierce early struggle to establish themselves and spread their rule. Their brand of criminality disguised as heroism was designed to unnerve and frighten the weak. The second performance is tonight.

The Foundation of the Camorra could have been scripted from one of the criminological guidebooks to the Honoured Society.

The audience captivated by this spectacle was peculiarly knowledgeable. For *The Foundation of the Camorra* was staged at the San Ferdinando theatre, which stood just a few metres from the infamous Vicaria prison where the play was set. During any given performance the spectacle in the auditorium was as colourful as whatever happened on stage. And as noisy: the din of chatter, catcalls and fragments of song was incessant. In the stalls, under a constant rain of orange peel and seed husks from above, ink-stained printers argued with smoke-blackened railwaymen, and breastfeeding mothers gossiped with fat prostitutes. Surveying it all from the rickety boxes just above was what passed for a middle class in the Vicaria quarter: shabby-smart teachers, or pawn-brokers with their wives and kids decked out lavishly in unreclaimed loan collateral. Here in the San Ferdinando was a hyper-condensation of the already impossibly cramped life of the Vicaria quarter. So it is hardly surprising that when *The Foundation of the Camorra* was on, *camorristi* came to see it too.

So many *camorristi* came, in fact, that the play drew the attention of law enforcement. On 4 November the local inspector wrote to the Chief of Police to express his concerns.

Given that the aforementioned theatre is frequented by an audience entirely made up of members of the underworld and men with prison records, the action being performed there is one big lesson at the school of crime.

What worried him was the play's dangerously ambiguous message. Of course it had a happy and morally instructive ending, as did everything else staged at the San Ferdinando. But the audience seemed far more excited by what came before: displays of delinquent bravado that mirrored their own twisted values. Worse still, certain passages in the play were little more than propaganda for the Honoured Society. The police inspector's letter quotes from one offending speech by the stage *capo*.

Our rulers act like *camorristi* on a big scale. So there's nothing wrong if the people do it on a small scale.

Nonsense, of course; but alluring nonsense all the same.

Popular melodramas were churned out at staggering speed for the unruly punters at the San Ferdinando. Edoardo Minichini, the author of *The Foundation of the Camorra*, is thought to have written around 400 plays; he died in poverty, leaving his wife and ten children to fend for themselves. (The fact that the camorra notoriously took protection payments from theatres probably helps explain his economic difficulties.) Many of Minichini's plays featured *camorristi*. In fact there was a fashion for such dramas in 1890s Naples. Titles like *The Boss of the Camorra* (1893) and *Blood of a Camorrista* (1894) sucked in large and enthusiastic audiences from the tenements. In fact these plays were only the latest manifestations of Honoured Society folklore. Ever since the 1860s, singers, storytellers and puppet shows had been thrilling plebeian audiences with phoney tales of camorra honour and derring-do.

The star of the San Ferdinando stage, an actor appropriately named Federigo Stella, always played the good guy, and always played him in the same histrionic, declamatory style. One of Stella's stock characters became what one contemporary man of the theatre called the 'old-school, valorous *camorrista* who dishes out good deeds, clubbings and oratory with the same spirit of fair play'. It mattered little to Stella's audience that there was no such thing as the noble *camorrista*, nor had there ever been.

Mafiosi and *camorristi* have always had a narcissistic fascination with their own image as reflected on stage, in verse and in fiction. There is nothing at all new about the feedback loop that links gangster art and gangster life. The Hollywood filmmakers who are fascinated by the mob, and the mobsters who make their villas look like the house in the climactic scene of *Scarface* (I know of two cases in Italy), are both heirs to a tradition as old as organised crime itself. As we have already seen, the camorra assembled a myth of its own Spanish origins from whatever cultural flotsam and jetsam it could find. The mafia was scarcely less stage-struck. The very name 'mafia' almost certainly entered common use in Palermo because of an enormously successful play in Sicilian dialect first performed in 1863, *I mafiusi di la Vicaria* ('The mafiosi of Vicaria prison' – the Vicaria being, as well as the notorious Naples prison, the other name for Palermo's Ucciardone jail). *I mafiusi* is the sentimental tale of an encounter between prison *camorristi* and a patriotic conspirator in the years before Italian unification. In other words, the play that gave the mafia its name has eerie echoes of the real meetings between patriots and prisoners that played such a crucial role in the history of Italian gangland. It is said that a Man of Honour was consulted on the script.

Mafiosi also loved adventure stories. Their favourite author was not Alexandre Dumas, as Chief Prosecutor Morena claimed, but the Sicilian, Vincenzo Linares, famous for his fictional tale of *The Beati Paoli,* which was first published in 1836.

The Beati Paoli of Linares's imagination was a mysterious brotherhood in the Palermo of the 1600s. They would meet before a statue of the goddess justice in a grotto full of weaponry under a church in piazza San Cosimo; here they would pass solemn and lethal judgement on anyone who abused the weak and innocent.

The fable proved so popular in Palermo that in 1873 piazza San Cosimo was renamed piazza Beati Paoli. Then in April 1909 the police discovered that *mafiosi* were holding their own tribunals in a cellar just off piazza Beati Paoli – the very cellar that popular legend identified with the HQ of the secret society in Linares's story. Later still, in the 1980s, many Sicilian Men of Honour who turned state's evidence would tell the authorities, with not a hint of irony, that the mafia and the Beati Paoli were the same thing. Clearly, *mafiosi* had long since begun to believe their own propaganda.

The slack society

Pseudo-scientific criminologists and opportunistic men of the theatre did not have a monopoly on public discussion of the mob in the new criminal normality of the 1880s and 1890s. A pioneer of serious-minded analysis of the issue was Pasquale Villari, a Neapolitan historian who held a university chair in Florence.

Villari was a lifelong campaigner for good government and social progress in the south. The squalor of the low city and the camorra that grew out of it was his consistent concern. In 1875 he created a furore by writing an open letter in which he claimed that the state of Naples was so desperate that the camorra was 'the only normal and possible state of things, the natural form that the city takes'. One of the most revealing passages in the letter was an interview with a former deputy mayor who told him that most public works contracts were impossible to implement without the approval of the camorra.

Villari's call to moralise Naples from top to bottom gained new resonance when the Left assumed power, with a brand of pork-barrel politics that gave *camorristi* even greater access to public spending. Villari inspired a generation of radical conservative campaigners to raise what became known as the 'Southern Question'. One of those to follow Villari's call was Pasquale Turiello, who in 1882 diagnosed what he termed the individualism, indiscipline and 'slackness' in Neapolitan society. Turiello argued that the Left's shambolic sleaze both reflected and cultivated Neapolitan 'slackness'. The city was being divided up between bourgeois political clienteles from above and proletarian camorra gangs from below.

The events of the 1880s and 1890s would confirm Turiello's

grim diagnosis and demonstrate his belief that it applied across much of southern Italy and Sicily, and even to the national political institutions. In 1882, the right to vote in general elections was finally extended to include about 7 per cent of the population. Anyone who paid some tax or had a couple of years of primary school education could now go to the polls. Another reform followed in 1888: the electorate for town and provincial councils was broadened; and the mayors of larger towns were now to be elected. The spread of democracy swelled the market in political favours. *Mafiosi* and *camorristi* – either directly, or through their friends in national and local government – gained the power to share out such appetising perks as exemptions from military service, reduced local authority tax assessments, and town hall jobs. Other quasi-public bodies, like charities, banks and hospitals, helped grease the wheels of patronage.

Meanwhile, in Naples, the paradigm of the slack society, an appalling cholera epidemic struck in 1884. The entire bourgeoisie and aristocracy fled in panic. Some 7,000 people died, most of them from the alleys and tenements of the low city, which one contemporary said were like 'bowels brimming with ordure'. In the epidemic's aftermath the call went up to 'disembowel' the city. Tax incentives and public money were quickly allocated to support ambitious plans for slum clearance and sewer construction. For the next twenty-five years, the modernisation of Naples proceeded with agonising slowness and inefficiency. All the while, the city's political cliques squabbled over the trough.

At every level of government, the slack society had enormous trouble creating and enforcing good reforms that benefitted all of society. Instead, it produced endless political fudges that fed temporary alliances of greedy politicians and their hangers on. Indeed, when it came to dealing with the mafia and the camorra, the most important reforms were often the least likely to be implemented: policing is a prime example. On this point, as on others, there is no clearer way to illustrate the weaknesses of the slack society than through the life of an individual policeman.

In 1888 Ermanno Sangiorgi, the policeman who had first discovered the Sicilian mafia's initiation ritual, was working in Rome as a special inspector at the Ministry of the Interior. By that time he had found happiness in his personal life, although that happiness once more brought down trouble from above. While he was still in Sicily, six years after his wife's death, he began an affair with a colleague's wife. He was punished for what a senior civil servant called his 'scandalous conduct' by being transferred immediately, in December 1884. (The Ministry evidently regarded sexual morality as a more serious matter than consorting with gangsters.) Sangiorgi's new love, a Neapolitan called Maria Vozza, twenty years his junior, followed him. She had to live in separate accommodation to avoid damaging his career any further. The two would remain together for the rest of his life.

In September 1888 Sangiorgi was sent back to Sicily on a secret mission to inspect the island's unique mounted police corps, in preparation for a root and branch reform. He found that Palermo police headquarters was 'in a complete state of confusion and disorder'; Trapani was worse. The mounted police corps did not even keep proper records of what crimes had been committed. Two of its most senior officers in Palermo had 'intimate relationships with people from the mafia'. The result was not a surprise. As Sangiorgi wrote, 'It would be dangerous to be deceived: the mafia and banditry have incontrovertibly raised their heads.'

No action was taken. Not for the last time, Sangiorgi's hard work failed to produce any political effects.

The results for Sangiorgi's career were positive, however. In 1888 he was picked to manage security when the King visited the turbulent region of Romagna. He did the job so well that in 1889, in Milan, he became Italy's youngest Chief of Police. His rapid progress earned him the rare accolade of a newspaper profile.

Sangiorgi is only forty-eight. He is reddish-blonde, like-able, and knows how to conceal the cunning required by his job beneath a layer of affable bourgeois calm. He is as alert as a squirrel, an investigator endowed with a steady perspicacity.

The year after this profile was published he was transferred to Naples, a city where the police still enjoyed one of the worst reputations of any force in Italy, a city in ferment in the aftermath of the cholera epidemic of 1884 and the 'disembowelling' that followed it. As he had done in Sicily, Sangiorgi immediately set about breaking up the traditionally cosy relationship between the police and organised crime. On 21 February 1891, one of Sangiorgi's officers, Saverio Russo by name, paid the ultimate price for this 'open fight' against the camorra when he was murdered by a *camorrista* he was trying to arrest. One well-informed newspaper commentator warned his readers against taking this shocking incident as an indication that gangsterism was out of control. Indeed, crime had decreased considerably in recent months:

> Without any doubt a great deal of the credit for this must be given to the new Police Chief Sangiorgi. Of course it is no easy matter purifying the environment inside Police Headquarters and the local stations. Nor is it an easy job to shake up officers who are not always diligent and who previously went as far as to protect gangland. But the good results that Police Chief Sangiorgi has obtained so far, his sharp sagacity and great experience, constitute a guarantee for the government and citizenry alike.

Trouble cropped up in Sangiorgi's personal life while he was in Naples. In February 1893 he was mortified to learn that his son from his first marriage, Achille, by now a coal merchant in Venice, had been arrested for cheque fraud; to Sangiorgi's great shame, the story was covered in the press. The Ministry of the Interior looked into the case, but could only express sympathy for a hard-pressed father's lot.

The supreme boss of the Honoured Society when Sangiorgi arrived in Naples was Ciccio Cappuccio, known as 'Little Lord Frankie'. His specialism was a traditional area of camorra dominance: the market in horses, particularly the army surplus nags that were occasionally auctioned off to the general public. Rigging auctions was easy: the *camorristi* only had to bully other bidders. But the camorra's control over the horse trade was also more insidious.

Marc Monnier's father had been a keen equestrian and occasional horse dealer back in the 1840s and 1850s, so the Swiss hotelier had witnessed first hand how *camorristi* used the uncertainties of the business to wheedle themselves into every possible economic transaction. Buying a horse from a stranger in Naples was always risky. No one could guarantee that, once the money had been handed over, the animal would not turn out to be frightened of the city's clamour or too weak to cope with its hills. No one, that is, except a *camorrista*. For a share of the price, *camorristi* promised to make business deals run smoothly – on pain of a beating, or worse. The camorra also controlled the supply of horse fodder: many bosses, including Little Lord Frankie, doubled as dealers in bran and carobs. From this base they could exercise total control over the city's ragged army of hackney-carriage drivers.

Little Lord Frankie passed away, of natural causes, in early December 1892. His death became the occasion for a disturbing display of just how deeply dyed by illegality was the slack fabric of Neopolitan society. From Police Headquarters, Sangiorgi could do little more than watch.

Little Lord Frankie's obituary in an important new Neapolitan daily, *Il Mattino*, was lavish in its praise. Here was a righter of wrongs, a proletarian justice of the peace. With a flush of pride, *Il Mattino* recalled the time when he had single-handedly downed twelve Calabrian *camorristi* in a knife fight in prison. But it was wrong to call him a 'bloodthirsty, born delinquent'.

> He was exceptionally nice: a model of decorum, respectful and deferential. He had a grim look in his grey eyes. But he strove constantly to moderate it by applying the sweetness and docility of a man who knows his own strength – a man who is absolutely sure that nothing in the world can resist his will.

Evidently it was not only the lumpenproletariat of the Vicaria quarter who embraced the myth of the noble, old-style *camorrista*. *Il Mattino*, like its notorious editor Edoardo Scarfoglio, was hysterically right wing and utterly corrupt – the mouthpiece of the worst elements in the Neapolitan political class. But what is both shocking and revealing about its coverage of Little Lord Frankie's death is the way it tolerates, and even celebrates, the private statelets that camorra bosses were able to carve out in large areas of the city.

Little Lord Frankie's last journey was a statelet funeral. Six horses drew an elaborate hearse, covered in wreaths, on a tour of half the city. The mourners were led by every cab driver in Naples, and a procession of sixty hackney carriages. Then came a huge crowd of awestruck followers, all telling tales of the dead man's 'heroic and chivalrous deeds', according to *Il Mattino*. The paper even published a poetic lament for Little Lord Frankie.

> *Who will defend us now?*
> *Without him, what will we do?*
> *Whoever can you run to*
> *If a wrong is done to you?*

Naples was still a city where the rule of law and honesty in public affairs seemed alien concepts.

A few months after Little Lord Frankie's posthumous show of force, Sangiorgi found himself at the centre of a riot that, for one brief moment, laid bare the contorted entrails of the slack society. And despite his 'steady perspicacity', and 'sharp sagacity', the notorious hackney cab drivers' strike of August 1893 would prove too tough an assignment for the determined Police Chief. For the first time in decades, the camorra took to the streets in force.

The events of the strike itself can be quickly related. The cab drivers' anger was triggered by a proposal to extend the city's tram system. So on 22 August 3,000 cabbies launched a violent street protest to coincide with patriotic demonstrations against the murder of some Italian workmen in southern France. Socialists, anarchists and a hungry mob from the low city soon joined in. Sangiorgi was in bed with a severe fever when the disorder broke out. While he was away from work, a scrum of his officers on the hunt for rioters assaulted customers in the Gambrinus, the most prestigious café in the city. Sangiorgi crawled back to his desk the following morning to find that the police had become the targets of mass fury: there were pitched battles in the alleys between rioters and the forces of order. A boy of eight, Nunzio Dematteis, was shot in the forehead by a *Carabiniere* defending a tram from the mob. News quickly spread that the police were to blame for the boy's death. The crowd carried his bleeding body aloft and marched on the Prefecture. Sangiorgi's officers blocked their path and a grotesque tug of war over the corpse ensued. Some local parliamentarians demanded that the police withdraw their 'provocative' presence from the streets. The army was called in to restore calm.

Thus far, with the possible exception of the botched police operation, there is little that is particularly Neapolitan about the events of August 1893. Trams represented an obvious threat to the hackney-carriage business. A violent industrial dispute like this could have happened in any big city in Europe, where police aggression would have been the likely response. But in Naples there were of course many *camorristi* among the cab drivers. After all, these were the same men who had filed along behind Little Lord Frankie's coffin just a few months earlier. Sangiorgi's police learned that the riot of August 1893 had been planned the night before, at a meeting between *camorristi* and anarchists. The Chief of Police compiled a list of several hundred cabbies involved in the disturbances, marking out many of them as *camorristi* and men with criminal records.

And where the camorra had interests, so too did its eminent friends. Street gangsters may have performed the strike but it was orchestrated by city politicians. Those politicians had two notable beefs against the central government in Rome: first, the proposal to award the contract for extending the tram network to a company from Belgium, of all places; and second, the threat to take away control over the reconstruction programme set in motion after the cholera epidemic of 1884. One of Sangiorgi's officers later reported that the origins of the riot lay in 'the great shifting of interest groups caused by the disembowelling work'. By engineering anarchy in the streets of Naples, the interest groups clustered around city hall and the building industry hoped to win concessions from Rome.

Over subsequent days the strike was quelled by a mixture of negotiation and deceit. First the negotiations: the cab drivers were invited to talks with the town council. Then, presumably on the orders of the Interior Ministry, and 'in order to favour the resolution of the dispute', as Sangiorgi put it, he released the cabbies who had been arrested – *excluding* the ones with criminal records. A camorra-backed politician called Alberto Casale then acted as intermediary during the talks; in all likelihood, Casale was one of the politicians who had helped orchestrate the strike in the first place. Concessions were duly made: the tram timetable would be curtailed, and the tram network would not be extended.

Then came the deceit: a few weeks later this agreement was torn up and the original plans for the tram network were re-instated. It would later emerge that Alberto Casale had accepted a sturdy backhander from the Belgian tram company. His favourite *camorristi* received their share of the cash too – or at least we can surmise as much because the town council's flagrant bad faith during the negotiations did not reignite the cab drivers' protest. More importantly, the city council retained its control over a large chunk of the reconstruction funds. The manoeuvrings behind the scenes of the hackney-cab strike showed, as Turiello had argued, that the camorra and the political clienteles were operating at different ends of the same market for favours. The slack society was also the sly society.

By the time the dispute was resolved, Sangiorgi had left Naples. The disastrous way the cab drivers' protest had been tackled led to a purge in Police Headquarters. Sangiorgi was transferred to Venice only two weeks after the end of the strike. The rioting of August 1893 was one of the worst moments of his career, but he took much more than his fair share of the blame for the chaos.

Meanwhile, among the many jails, penitentiaries and penal colonies of the peninsula, mob rule persisted unchecked throughout the last quarter of the nineteenth century. Overhauling the prisons would have been an incisive reform directed against organised crime, drying up its traditional sump of strength. Yet the forces of law rarely concerned themselves with the mafia and camorra's prison activities. One exception was a case in the late 1870s: following the murder of a police informer in Naples that had been ordered from behind bars, fifty-three prison *camorristi* were successfully convicted, a rare investment of precious institutional resources in trying to tackle this chronic problem.

Evidently the prisons still hosted a dense gangster network. In 1893 a positivist criminologist published *The Story of a Born Delinquent*, an autobiography – no less – by a senior prison *camorrista* known only as Antonino M. Antonino M recounted taking part in several vicious battles in prison, including one that saw Neapolitans and Sicilians line up against Calabrians and Abruzzesi: many were killed and a warden was left holding his intestines in his hands.

But it is the unity of the prison confraternity, rather than its divisions, that emerges most clearly from Antonino M's account. He related that every time he was transferred from one jail to another (usually for violent conduct), he used code words to prove his camorra credentials. His status was duly recognised wherever he went: in jails in Puglia and the Marche, as in the Castello del Carmine in Naples (the very jail where Duke Castromediano had been clapped in irons in 1851). Nor was this the only way that *camorristi* in different regions were connected: punishments decreed in a prison in Cosenza, northern Calabria, could be carried out in the penal colony on Favignana, an island off the western coast of Sicily.

There was plenty more evidence where Antonino M's story came from. Undeniably, all the things that Duke Castromediano had observed back in the 1850s were still going on in Italy's prisons: organised violence and vendettas; corruption, extortion, smuggling and the trade in favours; ritual initiations and knife fights; and training in the skills and protocols of the sect. But instead of reform, such information only triggered a depressingly repetitive pattern of political failure. Now and again a particularly savage prison riot or an unusually alarming government report would generate fervent calls for change. Just as predictably, those calls would echo pointlessly into silence: lack of funds and the sheer political irrelevance of the prisons issue meant that Italy's slack society could not muster the will to tackle the problem.

Soon Italy would pay a very heavy price for failing to reform the prisons.

The criminologist who published Antonino M's autobiography also subjected him to a close physical examination. Not surprisingly, the tests came up positive: Antonino M was a born delinquent, a mixture of 'the savage, the epileptic and the moral lunatic'. He had a series of telltale bodily deformities, such as jug-handle ears, large testicles and slow reflexes in his pupils. He also had tattoos, including the slogan 'DOWN WITH DISHON-OURED SCUM' across his chest. But the giveaway was the specimen's broad, flat skull – his brachycephaly, to use the scientific term. Antonino M was Calabrian, the criminologist explained; and typical Calabrians were dolichocephalic, meaning that they had long, thin heads. Manifestly, Antonino M was a degenerate member of the Calabrian race.

Many Italians would probably have believed the criminologist if he had said that Calabrians had four arms and a single eye in the middle of their brow. Calabria was Italy's poorest region, its most politically marginal. But by the time Antonino M came to have the criminological callipers applied to his cranium, born Calabrian delinquents like him had already surfaced from the prison system to form a new criminal fraternity.

THE 'NDRANGHETA EMERGES

1880–1902

4

Harsh mountain

A single geographical fact defines the landscape at the southernmost tip of Calabria: Aspromonte. The 'Harsh Mountain' is a place of bitter beauty. To the south and east, where Aspromonte looks down past Mount Etna and out towards North Africa, its flanks are toasted by the sun. Here valleys gouge their descent, spilling cement-grey grit towards the turquoise expanse of the Ionian Sea. In spring, the more sheltered hollows host embattled blooms of pink oleander and yellow broom. Aspromonte's higher reaches, by contrast, are dark with pine and slender beech. Among the trees, tortuous paths seek out the peaks and exquisite high meadows before skirting down into sudden gorges that springtime fills with the smell of oregano. The woodland canopy extends down the lush eastern slopes where the panoramas are even more captivating: the Straits of Messina separating Calabria from Sicily, the smoky Aeolian Islands, and the Tyrrhenian Sea.

Nothing in this landscape is permanent. Human inhabitants cling to the coastal strips or create improbable, eagle's nest villages above the gorges. Every winter torrents tear rocks from the fragile valley sides and landslips rake brutal shortcuts down through the roads' painstaking meanders. Whole villages, like Roghudi and Amendolea, have been abandoned from one day to the next, their inhabitants pushed down from the mountain to the coast.

Massive earthquakes give history a deadly, arrhythmic beat in southern Calabria. In 1783 as many as 50,000 people died, and there was a sequence of lethal quakes in 1894, 1905, 1907 . . .

Even to the north of Aspromonte the mountains hog most of the terrain in Calabria, leaving precious little space for the coastal plains, and posing a formidable obstacle for travellers. As a result, most nineteenth-century tourist guides covered the region with little more than a cursory reference to its rugged scenery and stubborn inhabitants. Baedeker, the obligatory companion volume for the well-to-do northern European traveller, all but told its readers not to bother going to Calabria in 1869.

> The length of the journey, the indifference of the inns and the insecurity of the roads, which has of late increased, at present deter all but the most enterprising.

Such words of warning were not misplaced. At that time the railway stopped at Eboli. But Eboli was still a long way above Calabria's northern border, and 327 miles from Reggio Calabria, the small city at the tip of Italy's toe where Aspromonte overlooks the Straits of Messina. At Eboli, if the visitor were lucky enough to grab one of the three places available in the coach and then lucky with the roads, the weather and the outlaws, he could make the journey to Reggio in three and a half days. Along the route, he would stare nervously out at the forests and crags, recalling recent tales of bandit atrocities.

In 1871 the government census recorded that 87 per cent of Calabrians could not read or write. Across much of the region, callous landowners imperiously exploited vast swarms of peasants. Leopoldo Franchetti, a Tuscan Jewish intellectual who was one of the few men intrepid enough to investigate Calabrian society, wrote in 1874 that

> Among the oppressed there is no middle stage between two extreme states of being: on the one hand, fear, obedience and the most abject docility; and, on the other, the most brutal and ferocious rebellion.

Franchetti tells us that local government was a grubby and violent business in Calabria. There were many places where the mayor and his relatives cornered common land for themselves, or lived off the trade in timber stolen from common woodland. Any forest wardens who tried to impose the law, 'ran a serious risk of getting a bullet'. The 'grain banks' created to lend seed corn and money to the poor at planting time often served only as a source of easy credit for the rich. As elsewhere in the south and Sicily, the government in Rome tolerated such abuses because Calabria's corrupt mayors mustered votes for the ruling national factions. Calabria was one of the slackest parts of the slack society.

Yet one thing that Franchetti was not particularly worried about was organised crime. In the 1860s and 1870s, at a time when copious evidence attests to the shocking extent of mafia and camorra power, there are only a few intermittent reports of gangsterism in Calabria. Together, those reports do nothing to suggest that southern Calabria would become a hoodlum fief on a par with Sicily and Campania. There is no government document from the 1860s or 1870s, no traveller's tale, no faded local memoir that speaks of a strong and insistent mafia presence here. The region had many serious problems but delinquent fraternities were not among them.

By the mid 1880s, there were some signs of improvement in Calabria's fortunes. Trains now crawled to Reggio along a single-track railway that clung to the Ionian coast; and the line along the Tyrrhenian coast was under construction. Yet it was precisely at this historical moment that the first official reports tell us that 'a nucleus of *mafiosi* and *camorristi*' was in operation in Reggio Calabria and 'the ranks of the maffia's criminal associations' were growing elsewhere in Aspromonte's shadow. As if from nowhere, a new criminal sect was being born. By the end of the 1880s the province of Reggio Calabria and some adjoining parts of the province of Catanzaro were enduring an explosion in gang crime from which they have never recovered.

Mafiosi and *camorristi*: the earliest labels were borrowed from Sicily and Naples. Other names would soon be used: Calabrian mafia, Honoured Society, Society of *Camorristi*, and so on. But as police and magistrates became more knowledgeable about this new threat to public order in southern Calabria, they most often referred to it as the picciotteria. The word is pronounced roughly 'peach-otter-ear', and there is no mystery to its derivation. *Picciotto* ('peach-otto') was a southern Italian or Sicilian dialect word for 'lad'. *Picciotti* were also the lower ranking members of the Neapolitan camorra. Picciotteria sometimes means a young man's air of arrogant self-confidence. So 'Lads with Attitude' is a handy translation of the new association's informal title.

The Lads with Attitude were a lowly bunch: herdsmen and bagpipers, by and large, men whose grandest ambition was a flask of wine and a piece of goat meat. At the time when the picciotteria first appeared, the great Sicilian novelist Giovanni Verga was evoking the lives of poor people like them in some of the greatest fiction in the Italian language. Verga knew that he faced a hard task convincing his bourgeois readership to dare an imaginative leap into the mental universe of the peasantry. 'We need to make ourselves tiny like them', Verga pleaded. 'We need to enclose the whole horizon between two clods of earth, and look through the microscope at the little causes that make little hearts beat.'

From today's perspective, we need to make a similar imaginative leap. But we have no need to be patronising towards the 'little hearts' of the farm hands and woodcutters who became members of the picciotteria. For these humble folk were the direct ancestors of a fearsome Calabrian criminal brotherhood whose definitive name would only appear for the first time in the 1950s: the 'ndrangheta, Italy's third mafia, and now its richest, its most secretive and the most successful at spreading vile metastases around the globe.

Soon after it was born, the picciotteria was subjected to a

judicial offensive that was sporadic but nonetheless more effective than any faced so far by organised crime in either Naples or Sicily. In the years following the first signs of alarm, around Aspromonte and on either side of the first stretch of the Apennines, hundreds of Calabrian *picciotti* – precisely 1,854 of them between 1885 and 1902 according to one local prosecutor – were tried, convicted and put behind bars. This fact alone tells us something significant: Calabria's gangsters did not yet enjoy the same degree of VIP protection enjoyed by the Neapolitan camorra, let alone the Sicilian mafia.

Yet the picciotteria remained almost entirely unknown in the rest of Italy. Unlike the mafia and camorra, it provoked no parliamentary inquiries or debates, no bouts of national newspaper outrage, no investigations by sociologists, no poems or plays. Nobody cared: this was Calabria, after all.

The lack of interest in the picciotteria together with Calabria's history of maladministration and natural disaster often leaves historians with a shortage of evidence. The city of Reggio Calabria was undoubtedly where the picciotteria was first spotted in the early 1880s, but there is not enough surviving documentation to explain how and why. Yet elsewhere the early trials did deposit a thin but precious seam of paper that can now be mined for clues about how organised crime in Calabria began. And as it turns out, the 'ndrangheta's beginnings were much more straightforward than the camorra's or mafia's. There are two places in particular where enough nineteenth-century policework survives to give us a clear picture of those beginnings. A later chapter deals with the most notorious of those places: the village of Africo, sited 700 metres above the Ionian coast. Until it was finally abandoned in 1953 as a result of devastating floods, Africo was a byword for the isolation and poverty of Calabria's highland communities – and a byword for organised crime.

But before going to Africo, the story of the 'ndrangheta's origins takes us to the opposite flank of Aspromonte, and to a place of relative wealth and power. One of the secrets of the 'ndrangheta's survival and success over the years has been its ability to straddle the distance between prosperity and hardship, as between the contrasting faces of the Harsh Mountain.

The tree of knowledge

Palmi sits on a shelf where Aspromonte meets the Tyrrhenian Sea. Gazing to the north-east, it affords a seductive panorama over the Plain of Gioia Tauro, a fertile amphitheatre of land descending gently from the mountains. The Plain was Calabria's answer to the 'Golden Shell' around Palermo in the late nineteenth century. Land was owned in smaller farms rather than great estates, partly because a great deal of Church property was confiscated and privatised after Italian unification. There were many citrus fruit groves in the Plain too, although the irrigation was not as sophisticated as it was in Sicily. More important to the economy of towns like Palmi were the famous olive trees, as tall and venerable as oaks. Recently the wine industry had come to the fore, after French vineyards were devastated by phylloxera, an aphid-like insect that feasted on the roots and leaves of vines. Italian producers moved to fill the gap in supply, and in the plain of Gioia Tauro they even cut down olive trees to make room for the grape.

In the 1880s Palmi was a town of some eleven or twelve thousand inhabitants, which was not small by the standards of the region. Southern Calabria is a place where the population is spread out in little centres, and in the 1880s few of them housed more than five thousand people. Even the provincial capital, Reggio Calabria, could only muster its 40,000 population by including the villages that surrounded it. Palmi was the administrative capital for the whole of the Plain of Gioia Tauro, an area encompassing 130,000 souls. And as the administrative capital it had an outpost of the Prefecture, a police station, a courtroom, and a prison. Men from that prison would turn Palmi into Calabria's most notorious mafia stronghold in the 1880s and 1890s.

It all began in the spring of 1888. The local newssheet started to report razor slashings and ritual knife duels. In Palmi's taverns and brothels, gang members battled it out with clubs and blades. In classic mafia and camorra fashion, the bleeding losers refused point blank to name the men who had wounded them.

Within weeks of these first reports, Palmi's hoodlum problem was out of control. Ordinary citizens were afraid to leave their homes. Anyone who stood up to the thugs received the razor treatment. The *picciotti* settled their bloody accounts in the centre of town, on corso Garibaldi and in piazza Vittorio Emanuele. They had begun by extorting money from gamblers and prostitutes. Now they also fleeced landowners who were afraid to report thefts and vandalism for fear of worse: the Lads with Attitude were setting up protection rackets, the very foundation of any mafia's territorial authority. The gang threatened a local *Carabiniere*, and pelted him with stones; they even silenced the local newspaper, whose editor received a threatening letter telling him not to 'persecute the lads'. From Palmi the sect spread to the smaller towns and villages right across the Plain of Gioia Tauro, and up onto the surrounding mountain slopes.

Only in June 1888, when a clerk at the local branch of the Prefecture was slashed across the face as he came out of the theatre, did the police round up the first large batch of suspects. The twenty-four men arraigned early in 1889 give us our first glimpse of the *kind* of person who became a Lad with Attitude. Many of them were young – late teens or early twenties – and all of them were labourers or artisans: the legal documents list job titles such as peasant, carter, waiter, tailor, mule driver, shepherd. There were also one or two men who farmed their own plot. The boss, one Francesco Lisciotto, was a cobbler; at sixty, he was comfortably the oldest man in the gang. More importantly, like all but three of the Palmi *picciotti*, he had already spent time behind bars.

The police and magistrature continued their fight. In June 1890 one trial targeted a picciotteria network based in Iatrìnoli and Radicena, two towns that sat one just above the other about fifteen kilometres from the coast at Gioia Tauro. Many of the ninety-six defendants were workers and craftsmen like their fellow *picciotti* in Palmi. The judges in the case explained that the sect began in 1887; they had no doubts about where it came from.

> The association originated in the district prisons [in Palmi], under the name of 'Sect of *camorristi*'. From there, as and when its bosses and promoters were released, it spread to other towns and villages where it found fertile soil among the callow youth, old jailbirds, and especially goatherds. The Society, with the protection it afforded to its comrades, offered this last group a way to pasture their animals illegally on other people's land, and to impose themselves on landlords.

Men like the Palmi *capo* Francesco Lisciotto came out of jail with their status in the Society already well established. The 'ndrangheta was not founded, in other words; it *emerged* almost fully formed from inside the prison system.

More arrests and further trials followed over the coming years. Early in 1892 the court in Palmi tried some 150 men from right across the Plain of Gioia Tauro. The *picciotti* did their best to evade justice by killing one witness and threatening many others into silence. But the evidence against them proved overwhelming. The new boss of Palmi, Antonio Giannino, aged only 20, was his gang's knife-fencing instructor. Indeed he was so proud of his skills that he had himself photographed in fighting pose. The image helped convict him.

The 1892 trial added more detail to what the police knew about the picciotteria: the characteristic appearance of its affiliates, for example. The *picciotti* had tattooed hieroglyphs that signalled their rank. They also wore tight trousers that flared over their shoes, tied their silk scarves in a special way to leave the ends fluttering as they swaggered, and combed their hair into a distinctive butterfly-shaped quiff.

If peace returned to Palmi following the huge and successful prosecution of 1892, it certainly did not return for long. In 1894 the town was reduced to rubble by an earthquake. By the following year the picciotteria was active again, robbing and extorting among the temporary shacks in which much of the population still lived. Yet the police seemed inert. Commentators in the press muttered that the police in Palmi had 'evening conversations' in the very wine cellars where the hoods hung out, and that the forces of law and order were less interested in tackling organised crime than they were in arresting opposition voters during elections. In Calabria's bigger towns, just as in Naples and Sicily, the police soon learned to co-manage crime with gangsters.

Eventually, in September 1896, another wave of arrests elicited more confessions. Early in 1897 the resulting trial provided full details of the Calabrian mafia's ranks and rituals for the first time. The picciotteria formed itself into locally based cells or 'sections'. Each cell was subdivided between a Minor Society and a Major Society. The Minor Society contained men bearing the lower rank of *picciotto*. The Major Society contained the more senior criminals, known as *camorristi*. Both the Major and the Minor had their own boss and a *contaiolo*, or bookkeeper, who gathered and redistributed the gang's income from crime. Each new member had to undergo an initiation ritual to join the Society before he was awarded the lowest rank of all, that of 'Honoured Youth'. The boss of the Major Society would call his men into a darkened room, form them into a circle and begin the long ceremony with the words, 'Are you comfortable?' to which the assembled gangsters would reply, 'Very comfortable!'

On 24 February 1897 a crucial witness in the resulting trial, a man by the name of Pasquale Trimboli, took the stand in Palmi's courthouse. The defendants in their cage, and the public squeezed into the tiny gallery, all craned to hear what he had to say.

Trimboli had been a member of the picciotteria, and therefore knew everything about the sect – including the terrible secret of its origins. Mention of the mysterious genesis of the picciotteria transfixed the court. But the mood of intense concentration soon gave way to puzzled laughter as he told his childish tale of how the Calabrian mafia was born.

> The society was born from three knights, one from Spain, one from Palermo, and one from Naples. All three of them were *camorristi*. The Spanish knight took a camorra, a bribe, on every hand of cards the other two played. With time, he gathered in all their money and the others could not play any more. So he gave 10 *Lire* back to each one, and told them, 'Here are 10 *Lire* for you, and I've got all the rest in my hand, so that means that I'm the strongest.'
>
> Metaphorically speaking, these three *camorristi* were a *tree*. The boss, the Spanish knight, was the *trunk* of the tree. The Palermo knight, who was the oldest, was the masterbone, *Mastrosso*. And the third knight, the one from Naples, was the bone, *Osso*. The other members were the *branches* and the *leaves*. The 'honoured youths', who aspired to become *picciotti*, were the *flowers*.

To my knowledge, this is the first recorded (and garbled) version of the 'ndrangheta's founding myth. What it suggests is that Calabrian gangsters were seeking out fables to build their *esprit de corps*, to endow their newly surfaced fraternity with the same aura as their brethren in Campania and Sicily.

The success of the judicial assault on the picciotteria can be judged from the testimony of a priest who was called to give evidence in yet another trial just three years later. He said that in Palmi,

> the criminals' audacity makes walking through the streets extremely dangerous, even before the Angelus [i.e. sunset].

> Honest people are now in the habit of going home as soon as they can, because at any time in the busiest parts of town you can hear the wails of the wounded and dying.

But if the trials in Palmi failed to shake the grip of the picciotteria in the Plain of Gioia Tauro, they did at least provide historical documentation that has a familiar ring. Doubly familiar, in fact. On the one hand there is a great deal about the picciotteria that resembles the Honoured Society of Naples. (One early picciotteria trial in 1884 even found that the criminal boss of the small town of Nicastro 'had relations with the famous Neapolitan *camorrista* Ciccillo ["Little Lord Frankie"] Cappuccio'.) Like their Neapolitan cousins, the Calabrians duelled with knives, and slashed their victims' faces with razors. Both sects exploited prostitution and gambling; both blew their illicit earnings on feasting and getting drunk; both had a similar dress code (flared trousers and all that); and both divided their gangs between a Minor Society and a Major Society, between aspiring 'Honoured Youths', junior *picciotti*, and senior *camorristi*. Like the Neapolitans, the Calabrians punished their members' transgressions with a distinctively disgusting punishment they called *tartaro* ('Tartarus' or 'Hell'): it involved daubing the culprit with urine and faeces. There are many, many other similarities that it would be tiresome to list here: in the coded jargon they spoke to try and conceal what they were talking about, for example. What these likenesses confirm is that both the Neapolitan camorra and the Calabrian mafia share the same genealogy. Both were born from the *same* prison camorra.

On the other hand the picciotteria is also familiar in that it closely resembles the 'ndrangheta of today, with its Minor Society and its Major Society, its foundation myth of the three Spanish knights, and so on. In fact even the most confused bits of Pasquale Trimboli's testimony chime strongly with what we know about the 'ndrangheta's contemporary practices. *'Ndranghetisti* habitually refer to their organisation metaphorically, as what they call a 'Tree of Knowledge': the trunk being the boss, the branches the officers, and so on.

The 'ndrangheta of today, with its unique admission rituals for every rank in the organisation, is more obsessed with ceremony than any other Italian mafia. The archival papers tell us that the Calabrian mafia of the late 1800s was developing the same obsession. Today's 'ndrangheta also has a great variety of specialised job titles within each local gang – far more than either the Sicilian mafia or the Neapolitan camorra. Echoes of that level of specialisation reach us from the nineteenth century too. Both the Minor Society and the Major Society of the Palmi section of the picciotteria had other posts in addition to the boss and the bookkeeper: such as the '*Camorrista* of the Day', whose duty was to inform the boss of local goings on; and the '*Picciotto* of Correspondence' who handled communications between members in prison and members at large. In short, there can be no doubt that the Lads with Attitude were the 'ndrangheta by an earlier name.

A long and gruesome history had begun.

Darkest Africo

The *zampogna*, or southern Italian bagpipe, is an ancient and unlovely instrument. It is made from a whole goat- or sheepskin that has been cured, turned wool side in, and sealed. A cluster of wooden pipes lolls where the sheep's head was once attached and a mouthpiece protrudes from the stump of a front leg. When the *zampogna* is pressed under the player's arm, nasal melodies are emitted over a hypnotic wheeze that sounds like the infinite bleat of the departed animal's soul.

In the hilltop towns of nineteenth-century Calabria, dancing to the *zampogna* was one of the few things that passed for entertainment. So any student of Calabrian folklore who had ventured into the streets of Africo on the mild evening of All Saints, 1 November 1894, would not have been surprised to see a circle of men taking turns to perform a skipping dance around the local *zampogna*-player. But as the *zampognaro* himself – his name was Giuseppe Sagoleo – would later tell an investigating magistrate, there was nothing folkloristic about his performance that evening. This bagpipe party was a carefully choreographed prelude to a murder that would precipitate one of the biggest early picciotteria trials. By luck, the complete papers from that trial have survived the upheavals of Calabrian geology and history to give us a priceless insight into this newly emerged criminal organisation in one of its heartlands.

But to make sense of the bagpipe party of All Saints, we need to take a few steps further back in time. For the brutal execution carried out that evening was the culmination of a campaign by the recently established Africo section of the picciotteria to take control of the town for the first time. The *zampogna* had a central role in that campaign. Combined with the testimonies of witnesses, Giuseppe Sagoleo's story takes us deep into the world of the 'ndrangheta in its primitive form.

The *zampognaro*'s woes began, he testified, early the same year when Domenico Callea, age 34, returned to his home town after serving ten years in prison for the kidnap and violent rape of a woman. Once his hair grew back from his prison crew cut, Callea cultivated a butterfly-shaped quiff. He made the transition from prison *camorrista* to senior Lad with Attitude smoothly: he immediately became both the bookkeeper for the Africo section, and also its duelling instructor.

Domenico Callea approached the *zampognaro*, offering to propose him for membership of a 'society' that existed in Africo. Because Callea was one of the society's leaders, he said, he could even offer to waive the 7½ *Lire* enrolment fee. But Sagoleo was smart enough to make inquiries about the society before accepting Callea's invitation. When he was told that the members were obliged to follow the bosses' orders, even if that meant committing robbery or murder, he refused to join.

Across southern Calabria, Lads like Callea were making similar offers. They nearly always charged a membership fee of 7½ *Lire* – about three quarters of the value of a goat, or about 8 per cent of the price of a pig. They usually claimed that the society just existed to drink wine and have a good time. And very frequently they beat people up or flicked them with a razor if they refused to pay. Sagoleo the *zampognaro* was lucky.

This simple method of squeezing money from new recruits was a classic prison camorra technique. The picciotteria would use it for years to come. So the early 'ndrangheta was based partly on a kind of pyramid selling scam that benefitted only the bosses at the top. As the case of the bagpipe player of Africo also illustrated, this method had an inbuilt weakness in that it created a great many new members who had little genuine loyalty to the picciotteria. One of the reasons we can know so much about the early 'ndrangheta is that so many of these new recruits would confess everything to the police. The 'ndrangheta came into the world with a birth defect that would take decades to shed.

Although the *zampognaro* refused Domenico Callea's offer, he did not save himself from the attentions of Callea's friends. As he explained to the investigating magistrate

> The association's members were always coming to me and asking me to play. There were times when they told me I had to do it whether I wanted to or not because they were in charge. Sometimes they paid me, and sometimes they didn't. And I couldn't complain because they threatened to break my bagpipes.

Domenico Callea's *picciotti* were subjecting the bagpipe player to what the police called a *prepotenza*, an act of petty bullying – like refusing to pay in a shop or pestering another man's wife. But this *prepotenza* had a clear strategic purpose. The picciotteria may have been a secret sect, but its secrecy, like that of other Italian criminal fraternities, was of a paradoxical kind: the Lads were, after all, not yet so guarded that they could resist sporting distinctive haircuts and trousers. This is because their power depended on their ability to make their presence felt in the most public of ways. Indeed by strong-arming the poor *zampognaro* into playing at their parties, the Lads were imposing themselves on one of the few expressions of a collective social life in Africo. This was a flagrant *prepotenza* committed against the whole community. More than that, it was a deliberate attempt to undermine any sense of community, and replace it with fear.

On 12 May 1894, the day devoted to Africo's patron, Saint Leo, Domenico Callea called upon the bagpiper to welcome a very important guest: Filippo Velonà, a 38-year-old cobbler from the nearby village of Staiti. The official files on Velonà give us a clear but hardly very expressive description: he was 1.70m tall with brown hair and eyes, a 'regular' forehead, a 'natural' complexion, a 'robust' physique and no distinguishing marks. In short, Velonà could have been any one of the countless artisans who eked out a life by servicing the poor mountain communities of Calabria. The only clue to his real identity is in the local mayor's description of his conduct as *cattivissima* – 'exceptionally bad'. This after all, was a man who had two convictions for wounding and who had served seven years in jail for dishing out a beating from which the victim subsequently died. When he was released in 1892 he led the emergence of the picciotteria in the district of Bova which lay either side of the rugged valley blasted out by the Amendolea torrent.

The villages of the Bova district, including Africo, were a cultural island even on Aspromonte: their inhabitants spoke not Calabrian dialect, but Greek – or at least Grecanico, an archaic dialect of Greek that survives from the early Middle Ages when Calabria was part of the Byzantine Empire. One sign of how important this cultural island is to the Calabrian mafia today is the fact that the word 'ndrangheta derives from the word for 'manliness' or 'heroism' in Grecanico.

But boss Velonà's prestige extended beyond the Grecanico-speaking area: further round the coast to the north-east, he was acknowledged in Bovalino, San Luca and even as far as Portigliola and Gerace. This was a huge stretch of the Calabrian coast – as big as the Plain of Gioia Tauro just over the mountains; it corresponds more or less to the *Mandamento ionico*, or 'Ionian Precinct', which is one of the three areas into which the 'ndrangheta's jurisdiction is divided today. No wonder the rank and file called Velonà 'President'.

Velonà came to Africo on 12 May to initiate a new Lad with Attitude. The formalities were completed indoors. The young man ritually submitted himself to the boss's authority by kneeling before him, kissing his hand, and uttering the following words: 'Father forgive me if I have strayed in the past, and I promise not to stray in the future.'

The initiation, as always, was celebrated with a banquet

attended by members from across the area. They drank a great deal of wine and ate a goat purloined from the man who had been forced to put Velonà up during his stay. Everyone laughed when one *picciotto* loudly asked the wife of the very man from whom the animal had been stolen for some salt to preserve a piece of it. The lads clearly appreciated such a creatively framed *prepotenza*. Then, after eating copiously, the bosses settled down to play cards while the younger affiliates danced to the sound of the bagpipes. 'All of this happened publicly, in front of everyone', as one witness explained.

By stealing animals, and eating stolen meat in such demonstrative assertions of their *esprit de corps*, the *picciotti* were proclaiming themselves to be at the top of the food chain; for this was a part of the world where the peasant diet was mostly vegetarian. Elsewhere, the picciotteria went to even greater lengths to show that its members were in the protein elite. In Bova, the town's mayor would indignantly testify, one local mobster (a cobbler like his boss) once treated his brethren from other towns to a fish banquet. Now, Bova is only about nine kilometres from the sea, as the crow flies. But those 9 kilometres may as well have been 90: nothing perishable could be relied upon to survive the arduous trip on a mule's back up into the mountains from the coast. As the mayor explained, fish 'arrives only very rarely in our town, and people from a humble background are not accustomed to eating it'. For a cobbler to serve fish to his guests was the dietary equivalent of gangster bling.

On Aspromonte, there were many who were impressed by these rudimentary advertisements for power. While the boss Velonà was in Africo he was approached by a woman who presented him with a sheep and begged him 'to do her the honour of admitting her son to the association'.

Callea's crew were doing more to earn such admiration than bullying the bagpiper and pinching the odd goat for their team-building banquets. According to the mayor of Africo, seventy pigs had been stolen in 1893 alone. Many other beasts went missing too. The victims – men like the schoolteacher, the arch-priest, and the mayor himself – were too afraid even to report their losses to the authorities. Rumours said that the animals were sold cheaply to butchers who were also in the association; goats had been found with their ears – and therefore their owners' marks – cut off. Butchers in Bova later reported that the legal livestock trade had virtually collapsed because people were just too afraid to go around buying and selling animals.

The accumulating evidence from Africo points inexorably to an important conclusion: even in the most isolated mountain villages of Grecanico-speaking Aspromonte, the Lads with Attitude were part of an organisation that was much bigger, and more coordinated, than some loose constellation of local gangs. Not only did they have common rituals and structures and a shared past behind bars, in Filippo Velonà they also had a charismatic boss whose prestige traversed a wide territory. They even placed themselves under the jurisdiction of a single judge: his name was Andrea Angelone.

Angelone was an old prison *camorrista*, fifty-nine years old to be precise. He was released from jail for the last time following a twelve-year stretch in 1887 and immediately set up a branch of the picciotteria in his home village of Roccaforte del Greco, in the Grecanico-speaking district. Although he did not take an active role in the sect's day-to-day criminal activity thereafter, he still received his regular cut of the takings in return for dispensing his wisdom at tribunals. The Grecanico-speaking Lads also had contacts in Reggio Calabria and in the district of Palmi.

The authorities in Palmi reported similar long-range connections. The various sections of the organisation on the Plain of Gioia Tauro had 'emissaries so they could correspond with one another'. And while the local branches each had their own boss and underboss, clusters of them operated under the authority of one gang.

As in Sicily, cattle rustling was almost certainly one of the main reasons for these links. Many of the Calabrian *mafiosi* were woodcutters and herdsmen who thought nothing of spending days on end in the mountains, and who were born with a map of Aspromonte's numberless pathways imprinted on their minds. The rustling technique was simple and virtually foolproof: steal animals in one place, and then avoid detection by sending them off through the mountains to trusted brethren in other towns who could put them on the market. The *picciotti* also moved around the area to exact an extortion tribute on the regular fairs that were still an important part of the Calabrian mountain economy.

What were the authorities doing in the late 1880s and early 1890s, while the picciotteria was building its numbers and thickening its networks? The answer is, very little. Africo, Roccaforte, Bova and the other centres of gang activity were still among the many places in the peninsula where 'Italy' did not mean very much beyond taxes, military service and the occasional visit from *Carabinieri* on patrol. In April 1893, two forest guards (auxiliary policemen) sent a letter to the local magistrate denouncing the existence of 'a terrible sect of so-called maffiosi' in Africo and the surrounding area. Their warning was ignored and buried in a pile of paperwork.

Which is where, more than a year later, it was found by a dynamic new representative of the Italian state's feeble authority in Calabria: Sergeant Angelo Labella, commander of the Bova station of the *Carabinieri*. On 21 June 1894, Labella wrote his first report on the criminal association he had unearthed: he named fifty members, including Domenico Callea and Filippo Velonà. Over the coming weeks Labella added to his roll call of suspects, and laid the groundwork for a huge prosecution by detailing witnesses who could provide evidence against the gang. At last, it seemed, the Italian state was set to challenge the picciotteria regime in this forgotten place.

In September 1894 investigating magistrates came to the district capital of Bova and began summoning the witnesses Labella had cited. The Lads quickly mobilised in response to this challenge to their authority. They verbally threatened anyone prepared to give evidence against them, including the wealthier citizens of Africo. They slaughtered animals and left them in the fields for the owners to find; they vandalised vines. In late October they cut down twelve fruit trees belonging to one landowner and carved funeral crosses into the stumps, just in case the message in the damage was not clear.

The *picciotti* also enlisted the bagpiper to their campaign of intimidation. He was forced to play while they went through the streets improvising menacing songs about their enemies, including literate folk like town councillors, the archpriest, the tax collector, and Sergeant Angelo Labella. They were heard bellowing the following clumsy ditty outside one landowner's balcony.

> Now take up your pen and inkpot to do a new trial. But if we win our freedom, we'll take vengeance with our own hands.

While their Lads were intoning their threats, Domenico Callea and the other bosses had already decided on the fate of the most dangerous of the witnesses named in Sergeant Labella's first report: a fifty-year-old swineherd named Pietro Maviglia.

Maviglia did not cut a very impressive figure. His crippled leg meant that he walked with the aid of a stick and he could not hobble very far without gasping for breath. (The post-mortem would identify the signs of pleurisy in his wounded lungs.) But Maviglia's importance lay in the fact that he was a member of the gang – one of the earliest members, in fact.

Back in 1892 Maviglia had become involved in a dispute with Domenico Callea's equally nasty younger brother Bruno, who had beaten him up as a result. To take revenge, Maviglia leaked news of a burglary that Bruno Callea had committed. As a result of Maviglia's testimony, Callea was sentenced to two years for the burglary, and another fourteen months for beating the crippled old swineherd up a second time.

Maviglia was expelled from the picciotteria. From that point on, he lived his life under the threat of death. With Sergeant Labella's detective work continuing, and prosecuting magistrates conducting their first interrogations in the case, silencing Maviglia now became an urgent priority for the bosses.

In a place like Africo, rumours took the place of newspapers, especially when it came to informing the citizenry about the internal affairs of the criminal fraternity. In October 1894 whispering voices began to relate the surprising news that the Calleas had settled their quarrel with Pietro Maviglia. In the face of the ongoing judicial investigation, harmony had returned to the brotherhood, it was said. Maviglia himself was unsure of how to respond to the peaceful proposals directed at him; he asked his brother for advice, confiding that the *picciotti* wanted to readmit him into what he referred to as 'the sect'.

The *picciotti* held the bagpipe party on the evening of All Saints for two reasons. First, to reassure Maviglia that the offer to readmit him to their fraternity was genuine. Second, to provide cover for his killers. While the bequiffed members of the gang danced and drank and sang in the streets that evening, one *picciotto* approached Maviglia and explained to him that the Lads had stolen a goat, and would eat it together in a shack out in the countryside to celebrate the swineherd's return to the brotherhood. Pulling his fist from his pocket, he showed its contents: 'I've even got some salt', he smiled.

About an hour after dark that night, Pietro Maviglia was seen for the last time by anyone but his assassins. Leaning on his walking stick, with his jacket slung over his shoulder, he set off along the via Anzaro that led towards the cemetery.

Shortly afterwards, one of the Lads told the bagpiper to bring the dancing to an end and then followed the direction that his intended victim had taken.

Late on the morning of 4 November 1894 the local deputy magistrate and doctor arrived in Africo to perform a grisly duty. They were 'local' in the sense that they had only had to trudge for four hours to reach Africo from the district capital of Bova, along mountain tracks that horses refused to tackle. They found Pietro Maviglia lying where he had been found the previous evening: face down on top of his walking stick, in a field about fifteen minutes from where he had last been seen among the *picciotti* dancing to the bagpipes.

The doctor worked quickly once the body had been moved to the cemetery and formal identification had taken place. Five lesions spoke the likely narrative of Maviglia's last minutes. The old man was stabbed in the small of his back first. Perhaps the head injury came next: a hatchet blow had notched the back of his skull. Maviglia was then stuck twice with a dagger, both blows entering the chest cavity just to the left of the breastbone. The heart was pierced through both ventricles. Either of these injuries would have been fatal, but the killers – at least three of them – were remorseless, inflicting the fifth and final wound when their victim was already prostrate. It seemed a reasonable deduction that, as Maviglia's head was heaved backwards by the hair, his throat was cut by a very sharp blade: a clean-edged, ten-centimetre gash bisected his right jugular vein, his voice box and his oesophagus. 'Undigested food is coming out', the doctor jotted dispassionately.

> I must also point out that there was coarse cooking salt
> on the throat wound. The authors of the murder sprinkled
> it there, perhaps in order to achieve greater satisfaction
> for their feelings of vendetta.

Pietro Maviglia was butchered like a goat. In the days following his death, the people of Africo said that his butterfly quiff had been sliced off too, 'so as to demonstrate that he was not fit to belong to the association'. The doctor neither confirmed nor denied the rumour.

The revolting details of Pietro Maviglia's murder give the lie to the first of many historical misconceptions about the picciotteria. The early Calabrian mafia, it is still sometimes said, had a social function. In a desperately deprived and backward part of the country, *mafiosi* got together to create a source of authority and a system of mutual assistance. Or so the argument goes.

It may be true that, on the slopes of Aspromonte, the early 'ndrangheta moved into a vacuum where the state should have been. But they ruled by fear – that much is evident from one statement after another that the magistrates collected in the aftermath of Maviglia's death. That fact is not changed if, in the absence of state authority, some people – including landowners – made the best of their situation, and allied themselves with bullies they could not fight. Pietro Maviglia's murderers, it is worth remembering, made no attempt to hide his corpse: those horrific injuries and even the fistful of salt thrown on his slit gullet, were meant as a warning to others – a public, poetic 'justice'.

After the post-mortem, investigations into the picciotteria in Africo finally began to make real progress. More *Carabinieri* arrived in the village, and were billeted in a house right next door to Domenico Callea's. The picciotteria's bookkeeper and fencing instructor had gone on the run after ordering Pietro Maviglia killed. His new wife was left alone in the house. She kept the *Carabinieri* awake all night with the sound of her sobbing.

The strong military presence in Africo encouraged more witnesses to come forward. With Sergeant Labella's energetic help the magistrates preparing the prosecution case were able to tease out more and more evidence. Maviglia's murderers were arrested. Under interrogation, they broke: blaming one another at first, and then finally confessing. In the Grecanico-speaking communities, the wall of *omertà* around the picciotteria collapsed.

Perhaps the most historically significant truth to surface after Maviglia's brutal demise was that the criminal network that the

Lads with Attitude rapidly created in the 1880s and 1890s had an enthralling religious symbol at its centre.

The Sanctuary of the Madonna of Polsi lies hidden in a valley in Aspromonte's upper reaches. Legend has it that in 1144 a shepherd came to this secluded spot looking for a lost bullock. He was greeted by a miraculous vision of the Blessed Virgin. 'I want a church erected', she declared, 'to spread my graces among the devout who will come here to visit me'. For centuries, in early September, poor pilgrims have made their way up the twisting mountain roads to Polsi in joyous conformity with the Virgin's wishes.

Calabria's greatest writer, Corrado Alvaro, described Polsi as it would have been in the late nineteenth century when twenty thousand men and women flooded the churchyard and the woods round about in preparation for the Festival. Some had walked barefoot all the way; others came wearing crowns of thorns. The men drank heavily and fired their guns in the air. Everyone feasted on roast goat, bellowed ancient hymns, and danced all night to the music of the bagpipe and the tambourine.

On the day of the Festival itself, the tiny church was filled with the imploring wails of the faithful, and with the bleating and mooing of the animals brought as votive offerings. Hysterical women shrieked vows as they elbowed their way through the crowd to place eerie *ex-votos* at the Madonna's feet: brass jewellery, clothes, or babies' body parts modelled from wax. When evening came and the Madonna was paraded around the sanctuary on a bier, the pilgrims prayed, wept, beat their chests, and cried out 'viva Maria!'

The Festival of the Madonna of Polsi has a special symbolic significance for the 'ndrangheta. To this day the Chief Cudgels from across the province of Reggio Calabria use the Festival as cover for an annual meeting. In September 2009, prosecutors maintain, the newly elected 'Chief of the Crime', Domenico Oppedisano, came to have his appointment ratified at Polsi. Senior positions in the 'ndrangheta's coordinating body, the Great Crime, come into force at midnight on the day of the Festival.

The nearest town to the Sanctuary at Polsi is San Luca, where the writer Corrado Alvaro grew up, and where the *'ndrine* (local mafia gangs) involved in the Duisburg massacre of 2007 originated. *'Ndrangetisti* refer to San Luca as their Mamma; the 'ndrangheta there is traditionally the guardian of the whole association's rules, and the arbiter in disputes. San Luca has been called the 'Bethlehem' of Calabrian organised crime.

We can now be sure that the Polsi crime summit is a tradition as old as the 'ndrangheta itself. For in June 1895 a shopkeeper from Roccaforte del Greco told the magistrates investigating Pietro Maviglia's murder what he had seen in Polsi.

> On 3 September 1894 I went to the Festival of the Madonna of the Mountain. There I saw several members of the criminal association from Roccaforte in the company of about sixty people from various villages who were all sitting in a circle eating and drinking. When I asked who paid for all that food and wine at the Festival, I was told that they paid for it with the camorra they collected.

Evidently the pilgrimage to the Sanctuary at Polsi was, from the outset, a chance for the Lads to make a profit and talk shop rather than to worship.

Sergeant Labella's investigations also threw up more scattered evidence about how the picciotteria began. Although he could not be precise about the year of its emergence, he thought that it was no later than 1887, the year that the sect's 'judge', Andrea Angelone, was released from prison. Other witnesses pushed the starting date back further. One resident of the same village said he thought Angelone had been a member of a criminal association 'sixteen or seventeen years back' (i.e. in about 1879).

The elementary-schoolteacher in Africo proved to be a particularly insightful witness. He had first taken up his post in the mid 1880s and had immediately heard talk of a criminal sect in town. But 'this association, it was said at the time, comprised three or four people'. Its numbers increased rapidly over the coming years, particularly during Domenico Callea's recruitment drive in 1893–94.

The story that these fragments of evidence tell – a story that was being repeated in Palmi, and indeed all around Aspromonte – goes something like this. Until the mid 1880s, a few Calabrian ex-cons, the senior *camorristi* from within the prison system, would keep in touch when they returned home from jail. They might offer one another help and even get together for the odd criminal venture: the trial records and other sources tell us of occasional outbreaks of gang activity in various parts of the province of Reggio Calabria in the 1870s and even before. But the *picciotti* as yet lacked the numbers and the strength to impose themselves on other felons on the outside world in the way that they had done in the confined environment of prison. Needless to say, they also lacked the power to browbeat whole towns. Then in the 1880s there were changes that gave Calabria's prison camorra the chance to project itself into the outside world. The question, of course, is what exactly those changes were.

It is telling that no representative of the state seemed at all curious to answer that question. In 1891, Palmi's Chief Prosecutor wrote his annual report on the work of the court during the previous year. The picciotteria did not even merit a mention: it was only a superficial symptom of Calabria's chronic backwardness, after all. The reason for the high rate of violence in the Palmi district was not organised crime, he wrote, but the 'ardent and lively nature of this population, their touchiness, the stubborn way they stick to their plans, the unwavering tenacity of their feelings of hatred – which very often drive them to vendetta'.

If a Sicilian Chief Prosecutor had written such claptrap we would have very good reason to be suspicious of his motives. But in Calabria, such suspicions are probably not merited. (Not yet, at any rate.) After all, the Palmi court had just sent dozens of *picciotti* back to jail. But the Chief Prosecutor's stereotypical views of the Calabrian psyche are significant all the same. Railway or no railway, Calabria was still seen as a semi-barbaric, faraway land about which Italy knew very little and cared even less. Despite its ties to the international market for olive oil, wine and lemons, Palmi was simply not important enough to draw much government curiosity down on the picciotteria, which means that historians have to work harder to solve some outstanding mysteries about its emergence.

Sworn sects have dominated prisons in many different times and places. The long-established South African number gangs, the 26s, the 27s, and the 28s, for example, who take their mythology from the story of a Zulu chief. Or the vast network of *vory-v-zakone* ('thieves with a code of honour') who infested the Soviet Gulag system from the 1920s. The *vory* had a 'crowning' ritual for new members, sported tattoos, and had a distinctive look comprising an aluminium cross round the neck and several waistcoats.

But by no means all of these gangs manage to establish their authority in the world outside the prison gates. The 26s, the 27s, and the 28s only did it in the 1990s, when Apartheid fell and the country was opened to narcotics traffickers who needed local manpower and a local criminal 'brand'. When the Soviet Union collapsed the *vory-v-zakone* did not simply step out of the Gulag to assume leadership of the crime bonanza that ensued. Rather they had their traditions hijacked by a new breed of gangster bosses who wanted to add an air of antiquity to their territorially based bands: the result was the Russian mafia. Examples like these show just what an achievement it was for Calabria's prison *camorristi* to carve up territory in the outside world between themselves.

The economy is surely a big part of the reason why they pulled it off. An economic crisis hit Calabrian agriculture with increasing force in the 1880s. Phylloxera reached Italy and the wine boom went sour. Then a trade war with France threw agricultural exports into crisis. Smallholders like those in the Plain of Gioia

Tauro, who had run up debts to buy a plot of former Church land and plant it with vines, were driven to penury. The poorest labourers, like those in Africo, struggled even harder to feed themselves. There were plenty of recruits for the picciotteria.

The arrival of the steam train was also partly to blame, in Palmi at least. Contemporaries noted that the initial upsurge of razor attacks and knife fights coincided with the presence of navvies working on the Tyrrhenian branch of the railway in the spring of 1888. A dozen years later, in around 1900, some observers began to claim that the Lads with Attitude had been *imported* into the Plain of Gioia Tauro by Sicilian *mafiosi* among the navvies. But since none of the men convicted in Palmi's court house were Sicilians, this theory is almost certainly wrong. A more likely scenario is that there were ex-con *camorristi* among the railway workers. The fighting in Palmi could have been the result of competition for jobs with local *picciotti*.

Either way, the role that the railways played in the emergence of the Calabrian mafia makes for a bitter historical irony. As one magistrate opined at the time

> Whether the railway brought more evil than advantage is unclear. It is painful to ascertain that such a powerful influence for civilisation and progress served to trigger the cause of so much social ignominy.

The 'ndrangheta began just when Calabria's isolation ended.

There is a third likely reason why the picciotteria appeared when they did. In 1882 and 1888 two important electoral reforms inaugurated the era of mass politics in Italy. The number of people entitled to vote increased. Local government obtained both more freedom from central control, more responsibilities for things like schooling and supervising charities, and with them, more resources to plunder. With around one quarter of adult males now entitled to have a say in who governed them, politics became a more expensive and more lucrative business.

More violent too. Shootings, stabbings and beatings had always been part of the language of Italian politics, particularly in the south. Much of the violence was administered from Rome. On orders from the local Prefect, the police would rough up opposition supporters, arrest them or simply take away their gun licences, leaving them vulnerable to attack by goons who worked for the candidate the government wanted to win. The reforms of the 1880s greatly increased the demand for violence at election times and encouraged more aspiring power brokers to enlist support from organised enforcers.

Strong-arm politics was not something that the police were particularly keen to investigate, understandably enough. But there are nonetheless clear signs from deep within the dusty folders of trial papers that even in Africo the picciotteria had friends among the elite. The press remarked that the men who sliced up the crippled old swineherd Maviglia were defended by the best lawyers in Reggio Calabria. And among the *picciotti* in the case were 'people who, because of their prosperous financial state, can only have been driven to crime because they are innately wicked'.

The 'innately wicked' inhabitants of Africo included the former mayor, Giuseppe Callea, whose sons were prominent *picciotti*: Domenico, the sect's bookkeeper and fencing instructor who tried to recruit the bagpiper into the gang; and his brother Bruno, the *picciotto* who was sent to prison for robbery on the evidence provided by the crippled swineherd Pietro Maviglia. Former mayor Callea clearly endorsed his sons' criminal career path: he himself physically threatened Maviglia.

The rise of the picciotteria brutally exposed the fragmentation of Calabria's ruling class, which proved utterly incapable of treating the newly assertive criminal brotherhood as a common enemy. In Africo, some men of education and property testified against the *picciotti*, and were duly threatened to the music of the *zampogna*. Others, like Giuseppe Callea, were more than happy to ally themselves with the gang. But it would be naïve of us to think that such cases saw good citizens pitted against shady protectors of gangsters. Legality and crime were not what divided Calabrians; ideology of one colour or another was not what brought them together. On Aspromonte, family, friends and favours were the only cause of conflict, and the only social glue. The law, such as it was, was just one more weapon in the struggle. The few sociologists who took an interest in Calabria after Italian unification noted that the propertied class 'lacked a sense of legality', and even 'lacked moral sense'. Whatever terms one used to describe it, the rise of the picciotteria showed that the lack was now infecting the other social classes.

Despite this proliferation of organised criminal activity, the prosecution of the early 'ndrangheta in Africo was a success. The butchers of Maviglia were convicted, as were dozens and dozens of the *picciotti*. Across southern Calabria the police and *Carabinieri* registered similar results, and would continue to do so for years to come. But the struggle to assert the state's right to rule was close to futile from the start. The Lads convicted of 'associating for delinquency' served their risibly short sentences in the very same jails where they had learned their Attitude in the first place. And there was no sign of an end to the fundamental weaknesses in Calabrian society that gave them their foothold outside the prisons.

The criminal emergency in Calabria utterly failed to capture the attention of national public opinion. All too few Italians were prepared to 'look through the microscope at the little causes that make little hearts beat'. In the long term, Italy would pay the price for this collective failure of the imagination. Nothing that happened to Calabrian shepherds and peasants could ever be news. Nothing that is, until the exploits of a woodsman called Giuseppe Musolino turned him into the Brigand Musolino, the 'King of Aspromonte', and perhaps the greatest criminal legend in Italian history.

The King of Aspromonte

The facts of Giuseppe Musolino's life would count for little, in the end. But the facts are nonetheless where we must begin.

Musolino was born on 24 September 1876 at Santo Stefano in Aspromonte, a village of some 2,500 inhabitants situated 700 metres up into forests overlooking the Straits of Messina. His father was a woodsman and a small-time timber dealer just successful enough to set himself up as the owner of a tavern. Musolino grew into a woodsman too. But it was the violent tendencies of his youth that would most attract the attention of later biographers: before his twentieth birthday he got into trouble several times for weapons offences and for threatening and wounding women.

The Musolino saga really began on 27 October 1897, in his father's tavern, when he became involved in an argument with another young man by the name of Vincenzo Zoccali. The two arranged to have a fight and Musolino suffered a badly cut right hand. Musolino's cousin then fired two shots at Zoccali, but missed.

Two days later, before dawn, Zoccali was harnessing his mule when someone shot at him from behind a wall. Again the bullets failed to find their target. Musolino, whose rifle and beret were found at the scene, went on the run in the wilds of Aspromonte. He was recaptured just over five months later, and in September 1898 he was given a harsh twenty-one year sentence for attempted murder. Enraged at the verdict and proclaiming himself the innocent victim of a plot, Musolino swore vendetta. He would eat Zoccali's liver, he cried out from the dock.

On the night of 9 January 1899 Musolino and three other

inmates, including his cousin, escaped from prison in Gerace by hacking a hole in the wall with an iron bar and lowering themselves to the ground with a rope made from knotted bedsheets. The promised vendetta began on the night of 28 January, when Musolino gunned down Francesca Sidari, the wife of one of the witnesses against him. He apparently mistook her for his real target as she stooped over a charcoal mound. When the gunshots and screaming attracted the attention of her husband and another man, Musolino shot them too. He left them for dead, and fled once more into the mountains.

The brigand Musolino (as he soon became known) now entered a twin spiral of vengeance: his targets were both the witnesses against him in the Zoccali case and the informers recruited by the police in their efforts to catch him.

A month after his first murder, Musolino killed again, stabbing a shepherd whom he suspected of being a police spy. In mid-May the bandit returned to Santo Stefano and caught up with Vincenzo Zoccali – the man whose liver he had vowed to eat. He planted dynamite in the walls of the house where Zoccali was sleeping with his brother and parents; but the charge failed to detonate. (The family subsequently fled to the province of Catanzaro.) Musolino badly wounded another enemy a few days later.

The sequence of attacks continued through the summer of 1899. In July he killed one suspected informer with a single shotgun blast to the head. A week later he shot another in the buttocks.

In August the brigand went all the way to the province of Catanzaro in pursuit of Vincenzo Zoccali and his family and succeeded in killing Zoccali's brother. He then returned quickly to a village just below Santo Stefano where he murdered another man he may have suspected of being an informer.

Musolino then vanished for six months.

The next the world heard of Musolino was in February 1900 when he reappeared on Aspromonte with two young accomplices; he shot and wounded his own cousin by mistake. The brigand apparently kneeled before his bleeding cousin, offered him his rifle, and begged him to take vengeance for the error there and then. The request was declined and the brigand continued with his attacks.

Musolino found his next prey in the Grecanico-speaking village of Roccaforte, blasting him in the legs with a shotgun. The prostrate victim then managed to convince the bandit that he was not, as suspected, a police spy. Musolino tended the man's wounds for half an hour and then sent a passing shepherd to fetch help.

On 9 March 1900 one of Musolino's accomplices, a man from Africo called Antonio Princi, betrayed him to the police. As part of the plan to capture Musolino, Princi left some *maccheroni* laced with opium in the bandit's hideout, which at the time was in a cave near Africo cemetery. Princi then went to get the police. Five policemen and two *Carabinieri* followed him back to the hideout. But the opium had been sitting on the shelf of a local pharmacy for so long that it had lost much of its narcotic power. Even after eating the *maccheroni*, Musolino still had sufficient command of his faculties to fire at his would-be captors and then escape across the mountain, with the police and *Carabinieri* in pursuit.

In the early hours of the following morning Musolino was surprised while urinating by Pietro Ritrovato, one of the two *Carabinieri*; the brigand fired first from close range. The young *Carabiniere* suffered a gaping wound in his groin, and died in torment several hours later.

After another six months of silence Musolino and another two accomplices killed again on 27 August 1900. They chased their victim, Francesco Marte, onto the threshing floor of his own house, where he stopped, turned and begged them to be allowed the time to make his peace with God before dying. They allowed him to kneel down, and then shot him repeatedly in front of his mother, continuing to fire even when he was already dead. Musolino would claim that Marte was a traitor who was involved in the *maccheroni* plot against him.

Subsequently the same two accomplices, perhaps acting on his behalf, also tried and failed to kill the former mayor of Santo Stefano who had testified when Musolino went on trial for attempted murder.

The brigand's last violent attack came on 22 September 1900, when he wounded yet another alleged informer in Santo Stefano.

Musolino's bloody rampage and the continuing failure to arrest him had long since become a political scandal. The Aspromonte woodsman was discussed in parliament. The government's credibility was at stake. Hundreds of uniformed men were sent to southern Calabria to join the hunt. Yet still, for another year and more, Musolino would manage to evade them all . . .

There is one more important fact about Musolino: he was a Lad with Attitude.

At the height of the political furore over the brigand, Italy's most valiant journalist, Adolfo Rossi, took the very rare step of actually going down to Calabria to find out what was going on. From police and magistrates he learned all there was to know about the new mafia.

Rossi toured the prisons and saw the *picciotti* in their grey- and tobacco-striped prison uniforms. He went to Palmi, which he learned was 'the Calabrian district where the picciotteria was strongest'. Palmi's Deputy Prefect glumly explained that, 'one trial for "associating for delinquency" has not even finished by the time we have to start preparing the next one'.

Rossi visited Santo Stefano, Musolino's home village, and even climbed all the way up to Africo. He was shocked by the squalor he found there, writing that 'the cabins are not houses being used as pig sties, but pig sties used as houses for humans'. The *Carabinieri* told him how, a few years earlier, members of the sect had 'cut a man to pieces, and then put salt on him like you do with pork'.

Adolfo Rossi's long series of reports from Calabria is still the best thing ever written about the early 'ndrangheta; it deserved to be read far more widely than in the local Venetian newspaper in which it appeared. And everyone Rossi interviewed agreed that Musolino was an oathed member of the picciotteria – albeit that opinions varied on when exactly Musolino was oathed, and what rank he held. Rossi saw reports that showed how the *Carabinieri* in Santo Stefano had Musolino down for a gangster from the beginning. On the day after Musolino's first knife fight with Vincenzo Zoccali, they wrote that he belonged to the 'so-called maffia'.

While Musolino was in custody awaiting trial for attempted murder, the jailers observed him behaving like a *camorrista*. One guard stated to Rossi that

> Musolino entered this prison on 8 April 1898. Later some of his cellmates informed me that in June of the same year he was elected a *camorrista* [i.e. a senior member of the Society].

In Africo Rossi spoke to a police commander who explained that Musolino had avoided capture for so long because he had the support of the picciotteria network across Aspromonte and beyond. One man who confessed to Rossi that he had sheltered Musolino was the mayor of Africo, a shady figure who testified *against* the picciotteria back in 1894. In Santo Stefano, Rossi learned that some of the brigand's accomplices were Lads, and that some of his escapades, including his original spat with Vincenzo Zoccali, had more to do with the internal politics of the mob than with his personal programme of vengeance.

Despite these facts Musolino became a hero: a wronged avenger, a solitary knight of the forest, a Robin Hood, the 'King of Aspromonte'.

His fame began to grow rapidly after his prison breakout in 1899. It was a local phenomenon at first. Most people on Aspromonte firmly believed that Musolino was innocent of the charge for which he was originally imprisoned – that of attempting to murder Vincenzo Zoccali. And, in truth, there are one or two residual doubts about how sound the conviction was. Musolino's 'innocence', genuine or not, proved to be the seed of his fame. The peasants of Aspromonte, ignorant and pitiably poor, regarded the state with inborn suspicion. For such people, in such circumstances, a renegade hero who only killed false witnesses was all too captivating a delusion.

Musolino found food and shelter everywhere he went on Aspromonte. For his sake, women kept lanterns lit for the Madonna of Polsi and for Saint Joseph (San Giuseppe, the patron saint of woodworkers, from whom Musolino took his Christian name). Much of this support was managed by the picciotteria. Much of it can be explained by perfectly understandable fear. Some of it – and it is impossible to tell just how much – was down to the brigand's burgeoning popular aura.

Stories soon spread that aura further afield. Stories about how, while Musolino was in prison, Saint Joseph came to him in a miraculous vision and revealed the weak points in his cell wall. Stories about how he never stole from anyone, always paid for what he ate, never abused women, and always outwitted the clodhopping *Carabinieri*.

From Aspromonte, the Musolino legend was broadcast by the oral folklore of the entire south. He became a star of the puppet theatre. Children played at being Musolino in the street. Wandering players dressed up as brigands to sing of his adventures or had their poems in praise of him printed on grubby sheets of paper to be sold for coppers. The authorities arrested some of these minstrels, but the cult was now unstoppable. The 'King of Aspromonte' himself capitalised on it. Musolino sent a letter to a national newspaper in which he impudently put himself on the side of the ordinary people against authority.

> I am a worker, and the son of a worker. I love people who have to sweat in the fields from morning until night so as to produce society's riches. In fact I envy them,

because my misfortune means I cannot make a contribution with my own hands.

The Italian state now found itself losing a propaganda war against
the delinquent artisans and peasants of Aspromonte. The whole
Musolino affair was turning into what today we would call a PR
disaster for the rule of law. Perhaps its most worrying dimension
was that the illiterate were not the only people seduced by the
myth. Although right-thinking opinion-formers of all political
persuasions condemned the popular cult of Musolino as a sign
of Italy's backwardness, books and pamphlets about him still
sold in their thousands. In Calabria, only one newspaper dared
to suggest that the King of Aspromonte might actually have been
guilty of attempting to murder Vincenzo Zoccali. In Naples,
where the myth of the noble *camorrista* had such currency, the
Corriere di Napoli reported fables about the brigand's supposed
acts of generosity without critical comment and came very close
to justifying his campaign of retribution.

Musolino only harms his enemies, because he thinks he
has a mission and wants to carry it through to the end.

Between the brigand and the law, there was right and wrong on
both sides – so went the argument. Accordingly, some press
commentators entertained the idea that a fair solution would be
to offer Musolino safe passage to the United States.

Eventually the authorities acted on the intelligence that told
them Musolino was no lone wolf. Early in 1901, a zealous young
police officer, Vincenzo Mangione, was sent to Santo Stefano to
implement a more radical strategy than blindly chasing the bandit
around the mountain and trying to bribe informants (especially
picciotti) to betray him.

Mangione compiled a series of highly revealing reports on the
picciotteria in Musolino's home village. Drawing on sources who
were mostly disaffected *picciotti*, he describes a 'genuine criminal

institution', with its own social fund, tribunal, and so on. It was founded in the early 1890s by Musolino's father and uncle, who both now sat on the organisation's 'supreme council'. There were 166 affiliates of the mafia in Santo Stefano.

Musolino's possible motives emerged with a new clarity from Mangione's research. The bandit was of course an affiliate like his father. Nothing he had done could be separated from his role inside the criminal brotherhood. For example, the attempt on Zoccali's life that began the Musolino saga was ordered by the picciotteria as punishment because Zoccali had tried to duck out of his duties as a *picciotto*. Musolino was now a roving contract killer for the whole sect.

Most revealingly of all, Mangione learned how the Lads earned favours from 'respectable people . . . political personalities, lawyers, doctors, and landowners'. The most important of those favours were character references and false witness statements. A more tangible example of the favours that the picciotteria could command stood, ruined and smoke-blackened, at the very entrance of the village. It was the Zoccali family's house. When Musolino failed to dynamite it, the *picciotti* simply burned it to the ground and then persuaded the town council to deny the Zoccali family a grant to rebuild.

The notables of Santo Stefano were not remotely concerned to keep their friendship with the picciotteria secret. When the King of Aspromonte's sister Anna got married, the new mayor and his officers, the town councillors, the general practitioners, teachers, municipal guards, and the town band all came to the wedding reception. The mayor chose the occasion to circulate a petition asking the Queen to grant Musolino a pardon.

The outcome of Mangione's intelligence was a two-pronged strategy to capture Musolino: first, his support network would be attacked; second, the whole picciotteria in Santo Stefano would be prosecuted. Accordingly, there was a series of mass arrests in the spring and summer of 1901. With many of his supporters in custody, Musolino struggled to find a place to hide on his home territory.

On the afternoon of 9 October 1901, in the countryside near Urbino – more than 900 kilometres from Santo Stefano – a young man in a hunting jacket and cyclist's cap was spotted acting suspiciously by two *Carabinieri*. He fled across a vineyard when they hailed him and then tripped over some wire. He pulled out a revolver but was smothered before he could pull the trigger. 'Kill me', he said as the handcuffs went on. He then tried bribery, unsuccessfully. When searched he was found to be carrying a knife, ammunition and a large number of amulets, including a body pouch full of incense, a crucifix, a medallion showing the Sacred Heart, a picture of Saint Joseph, and an image of the Madonna of Polsi. Five days later he was identified as the brigand Giuseppe Musolino.

Musolino was sent for trial in the pretty Tuscan city of Lucca for fear that a Calabrian jury might be too swayed by the myth surrounding him. His long-delayed encounter with justice was set to be one of the most sensational trials of the age.

But before it could begin, the second arm of the government's strategy failed. The witnesses Mangione had relied upon to gather evidence about the picciotteria in Santo Stefano were intimidated into retracting their statements. The case never even reached court.

So when national and international correspondents gathered in Lucca to report on the eagerly awaited Musolino trial in the spring of 1902, what they witnessed turned out to be a prolonged exercise in self-harm for the law's reputation in Italy. The problem was that Musolino's lawyers objected vociferously every time the prosecution tried to demonstrate that he was a sworn member of a local criminal sect. After all, had not the case against this supposed sect in Santo Stefano been thrown out before it reached court? Where was the evidence? In this way, the real context of the Musolino saga was obscured. So a multiple murderer was largely left free to pose as the heroic outlaw that the marionette theatres of southern Italy had made him out to be.

Musolino had spent the time since his capture the previous

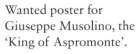

Wanted poster for Giuseppe Musolino, the 'King of Aspromonte'.

The original cause of the King of Aspromonte's killing spree? A diagram showing the damage inflicted on Musolino's skull in infancy by a falling flowerpot.

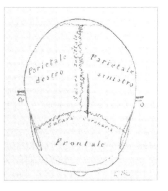

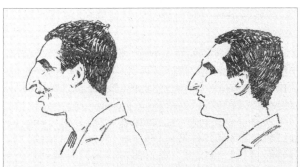

Sketches of Musolino made in court.

October writing a verse narrative of his adventures and having his body meticulously measured by positivist criminologists. Over the same period he received countless admiring letters and post-cards, particularly from women. They pledged their love, sent him religious tokens and sweets, promised to pray for him and begged for locks of his hair. The judge in Lucca was so concerned about Musolino's effect on the morals of the town's womenfolk that he stipulated that only men would be allowed into the hearing. But the stream of fan mail only increased once the trial started. Mysteriously, signed postcard portraits of the King of Aspromonte went on sale near the courtroom. Interviewed by journalists in his cell, Musolino would relish recounting his erotic adventures while he was on the run.

From the outset, Musolino's lawyers did not contest the fact that he had committed a long trail of murders and attempted murders after escaping from prison. Their defence rested instead on the claim that he was innocent of the crime for which he had been imprisoned in the first place: the attempted murder of Vincenzo Zoccali. The lawyers reasoned that his bloody deeds could be explained, and perhaps even justified, by the conspiracy against him in the Zoccali case.

A visiting French judge was understandably astonished that this argument could even be considered a defence at all; it seemed like evidence of Italy's 'moral backwardness' to him. Musolino did not share the same doubts. When he was called to the dock he told the court that he had concluded his campaign of righteous retaliation now, and would never break the law again if he were allowed to go free. He claimed to be the descendant of a French prince and compared his plight to that of Jesus Christ.

Now and again Musolino did blot the script that portrayed him as a noble desperado: such as when he repeatedly screamed 'slut!' at Vincenzo Zoccali's mother as she came to the witness stand. But that did not prevent many onlookers from sympa-thising with him. One of Italy's greatest poets, a sentimental socialist called Giovanni Pascoli, lived in the countryside not far from Lucca and observed the trial with his habitual compassion. 'Poor Musolino!' he wrote to a friend. 'You know, I'd like to write a poem that shows how every one of us has a Musolino inside.'

Many commentators on the trial argued that the underlying problem in the Musolino case was not one lone brigand but the isolation of Calabrian society as a whole. Modern means of communication like the railway would surely bring the light of civilisation to the primitive obscurity of Aspromonte. The sun-weathered peasant witnesses who came up to Lucca for the case made for a spectacle that seemed only to confirm this view. Most of them were Calabrian dialect speakers who had to testify through an interpreter. There was loud laughter on one occasion when, as a witness started to talk, the interpreter turned to the judge and admitted that even he could not understand a word of what was being said. There was probably not a single Grecanico-Italian interpreter available in the whole of Italy.

Positivist criminologists were called on to explain the results of their painstaking physical and psychological examination of Musolino. He had a contradictory mix of symptoms, they explained. There seemed to be no clear aetiology for his criminaloid tendencies. Musolino had suffered a head injury at age six when a flowerpot fell on his head. The accident caused a dent in his skull, and may have given him epilepsy – an obvious delinquent trait. But then again he did not masturbate at all frequently and was very intelligent. Racially speaking, they concluded lamely, he was an exaggeration of the 'average Calabrian type'.

The most moving speech of the trial came from the lawyer representing the parents of Pietro Ritrovato, the young *Carabiniere* who had died of the horrible injuries inflicted on him by Musolino the morning after the drugged *maccheroni* episode. The old Ritrovato couple had filed a civil suit against the 'King of Aspromonte'. But they sobbed so much in court that they often had to withdraw. Their lawyer explained that his aim was not to ask for money, but to 'bring a flower to the memory of a victim who fell in the line of duty'. To that end, he wanted to destroy what he called 'the legend of Musolino' by insisting on the one crucial thing that the trial had neglected: Musolino was a member of a criminal association called the picciotteria.

The most squalid testimony came from the mayor of Santo Stefano – the one who had attended Musolino's sister's wedding and circulated a petition for a royal pardon. Aurelio Romeo was a chubby man with a sleek black beard who was a major player in one of the two dominant political factions in Reggio Calabria. In court he affected a flaming moral outrage about how the people of Santo Stefano had been mistreated by brutal and incompetent police. 'The picciotteria is an invention, an excuse for the police's weakness,' he said. Asked about the character of Musolino's two accomplices who were accused of trying to kill his predecessor as mayor, he said they were just honest, hardworking men.

The trial's outcome was inevitable: Musolino was found guilty and sentenced to life imprisonment. But equally inevitably Italy had lost a priceless opportunity to draw public attention to the acute criminal emergency in southern Calabria. The early 'ndrangheta would remain shrouded in obscurity and confusion, a little known curiosity of a little known region.

Musolino, by contrast, was destined for enduring fame, even as he languished in confinement. Just before the First World War, the English writer Norman Douglas went walking on Aspromonte and heard tale after tale about the brigand's adventures from his peasant guides.

> God alone can tell how many poor people he helped in their distress. And if he met a young girl in the mountains, he would help with her load, and escort her home, right into her father's house. Ah, if you could have seen him, sir! He was young, with curly blonde hair, and a face like a rose.

Musolino's hair was actually black. That, at least, the criminologists at the trial had demonstrated beyond doubt.

Under Fascism, Benito Mussolini blocked any attempt to make a film of Musolino's life because of the similarity in their surnames. A biopic finally came out in 1950: it presented Musolino as a man who suffered such wrongs at the hands of the Calabrian mafia that he was forced to take the law into his own hands.

5

MEDIA DONS
1899–1915

Bankers and Men of Honour

One reason why Italy barely noticed the rise of the picciotteria was that the country had much graver worries. In the late 1880s a building bubble burst, leaving lending institutions with huge liabilities. In 1890 the economy went into recession, piling further pressure on the financial system. Several banks subsequently failed, including two of Italy's biggest. Another, the Banca Romana, tried to stave off implosion by effectively forging its own money and then using the phoney cash to buy off dozens of politicians. 'Loans' from the Banca Romana also helped the King maintain his lavish lifestyle. The Prime Minister was forced to resign in November 1893 when his involvement in the scandal was exposed in parliament.

To many, it seemed as if it was not just the Italian banking system that was about to collapse, but the monarchy and even the state itself. The politician called upon to save the nation was Francesco Crispi, an old warhorse of the Left, a Sicilian who had been one of the heroes of Garibaldi's expedition back in 1860. Crispi also faced an unprecedented political challenge in the form of the trades unions, the Socialist Party and other organisations recruiting among the peasants and labourers. Crispi responded with repression, proclaiming martial law in some areas of the country and banning the Socialist Party in 1894. Desperate for military glory to reinforce the feeble credibility of the state, Crispi launched a reckless colonial adventure in East Africa. In March 1896, at the battle of Adowa, the Italian army that Crispi had spurred into action was destroyed by a vastly superior Ethiopian force. Crispi resigned soon after the news from Adowa reached Rome.

After Crispi the clampdown on the labour movement was relaxed, but politics continued on its reactionary course. For the next few years conservative politicians would talk openly of putting Italy's slow and hesitant advance towards democracy into a brusque reverse. In the spring of 1898 a hike in food prices caused rioting. Cannon fire resounded in the streets of Milan as troops mowed down demonstrators. Another new Prime Minister then embarked on a long parliamentary battle to pass legislation restricting press and political freedoms.

In the summer of 1900 a Tuscan anarchist called Gaetano Bresci returned to Italy from his home in Patterson, New Jersey; he was bent on revenge for the cannonades of 1898. On 20 July he set a suitably violent seal on the most turbulent decade in Italy's short history when he went to Monza and assassinated the King.

By that time, though, Italy was already striding into a very different age. An overhauled banking system, including the newly established Bank of Italy, helped the economy revive. The north-west was industrialising rapidly: in Turin, FIAT started making cars in 1899; in Milan, Pirelli started making car tyres in 1901. Over the next few years Italian cities would fill with noise and light: automobiles, electric trams, department stores, bars, cinemas, and football stadia. In politics, reform was the order of the day. More people became literate and thereby earned the right to vote. The Socialist Party, though still small, was strong enough to bargain for concessions in parliament. In 1913, Italy would hold its first general election in which, by law, all adult men were entitled to vote.

A surge in newspaper readerships was another symptom of the new vitality. In 1900, the year that Bresci shot the King, the *Corriere della Sera* had a print run of 75,000 copies. By 1913, it was up to 350,000. So the Italy that followed the King of Aspromonte's trial in 1902 was a country undergoing a media revolution. Indeed all three of Italy's Honoured Societies now had to test their aptitude for brutality, networking and misinformation in a much more democratic society – one where public opinion shaped the political decisions that in turn shaped criminal destinies.

The Neapolitan camorra would not survive the challenge.

But in the case of the Sicilian mafia, the new media era made no more impact than the puff of a photographer's flash powder: it illuminated a crepuscular landscape of corruption and violence for an instant, and then plunged it back into a darkness deeper than before.

The Sicilian mafia dramas of the early twentieth century all arose from the single most sinister moment of the banking crisis of the early 1890s, a murder that would remain the most notorious of mafia crimes for the best part of the next century. Notorious partly because the victim was one of Sicily's outstanding citizens, and partly because the killers got away with it, but mostly because the resultant scandal, known as the Notarbartolo affair, briefly exposed the mafia's influence in the highest reaches of Sicilian society.

Marquis Emanuele Notarbartolo di San Giovanni fought with Garibaldi in 1860 but he was constitutionally averse to violence. In an age when questions of honour were often settled with swords at dawn, Notarbartolo was only ever drawn into one duel: it lasted three hours because he only fought defensively. He was a devoted family man who wrote his wife short, tender notes every day of their life together. Notarbartolo was also a public servant of rare dedication. As Mayor of Palermo between 1873 and 1876, he tackled corruption. In 1876 he began a long stint as Director General of the Bank of Sicily, where he made himself unpopular with a policy of tight credit. The reputation for rigour that Notarbartolo earned at the Bank of Sicily would lead directly to his atrocious murder.

Notarbartolo's fine record found its malevolent shadow in the career of don Raffaele Palizzolo, whom the police would define as 'the mafia's patron in the Palermo countryside, especially to the south and east of the city'. Palizzolo's fiefdom centred on the notorious *borgate* of Villabate and Ciaculli, where he owned and leased land, and where his friends exerted their characteristic control over the citrus fruit groves and coordinated the activities of bandits and cattle rustlers.

In the 1870s don Raffaele began amassing a fortune by installing himself in town and provincial councils and on the boards of countless charities and quangos. When Notarbartolo was mayor of Palermo, he caught Palizzolo palming money from a fund that stockpiled flour for the poor.

Palizzolo was a master of what Italians call *sottogoverno* – literally 'under government' – meaning the bartering of shady favours for political influence. Come election time he would tour the area on horseback, flanked by the mafia bosses and their heavies. Indeed the Villabate mafia would often disguise their sect summit as political meetings in support of their patron. In 1882 Palizzolo was elected to parliament.

At the Bank of Sicily, Emanuele Notarbartolo also found Palizzolo in his path. As Director General, Notarbartolo was supposed to be supervised in his work by a General Council of forty-eight dignitaries from local government, chambers of commerce and the like. Palizzolo was one of them, as were other notorious shysters linked to organised crime, and a number of businessmen with a manifest conflict of interests: they were among the people that owed money to the bank. No wonder Notarbartolo's policy of tight credit was unpopular.

In 1882 Notarbartolo was kidnapped by four men dressed as soldiers, and only released on payment of a ransom. Acting on a tip-off, the police found the kidnappers hiding out in any empty house. The ransom was never recovered, although we can make a good guess at who took a hefty share of it: both the site of the kidnapping and the kidnappers' hideout lay on territory controlled by the same Villabate *mafiosi* who made Palizzolo the guest of honour at their banquets.

In 1888 Notarbartolo found himself working alongside his great enemy day-to-day when Palizzolo was voted onto the Bank of Sicily's board. The smouldering confrontation between the Director General and the General Council exploded when Italy's building boom collapsed. Notarbartolo tried to persuade ministers to have the Bank of Sicily's constitution amended so as to lessen the power of the General Council and give the Director General the power to respond to the credit crisis. But he was out-lobbied by Palizzolo *et al*, and lost his job in February 1890. His victorious enemies then tried to withhold his pension.

With Emanuele Notarbartolo out of the way, the bank's money was used illegally to inflate the share price of Italy's biggest shipping company, *Navigazione Generale Italiana*, or NGI. NGI's major shareholder happened to be the wealthiest man in Sicily. Who happened to be a great supporter of the dominant politician of the moment, the Sicilian Prime Minister Francesco Crispi. Who happened to have a close ally in the Bank of Sicily's new Director General. Who happened to have a pot of NGI shares of his own.

Palizzolo greased the cogs of this mechanism. As a Member of Parliament, don Raffaele lobbied hard, as he had always done, for NGI's cause. As a member of the Bank of Sicily's board, he approved the NGI share operation. As a member of the mafia, he took some of the bank's cash to buy more of those artificially boosted NGI shares, and made generous loans to friends of his who exported lemons and oranges for a living.

Then, late in 1892, the sleaze at the Banca Romana (the bank that was forging its own money) was exposed in parliament. Credit institutions across the country were wobbling. The calls for a clean-up in the banking system were now too loud to ignore. Emanuele Notarbartolo was strongly tipped to return to the Bank of Sicily with a mandate to crack down on corruption once more. And if Notarbartolo regained his job as Director General of the Bank of Sicily, he would surely expose a fraud that implicated the most powerful economic and political interest group on the island – and linked them squarely with Raffaele Palizzolo and the mafia.

At dusk on 1 February 1893 Emanuele Notarbartolo was stabbed twenty-seven times on a train heading for Palermo; his body was thrown out onto the track.

Months later, Notarbartolo's wife was seen, still in tears, as she burned the hundreds of notes he had sent her. While she wept, and Italy descended into a financial, social and political crisis that threatened to bring the young country to its knees, the mafia and its accomplices quietly covered the murderers' tracks, burying the story in artful layers of deceit and obfuscation.

The reason we know all about the shenanigans at the Bank of Sicily, indeed the reason why Emanuele Notarbartolo's murder ever came to court at all, was because of the grief-stricken determination of his son Leopoldo, a young naval officer who was a man in his father's mould.

Right from the outset, no one seriously doubted that Emanuele Notarbartolo was a victim of the mafia, although the mafia had never killed anyone of such status before. (Nor would it do so again until the 1970s.) Right from the outset, the authorities heard the strong rumours that the Honourable don Raffaele Palizzolo had orchestrated the murder. Leopoldo Notarbartolo, well aware of Palizzolo's long history of run-ins with his father, had more reasons than anyone to suspect the notorious MP of being involved. Yet nothing was done. In 1894, just over a year after Notarbartolo was found lying on the trackside, a senior magistrate wrote to the Minister of Justice to explain the reasons why no one had yet been charged.

> This failure can be attributed to the following two causes: first, the high mafia planned the murder long in advance, and carried it out with the greatest of care; second, the authorities receive no help from society, because all the witnesses are either reticent or afraid.

Knowing what we know about the mafia's history so far, we can also add a third cause that the magistrate neglected to mention: the police and judiciary in Palermo were profoundly infiltrated.

Leopoldo Notarbartolo witnessed the scandalously lax handling of the investigation and began to make inquiries of his own. He was one of many Italians whose quest for truth and justice was a long and solitary one: it took over a decade out of his life. Like most such quests, Notarbartolo's was a tale of meticulous endeavour: sifting through his father's papers, interviewing reluctant witnesses, travelling far and wide to check dubious alibis. And like most such quests, it was also a search for political help.

Leopoldo Notarbartolo knew that his only chance of exposing the high-level intrigues that had led to his father's death, and protected his murderers from the law, would come if he exploited high-level contacts of his own. Sometimes, in Italy, the forces for good have to operate through the same personal channels as the forces for evil.

When Francesco Crispi – the Prime Minister close to the NGI shipping lobby – fell from power following Italy's humiliating defeat at the battle of Adowa in March 1896, his successor as Prime Minister was another Sicilian: someone that Leopoldo thought he might just be able to talk to; someone who has already had a part to play in the history of the mafia.

Antonio Starabba, Marquis of Rudinì, was the mayor of Palermo who made his name by defending the Royal Palace during the Palermo revolt of September 1866. Standing side-by-side with Rudinì during the siege was Emanuele Notarbartolo – indeed Notarbartolo had carved the mould from which the Royal Palace's defenders made musket balls out of lead piping. We last saw Rudinì as he stood on the edge of the political wilderness, desperately expounding his baffling theory about the 'benign maffia' to the parliamentary inquiry of 1876. By the 1890s Rudinì's trim blonde beard had become broad, grizzled and forked. The financial and political crises of the day had pushed Italy right-wards, and in doing so had revived the Marquis's fortunes.

Leopoldo Notarbartolo had few illusions about Rudinì: 'slimy' was the adjective he used to describe him. In truth Rudinì was now so powerful he could rely on someone else to wade through the slime on his behalf. His constituency election manager at the time was one Leonardo Avellone, a local mayor. In 1892 a Sicilian newspaper gave an unforgettable portrait of Avellone.

> *Commendatore* Avellone is a well-to-do man who is nearing sixty. He is chubby, friendly, with the cunning of a peasant and the polite, helpful nature of a Jesuit priest. But he is also vengeful and treacherous with everyone, especially his friends. He is ignorant, but quick-witted and equally adept in doing good as in doing harm. He makes friends with the virtuous and the wicked alike, without the slightest distinction. He is a father figure not just to his numerous children, but also to his relatives and hangers-on who, in his shadow, exercise an absolute tyrannical dominion in the Termini area. He always strikes the pose of a man of order who is extremely conservative, a classic figure of the Right. On occasion, he has given the police some excellent assistance. But then at other times he has had no scruples about helping or setting free criminals of all kinds who are either employed by him or have placed themselves under his protection.

Avellone, in short, was the very archetype of a mafia boss; he was happy to take care of local business – both legal and criminal – while his sponsor Rudinì dealt with grand affairs of state in Rome. Avellone did very well out of Rudinì's return to the forefront of Italian politics. He acquired a decisive influence over everything that moved in his little realm: from giving out licences to sell lottery tickets and tobacco to awarding government positions and public sector jobs; he was even said to control policing policy. This then, was what Rudinì had meant by a 'benign *maffioso*' back in 1876. There were many such benign *maffiosi* in western Sicily – don Raffaele Palizzolo being the most influential of them all.

The one thing that persuaded Leopoldo Notarbartolo that it was worth talking to Rudinì was that the new Prime Minister was a sworn political enemy of the previous premier, Francesco Crispi. So Notarbartolo used his family name to get access to Rudinì's study and then set out the gist of his case against Raffaele Palizzolo. Could Rudinì do anything to bring justice?

Rudinì's reply was brief, jocular and chilling: Notarbartolo should find 'a good *mafioso*', pay him well, and let him take care of Palizzolo.

The Prime Minister subsequently called on don Raffaele's services in Palermo when it came to ousting Crispi's supporters from their positions in the city.

Only in 1898, more than five years after his father's death, did Leopoldo finally find the political help he needed. Rudinì fell from power soon after the events of May of that year, when troops fired cannons into the crowds in Milan. His successor was a military man, General Luigi Pelloux. Pelloux had no political interests in Sicily and he was also a friend of the Notarbartolos. Through General Pelloux, Leopoldo Notarbartolo got access to the documentation he needed: from inside the Bank of Sicily, from Palermo police headquarters, and even the Interior Ministry. Finally, the murdered banker's son could look forward to his day in court.

Within weeks of taking office, General Pelloux also opened another front against the mafia. He recruited the country's foremost mafia-fighter to lead the most serious assault on organised crime's territorial dominance in Sicily since the 1870s.

Floriopolis

On 4 August 1898 the new Prime Minister telegraphed a peremptory order to the Prefect of Genoa: 'Chief Police Ermanno Sangiorgi transferred Palermo. He must go as soon as. With expenses.'

Ermanno Sangiorgi was now fifty-eight years old and Italy's most experienced senior police officer. Since leaving Naples following the cab drivers' strike in 1893 he had been posted to Venice, Bologna, Livorno and Genoa. While his career resumed its upward course, he found moments of great happiness in his personal life. He had another daughter, Maria Luigia, in 1890. In 1895 he married her mother, Maria Vozza, in a civil ceremony: the two could finally live together without causing a scandal. But Sangiorgi's older children were still a source of anguish. His daughter Italia was often unwell. His son Italo had turned out to be a ne'er-do-well: abandoning one steady job after another, roaming the Orient in search of something to do, constantly begging his father for cash to save him from what he called his 'squalid poverty'.

Sangiorgi's transfer to Palermo was to be his last posting, the culmination of nigh on four decades of service to the cause of law and order. A month after he arrived back in Sicily, a new Prefect was installed too. The Prefect announced the radical new policy that he and Sangiorgi would be implementing: an attack on the protection rackets that were the very base of mafia power.

> The crime of extorting money with menaces is the most terrible curse pervading the rural territory of the province of Palermo. The mafia has found a way to live an easy

life by shaking down landowners; it has organised what amounts to nothing less than a tax system in its own favour.

Suddenly, in the middle of Italy's darkest political crisis, Sangiorgi had the political backing to carry through the 'open fight against the mafia' he had first embarked on all those years ago. His efforts would be concentrated in the Piana dei Colli, to the north-west of Palermo – the same beautiful and dangerous landscape that was the theatre of Giovanni 'Darky' Cusimano's persecution of old man Gambino and his sons in the 1860s and 1870s.

Sangiorgi arrived in Palermo in the middle of a mafia civil war. At stake, as always, was territory in the rich citrus fruit groves of the Conca d'Oro. The trail of death and bereavement was not particularly long by the mafia's standards: five *mafiosi* shot dead, another driven to suicide and a seventh poisoned when he escaped to New Orleans. There were also two innocent victims: an eighteen-year-old shop girl and a seventeen-year-old cowherd who were both murdered in case they talked. But what was historically unprecedented about the mafia war of the late 1890s was that Sangiorgi skilfully used it to recruit witnesses, both among the *mafiosi* and their innocent casualties. He then used their evidence to put together the most detailed and convincing description of the criminal sect's structure that had ever been compiled. Sangiorgi set out that description in a report he sent back to Rome in instalments between November 1898 and January 1900.

The first striking thing about Sangiorgi's report is that it started from scratch. He had to assume that his readers (notably senior magistrates and the Prime Minister) knew nothing about the mafia because nothing had yet been proved. Accordingly he began with the basics.

The association's aim is to bully landowners, and thereby to force them to hire stewards, guards, and labourers, to impose contractor-managers on them, and to determine the price paid for citrus fruit and other produce.

From these simple first steps, Sangiorgi advanced a long way. He got the chance to confirm what he knew about the mafia's initiation ritual. And he ended by listing the bosses, underbosses and over two hundred soldiers in eight separate mafia cells. He exposed their links beyond Palermo – even as far as Tunisia, an outpost of the citrus fruit business. He explained how they came together for meetings and trials, and how they performed collective executions of any members deemed to have broken the rules – especially the rule that stipulated blind obedience to the bosses' wishes. Sangiorgi even named the mafia's 'regional or supreme boss', the fifty-year-old citrus fruit dealer and *capo* of the Malaspina *cosca*, Francesco Siino.

The Siino name echoed in Sangiorgi's memory. Francesco's older brother Alfonso, now in charge of the Uditore branch of the sect, was one of the two hit men who shot dead old man Gambino's son in 1874, and then went unpunished thanks to the 'fratricide' plot. Many other names in Sangiorgi's report rang a malevolent bell: names like Cusimano, and above all Giammona. Antonino Giammona was the poetry-writing boss whose gang's initiation ritual Sangiorgi had exposed in 1876. The old mobster was now close to eighty, but he still carried huge authority.

> He gives direction through advice based on his vast experience and his long criminal record. He offers instructions on the way to carry out crimes and construct a defence, especially alibis.

Linking these surnames there was now much more than a shared history of murder and extortion. The hoodlum families of the Palermo hinterland had intermarried, and many had passed on their wealth and authority to their offspring: Antonino Giammona's son Giuseppe was *capo* in Passo di Rigano; Alfonso

Siino's boy Filippo was underboss in Uditore. A generation on from his last encounter with the Palermo mob, Sangiorgi could see that the mafia's marriage strategising had founded criminal dynasties. If the structure of bosses, underbosses and *cosche* gave the mafia its skeleton, then these kinship ties were its bloodstream.

Sangiorgi also identified intimate ground-level contacts between this new criminal nobility and some of Palermo's longer established dynasties, among them the richest family in Sicily, the Florios. The head of the house of Florio, Ignazio, was a fourth generation entrepreneur whose father had married into some of the bluest blood in Sicily. The fortune that Ignazio inherited included the principal stake in NGI, the shipping company whose share price was covertly pumped up with Bank of Sicily money. A man of dash and style who was not yet out of his twenties when Sangiorgi became Chief of Police, Ignazio set the decadent tone in the Sicilian *monde*. Florio turned Palermo – or Floriopolis, as it became known – into a prime destination for the European yacht set. His sumptuous villa, located in its own parkland amid the fragrant hues of the Conca d'Oro, was the epicentre of polite society. But as Sangiorgi discovered, the Florio villa was also an important place for the Sicilian Honoured Society.

The men responsible for security at the Florio villa were the 'gardener', Francesco Noto and his younger brother Pietro – respectively the boss and underboss of the mafia's Olivuzza *cosca*. Sangiorgi did not discover just what were the terms of the deal between the Noto brothers and Ignazio Florio. But protection was almost always how *mafiosi* got their foot in the garden gate. Kidnapping was a serious risk, the Notos would have explained to Ignazio Florio, deferentially. But we can make sure of your safety. And once the Florios' safety was in the hands of the mafia, there was no limit to the turns the relationship might take – many of them mutually beneficial. Having murderers to call on can be a very tempting resource.

One morning in 1897 Ignazio Florio woke to learn that his

safety had been scandalously compromised: the villa had been broken into, and a large number of *objets d'art* were missing. He summoned the Noto brothers and delivered a humiliating tirade. A few days later, Florio woke up again and found that the stolen valuables had reappeared during the night – in exactly their original positions. This was a criminal gesture of astonishing finesse: both an apology, and a serene reminder of just how deeply the mafia had penetrated the Florio family's domestic intimacies.

Sangiorgi learned that the culprits in the Florio burglary were two of the Notos' own soldiers, who were unhappy because they felt they had not received a fair share of some loot from a kidnapping. The Notos strung the burglars along, promising more money on condition that the Florios' property was put back – which it duly was. Then they reported the episode to a sitting of the mafia tribunal, which ruled that it was an outrageous act of insubordination. Several months later, in October 1897, an execution squad comprising representatives from each of the eight mafia *cosche* lured the burglars into a trap, shot them dead, and heaved their bodies into a deep grotto on a lemon grove.

What shocked even Sangiorgi about the whole story was that the Noto brothers had told the Florios just what they had done to the burglars. In November 1897, soon after the police had found the bodies in the grotto, but before anyone outside the mafia had the slightest idea how and why they had ended up there, Ignazio Florio's mother was heard explaining that the dead men had been punished for the break-in earlier in the year. Justice had been done – discreetly and with due force – to the satisfaction of both the Florios and the hoodlums they sponsored. A kind of justice that could never have anything to do with the police.

The Florios inhabited a world of garden parties and gala balls, of royal receptions and open-top carriage rides, of whist soirées and opera premieres. An inconceivable distance separated their milieu from the rat-run tenements where the Neapolitan camorra was incubated, or from the dung-strewn hovels of Africo's *picci-otti*. Yet between the Florios and the Sicilian mafia there was almost no distance at all. If it came to an 'open fight' between the state and the mafia, there was little doubt about which side the House of Florio would take.

On the night of 27 April 1900 Sangiorgi ordered the arrest *en masse* of the Men of Honour named in his reports. He hand-picked his officers, trusting his judgement of their honesty and courage. Even so, Sangiorgi had to keep the operation a secret until the last minute to avoid leaks: the mafia's spies were everywhere. By October the Prefect of Palermo reported that Sangiorgi had reduced the mafia to 'silence and inactivity'. That silence was the reward for months of brilliant policework. But it was also the mafia's response to what had now happened to its favourite Member of Parliament, don Raffaele Palizzolo.

Four trials and a funeral

Between November 1899 and July 1904 the mafia issue went on a national tour. Prime Minister General Luigi Pelloux had to put direct pressure on the Palermo prosecutors' office to make sure the Notarbartolo murder finally came to court. The case was transferred away from Palermo lest the peculiar local atmosphere influence the outcome. There would, in the end, be three Notarbartolo murder trials, each in a different Italian city, each covered in depth by the country's growing press corps. For the first time, Sicily's shadiest machinations became a scandal across the whole country.

The first trial took place in the north, in foggy Milan, which was still a political tinderbox following the army massacre of the previous year. Here the ground itself seemed to throb with industry: hydroelectric power, Italy's 'white coal', was cabled in from the Alps; smoke stacks were reaching skywards in the periphery; and a grand stock exchange building was taking shape in the city's core. Milan was Italy's shop window to the world. With its strong radical traditions, home of the Socialist Party and its mordant newspaper *Avanti!*, Milan would also turn into the perfect resonance chamber for the Notarbartolo scandal.

Yet when the trial finally opened, only two people were in the dock: the brakeman and the ticket collector on the train where Notarbartolo had been stabbed to death more than six and a half years earlier. General Pelloux would only apply so much leverage on the Palermo judiciary. For the prosecution, the two railwaymen were accomplices to the mafia's assassins. For the defence, they were, at worst, merely terrified witnesses. For Leopoldo Notarbartolo, they were a chance to spark a publicity firestorm that would finally drive don Raffaele Palizzolo into the open.

On 16 November 1899 Leopoldo Notarbartolo gave an assured testimony from the witness stand in Milan, of which his father would have been proud. Speaking briskly in his deep voice, Leopoldo explicitly accused Palizzolo of ordering his father's murder and then went on to set out everything he had learned about the mafia and the Bank of Sicily. He also cast grave suspicions over the police and magistrates who had never even interviewed Palizzolo about the case.

Calls for Palizzolo to resign began immediately. The political pressure on him intensified day-by-day, until Parliament voted in a special session to remove his immunity from prosecution. The very same evening, Chief of Police Ermanno Sangiorgi enacted the order to arrest him.

Leopoldo Notarbartolo got the publicity firestorm he wanted. The newspapers at home and abroad carried lurid stories about Palizzolo, real or imagined. He seemed like a satirical grotesque come to life. One American resident in Italy, who understandably chose to remain anonymous, claimed to have gained access to one of the open receptions that Palizzolo held every morning at his sumptuous house on Palermo's main thoroughfare.

Palizzolo's bed was his throne: its heavy mahogany frame was inlaid with mother of pearl and surmounted by a baldachin; it stood, surrounded by numerous gaudily ornamented spittoons and shaving mirrors on stands, at the centre of a hall hung with pink silks. A crowd of petitioners gathered round about: council commissioners in search of seats on committees, policemen who wanted to get on in the force, and former convicts still sporting their penitentiary crew cuts. One by one, Palizzolo's major-domo would pick out the suppliants and guide them to a perch on one of the great bed's broad, upholstered flanks. Palizzolo greeted them all effusively, sitting up in his nightgown, holding a cup of chocolate with one hand and making extravagant gestures with the other.

Palizzolo is a small man with the short, thick neck of a bull and black, shining hair, parted in the middle. Except for his bushy eyebrows, he has few masculine features. His chin is weak and his forehead denotes cunning rather than breadth of thought and strength of character.

The fingers of both his fat, stubby hands were covered with rings – rings of all sorts, marquis, snake and signet rings, set with diamonds, rubies and opals, a whole jeweller's tray full. Yet under this rather vulgar display, under this half-womanish, half-foppish mask, lies hidden a shrewd personality and a calculating mind of no mean order.

As the trial in Milan progressed, there were more and more sensational revelations. A stationmaster turned out to have recognised one of the killers in an identity parade, but his testimony was ignored until he was frightened into retracting it. A police Inspector close to Palizzolo was arrested in the witness stand for concealing evidence; some twenty other witnesses faced charges of perjury. The Minister of War was forced to resign when a Republican paper exposed that he had lobbied to have an influential *mafioso* released in time for the elections. The court learned that former Prime Minister Rudinì had bestowed an official decoration on Palizzolo in 1897.

One of the men suspected of actually stabbing Emanuele Notarbartolo to death was named in the Milan courtroom too: Giuseppe Fontana was a lemon trader and a member of Palizzolo's favourite Villabate *cosca* of the mafia. He also turned out to be the manager on an estate owned by an aristocrat and Member of Parliament.

When the order went out to arrest Fontana, his aristocratic sponsor had to have his arm twisted by Chief of Police Sangiorgi before he would agree to talk to Fontana about surrendering. In the end, the *mafioso* Fontana did give himself up to Sangiorgi; but only on his own terms, and only in a style that confirmed the wildest journalistic guesswork about the mafia's influence in high places. Fontana came to town in a coach bearing his protector's family crest, in the company of his protector's lawyers. He then refused to enter Police Headquarters, insisting instead that Sangiorgi receive him in his own home. On hearing how Fontana dictated the terms of his own surrender, Leopoldo Notarbartolo acidly quipped that the *mafioso* had forgotten to demand that the guard at Sangiorgi's gate present arms as he passed.

The whole country was shocked by what was emerging in Milan. Even Prime Minister Pelloux began to worry about how far the scandal might reach, and thought it might be necessary to call a general election early. The Notarbartolo case reeked of a cover-up, and that reek increased public revulsion at the political system: while politicians were ordering troops to shoot at starving demonstrators and trying to quash press freedom, they were also pocketing illegal loans from banks and consorting with *mafiosi*.

Palizzolo had become a political leper. On 15 December 1899 an estimated 30,000 people filed through the streets of Palermo to show their support for the Notarbartolo cause. A hastily sculpted bust of the murdered banker was born aloft at the head of the procession and then set in a little temple opposite the Politeama theatre in the city centre; soon afterwards it was moved to the atrium of the Bank of Sicily's headquarters. As well as the Socialists and representatives from Palermo schools and clubs, the city's political class were out in force – even many whose conduct was called into question in the Milan hearings. Clearly there had been some shamelessly swift conversions to the cause of law and order in recent weeks. London's *Morning Post* pinpointed the hypocrisy.

> If any one of the numerous politicians who now compete in doing honour to Signor Notarbartolo's memory had energetically set about forcing the Government to punish his murderers, justice would have been done long since.

In January 1900, two months after the Milan trial began, proceedings were halted to allow a much more far-reaching case to be prepared. Here was a significant victory for the Notarbartolo cause, and for the struggle against Sicilian organised crime. Leopoldo Notarbartolo later recalled these moments as 'the culmination of the short-lived tide in our favour'.

In the summer of 1900 Prime Minister General Pelloux resigned. Leopoldo Notarbartolo had lost his key supporter in the Roman palaces of power. But the public indignation at the Notarbartolo cover-up was still strong. The destiny of the whole case hung in the balance.

The second important mafia trial of the day began back in Palermo in the spring of 1901. It did not arise directly from the Notarbartolo-Palizzolo affair, but from the determined police-work of Chief of Police Sangiorgi: the *mafiosi* named in his reports stood accused of forming a criminal association.

Because Sangiorgi's investigations had no direct bearing on the banking scandal he did not benefit from the public fury that still resonated from Milan. There were no foreign correspondents in Palermo when the trial began, and proceedings barely rated a mention in the mainland press. Yet in many ways the Sangiorgi trial was just as historically important as the Notarbartolo affair: this was a case that could have proved once and for all that the mafia existed.

Sangiorgi, veteran of Sicilian affairs that he was, must have had a weary sense of inevitability about the outcome of the trial he had spent the best part of three years preparing. With General Pelloux gone Sangiorgi was once more vulnerable to the system of friendships that the mafia had created to protect itself in its capital. Most of the *mafiosi*, including the venerable *capo* Antonino Giammona, were acquitted before the case even reached court. The likely explanation for these acquittals was that, just

The great enemy of the early Sicilian mafia: Ermanno Sangiorgi. A newspaper described this career cop as being 'as alert as a squirrel, an investigator endowed with a steady perspicacity'.

Men of Honour briefly caught in Chief of Police Sangiorgi's net in 1900.

Giuseppe Giammona, boss of Passo di Rigano, and son of the venerable *capo* Antonino Giammona.

Francesco Siino, the recently deposed 'regional or supreme boss'.

Brothers Francesco and Pietro Noto, respectively boss and underboss in Olivuzza, and responsible for 'security' at the home of Sicily's wealthiest family, the Florios.

Courtroom sketches from newspapers of the day.

as during the 'fratricide' affair in 1876–77, Sangiorgi faced insidious opposition from Sicily's most senior magistrate. Days before proceedings began, the Chief Prosecutor of Palermo, one Vincenzo Cosenza, wrote to the Minister of Justice to explain that 'in the course of exercising my duties I have never noticed the mafia, because the mafia has no desire to ensnare the priests of Themis'. (He meant magistrates, because Themis was the ancient Greek personification of order and justice.) Any Palermo judge who was incapable of imagining why the mafia might want to corrupt the legal system was, at best, culpably naïve. But Vincenzo Cosenza was not naïve: he was identified by Leopoldo Notarbartolo as a protector of Palizzolo's, the main obstacle in the way of bringing don Raffaele and his hitmen to justice.

The trial itself went as badly as Sangiorgi feared. One after another, most of his key witnesses retracted their statements. The mafia's protectors among the elite took the stand to give immaculate character references for their friends in the criminal sect: 'the Giammonas are highly esteemed in the area', one local politician explained. Another man of property was effusive.

> The Giammonas have been very generous to anyone who has a business relationship with them, and no one has a bad word to say about them.

An utterly implausible statement, of course, but understandable given that this particular witness owned land next to both Francesco Siino and the Giammona clan.

The House of Florio was simply too powerful to get mixed up in the case: no one from the shipping baron's family was called to court to explain what *exactly* the Florios' relationship was with the Olivuzza mafia. Ignazio Florio limited himself to a written statement, denying everything.

Defence lawyers portrayed the mafia war as a feud between unconnected families. One after another, they ridiculed Sangiorgi's theory that men who had been at one another's throats could secretly be members of the same sect. *Omertà*, they said, was not part of the rulebook of an organisation. As anthropologists had ascertained, it was a typically Sicilian 'hypertrophy of individualism – something that undoubtedly has its positive side'. Mafia was a kind of *cavalleria rusticana*, of 'rustic chivalry', and as such it was merely the degenerate form sometimes taken by the most noble features of the Sicilian character; getting rid of it – if that were even possible – would mean changing Sicily entirely.

Most of the *mafiosi* were acquitted, and the rest received the usual short prison terms that went with the crime of 'associating for delinquency'. Sangiorgi had been beaten again.

In September 1901 the second Notarbartolo murder trial opened. The city chosen to host the eagerly awaited proceedings was Bologna. With its arcades and ancient university, Bologna was one of the best-administered towns in Italy. Like Milan, it was still safely distant from the judicial snake pit in Palermo. But unlike Milan, it was conservative: a Bolognese jury was unlikely to be swayed by subversive propaganda.

Perhaps it was an optical illusion generated by the publicity. Or perhaps it was the toll taken by months of confinement before the trial. But when don Raffaele Palizzolo stood up to give evidence just a few days into proceedings, he seemed to have shrunk. There were no rings on his fingers and for a prop he only had the back of a chair rather than his mahogany bed. Whether he was pleading with the jury, shouting to the gallery or rambling to himself, Palizzolo seemed incapable of striking the right tone. It was as if he were so habituated to the body language of pork-barrelling – the glad-hands and corridor mutters – that he could find no pose to strike for open, public discourse.

> I was the only Member of Parliament who was accessible to the voters . . . I went down and lived among the people, trying to be their adviser and friend. And the people felt grateful.

In London *The Times* commented on his uneasy performance with typical understatement, saying that Palizzolo's testimony lacked the 'element of simple straightforwardness which carries conviction'. Leopoldo Notarbartolo, still dressed in his navy uniform, was the same assured witness in Bologna that he had been in Milan. *The Times* again:

> The statement of Lieutenant Notarbartolo, with its sobriety, scrupulous attention to fact and careful separation of deduction from premise, held the Court spellbound.

Chief of Police Sangiorgi was also called to the witness stand, although to my knowledge his testimony did not rate a single mention in any foreign newspaper. At least he was well known in Bologna, where he had served as Chief of Police in the mid 1890s. The local press commented that he had changed little: only a few more grey hairs in the blonde of his beard and receding hair. He was forthright in his account of the mafia's power.

> The mafia is powerful and it has relations across five Sicilian provinces and also abroad, where there are colonies of Sicilians.

Lawyers for the defence swept his testimony aside: the recent trial in Palermo hardly backed up this highly improbable assertion.

Sicily's wealthiest man, Ignazio Florio, may not have appeared in court in Palermo, but he could not avoid giving evidence in Bologna. He said that the mafia was 'an invention created to

236

calumny Sicily'. An 'invention', of course, that was protecting his luxurious villa and helping him boost the share price of his shipping line, NGI. Florio was a figure at the very heart of the prosecution case. The NGI stocks scam involving the Bank of Sicily's money was thought to be the whole reason why Palizzolo ordered Emanuele Notarbartolo murdered. Yet Florio somehow avoided being interrogated on the whole subject. One historian has wryly called his easy ride 'miraculous'.

The verdict, which finally arrived after nearly eleven months of hearings, came as a surprise to most. Palizzolo folded his arms and laughed convulsively when he heard that he, like the alleged assassin Giuseppe Fontana, had been sentenced to thirty years in jail. By a majority, the jury had evidently deduced that Palizzolo's guilt was the only possible explanation for the whole cover-up, despite the lack of positive proof against him.

Palizzolo's conviction marked the climax of a countrywide debate about the mafia that had been set in motion two and a half years earlier in Milan. There was a minor publishing boom, and a major outbreak of muddle. Most commentators agreed that the mafia could not possibly be a single criminal fraternity. That was surely preposterous. But if there was broad agreement about what the mafia was not, then only riddles lay in store for any Italian reader curious to know what the mafia actually was.

The very worst book on the subject was one of the most prominent. Its author was Napoleone Colajanni, a firebrand Republican MP from central Sicily who had been the first to lift the lid on the scandal at the Banca Romana back in 1892. Colajanni explained that the mafia was a 'particular moral criterion' left over from feudal times, an underlying feature of the Sicilian character. The isolated gangs that cropped up in Sicilian villages from time to time were merely surface manifestations of this archaic mentality. The Arab invasions of the early Middle Ages were a factor here, probably. Poverty and illiteracy were obviously to blame, mostly. Although there were sometimes rich and well-educated *mafiosi*. And politicians. And aristocrats. But in any case, Colajanni mused

> The *mafia* does not always have evil as its aim; on occasion, indeed not infrequently, it works towards what is good and just. But the methods it uses are immoral and criminal – especially when its actions include violent crime. It would also be false to say that all *mafiosi* are shirkers who live an easy life based on violence, deceit and intimidation. In fact often a *mafioso*, in order to keep his standing as a *mafioso* and show it off, will deliberately stop being wealthy and embrace poverty.

The hopelessly misinformed public debate over the Notarbartolo affair raises one of the most vexing puzzles about the mafia – one that would become more vexing over the decades as Italy's other criminal fraternities acquired power to rival the Sicilian mafia's. The Notarbartolo trial triggered the first organised crime scandal to take place in the era of modern media and mass politics. The vast majority of Italians did not take kindly to the murder and corruption that the word 'mafia' conjured up – whatever that word really meant. So why did the mafia not shrivel, like a vampire, when it was trapped by the rays of the media dawn?

The befuddlement created by books like Colajanni's counted for a great deal. And although Colajanni was not one of them, the mafia also had its own ideologists – lawyers and hired pens keen to spread fallacies about 'mafiosity' and the Sicilian mentality. Their views were eagerly amplified by one of Sicily's most important newspapers, *L'Ora*, which was founded, owned and controlled by none other than Ignazio Florio.

The mafia's influence on the fourth estate could also be brutally direct. On the day after the Milan trial was suspended, the head of the Sicilian press association wrote to Prime Minister General Pelloux to explain that he had twice been threatened, and challenged to a duel, by Palizzolo supporters. 'Timid journalists are keeping quiet, and honest ones are afraid', he warned.

But it is the political backstory to the Notarbartolo affair that really explains why media attention does not hurt the mafia nearly as much as one might expect. The new press of the early 1900s in Italy was ideologically riven, and its divisions reflected a divided nation.

The Notarbartolo cause had the Socialists among its most vocal supporters. Most grass-roots Sicilian Socialists were inveterate enemies of *mafiosi*. In the 1890s the mafia had used all of its tricks – corruption, infiltration and violence – to undermine new labour organisations that recruited among the peasantry. So we should not be surprised that Leopoldo Notarbartolo, despite being a man of the Right like his father, employed a highly able Socialist lawyer.

But other conservatives, who lacked Leopoldo's intimate yearning for justice, were loath to reach out across the political gulf. The barricades of 1898 may have come down, but early twentieth-century Italy remained a country permanently at risk of internal conflict. For men of both Right and extreme Left, the Italian state was a ramshackle edifice that could only be salvaged by being rebuilt. Both sides thought it was naïve to invest much hope in such a state when it came to enforcing real justice. As a result, when mafia issues were at stake in the game of political power, ideology trumped legality.

And Italy's notorious regional divisions often trumped them both. Even the bestselling newspapers, like Milan's *Corriere della Sera*, spoke overwhelmingly to a local readership. There was no such thing as a 'national' public opinion. Prejudices were rife. In Milan, even some of the Socialist Party's leaders viewed the whole south with open disgust, as a land peopled by aristocratic reactionaries, parliamentary pettifoggers, and racially degenerate peasant morons. All the inscrutable talk about how 'mafiosity' was part of Sicilians' make-up only served to harden the stereotypes.

Even the most open-minded Italians from the north and centre did not feel that the mafia, however dastardly it might be, had much bearing on their lives. Sure, they were indignant when they read how Sicilian politicians got into bed with toughs and crooks. But it was hard to sustain that indignation when the people they themselves voted for then got into bed with suspect Sicilian MPs. For most Italians outside the south and Sicily, the mafia lay at two removes.

Regionalism worked in both directions. The Florio family organ, *L'Ora*, stuck to a consistent line throughout the Notarbartolo affair: the mafia was a fiction, a pretext for northerners to get one over on Sicily. Partly because of *L'Ora*'s influence, when Raffaele Palizzolo was found guilty in Bologna in the summer of 1902, a broad section of opinion in Sicily greeted the news with a show of hurt regional pride. The Notarbartolo murder verdict, they lamented, was only the latest haughty swipe that the north had taken at the island. A *Pro Sicilia* Committee was set up, recruiting quickly from the constituency created by Florio wealth and mafia traction, but also drawing in support from many conservatives. The Palizzolo cause became the latest excuse to crank up Sicilian indignation, and thereby lever more money and favours out of the government in Rome. As a side effect of the *Pro Sicilia* turn in the island's politics, Palizzolo was cured of his leprosy and converted into a martyr to northern prejudices.

The old regionalist ploy worked. Someone in Rome almost certainly had a quiet word with the senior judiciary, and within six months Italy's Supreme Court quashed the whole Bologna trial on a tiny and highly questionable technicality.

Palizzolo and the mafia cut-throat Giuseppe Fontana faced a third jury, amid the Renaissance glories of Florence this time. But by now public opinion was exhausted. Not even the death of a crucial new witness, who was found hanging from the stairs of his Florence hotel, raised many eyebrows.

240

Ermanno Sangiorgi, still Chief of Police in Palermo, testified once more in Florence, despite the recent death of his beloved daughter Italia following a long illness. For his pains, Sangiorgi immediately became the target of a mafia smear campaign. The allegations – a convoluted yarn about bad debts, bully-boy policing, and favours to *mafiosi* – appeared first in a long letter published in the Florios' newspaper *L'Ora*. The story was soon picked up in Naples where the *Tribuna Giudiziaria*, a local rag specialising in courtroom dramas, told its readers that the episode shed a disturbing light on Sangiorgi, who had attracted such attention to himself by delivering 'a testimony against the defendants in Florence that was as fierce as it was slanderous'.

> Our conclusion? In Palermo, you won't find the real mafia among the People, but among the police. Just like in Florence, where the real *camorristi* are standing outside the dock, not inside it.

The original slurs were made by an ex-con in the orbit of organised crime. The brains behind him belonged to Palizzolo's lawyer, and possibly also to Vincenzo Cosenza, the Chief Prosecutor of Palermo who claimed never to have noticed the mafia during his career as a 'priest of Themis' – Cosenza was known to be close to the *Tribuna Giudiziaria*'s editors.

The Florentine jury acquitted Palizzolo and Fontana in July 1904. In London, the *Daily Express* gave the news in a few weary lines, under the title 'Victory for the mafia'. In Palermo, that victory was celebrated by a procession with flags and music: men wore Palizzolo's picture on their lapels, women waved handkerchiefs from the balconies. The mafia-backed *Pro Sicilia* Committee hailed the verdict as a great confirmation of patriotic harmony, and sent the mayor of Florence a telegram of thanks.

> A most solemn and imposing meeting of this Committee acclaims the city of Florence, which, by giving heart to

Sicily's juridical conscience, has reunited the Italian People
in the ideal of justice.

Leopoldo Notarbartolo was almost destroyed psychologically by
the outcome of his eleven-year struggle. In 1900, after the Milan
trial, when Palizzolo was first arrested and Chief of Police
Sangiorgi rounded up the *mafiosi* of the Conca d'Oro, the
murdered banker's son had been lured into believing that the
mafia could be defeated in one swift strike, like a monster run
through by a knight's lance. The second and third trials ground
those illusions into a bitter dust.

> What is the result of my efforts? Palizzolo free and serene.
> As for the mafia and its methods: the *Pro Sicilia* Committee
> proclaims and glorifies them; the government bows down
> to them and sustains them; and the wretched island of
> Sicily reinforces them ever more . . . Do I live on an earth
> that is watched over by God the Father, or amid a chaos
> of brutal forces unleashed by loathsome, wicked gnomes
> like the ones in Scandinavian legends?

Leopoldo continued his naval career but spent a further seven
years reflecting on his experience, and then another five pouring
his anguish into a meticulous and moving account of his father's
story, and his own. He found little consolation other than in
contemplating sea life, which offered him a less heroic metaphor
of how the forces of good might one day defeat the mafia. He
observed how, over generations and generations, tiny undersea
creatures live and die, all the while creating their miniature dwell-
ings from limestone deposits, piling them higher and higher until,
following some minor seismic shift, an entirely new island appears
above the waves.

> The people working humbly in the cause of good are like
> those ocean creatures. One day, the marvellous little island

will emerge! God has written his promise in the holy book
of nature.

Back on the 'wretched island' of Sicily, Ermanno Sangiorgi, one
of the people working in the cause of good, took until the summer
of 1905, a year after the conclusion of the Notarbartolo affair,
to win a libel suit against his accuser.

Italy reserves a peculiar cruelty to those that love it the most.
Soon afterwards Sangiorgi's son-in-law, who worked in Pisa as
an administrator for the royal family, the House of Savoy,
committed suicide after being caught with his hand in the till.
Sangiorgi was entirely blameless in the disgrace of his daughter's
widower. But the Royal Household held him liable for some of
the losses, which cost him more than a month's salary.

In March 1907, Sangiorgi formally requested permission to
retire from his position as Chief of Police of Palermo; he was
showing signs of ill health, in the form of a creeping paralysis.
His life in law enforcement – forty-eight years of service,
eighteen of them as Chief of Police – had begun even before
Italian unification. But passing time had not made him any
coyer: he bluntly asked for a special pension and the honorary
title of Prefect. He concluded the letter in a typically patriotic
fashion.

> I began my career during the war of Italian Independence
> when Northern Italy was echoing to the cry of 'Long live
> King Victor Emmanuel II!' I now end it with another cry
> on my lips and in my heart, 'Long live Victor Emmanuel
> III! Long live the House of Savoy!'

Sangiorgi retired in May 1907, with his honorary title but without
his special pension. The creeping paralysis that had hastened his
retirement also hastened him to his death, in November 1908.
The press in Naples and Palermo recalled him to readers as the

Police Chief whose botched handling of the cab drivers' strike in 1893 had brought anarchy to the streets.

Sangiorgi's passing marked the loss of a unique store of expertise on the mafia's early years: the hugely important report on the mafia that he had written for Prime Minister Pelloux would remain hidden in the archives until the 1980s. Fundamentally, the knowledge he had worked so hard to accumulate would remain valid long after his death: as times changed, the Sicilian mafia changed remarkably little. Nevertheless, the ingenuity and ferocity with which the mafia adapted to the changing times to come would have astonished even Sangiorgi.

Sangiorgi had played by the rules in Palermo; he had fought a clean, 'open fight' against the mafia, and it had ended in defeat. He died in his wife's city, in Naples, where the *Carabinieri* had already begun a campaign against the camorra that was both devious and very dirty – a campaign that would end in victory.

The 'high' camorra

In Naples, just as in Palermo, corruption and organised crime reached the top of the news agenda as the economic and political crises of the 1890s petered out. In 1899 a new Socialist newspaper, *La Propaganda*, began a campaign against sleaze and gangsterism. Certain high-minded politicians joined in from the Right. The campaign was such a success that a Socialist MP was elected in Vicaria – the most densely populated constituency in Naples and, of course, the very cradle of the camorra.

The main target of *La Propaganda*'s vitriol was Alberto Casale, a Member of Parliament and influential local government power broker who had extensive contacts with the Neapolitan underworld. We have already had a passing encounter with Casale: back in 1893, he used his purchase with the Honoured Society to bring an end to the camorra-backed cab drivers' strike. Casale responded to *La Propaganda*'s attacks by reporting the newspaper to the authorities for slandering him, and a criminal trial ensued.

The outcome of the Casale case was a disaster for a whole crooked system that linked the city's politicians, bureaucrats, businessmen and journalists. *La Propaganda* successfully defended itself against the slander charge by proving that Casale, among many other corrupt deals, had banked a kickback from a Belgian tram company for his role in the cab drivers' strike.

The shock waves from Casale's judicial humiliation sped to Rome. Casale resigned, the Naples city council was dissolved, and an official investigation into corruption in city government was launched under the leadership of an owlish old law professor from Liguria, Senator Giuseppe Saredo. The Saredo inquiry would once more lay bare the 'slack society'; indeed it would prove to be one of the starkest portraits of political and bureaucratic malpractice in Italian history.

Shining a light into the tenebrous passages of Naples city hall was no easy task. Senator Saredo and his team needed to study the paperwork to discover why the system was so corrupt and inefficient. But the paperwork was in chaos because of all the corruption and inefficiency. Bagfuls of official files had been smuggled away by bureaucrats keen to cover their tracks. The commissioners received a sullen or angry response from many of the key people it interviewed.

Despite all the obstacles, after ten months of wading through a slob-land of documents and testimonies, Senator Saredo and his team dredged up hard evidence aplenty. Appointments to public service were supposed to be made on an impartial, competitive basis. In Naples the regulations had been systematically evaded. Half of all local government employees had no educational qualifications whatsoever. Staggeringly, even the chief accountant whose job it was to draw up the council's budget had no qualifications. Some local government employees drew two or even three separate salaries. Several well-known journalists had no-show jobs with the council.

The reason why government posts in Naples existed was *not* so that services could be carried out for the citizenry. Services like fighting fires, teaching children, caring for the parks, collecting taxes and rubbish, building sewers: these were secondary concerns, at best. For that reason, they were left to the minority of idiots who actually felt bound to do an honest day's work. No, the real reason a job existed in Naples was so it could be handed out to people who had the right friends or relatives. A post with the council was a favour bestowed in return for other favours. In a package with these posts came the power to give and withhold yet more favours: to move an application for a trading licence to the top of the in-tray, or to consign it in perpetuity to the bottom; to give a contract to one tram company rather than to another. Because most local government bureaucrats were not particularly interested in doing anything for anyone they did not know, a whole parasitical swarm of intermediaries grew up: the *faccendieri*, they were called. (They still are.) The term means 'hustlers', 'wheeler-dealers'. The only expertise these *faccendieri* had was knowing which ear to whisper in. In return for a small consideration, they would arrange for someone they knew to get you what you wanted – as a *favour*.

A system of political patronage made this foul mess possible. Politicians stood at the business end of the chains of favours that snaked through the corridors of the Naples municipality. Explosively, the Saredo report referred to the men who operated this patronage system as 'the high camorra'.

> The original *low camorra* held sway over the poor plebs in an age of abjection and servitude. Then there arose a *high camorra* comprising the most cunning and audacious members of the middle class. They fed off trade and public works contracts, political meetings and government bureaucracy. This high camorra strikes deals and does business with the low camorra, swapping promises for favours and favours for promises. The high camorra thinks of the state bureaucracy as being like a field it has to harvest and exploit. Its tools are cunning, nerve and violence. Its strength comes from the streets. And it is rightly considered to be more dangerous, because it has re-established the worst form of despotism by founding a regime based on bullying. The high camorra has replaced free will with impositions; it has nullified individuality and liberty; and it has defrauded the law and public trust.

As a direct result of the inquiry's findings a corruption trial was launched and twelve people, including Alberto Casale and the former Mayor of Naples, were convicted.

Low camorra / high camorra. No encapsulation of the Neapolitan malaise could have been better calculated to make headlines.

Whereas 'mafia' was still a vague notion, one enmeshed in woolly fibs about Sicilian culture, the term 'camorra' carried the distinctive reek of the dungeon, the tavern, and the brothel; it spoke clearly of primitive rituals and knife fights; it conjured up stark pictures of violent men with crude tattoos on their torsos and arabesques of scar tissue on their faces.

At the very same time, during the Notarbartolo affair, the press were referring constantly to a 'high mafia'. Raffaele Palizzolo was without doubt a *mafioso*, who profited from cattle rustling and kidnapping; and he was also, without doubt, at home in the 'high' world of banking and politics. So the label 'high *mafioso*' fitted him as snugly as did his expensively tailored frock coat.

But was 'high camorra' really an accurate description of the systematic spivvery the Saredo inquiry had unearthed in Naples? The politician at the centre of the whole scandal, Alberto Casale, was a proven crook and a master of undergovernment like Palizzolo. But it was not strictly true to call him a *camorrista*. While Casale was certainly a politician who was shameless about doing business with the camorra, he was not an integral part of the camorra in the same way that don Raffaele was an integral part of the mafia.

What this amounts to saying is that the camorra was not as powerful as the mafia. The camorra certainly had a steady partnership with pieces of the state. But it had not *become* the state in the way that the mafia had done in Sicily.

Senator Saredo did not give any evidence to back up his use of the phrase 'high camorra'. His inquiry found no trail of blood or money leading from the upper world of politics down into the underworld where the camorra, in the strict sense, operated. In fact the low camorra remained a mere peripheral blur in Saredo's field of vision.

Saredo's provocative language was therefore misleading, but understandable. Ever since Italy had found out about the criminal sect called the camorra, it had also used 'camorra' in a much vaguer way, as an insult. The c-word was a label for any shady clique or faction – for *other people*'s cliques or factions. As the nineteenth century drew to a close, this term of abuse was steeped in new bile. Italians were growing bitterly frustrated with the way their politics worked. The mysterious deal brokering, the jobbery, the strong-arm tactics: 'camorra', it sometimes seemed, was everywhere in the country's institutional life. A hostility towards politics – *antipolitica* as it is sometimes called – has been a constant feature of Italian society ever since. With his talk of a 'high camorra', the old law professor showed that he had a mischievous streak: he was knowingly appealing to what was by now a conditioned reflex in public opinion.

As soon as it became clear that the Saredo inquiry was doing its job seriously, some leading politicians began briefing against it: what Saredo had termed the 'high camorra' was mobilising to defend itself. Tame journalists heaped abuse on Senator Saredo. Knowing the threat posed by a wave of 'antipolitics', they appealed to another conditioned reflex of Italian collective life: a suspicious, defensive local pride. So the northerner Saredo had besmirched the image of Naples, the editorials wailed. There may have been a few cases of corruption. But that was because Naples was poor and backward. What the city needed was not haughty lectures, but more money from government. Lots more.

In Italy, public indignation has a short half-life. When it fails to catalyse change, it steadily decays into less volatile states of mind: fatigue, forgetting, and sullen indifference. By 1904 the indignation about political corruption and organised crime that marked the turn of the century had all but totally degenerated. Raffaele Palizzolo was finally acquitted of ordering the murder of banker Emanuele Notarbartolo in July of that year. In Naples too, the Casale trial and the Saredo inquiry no longer provoked the same anger. The Socialist Party, having tried to ride the scandals, was now divided and discredited by a failed general strike. The chiefs of the 'high camorra' could now go on the offensive.

The Prime Minister of the day was Giovanni Giolitti – *the* dominant figure in Italian politics between the turn of the century and the First World War. Giolitti was a master of parliamentary tactics, better than anyone else at the devious game of coaxing factions into coalitions.

In the early 1900s Giolitti presided over an unprecedented period of economic growth and introduced some very welcome social reforms. But his cynicism made him as loathed as he was indispensable. 'For your enemies, you apply the law. For your friends, you interpret it', Giolitti once said: a manifesto for undermining public trust in the institutions, and all too accurate an encapsulation of the pervading values within the Italian state. He also compared governing Italy to the job of making a suit of clothes for a hunchback. It was pointless for a tailor to try and correct the hunchback's bodily deformities, he explained. Better just to make a deformed suit. Italy's biggest deformity was of course organised crime, and Giolitti showed himself to be as expedient as any previous statesman in tailoring his policies around it. One later critic, incensed at the way the Prefects used thugs to influence elections in the south, called Giolitti 'the Minister of the Underworld'.

In the general election of November 1904, Giolitti (whose lieutenants in Naples had orchestrated the drive to undermine the Saredo inquiry's authority) deployed all the dark arts of the Interior Ministry to turn the vote. In Vicaria, the constituency in Naples that had elected a Socialist MP in 1900, *camorristi* – real *low camorristi* – were enlisted to bully Socialist supporters. On polling day, alongside the police, gangsters stood guard outside the places where votes were changing hands for government cash.

Someone deep within police headquarters that day was endowed with a cynical historical wit. For *camorristi* who enjoyed official approval were given tricolour cockades to wear in their hats. So, just as they had done in the days before Garibaldi's Neapolitan triumph in 1860, *camorristi* in patriotic red, white and green favours formed a flagrant alliance with the police. The traditional trade in promises and favours between the 'low camorra' and the 'high camorra' had resumed. Nothing, it seemed, had changed.

Barely eighteen months later, things changed more dramatically than they had done at any point in the camorra's history.

Among the *camorristi* in tricolour cockades on election day in 1904 was the boss of the Vicaria chapter of the Honoured Society, Enrico Alfano, known as Erricone – 'Big 'Enry'. In the summer of 1906, Big 'Enry became caught up in what the *New York Times* would call 'the greatest criminal trial of the age'.

The Cuocolo trial, as it was known, was the stuff of a news-paperman's dreams. Tales of a secret sect risen from the brothels and taverns of the slums to infiltrate the salons and clubs of the elite. Police corruption and political malpractice. A cast of heroic *Carabinieri*, villainous gangsters, histrionic lawyers and even a camorra priest. The drama that unfolded in Viterbo seemed to have been fashioned expressly for the new media age. Foreign correspondents, news agencies, and the fibrillating images of Pathé's *Gazette* could now relay the excitement to every corner of the globe. Nor was the Cuocolo trial just a media event: unlike the Notarbartolo affair, it was a turning point in the history of organised crime. Not only did it reignite the political controversy and emotion that the Saredo inquiry had generated. Not only did it threaten, once more, to expose the sordid deals between *camorristi* and politicians. It actually killed off the camorra. With the Cuocolo case, the secret sect known as the camorra ceased to exist. Big 'Enry was to be the last supreme boss of the Honoured Society in Naples. And it all began with the discovery of two bodies.

The camorra in straw-yellow gloves

Just before 9 a.m. on 6 June 1906 police entered an apartment in via Nardones, central Naples. They found the occupant, a former prostitute called Maria Cutinelli, on a bed soaked in blood; she was in her nightshirt and had died of multiple stab wounds – thirteen in total – to her chest, stomach, thighs and genitals. The police suspected a crime of passion and immediately began looking for the victim's husband, Gennaro Cuocolo.

The hunt was over before it began. News soon arrived from Torre del Greco, a settlement squeezed between Mount Vesuvius and the sea some fifteen kilometres from the city: Gennaro Cuocolo had been found dead at dawn. His body lay in a lane that ran along the coast behind the slaughterhouse. He had been stabbed forty-seven times and his skull had been smashed with a club. Much of Torre del Greco was still smothered in ash from a recent volcanic eruption. Traces of a struggle in the black-grey carpet allowed Cuocolo's last seconds to be outlined: there were several attackers; after killing their victim, they lugged the body onto a low wall overlooking the sea – as if to put it on display. Cuocolo's blood mingled with the gore seeping through a gutter that ran from the slaughterhouse onto the crags.

There were good grounds for guessing the real motive for the murders. Cuocolo made his living commissioning burglaries and fencing the resulting booty. He was notoriously enmeshed with organised crime – a former member of the Honoured Society in the Stella quarter, in fact. The conclusion was surely plain: the camorra killed the Cuocolo couple.

The chief suspects were soon identified. At the same time that Gennaro Cuocolo was being stabbed and bludgeoned to death, five men were eating a leisurely dinner of roasted eel at Mimì a Mare, a picturesque trattoria only a couple of hundred metres from the murder scene. The five were arrested: at least three of them were known gangsters, including Big 'Enry who, as the police were well aware, was the effective supreme boss of the Honoured Society.

Yet initial investigations failed to unearth anything concrete to connect the diners at Mimì a Mare with the carnage behind the slaughterhouse. None of the five had left the dinner table long enough to kill Cuocolo. Big 'Enry and his friends walked free, much to the outrage of the Neapolitan public.

The decisive breakthrough came only at the beginning of the following year, as a result of the longstanding rivalry between the two branches of Italian policing. The *Pubblica Sicurezza*, or ordinary police force, was run from the Ministry of the Interior. The *Carabinieri*, or military police, operated under the Ministry of War. In theory the two forces patrolled different areas: the police were based in the towns and cities and the *Carabinieri* in the countryside. In practice, their duties often overlapped. The Cuocolo investigation was to be a classic case of the tensions and turf wars that often resulted.

In 1907, the *Carabinieri* wrested control of the Cuocolo murder probe from the police, and soon submitted a startling testimony by what we would now call a supergrass: he was a young horse trader, groom, habitual thief, and *camorrista* called Gennaro Abbatemaggio.

Gennaro Abbatemaggio made history when he broke the code of *omertà*. He recounted every detail of the Cuocolo murders: motive, plan and execution. But his evidence was far more important than that. There had never been a witness like him. Of course plenty of gangsters had spoken to the authorities before, and plenty of trials had drawn on evidence from deep within the Sicilian mafia, the Neapolitan camorra, and the Calabrian picciotteria. But no one before Gennaro Abbatemaggio had stood up in court to denounce a whole sect. Before him, no self-confessed mobster had made his own life and psychology into an object of public fascination and forensic scrutiny. Gennaro Abbatemaggio would become the biggest of the many celebrities created by the Cuocolo affair.

Abbatemaggio explained to the *Carabinieri* that the murder victim, Gennaro Cuocolo, first became the target of the camorra's anger because he broke its most sacred rule by talking to the authorities. Cuocolo's breach of *omertà* came after he commissioned a burglary by one Luigi Arena. In order to keep all the loot, Cuocolo betrayed his partner in crime to the police.

The hapless thief Arena was sent to a penal colony on the island of Lampedusa, situated between Sicily and the North African coast. From there, smarting with understandable rage, he wrote two letters to a senior *camorrista* to demand justice.

The thief's plea for vendetta was debated at a camorra tribunal, a meeting of the entire leadership of the Honoured Society, which took place in a trattoria in Bagnoli in late May 1906. The tribunal sentenced Cuocolo to death and ruled that his wife, who knew many of his secrets, should die too. Big 'Enry, boss of the Vicaria quarter and the most authoritative *camorrista* in the city, took on the job of organising the executions. He nominated six killers, in two teams, to do away with Cuocolo and his wife. Big 'Enry also set up the eel dinner in Torre del Greco so that he could keep an eye on the gruesome proceedings.

So Abbatemaggio asserted. He also said he knew all of this because he had served as a messenger to Big 'Enry in the build-up to the Cuocolo slayings. He also claimed to have been present, both when the death squads were debriefed by their boss, and when the *camorristi* shared out the jewellery stolen from Maria Cutinelli's blood-spattered bedroom.

There was a subplot to Abbatemaggio's narrative, a subplot that would become the most loudly disputed of his many claims.

He said that Gennaro Cuocolo always wore a pinkie ring engraved with his initials. Cuocolo's killers were supposed to have pulled the ring from his dead hand and sent it to the penal colony of Lampedusa as proof that camorra justice had been done. However, said Abbatemaggio, one of the killers disobeyed orders and kept the trinket for himself. Many months later, when *Carabinieri* following Abbatemaggio's tip-off raided the house where the killer lived, they slit open his mattress and out fell a small ring bearing the initials G.C. Here was crucial material corroboration of the stoolpigeon's testimony.

With Abbatemaggio on their side, the *Carabinieri* could turn a simple murder investigation into a frontal assault on the whole Honoured Society. A huge roundup of *camorristi* followed. The people of Naples cheered from the sidelines.

Yet doubts about the evidence against Big 'Enry and his cohorts surfaced quickly after the *Carabinieri* handed over Abbatemaggio's testimony to the magistrates who would have the job of preparing and evaluating the prosecution before the case could come to court. The *Carabinieri* had very obviously trampled over the procedural rule book. The search that had led to the discovery of Cuocolo's pinkie ring looked particularly irregular. And the main motive for the murders, in Abbatemaggio's tale, was questioned when it became clear that Gennaro Cuocolo had played no part whatsoever in getting the thief Luigi Arena sent to the penal colony of Lampedusa. Why would Arena write to the camorra asking for vengeance against Cuocolo, when Cuocolo had done nothing wrong?

For the *Carabinieri* who were driving the prosecution, trouble also came from within their own ranks. One officer got wind of the real story of Cuocolo's pinkie ring. As it turned out, Abbatemaggio the stoolpigeon had bought the ring himself and arranged for it to be engraved with G.C. The *Carabinieri* had then planted it where their pet *camorrista* said it would be. This was the 'Ring Trick', as sympathisers with the defendants would come to call it.

The *Carabiniere* who discovered the Ring Trick threatened to expose it to the press. He was immediately straitjacketed and deposited in a lunatic asylum on the orders of his commanding officer. The poor man eventually proved his sanity and a sympathetic magistrate arranged for him to be released. But he decided not to tell what he knew about the Ring Trick after some comfy wadding was added to his pension package. Retirement on the grounds of ill health, went the official version.

The Naples police, fuming at having been elbowed out of the case by the *Carabinieri*, relaunched their investigations following a completely different line of inquiry: they believed that the Cuocolos were killed by two thieves whom Gennaro Cuocolo had cheated of some government bonds stolen in an earlier robbery.

But there was a big problem with the police's 'government bonds' theory too: it was based largely on evidence from a certain don Ciro Vittozzi, an obese priest who was godfather to one of Big 'Enry's children; don Ciro also had a record of helping *camorristi* evade justice. So the *Carabinieri* accused the police of believing a fib that the camorra had fed them. The government bonds story, they said, was fabricated by the camorra to protect the real culprits. The *Carabinieri* even prosecuted two police officers for falsifying evidence. They upped the stakes further still by bullying the robbers accused by the police into suing their accusers. New tangles were thus added to a case already matted with legal complexities.

Despite the best efforts of Abbatemaggio's handlers, his story was clearly a rickety construction. So he changed it. A year after his initial testimony, he issued a new improved version. The pivotal figure in Abbatemaggio's new narrative was now one Giovanni Rapi, known in camorra circles as 'Johnny the Teacher' because, when young, he had worked in local schools. He had also been a champagne dealer in France. Now in his fifties, Johnny the Teacher had risen to become Big 'Enry's *contaiuolo* – bookkeeper; he also ran a prestigious social club and gambling den. According to Abbatemaggio, Johnny the Teacher sidelined in fencing stolen goods. In other words, he was a rival in the same trade as the murder victim Gennaro Cuocolo. Because of this rivalry, and because Cuocolo was blackmailing him, Johnny the Teacher had asked Big 'Enry to do away with Cuocolo and his wife.

The obvious question raised by this new story was why Abbatemaggio had not accused Johnny the Teacher before, even though he had been one of the five men known to have dined on eel at Mimì a Mare on the night of the murders. Abbatemaggio replied that he had originally been afraid of two things: that no one would believe that an apparently respectable figure like Johnny the Teacher could be capable of such a horrific deed; and that he could not point the finger at the Teacher without implicating himself in some robberies he had carried out at the Teacher's behest. Abbatemaggio duly confessed to the robberies in question, and was arrested.

The stakes in the Cuocolo murder inquiry were rising inexorably.

Much of the prosecution evidence for the Cuocolo trial was made public while the case was still going through its drawn-out preparatory phases. (This is still the norm in Italy.) So the public followed the developing story closely, and newspapers quickly divided into opposing camps. Were Big 'Enry and his friends guilty or innocent? Who was right, the police or the *Carabinieri*? Some sensed a miscarriage of justice and mounted their own parallel investigations into both the crime and how the *Carabinieri* had obtained Abbatemaggio's confession. Others supported a clampdown on gangsters, regardless of the legal etiquette.

Much of the Socialist press joined the hue and cry, as was predictable given the success of the campaign that had led to the Casale trial and the blows struck against the 'high camorra' a few years earlier. But the Socialists now found they had a very unexpected ally in the right-wing daily, *Il Mattino* – the biggest-selling newspaper in Naples.

As we have already seen, *Il Mattino* liked to give flattering coverage to the Honoured Society's funerals; as the mouthpiece of the 'high camorra', it had also been among the most vocal in blasting the Saredo inquiry for throwing muck at Naples. *Il Mattino*'s venal but brilliant editor Edoardo Scarfoglio had close friends among the 'high camorra' politicians – men who helped him pay for his beloved yacht: with its permanent crew of eleven, it cost more than a Prefect's annual salary to run. Yet just a few years later, here was Scarfoglio's paper cheering the *Carabinieri* on as they launched a new drive to cleanse the city. The turnaround in the newspaper's line was something of a mystery.

One part of the solution to that mystery is that the alliance between 'high' and 'low' camorras was inherently weak and messy. Those 'high camorra' politicians were quite prepared to make use of the 'low camorra' at election time, and to trade squalid favours and promises with them whatever the season. But they had no second thoughts about turning on their gangland auxiliaries when there was a public outcry demanding a few felons' heads on posts.

Sales are another reason for *Il Mattino*'s switch to an anti-camorra line. The grisly Cuocolo murders made the city flinch with fear, and turned organised crime into a red meat issue for a canny editor like Scarfoglio. Unnervingly for many Neapolitans, even the 'low camorra' now seemed to operate behind a façade of respectability. Gone were the bell-bottom trousers, garish waistcoats and quiffs that had marked the early *camorristi* out among the urban unwashed. Gangsters now blended in with the bourgeoisie and even the upper echelons. The expression 'camorra in straw-yellow gloves' (*in guanti gialli*, or *in guanti paglini*) was often used at the time and still provides a useful tag for the new breed of gentleman mobster. Gloves in a delicate, light-coloured suede were an accoutrement of wealth. So 'to wear straw-yellow gloves' meant to put on a false appearance of refinement, to disguise yourself among your social betters. If the 'high camorra'

– one lodged within the government institutions like the mafia – did not really exist, the camorra in straw-yellow gloves certainly did. By the early twentieth century, *camorristi* were covering their tattoos in respectable garb and turning up uninvited among the well-to-do.

Johnny the Teacher, with his high-society gambling den, was an obvious example. As were the dead couple: Gennaro Cuocolo was a gangland fence and his wife Maria Cutinelli was a former dockers' tart. Yet they lived in a well-furnished apartment across the road from the local police station. Cuocolo's *modus operandi* was to win the trust of well-off families so that he could enter their homes and find out what was worth stealing. He then gave precise instructions to his team of housebreakers on how to get in and what to take: tailored burglary.

But the most alarming embodiment of the *camorrista* in straw-yellow gloves to be revealed by the Cuocolo investigation was Gennaro De Marinis, known in criminal circles as *'o Mandriere* ('the Cowherd'), because he once worked in an abattoir. According to Abbatemaggio, the Cowherd had been the recipient of the letters from Lampedusa. The Cowherd certainly had an interesting underworld CV: he was now a jeweller, fence, loan shark and pimp so successful that he lived in a big house with servants.

The Cowherd was portrayed in the press as a new 'ultra-modern' type of *camorrista*. Sophisticated crooks like him infil-trated the cafés and clubs frequented by wealthy and dissolute young men. By offering introductions to attractive 'actresses', invitations to exclusive gambling dens, and cash loans 'between friends', they laid out a cushioned velvet path to blackmail and financial ruin for their victims.

There were also strong rumours in Naples that the Cowherd had inadvertently incurred the anger of royalty, and in doing so brought the wrath of the *Carabinieri* down upon the Honoured Society. The dashing Duke of Aosta, who was one of the most head-turning presences on the Neapolitan ball circuit, was shocked to find himself mixing with *camorristi* at sporting galas;

and he was incandescent to hear that the Cowherd had even been bed-hopping among the ladies of the blue-blood set. So the Duke complained to his cousin the King, who had the police surrender control of the Cuocolo investigation to the *Carabinieri*. Faced with the camorra in straw-yellow gloves, the King told the *Carabinieri* to take the gloves off.

Like so much about the Cuocolo trial, these rumours are destined to remain unverified. Be that as it may, the Honoured Society had long since ceased to be confined to the slum quarters. The drama of the Cuocolo murders unfolded amid the scenery of middle-class city life. Under the pergola of Mimì a Mare in Torre del Greco, where Big 'Enry and his men ate eel, and where the legendary tenor Caruso once lauded the *maccheroni alle vongole*. Or beneath the marble columns and ornamental lamps of the Galleria Umberto I, a prestigious new arcade built as part of the massive reconstruction programme following the cholera epidemic of 1884. Abbatemaggio explained that Big 'Enry and his cohorts had planned the Cuocolo murders here in the Galleria, in full view of the public, at the tables of the elegant Caffè Fortunio. The police confirmed that the Galleria was a regular camorra hang-out. Troublingly, the biggest rats from the alleyways now had the run of the city's swankier milieus too.

These were only the most visible symptoms of the sickness. Naples may not yet have produced a 'high camorra' to match the 'high mafia' of Palermo, but the *camorristi* still lurked in the city's every recess. Money lending was the key. Debt was a way of life in a city with little productive economic activity. The poor lived on the edge of destitution, addicted to the regular buzz of an illegal lottery ticket. The middle classes teetered just above the humiliations of poverty, addicted to the little luxuries that proclaimed their status to the ragged folk who lived on the lower floors. Upper-class betting addicts borrowed to keep betting. The whole town was in hock. As one local journalist commented, usury was to the Neapolitans what absinthe was to the French. The Honoured Society specialised in feeding that addiction.

As the Cuocolo investigation ground along, amid exposés and controversies, the publicity that figures like the Cowherd generated was only magnified by the squalid way the evidence was being gathered. The *camorristi* listed among the accused tried to buy their way out of jail – as was only to be expected. But newspapers, especially *Il Mattino*, were also happy to pay for a scoop, however much truth or falsity it contained. The *Carabinieri* seemed to be involved too. Crooks from across Naples gravitated towards the *Carabinieri* barracks where the investigation was based, hoping to sell a specially crafted witness statement. The shrewdest witnesses touted their story to all three sides, it was said.

The *Carabinieri* converted the strong rumours of a bidding war for testimonies into political leverage. In December 1910, in a secret report sent to their high command in Rome, they complained that the camorra was using every trick it knew to thwart their investigations. Even some newspapers had become hang-outs for crooks. Who could tell how high the camorra's influence now reached? Defeat in the Cuocolo case would do 'irreparable damage' to the Corps, and to the future of public order in Naples. The report cashed out in a revealing plea for 'moral and material support'.

> We regard it as necessary, for now, that funds in the region of 20,000 *Lire* be made available. We need to subsidise able, well-paid and trustworthy informants so that they do not just sell themselves to the highest bidder. Otherwise they could provide false information that could give rise to serious incidents during the trial.

Or, put bluntly: 'can we have more cash to pay our witnesses please?'

It is scarcely a surprise that, in the end, four years and nine months of investigation and legal preparation would be required to prosecute the camorra for the murders of Gennaro Cuocolo and Maria Cutinelli.

The criminal Atlantic

Those years of investigation were packed with incident. When Gennaro Abbatemaggio gave his original statement to the police early in 1907, Big 'Enry fled to New York disguised as a stoker on a steamer.

By that time, Italian organised crime had long since entered a transoceanic age. The first mafia murder on American soil – the first we know about, at any rate – took place on Sunday 14 October 1888: the victim, a Palermitan by the name of Antonio Flaccomio, had just had a drink in a Sicilian restaurant when he was stabbed to death right in front of Manhattan's celebrated Cooper Union building. But the history of the mafia in America was under way well before that date. Sicilian fugitives from justice had been hiding out in the United States since before Italy was unified; New York and New Orleans were major outlets for Sicily's lemons, and therefore became the mafia's first bases in the USA.

At the turn of the twentieth century the tens of thousands who crossed the Atlantic every year became hundreds of thousands: an awe-inspiring 870,000 at the peak of the exodus in 1913. Emigration transformed the economy of the rural south: migrants sent money home and their absence drove up the wages of those who stayed behind.

Among the new tide of migrants there were also members of all three of Italy's major criminal associations. From being a local nuisance in New Orleans or Mulberry Bend, Italian organised crime quickly grew into a national problem for the United States.

The two shores of the criminal Atlantic were bound together by uncountable cunning threads. Just by tugging at one of those threads – Big 'Enry's dash to New York – we can glimpse just how vast and densely woven the history of Italo-American gangsterism really is. (Too vast to be told in these pages.)

Big 'Enry's bid for freedom did not last long: he was soon tracked down and sent back to Naples by Lieutenant Giuseppe 'Joe' Petrosino, a Salerno-born policeman who had risen through the ranks of the New York police by fighting Italian organised crime. We can think of Petrosino as a potential heir to the mantle just relinquished by Ermanno Sangiorgi: Petrosino was a suitably transatlantic cop for the new transatlantic crime.

In 1909, while the Cuocolo investigation was still progressing, Petrosino paid a brief visit to Italy in order to set up an independent information network on Italian-born gangsters. On 12 March 1909 he was standing under the Garibaldi statue in Palermo's piazza Marina when two men shot him dead. He left a widow, Adelina, and a daughter of the same name who was only four months old.

No one would ever be convicted of Petrosino's assassination. There were many lines of inquiry. The first, and most plausible, related to a gang of Sicilians whose counterfeiting operation Petrosino had disrupted in 1903 following the notorious 'body in the barrel' mystery – the body in question being one of the *mafiosi*'s victims. In 1905 the gang thought to be responsible for the 'body in the barrel' were joined by a *mafioso* and lemon dealer called Giuseppe Fontana – the same Giuseppe Fontana outrageously acquitted of killing banker Emanuele Notarbartolo the previous year. (In 1913, Fontana was shot dead in East Harlem.)

The chief suspect for the murder of Lieutenant Petrosino was, and still is, don Vito Cascio-Ferro, a Man of Honour who shuttled back and forth across the Atlantic in the early 1900s. Cascio-Ferro never stood trial because he had a seemingly impregnable alibi provided for him by a Sicilian MP who said that Cascio-Ferro was at his house when Petrosino died. The MP in question was called Domenico De Michele; as chance would have it, he was the son of 'Baron' Pietro De Michele, the Burgio rapist and *capomafia* involved in the 'fratricide' plot against Ermanno Sangiorgi in 1877.

In the course of their protracted investigations into the Petrosino murder, Italian police also questioned a Calabrian gangster: Antonio Musolino, the younger brother of the King of Aspromonte, whose cousin was suspected of having taken the contract to kill Lieutenant Petrosino. With surprising candour Antonio Musolino said he fled Santo Stefano in 1906 because he was afraid that his family's many enemies were trying to kill him. In Brooklyn, he joined up with some of his brother's former support team, among them the cousin suspected of the Petrosino murder. In a basement room in Elizabeth Street, the epicentre of Manhattan's Italian community, Musolino was initiated into a mafia gang that included both Calabrians and Sicilians. His name for the gang was the Black Hand – a catch-all label for Italian gangsterism in America that derived from the menacing symbols (bloody daggers, black hands, and the like) that *mafiosi* sometimes drew on their extortion letters.

Musolino's brief story is typical of the way that the *picciotti* who travelled from Aspromonte to New York were absorbed into a much more powerful and well-established Sicilian organisation: the poor Lads with Attitude came under the influence of the 'middle-class criminals'. Where the Sicilian presence was not so strong, such as amid the lunar landscape of the mining districts of Pennsylvania and Ohio, the Calabrians brought across the Atlantic to cut coal were able to organise among themselves, and directly apply the methods and traditions they had learned at home.

Big 'Enry's brief trip to New York set in motion a third theory about the murder of Lieutenant Joe Petrosino, one implicating the camorra: Big 'Enry himself was the suspect. Interest in the

Cuocolo case in the United States became intense after the Petrosino murder. The huge investigation in Naples seemed to have exposed something much more powerful than even the most disquieting speculation about the Black Hand in the United States. In the *New York Times*, journalist Walter Littlefield boldly asserted that Big 'Enry had issued the order to kill Petrosino, and that the Honoured Society he ruled was the umbrella organisation for all Italian-American criminals on both sides of the Atlantic.

> It is the fond hope of modern, civilised Italy that the trial will stamp out forever the largest and most perfectly organised society of criminals on earth, with its profitable ramifications in America and its willing slaves in Sicily. If this object shall be attained, it will be like severing the head from the body. It will mean the dissolution of the brains of the Black Hand in America and the Mafia in Sicily.

Around the world, the expectations surrounding the Cuocolo affair were becoming as acute as they were unrealistic.

The latest historical research reaches less panic-striken conclusions than Walter Littlefield. *Camorristi* from Naples and its surrounds were certainly operative in the United States at the time of Big 'Enry's visit, and some of them even created autonomous territorial pockets in Brooklyn, next door to the dominant Sicilian gangs. Johnny the Teacher, Big 'Enry's bookkeeper, seemingly had links with a savings institute in New York that gathered immigrants' money and sent it back home. Once Big 'Enry had been extradited, New York *camorristi* toured Italian-owned restaurants to pay for his lawyers.

Meanwhile the man at the centre of the approaching Cuocolo trial, the stoolpigeon Gennaro Abbatemaggio, spent his time in custody reading a serialised life of Joe Petrosino.

As the preparations for the Cuocolo trial ground on, the most newsworthy event of Italy's new media era occurred shortly after 5.20 a.m. on 28 December 1908 when a massive earthquake, with its epicentre in the narrow Straits separating Sicily and Calabria, devastated Messina, Reggio Calabria, and many of the towns and villages of Aspromonte. It is estimated that some 80,000 people died; many of the traumatised survivors emigrated to the New World. This cataclysm, the most lethal seismic event in the history of the west, aroused the whole world's sympathy for weeks.

Once the media agenda had moved on, the drab and sorry story of the reconstruction began. The stricken zones of Calabria had been a slack society before the disaster, they became slacker still in its aftermath. In Reggio Calabria, it took eleven years to rebuild the Prefecture, and six more to finish the Palace of Justice where the criminal courts were housed. The protracted struggle over reconstruction funding from the state became the new centre of gravity of political and economic life in much of the disaster area. The picciotteria wanted a share of the spoils. In Reggio Calabria, mobsters were spotted in the shebeens where the builders drank: such a large workforce offered plentiful opportunities to profit from gambling, extortion, robbery and gang-mastering. In 1913 the police would go on to successfully prosecute eighty-three members of a mafia group operating across the city. They had a hierarchy of ranks, like *picciotto*, *camorrista*, bookkeeper and *fiorillo* – little flower. But of course this was a matter of interest only for the local press, as were other trials of the early twentieth century that showed that the picciotteria was spreading north into the other provinces of Calabria.

Of the people who saw the way the picciotteria was quietly entrenching itself in Calabrian society in the years before the First World War, precious few have left us any kind of testimony. One of them is the San Luca-born writer Corrado Alvaro. In 1955 he retrieved a vivid memory from his adolescence which encapsulated how the picciotteria had become what he called an 'aspect of the ruling class', a normal and broadly accepted part of community life – scarcely a generation after it emerged. On one occasion Alvaro returned home to San Luca, which had avoided the worst of the 1908 earthquake, from a term spent at his distant grammar school. His mother casually told him that his father was busy in the upstairs room with 'men from the association'. Alvaro, full of his textbook notions of public-spiritedness, assumed she meant a group promoting some kind of local interest. 'So there is an association in our village at long last?' His mother gave a flat reply: 'It's the association for delinquency'.

Gennaro Abbatemaggio: **Genialoid**

At last, in March 1911, the Cuocolo trial opened in the cavernous Baroque church that served as the Court of Assizes in Viterbo, a small city between Rome and Florence that had been chosen to host the whole show for fear that a Naples jury might be swayed either by camorra threats, or by the camorra fever the case was generating.

Newspaper readers and newsreel viewers around the world could finally see the eloquent pictures of the defendants crammed into a large cage in the court, and put faces to the quirky nicknames in the Cuocolo story.

For his own protection, Gennaro Abbatemaggio was confined to a smaller cage by himself. Now twenty-eight years old, small and well-dressed, he had a long razor-slash scar running down his cheek to the point of his chin. He wore a short, pomaded moustache that turned perkily upwards at its points to form inverted commas around his mouth.

'The camorra is a career', he began in an attractive baritone, 'which goes from the rank of *picciotto* to that of *camorrista*, passing through intermediate ranks.' He joined the camorra in 1899, at age sixteen, as a *picciotto*. In 1903 he was promoted to the rank of *camorrista* in the Stella section of the Honoured Society.

> *Camorristi* in Naples exploit prostitution greedily . . . They demand a *camorra* [a bribe] on everything, and especially on all the shady activities that, precisely because they are illegal, have to pay the camorra's tax. They extort the *camorra* on illegal betting, on the gambling dens that

cover Naples like a rash. They extort the *camorra* on sales
at public auctions, and even show their arrogance during
national and local elections . . . The camorra is so base
that it takes money, sometimes even really tiny payments,
to massacre or disfigure people. The camorra is involved
in loan sharking. In fact its biggest influence is on loan
sharking.

Abbatemaggio went on to describe the camorra as 'a kind of
low-grade Freemasonry'. His description of the camorra's rules,
structure and methods confirmed the criminological 'textbooks'
that had been so popular in Naples for years. He ended with a
passionate plea.

> My assertions are the absolute truth. I want to carry my
> head high, and look anyone who might dare to doubt
> them straight in the face.

Abbatemaggio then began to reel off his account of how the
Cuocolos came to be so brutally slain on that June night nearly
five years previously. The letters from the Lampedusa penal colony.
The lobbying by Johnny the Teacher and the Cowherd to have
Gennaro Cuocolo punished. How the plenary meeting of the
camorra's top brass at the Bagnoli trattoria approved the decision. How Big 'Enry organised the executions in a series of
meetings in the Galleria. The savage actions of the two teams
of killers. The dinner at Mimì a Mare. The story of Cuocolo's
G.C. pinkie ring.

Abbatemaggio stood and spoke for so long that he had to cut
a hole in his shoe to relieve the pressure on a severe blister. During
breaks he passed his fan mail on to friendly hacks and explained
that, if he had ever had the chance to study, he too would have
become a journalist.

Il Mattino's correspondent had no doubts about Abbatemaggio's sincerity. Here was 'a man endowed with marvellous physical

and mental solidity, and with balanced and robust willpower' the Neapolitan daily opined. It was inconceivable that he could have dreamed everything up as the defence claimed.

> Even the most audacious imagination would not have been able to create all the interconnecting lines of this judicial drama. Every detail he gives is a page taken directly from life – albeit from a life of crime: it is intense, keen, overwhelming.

The defence also thought that Abbatemaggio's testimony was dramatic, although in a very different sense. In cross-examination, one lawyer announced that he would prove that this supposed inside witness had gleaned all he knew about the Honoured Society from downmarket plays. 'Has Abbatemaggio ever been to the San Ferdinando Theatre to see a performance of *The Foundation of the Camorra*?' Abbatemaggio replied calmly that he only liked comic opera – *The Merry Widow* and the like. 'Besides, why would I need to watch the camorra performed in the theatre, when I was part of it?'

The quip was greeted with approving laughs from the public gallery.

The defence also tried to discredit Abbatemaggio by questioning his sanity: he was a 'hysterical epileptic', they claimed, in the dubious psychological jargon of the day. One expert who closely examined him disagreed, but said nonetheless that he was a particularly fascinating case. Again and again Abbatemaggio responded to those who doubted his evidence with names, dates, and a torrent of other particulars. Perhaps he could be classified as a 'genialoid', a rare blend of the genius and the lunatic; his 'mnemonic and intuitive capacities are indeed phenomenal'.

Abbatemaggio's credibility as a witness also depended on his ability to tell a story about himself, a story of redemption. He claimed to have found personal moral renewal by exposing the camorra's secrets to the law. He had been saved, he said, by his love for the young girl he had recently married. 'Camorrist told all to win his bride', was the *New York Times* headline.

Meanwhile, in the defendants' cage, camorra boss Big 'Enry scowled and scoffed. Wiry, sunken eyed and heavy jawed, he had a disconcerting horizontal scar that ran from the corner of his mouth out towards his right ear. He wore mourning black because his younger brother Ciro, one of the five men who ate at Mimì a Mare on the night of the murders, had died of a heart attack in custody. During Abbatemaggio's testimony Big 'Enry was heard to mutter the occasional comment. 'This louse is like a gramophone, and if you turn his handle he goes on and on'. The label stuck: for the rest of the trial, the defendants would refer to Abbatemaggio as 'the gramophone'.

When Big 'Enry's own turn to give evidence came he made an impression that initially surprised many by how eloquent and convincing it was. He explained that he ran a shop in piazza San Ferdinando selling horse fodder – bran and carobs. He was also a horse dealer who traded with military supply bases in Naples and surrounding towns; he had made a lot of money exporting mules to the British army in the Transvaal during the Boer war. He denied being a *camorrista* but admitted that he was rather hot-headed and did sometimes lend money at very high interest rates. It was all a question of character.

> Gentlemen of the jury, you need to bear in mind that we are Neapolitans. We are sons of Vesuvius. There is a strange violent tendency in our blood that comes from the climate.

The *Carabinieri*, Big 'Enry concluded, were victimising him and had bribed witnesses. He had suffered so much in prison that he was losing his hair.

Several policemen of various ranks were subsequently called to testify, and reeled off Big 'Enry's catalogue of convictions. He had begun his career as a small-time pimp. Like many other *camorristi*, Big 'Enry dealt in horse fodder because it provided a good front for extorting money from hackney carriage drivers and rigging the market in horses and mules. They explained that he provided the protection for the high society gambling den run by Johnny the Teacher, and confirmed that he was the effective boss of the camorra. They noted that the nominal boss was one Luigi Fucci, known as *'o gassusaro* – 'the fizzy drink man' – for the prosaic reason that he ran a stall selling fizzy drinks. Big 'Enry used him as a patsy, while keeping the real power in his own hands.

Big 'Enry began to look like what he really was: a villain barely concealed behind a gentlemanly façade. Not many of the other defendants came across much better. Arthur Train, a former assistant District Attorney in New York, was one of many American observers at the trial. He noted that

> the Camorrists are much the best dressed persons in the court room. Closer scrutiny reveals the merciless lines in most of the faces, and the catlike shiftiness of the eyes. One fixed impression remains – that of the aplomb, intelligence, and cleverness of these men, and the danger to a society in which they and their associates follow crime as a profession.

The Cowherd, the 'ultra-modern *camorrista*' whose sexual conquests among the ladies of the aristocracy had reputedly so enraged the Duke of Aosta, was a particularly elegant figure. He too tried to present himself as an honest businessman who had begun by selling bran and carobs and had risen to become a successful jeweller. Only a freakish chain of bad luck had led him to spend several short spells in jail for extortion, theft and taking part in a gunfight, he said. The Cowherd's refined appearance was compromised by the two long scars on his cheek. 'Fencing wounds', he protested. He did at least make a telling point about the notorious ring engraved with Gennaro Cuocolo's

Individui della mala vita sfregiati
(*Riproduzione dal vero mercè il metodo foto-xilografico*)

The *sfregio*, or disfiguring scar, was one of many visible signs of camorra power in Naples. *Camorristi* handed out *sfregi* as punishments both to one another and to the prostitutes they pimped. Sicilian *mafiosi*, by contrast, refrained from both pimping and the *sfregio*.

initials: he demonstrated that it was not big enough to fit on his own little finger – and he was a much smaller man than Cuocolo.

Few of the accused had plausible alibis. Some denied knowing Abbatemaggio, only to be flatly contradicted by other credible witnesses. One *camorrista* thought it was a good idea to have his defence printed in pamphlet form. In it he admitted that the camorra existed but claimed that it was a brotherhood of well-meaning individuals who liked to defend the weak against bullies. This brotherhood's ruling ethos was what he termed *cavalleria rusticana* – 'rustic chivalry'. Evidently this particular defendant was trying to apply the lessons from the Sicilian mafia's successful ploy in earlier trials. He cited camorra history too, concluding his pamphlet on a patriotic note by recalling how, half a century ago, when Italy was unified, *camorristi* had fought Bourbon tyranny and contributed to 'the political redemption of Southern Italy'.

The judge in Viterbo attracted much criticism for allowing the defendants themselves to cross-examine witnesses. These exchanges prolonged proceedings enormously, and sometimes descended into verbal brawls. One *camorrista*, a fearsome one-eyed brute who stood accused of smashing Gennaro Cuocolo's skull with a club, shrieked colourful insults across the court at Abbatemaggio.

> You're a piece of treachery! And you've sold yourself just so you can eat good *maccheroni* in prison. But you'll choke on those nice tasty bits of mozzarella. You'll see, you lying hoaxer!
>
> Shut up you louse! Shut up you pederast! I'd spit in your face if I wasn't afraid of dirtying my spit.

Abbatemaggio had no such worry, and spat back across the court into the defendants' cage.

Weeks and weeks of witness statements, angry cross-examinations, and scuffles went by. Public interest slowly flagged as spring turned to summer. But it revived in July and August 1911 when the two great heroes of the Cuocolo spectacular were called to give their statements. In the words of the *New York Times*, these were the *Carabinieri* who 'finally succeeded in penetrating the black vitals of the criminal hydra and are now ready to exhibit the foul, noxious mass at the Viterbo Assizes'. They were Sergeant Erminio Capezzuti and Captain Carlo Fabroni.

Sergeant Capezzuti was Abbatemaggio's handler: he had persuaded the informant to break the code of *omertà* and protected him afterwards; he had also led the search team that claimed to have found the G.C. pinkie ring.

Ludicrously overblown tales of Capezzuti's heroism had circled the globe between the murders and the trial. It was said that he had disguised himself as a *camorrista* and even undergone a ritual knife fight and been oathed into membership of the Honoured Society. The *New York Times* claimed he had pulled off 'one of the most remarkable feats of detection ever accomplished'. The *Washington Times* reported that Capezzuti was set to become a monk after the trial because this was the only way he could protect himself from the camorra's revenge. Every newspaper in the world seemed to compare Capezzuti to Sherlock Holmes.

It is not clear quite where some of these fables about the 'Sherlock Holmes' of Naples began. Certainly little to justify them surfaced when Capezzuti came to Viterbo. The Sergeant stuck calmly to every detail of the prosecution case, including the G.C. ring story. His evidence was measured and, for those expecting Sherlock Holmes, rather dull.

Captain Carlo Fabroni's time on his feet was anything but dull. The *Carabiniere* officer who was in charge of the whole Cuocolo investigation hailed from the Marche region, and had arrived in Naples only shortly after the Cuocolo murders. One of the first things he did, he explained, was to read up on all the criminology published about the camorra. What he had learned during the course of his investigations precisely corresponded with what he had read.

As Captain Fabroni's testimony continued, his self-confidence tumesced into arrogance. He brushed aside any suspicions that Abbatemaggio might not be telling the whole truth.

> With my extremely honourable past in the military I would blush at the very thought of inducing a man to commit an act of nameless infamy by inventing an accusation.

Under cross-examination, Fabroni provoked the defence at every opportunity, and scattered accusations that the police, politicians and even the judiciary were in cahoots with the camorra. On one occasion, he claimed that Big 'Enry had only been acquitted on an earlier extortion charge because his defence lawyer was the judge's brother; the lawyers all took off their togas and walked out in protest at this collective insult to their profession.

But Captain Fabroni's most startling move was to drop a hand grenade in the lap of his key witness. Since the first hearings, there had been much comment on the sheer vividness of Abbatemaggio's narrative. The 'gramophone' told the court the order in which the *camorristi* stabbed each of the victims, and even the abuse they had shouted while they were doing it. Was it really plausible that the killers would tell Abbatemaggio about their own bloody actions in such detail?

Captain Fabroni's counter to this question was a highly risky move to undercut the stoolpigeon's character, but keep the testimony intact. Abbatemaggio had not broken the code of *omertà* because he wanted a cleaner life with his new wife, Fabroni explained: that was just a cover story. Fear was Abbatemaggio's real motive – fear that the camorra would kill him as it had done the Cuocolos. The reason for this fear was that he had tried to blackmail his fellow criminals. And the reason he knew enough to blackmail them was because, in all probability, he had been present at one or both of the murder scenes. Perhaps Abbatemaggio was himself one of the killers. As Captain Fabroni concluded, 'It's just not possible to reconstruct such an appalling tragedy in every particular unless you have taken part in it in some way.'

Having taken in Captain Fabroni's words, the world's press immediately upended their sentimental opinions of the 'gramophone'. One Australian newspaper called the informer 'a rascal of almost inconceivably deep dye'. Nor was Captain Fabroni the only man in Viterbo to point the finger at Abbatemaggio: the Cowherd also accused him of the murders, and referred to him constantly as 'the assassin'. Thus both prosecution and defence seem to have believed that Abbatemaggio was one of the Cuocolo hitmen. Quite what proportions of truth and cynical tactics were in these allegations may never be known. What is certain is that Abbatemaggio was never formally indicted with the murders.

The Viterbo trial still had a year to run when Captain Fabroni finished giving evidence. Through the months that followed, each of the defendants and many of the witnesses were called back time and again to answer further questions. But a decisive shift in the burden of proof had already taken place. For all its unfathomable obscurities, the Cuocolo case was now a simple credibility contest: either the accused were guilty, or the *Carabinieri* were slanderers. On one side was a cage full of crooked figures with scarred faces who gave mutually contradictory statements. On the other side were Captain Fabroni and Sergeant Capezzuti. Granted, these two *Carabinieri* had failed to live up to their 'Sherlock Holmes' billing. But it was hard to believe that they could be so devious as to fabricate the whole prosecution case.

The strange death of the Honoured Society

At just after five thirty in the afternoon of 8 July 1912, the forty-one accused were summoned back into the packed Viterbo courtroom to hear their fate. Almost all of them failed to move, immobilised by dread. Their nerves were understandable given the scale of the proceedings that were about to reach a climax: 779 witnesses had been heard in the course of sixteen exhausting months of hearings.

Finally, the familiar gaunt figure of Big 'Enry appeared, alone, in the defendants' cage. He looked around him. The lugubrious tension was broken only by the staccato sobs emitted by one of the defence lawyers. Big 'Enry saw, heard and understood which way the verdict had gone. He then destroyed the silence by aiming a shrill cackle across at the elevated box where the jury sat.

> You've found us guilty. So we are murderers? But why, if you are our judges, have you got your heads bowed? Why won't you look me in the face? *We* are the ones who have been murdered! *You* are the murderers!

More of the accused filed into the cage and began bawling, pleading with the jury and the public, screaming at Abbatemaggio. Suddenly a long jet of blood spurted out onto the marble floor. The Cowherd had used a piece of glass to cut his own throat. Doctors rushed to save him and the guards carried him away to recover.

One by one the defendants gave up their protests and flopped down onto their benches to weep. The loudest and angriest of them, Johnny the Teacher, also took the longest to exhaust himself. He alone was still raving when the Clerk of the Court could finally make himself audible and read out the guilty verdicts. The judge handed down more than four centuries of prison to those found guilty of murder and membership of a criminal association, among other crimes.

A crusade for justice, with no prisoners taken? Or a gross abuse of the state's power? In the aftermath of the Cuocolo trial, public opinion remained divided as to what this courtroom spectacular actually meant. The Cuocolo trial certainly achieved the highly desirable aim of striking at the camorra. Yet everyone in Italy could see that it had achieved that aim by lengthy, shambolic and perhaps even dubious means. The Cuocolo murders presented the Italian state with a unique opportunity to show off its fight against organised crime to a vast new audience at home and abroad. The result was confusion at home and national embarrassment abroad. Newspaper leader writers all over the globe lamented the state of Italian justice. The press in the United States was scornful: the trial had been a 'bear garden', a 'circus', a 'cage of monkeys'. Even an observer more sympathetic to Italy, like Arthur Train, could only plead with his readers to understand how difficult it was to administer justice when 'every person participating in or connected with the affair is an Italian, sharing in the excitability and emotional temperament of his fellows'. Still more sober, and no less damning, was the appraisal of the *Bulawayo Chronicle* in what is now Zimbabwe, where cinema-goers had seen newsreels from Viterbo.

> The Camorra trial stands as monumental evidence to the incapacity and inadequacy of the present system of criminal procedure in Italy.

Had more than a tiny minority of magistrates and lawyers been ready to heed them, there were plenty of legal lessons about the fight against camorra-type crime to be learned from the Cuocolo trial: about Italy's hazy laws against criminal associations; about the ungainly, agonisingly slow, and peculiarly Italian marriage of investigative justice with an adversarial system.

The most important lessons came from the story of Gennaro Abbatemaggio. Even on the *Carabinieri*'s account, his treatment was a legal outrage: for example, after first talking to the *Carabinieri*, he spent many months hiding out in a remote part of Campania in what happened to be Sergeant 'Sherlock Holmes' Capezzuti's home village. As Ermanno Sangiorgi found out as long ago as the 'fratricide' case of the 1870s, the authorities had absolutely no guidelines on how to handle defectors from the ranks of the criminal brotherhoods. What kind of deal should the law strike with them in return for what they knew? How could there be any certainty that what they said was true? Italian legislation offered no answers to these questions, and no way of distinguishing good police intelligence gathering from co-managing crime. Because the lessons of the Cuocolo trial were never learned, those questions would continue to vex, and continue to undermine the struggle against organised crime in southern Italy.

And yet remarkably, after the trial in Viterbo, there were to be no more reports of criminal activity by the sect that had plagued Naples since before Italy was unified. Somehow Gennaro Abbatemaggio, and the judicial monster he helped create, ended the history of the Honoured Society.

The trial in Viterbo left a legacy of puzzles. The hardest of them all is why, when so many earlier camorra prosecutions had merely pruned the branches of the Honoured Society, the Cuocolo case actually struck at its root.

One possible answer lies in the evidence given by the Neapolitan police, who had not enjoyed a good press in the build up to the Viterbo trial. Not only had they been overshadowed by the

Carabinieri, in the persons of Sergeant Capezzuti and Captain Fabroni; but they had been discredited by the insinuation that some of them were hand in glove with *camorristi*. Italians were quite ready to believe that this charge had purchase. Everyone knew that the police used the camorra to lend a hand at election time on behalf of the Interior Ministry. In Naples, as in Palermo, the police and gangsters co-managed crime. For all these reasons, evidence from policemen received only desultory media coverage.

Yet for the same reasons, the police understood better than anyone else how the Honoured Society worked. Just as importantly, because of their acrimonious rivalry with the *Carabinieri*, the police who gave evidence in the Cuocolo trial had no corporate interest in backing up either the *Carabinieri*'s textbook account of the camorra, or Abbatemaggio's story. So, in retrospect, the picture of the camorra the police gave the Viterbo jury becomes all the more credible – a picture of a criminal organisation that was already in serious decline before Gennaro Cuocolo and his wife were knifed to death.

Take agent Ludovico Simonetti, who spent four years as a street cop in Big 'Enry's own quarter of the city. Simonetti had no problem admitting to the judge in Lucca that the police regularly used camorra informers, and he was happy to confirm Big 'Enry's leading rank inside the criminal organisation. But Simonetti's evidence was most interesting where it diverged from the prosecution's line; it displays none of the frozen, 'idiot's guide' quality of what Captain Fabroni and the 'gramophone' testified.

Agent Simonetti explained that the Honoured Society was founded on two principles: dividing the profits of crime out among the members; and blind obedience or *omertà*. 'The camorra was so powerful that it could be called a state within a state.' *Was* so powerful: the camorra's supremacy was emphatically a thing of the past. Simonetti went on to say that the principles upon which the criminal sect had been founded were crumbling.

> Now the booty goes to whoever did the job, not to the collectivity. Except on the odd occasion when some more energetic boss manages to extract a bribe. The underworld doesn't have the blind obedience it once did: there are no longer any punishments.

Agent Simonetti pinpoints a crucial new weakness here. The Honoured Society had lost its ability systematically to 'tax' criminals – to extract bribes from them, in other words. Once, by means of this kind of extortion, *camorristi* had presided over petty criminals in the same way that a state presides over its subjects. Now that the power to tax crime had faded, the camorra was beginning to look like just one gang among many. For that reason, it had become more vulnerable to the kind of humdrum underworld rivalries that regularly tore other gangs apart. Blind obedience had gone.

Simonetti made it clear that clusters of *camorristi* still did all the things they had done for decades: robbing, pimping, loan sharking, rigging auctions, bullying voters, extorting money from traders, running the numbers racket. Almost all the most important fences in the city were still members of the Honoured Society. *Camorristi* still respected one another. The individual camorra cells in each quarter of the city still existed. But these days their power came simply from the ferocity and charisma of the individual criminals. In Simonetti's words, the camorra as an 'organised collectivity' did not exist any more.

The old sacraments were losing their magic. In the past, for a criminal to be elevated to membership of the Honoured Society was a life-changing rite of passage. Now existing members used the initiation ritual as a way of flattering other hoods and wheedling cash out of them. As agent Simonetti put it, 'Once it was a serious business that required a blood baptism. Now it's just a baptism in wine.'

Other grassroots police officers enriched Simonetti's account. One of them, Giovanni Catalano, had often seen Abbatemaggio eating pizza with Big 'Enry, Johnny the Teacher and other top *camorristi* in the old days. The camorra certainly still existed, Catalano went on to stress: in virtually every convicted felon's police file there was a telegram from a prison governor wanting to know if the crook in question was a member of the Honoured Society so he could be put in the segregated wing reserved for *camorristi*. But, Catalano went on, the potboilers on the camorra that filled the shelves of Neapolitan bookshops were based on out of date sources, and designed only to satisfy 'readers' morbid curiosity'. The chiefs of the Honoured Society were simply not capable of imposing total obedience now. Camorra tribunals had gone for good. The very fact that a *camorrista* like Gennaro Abbatemaggio could go over to the law was itself a sign of how much things had changed.

The most vivid police testimony of all was the last. A third officer, Felice Ametta, began by joking that he had started his career at the same time as many of the men in the cage had started theirs. He reeled off a list of the Honoured Society's top bosses since he had first arrived in Naples in 1893; he knew them all. But this was a time of crisis for the organisation, a time of infighting. Ametta then recalled the bizarre and revealing incident that led directly to the rise of the new supreme boss, Big 'Enry, an incident that beautifully encapsulates the divided state of the camorra in the early years of the twentieth century.

Needless to say, Big 'Enry was listening intently as Ametta began to tell his tale to the court.

The story revolved around a thief who wanted to be admitted to the Honoured Society. What made his case unusual and controversial was that many *camorristi* suspected the thief of being a pederast. In the old days there would have been no debate: cuckolded husbands, thieves and pederasts were all banned. Accordingly, the then *contaiuolo* (bookkeeper) of the Honoured Society invoked the old rules and obstinately refused to make him a member. But opinion within the camorra was split; the 'pederast' was lobbying hard among his *camorrista* friends. The dispute rumbled on until one evening, in a tavern in the Forcella quarter, the 'pederast' provoked a fight in which the *contaiuolo* suffered serious head injuries. The Honoured Society was suddenly on the brink of a civil war.

Felice Ametta heard news of this potentially explosive rift soon after the fight. Hard-nosed cop that he was, and very used to the business of using the camorra to manage crime, he called Big 'Enry in for a meeting in a coffee bar in via Tribunali.

Hardly had these words sounded across the Lucca courtroom, than the jury swivelled in their seats at the sound of Big 'Enry detonating with rage.

> Called *me* in for a meeting? I'm no stoolie! Never! I'd go to jail a thousand times before I stained myself by arranging a meeting with a policeman!

From a man who denied even being a *camorrista*, this was a highly revealing outburst.

When calm was restored, Ametta went on to explain that Big 'Enry took control of the Honoured Society at precisely this delicate moment, presenting himself as the man who could bring about peace. His leadership platform involved turning the clock back. In Ametta's words

> Big 'Enry wanted to found a kind of old-style camorra, with rigid regulations and statutes, with a tribunal including two advocates for first trials, four advocates for appeal hearings and a general secretary.

There were guffaws when the court heard this elevated legal vocabulary being applied to the sordid affairs of hoodlums. But Ametta's point was a serious and extremely insightful one. What he was implying was that the textbook camorra as Captain Fabroni and Gennaro Abbatemaggio had portrayed it in Viterbo was no longer a reality on the streets of Naples. Instead it existed only as a political project put forward by a new leader desperate – for his own selfish reasons, no doubt – to hold the Honoured Society's rapidly fragmenting structure together.

Thus when Big 'Enry was arrested, the last paladin of the old order was brought down and the Honoured Society was allowed to fall into ruin. The Cuocolo trial did not exactly destroy the camorra, it destroyed the only man who still believed in the camorra, who still wanted to take the criminological textbooks on the Honoured Society and make reality fit them once more.

The street cops who gave evidence at the Cuocolo trial give us a close-up description of the Honoured Society's decline. But being street cops, they did not have to try and *explain* that decline. So their vivid evidence begs a bit of educated guesswork from the historian.

In essence, it seems, the old Honoured Society could not cope with the way Naples was modernising. With Italy becoming more democratic, politicians were gaining access to greater sources of patronage of jobs, housing, and other favours. As a result, under-government could reach further down into the low city, competing with the camorra to win clienteles among the poor. The camorra's bosses were unable to respond by mutating into a 'high camorra', by producing their *own* politicians, by *becoming* the state rather than just performing services for *pieces* of the state. The Honoured Society remained at heart what it had always been: a criminal elite among the ragged poor. The leap from the tenements to the salons was just too great. And in the new more democratic age, when Neapolitan political life became as visible as it was volatile, the camorra had no political mask, leaving it too conspicuous and isolated to survive a serious onslaught by the forces of order. In short: the top *camorristi* might put on their straw-yellow gloves, but they could not cover the scars on their faces.

Here a comparison with the Honoured Societies of Calabria and Sicily is instructive. The picciotteria shared the camorra's lowly origins. But they did rapidly merge with local politics and – just as importantly – Calabria was all but invisible to public opinion in the rest of the country. The Sicilian mafia orbited around a city that rivalled Naples for its importance to national political life: Italy could not be governed if Palermo and Naples were not governed. Yet unlike the camorra, the mafia had its own politicians, its Raffaele Palizzolos and Leonardo Avellones, to say nothing of the Prime Ministers and shipping magnates who were its friends. Even the mafia's killers could rely on being shrouded by the elite if they fell foul of the law. Big 'Enry and the other *camorristi* were left naked by comparison.

Camorra legend has it that not long after the Cuocolo verdict, on the evening of 25 May 1915, the few remaining *camorristi* met in a cellar bar in the Sanità area of the city and dissolved the Honoured Society forever.

What of Gennaro Abbatemaggio? Once the newsreel cameras had ceased to whirr, the man who had snuffed out the Honoured Society followed an eccentric and even self-destructive path through life. The redemption parable that he tried to sell to the Viterbo jury would return to mock him.

Abbatemaggio was caught defrauding two members of the Cuocolo trial jury in a strange deal to buy some cheese, and spent time in jail as a result. Subsequently, during the Great War, he won a sergeant's stripes with the *arditi* ('the audacious'), a volunteer corps of shock troops who raided trenches with grenade and dagger. In 1919 he returned victorious from the front into the arms of the wife who had reputedly saved him from a life of crime – only to discover that she had been having an affair with one of the *Carabinieri* ordered to protect him from the camorra's vengeance. His marriage fell apart, and he attempted suicide in January 1920.

Then came Fascism. Abbatemaggio embraced the Fascist

revolution in Florence, murdering and plundering with one of Mussolini's most militant and corrupt squads.

Perhaps, through all these vicissitudes, Gennaro Abbatemaggio was trying to make a fresh start, to fashion a new self. If so, his efforts failed. Something was gnawing away inside his mind. On 9 May 1927, he finally found release from the inner torment when he deposited a statement with a lawyer in Rome. The statement began as follows.

> I feel it is my duty, dictated by my conscience, to make the following declaration. I do so belatedly, but still in time to bring an end to the worst miscarriage of justice in the legal annals of the world.
>
> ***I proclaim that the defendants found guilty in the Cuocolo trial are innocent.***

The man Big 'Enry had called 'the gramophone' went on to explain that he had played a pre-recorded lie of fabulous complexity and detail in Viterbo. The reason he had made up all that evidence was that the *Carabinieri* had threatened to charge him with the Cuocolo murders unless he helped them. They had arranged his release from prison and given him money and wedding presents. They had bribed key defence witnesses and leading journalists, spending a grand total of 300,000 *Lire* on sweeteners during the case. In particular, they had spent 40,000 *Lire* on a bung for *Il Mattino* editor Edoardo Scarfoglio who, in return for this hearty contribution towards the cost of running his yacht, became the prosecution's cheerleader through the whole affair.

The trial that destroyed the Honoured Society of Naples was a giant bluff. An early release was rapidly granted to the *camorristi* convicted a decade and a half earlier – or at least to those who had not died or gone insane in the interim.

The uncertainties about the Cuocolo case remain legion to this day. Ultimately, there is no way to tell whether even Gennaro

Abbatemaggio's 1927 confession exposed the full facts. He was an unreliable witness in Viterbo, and is doomed to remain one. We still cannot know for certain whether Big 'Enry and his crew murdered the Cuocolo couple. We still cannot explain the sheer ferocity with which the Cuocolos were slain that June night in 1906. Why stab Gennaro Cuocolo so many times? Why move his body and put it on display? Why mutilate his wife's genitals? Why risk the public outcry and political pressure that would inevitably follow such unprecedented acts of butchery?

My own view, for what it is worth, is that Big 'Enry was indeed guilty: the *Carabinieri* got the right man, but fabricated the evidence they needed to convict him. Even the street cops who testified in Lucca thought that the Cuocolo murders were a camorra vendetta.

The Cuocolo murders might make sense as part of Big 'Enry's political project, his plan to inject new vigour into the Honoured Society's wilting traditions. Big 'Enry's reasoning in the run-up to the murders ran along the following lines. Gennaro Cuocolo used to be a big player in the Honoured Society, an impresario of highly lucrative burglaries. But he had left the camorra and gone his own way; he now belonged to a bigger, less rule-bound criminal world. His wife could now be a partner rather than a streetwalker to be exploited and expended as camorra traditions demanded. Gennaro Cuocolo therefore represented a double threat: he was both a rival in the struggle to control the strategic market in stolen goods; and he was a living demonstration that the Honoured Society was falling apart. So camorra justice had to be done as it was in the old days. More flagrantly than the old days. More savagely than the old days. In a last, hopeless attempt to bring back the old days.

Whoever really murdered the Cuocolos, the whole affair became an awkward and contested memory for Naples. Abbatemaggio's final confession certainly reversed the verdicts, but in doing so it only compounded the debacle. Thus, even in Italy's epoch-making moment of victory over the Neapolitan

Honoured Society, truth and the law had been disgraced. For that reason, among many others, the camorra was destined to enjoy a long and bloody afterlife.

Between the crises of the 1890s and the First World War, Italy had lurched towards democracy and an open arena for public debate in the press. At the same time it had tried to fight organised crime. The results, in both cases, were distinctly mixed.

Italy entered the Great War as a deeply divided country. It emerged from it victorious, but on the brink of falling apart: its fragile democracy soon collapsed under the political strains that were the war's immediate legacy. Fascism took power. And where democracy failed in the battle with organised crime, Fascist dictatorship would trumpet success.

Two weeks after Gennaro Abbatemaggio's final confession, on 26 May 1927, Benito Mussolini delivered one of the most important speeches of his life – the Ascension Day speech, as it was known. In it he welded his political credibility to the war against gangsters with more conviction than any of his liberal predecessors. Not only that, he proclaimed that the end of mob rule on Italian territory was imminent.

6

MUSSOLINI'S SCALPEL
1922–1943

Sicily: **The last struggle with the mafia**

Fascism was founded in March 1919 by a handful of aggressively nationalistic war veterans in Milan. The first stage of the movement's rise was the most overtly violent: Fascist squads broke strikes, ransacked trades union offices, killed and crippled selected leftists, and generally posed as defenders of the *Patria* against the red menace. The typical *squadrista* dressed in a black shirt and fez and his signature weapons were the cudgel and the can of castor-oil, an industrial lubricant that was force-fed to victims, bringing on violent stomach cramps and diarrhoea.

Many industrialists and landowners were delighted at this ruthless purge of the Left. Prefects and senior police officers often stood by and did nothing. The old schemers in parliament were confident that they could domesticate the black-shirted bully-boys once the left-wing subversives had been humbled.

Mussolini soon showed that this confidence was badly misplaced. In October 1922, the Duce staged the 'March on Rome', daring a vacillating government to hand over power to him, or face a black-shirted invasion of the capital and the risk of civil war. Mussolini did not blink, and was duly installed as Prime Minister.

Before the March on Rome, the Blackshirt movement was overwhelmingly concentrated in the north and centre of Italy. However, when Fascism took power, it suddenly found that it had won lots of new southern supporters. With their traditional shamelessness, the old political grandees of southern Calabria and western Sicily, along with their mafia election-managers and tawdry clienteles, rushed to cosy up to Fascism now that it promised access to the Roman patronage trough. In the south, the *Partito Nazionale Fascista* risked being hollowed out into an alibi for the same old politics of faction and favour that so suited the gangsters. The few original Fascists were dismayed. Just a few weeks after the March on Rome, the Fascist groups in Reggio Calabria and Palmi were found to be suffering from 'acute factionitis'. In Sicily, early uptake Blackshirts decried the 'Fascistised mafias' that now took control of some town councils.

Fascism welcomed fairweather supporters like these in the early days. But Mussolini had bigger ambitions. In 1924 he changed electoral law to guarantee the *Partito Nazionale Fascista* an outright parliamentary majority. Just a few weeks after the subsequent election victory, Fascist agents kidnapped and murdered the Socialist Party leader Giacomo Matteotti. Outrage spread across the country. But once again the King and leading liberal politicians vacillated at the prospect of throwing the Duce out. Democracy's last chance had gone. On 3 January 1925 Mussolini declared himself dictator. Now he looked south to find an exemplary enemy for his new regime: the mafia. The fight against criminal associations was now a vital front in the Duce's belligerent nation-building project.

As so often, the tempo of criminal history was set in Sicily: in October 1925 Mussolini bestowed full powers to attack the mafia across the whole island on an ambitious northern policeman called Cesare Mori. Mori had dragged himself up the career ladder from nowhere, or rather from the orphanage in Pavia, near Milan, where he had been brought up. The Sicilian mission was his chance to make history; history has come to know him as the 'Iron Prefect' and his anti-mafia campaign as the Mori Operation.

The Iron Prefect began with a highly publicised assault on the hilltop town of Gangi, at the very eastern edge of the province of Palermo. All access to Gangi was denied, all communications cut. Criminals were flushed out of their hiding places with flagrant ruthlessness: their women and children were taken hostage, their goods sold off for pennies, their cattle butchered in the town square. There were as many as 450 arrests.

The Mori Operation involved deploying the same methods among the lemon groves of the Conca d'Oro, and among the many mafia-infested satellite towns of Palermo like Bagheria, Monreale, Corleone and Partinico. The roundups continued into the provinces of Agrigento, Caltanissetta and Enna.

The Mori Operation was still in full swing when the Duce decided it was time to tell the world about what he had achieved.

On 26 May 1927 – for Catholics, the anniversary of Jesus's ascent into heaven – Italy witnessed a little apotheosis of its own.

With his barrel chest and bull neck jemmied into a frock coat and wing collar, Mussolini entered the Chamber of Deputies to be greeted with volleys of cheering and applause. The effusive reception was to be expected: this was now the Duce's fifth year in power, and Italy's parliament had been entirely tamed. All the same, this was not a routine institutional occasion. The speech Mussolini was about to give was heralded as the most important he had ever delivered: a progress bulletin on the building of the world's first Fascist dictatorship. To mark the occasion, the ushers set a huge bouquet of roses before Mussolini's chair. And to mark the occasion, the dictator modulated his usual pout and strut. Toying almost meditatively with one of the roses, he addressed the chamber in a low, even voice.

Mussolini's Ascension Day speech betrayed what the *New York Times* diagnosed as 'signs of increasing megalomania'. But the speech was also undeniably seductive to many Italian ears. In 1922, Mussolini asserted, the Fascists had inherited a democratic governing apparatus that was shambolic, weak and seedy; it was merely 'a badly organised system of Prefects' offices in which each Prefect's only worry was how to hustle votes effectively'. In five short years,

Mussolini claimed, his regime had done 'something enormous, epoch-making, and monumental': for the first time since the fall of the Roman Empire, it had established genuine government authority over the Italian people. The Fascist regime had finally imposed order and discipline on an Italy debilitated for so long by politicking and corruption. The country now marched as one to the thumping beat of a totalitarian ideology: 'Everything within the state. Nothing against the state. Nothing outside the state.'

The supreme authority of the state was Fascism's blazon motif. The Sicilian mafia constituted a state within a state. Therefore Fascism and the mafia were on a collision course.

A centrepiece of the Ascension Day speech was Mussolini's proud bulletin on the Mori Operation. Sicily, he told parliament, was lying on the operating table, its torso sliced open by the Duce's 'scalpel' so that the cancer of delinquency was exposed. Thousands of suspected *mafiosi* had been captured in tens of Sicilian towns and villages. The result was a dramatic fall-off in crime. Murders had come down from 675 in 1923 to 299 in 1926, and episodes of cattle rustling from 696 to 126 over the same period. The Duce fired off more statistics before concluding with an oratorical flourish.

> Someone is bound to ask me, 'When will the struggle against the mafia come to an end?'
>
> It will come to an end *not just* when there are no longer any *mafiosi*, but when Sicilians can no longer even *remember* the mafia.

Here was a long-awaited show of political willpower: there was to be 'no holding back' against the mafia that was 'dishonouring Sicily', in Mussolini's words. After six decades of collusion and connivance, Italy seemed finally to have a leader who made it priority business to destroy the country's most notorious criminal organisation.

Mussolini's scalpel continued to slice into the island's flesh for another two years after the Ascension Day speech: by 1928, according to some calculations, there had been 11,000 arrests. Then in June 1929, the Iron Prefect was recalled to Rome. His part of the job of eradicating the mafia, Mussolini declared, had been completed; it was up to the judiciary to finish off the task. A long cycle of major mafia trials, the biggest of them with 450 defendants, began in 1927 and would not come to an end until 1932. By that time many people felt able to talk about the Sicilian mafia in the past tense. Among them was the Iron Prefect himself.

Cesare Mori published a memoir in 1932 and it was rapidly translated into English with the title *The Last Struggle with the Mafia*. Having brandished the scalpel against organised crime in Sicily, Mori now took up the chisel, with the intention of carving his own narrative of the mafia's demise into the marble of history.

The Iron Prefect told his readers that Sicilian psychology, which he called 'childlike', was at the root of the mafia problem. Sicilians, Mori believed, were easily impressed by haughty figures like *mafiosi*. So to win the Sicilians over, the Fascist state had awed them; it out-mafiaed the mafia; it had given itself a physical presence, and become embodied in men tougher and more charismatic than the *mafiosi* themselves – men like Cesare Mori.

The Iron Prefect was sceptical about the theory that the mafia was a sworn criminal association, an Honoured Society.

> The Mafia, as I am describing it, is a peculiar way of looking at things and of acting which, through mental and spiritual affinities, brings together in definite unhealthy attitudes men of a particular temperament, isolating them from their surroundings into a kind of caste . . . There are no marks of recognition; they are unnecessary. The *mafiosi* know one another partly by their jargon, but mostly by instinct. There are no statutes. The law of *omertà* and tradition are enough. There is no election of chiefs, for the chiefs arise of their own accord and impose themselves. There are no rules of admission.

In order to repress this 'peculiar way of looking at things', a certain amount of brutality was necessary, if regrettable. With their awe-inspiring toughness, Mori wrote, the great roundups of 1926 and 1927 caused the felons' morale to crumble.

> Dismayed and panic-stricken, they fell like flies, with no other gesture of resistance but a feeble attempt at flight to well-concealed hiding places. They were all struck down.

If Mori had bothered to follow the trials that had just concluded in Palermo, he would have found reams of evidence that the mafia was indeed more than a 'mental and spiritual affinity' between men with an 'unhealthy attitude'. But that did not matter much now. In his book's closing lines, Mori declared that Sicily, having won its last struggle with organised crime, had now begun an 'irresistible march towards her victorious destiny'.

The Iron Prefect was showily magnanimous to those he had vanquished and imprisoned, expressing the hope that *mafiosi* would 'come back to the bosom of their families better and wiser men, and then spend their life in honest toil until the mantle of forgiveness and oblivion is thrown over the past'. If the island had not yet had the mafia erased from its memory, as Mussolini promised, then that day could at least be envisaged with confidence. Fascism had beaten the mafia. Whatever the mafia was.

So confident was the regime of its success that, in the autumn of 1932, in celebration of the tenth anniversary of the Fascist March on Rome, hundreds of *mafiosi* convicted during the Mori Operation were released in an amnesty. The Sicilian mafia's history was not quite over yet.

Campania: **Buffalo soldiers**

What remained of the camorra after it was dismantled by the Cuocolo trial? Although the trial marked the end of the Honoured Society, it did not eliminate gang crime in some of the city's nerve centres, such as the wholesale markets or the docks at Bagnoli, where extortion and smuggling were endemic.

Another thing that survived was the myth of the good *camorrista*. Risen from among the poor, the good *camorrista* enforced a rough and ready justice in the alleyways, or so it was believed. Above everything else, such 'men of respect' protected the honour of women. One tale became an archetype in popular memory: the *camorrista* who, seeing a local girl seduced and abandoned, collars her rogue *innamorato* and forces him to do the decent thing. With telling and retelling, such stories hardened into a tableau utterly removed from reality and impervious to contrary evidence. What camorra honour had really meant for women was pimping, beatings, and disfigurement.

When the *camorristi* of the Honoured Society had gone, *guappi* were invested with the aura of 'men of respect'. A *guappo* was a street-corner boss. He may have lacked the formal investiture of Honoured Society membership; he may have lacked contacts with a brotherhood far beyond the alleys of his tiny fief. But the typical *guappo* certainly carried on in much the same way as the typical *camorrista* had done: contraband, usury, pimping, receiving stolen goods and of course farming his turf for votes. Many *guappi* were former *camorristi*, or the sons of *camorristi*.

But to discover the real forebears of the cocaine barons, building industry gangsters and political fixers who make up the camorra today, we need to return for a moment to the days of the Cuocolo trial; more importantly, we need to leave Naples and explore a very different criminal landscape.

On 4 August 1911, two jewellers, father and son, were waylaid by armed robbers on the fruit-tree lined road leading out of Nola, a town perhaps 30 kilometres north-east of Naples. There was a struggle when the father refused to give up the jewellery he was carrying. The attackers responded by shooting his son several times in the face, causing the old man to faint with shock. It was the kind of crime that would not normally have generated a great deal of interest in Naples. But with the Cuocolo trial priming the public's taste for camorra stories, journalists were drawn out into the countryside to cover the story. Nola, after all, hosted the livestock market where Big 'Enry sourced the mules he once sold to the British army fighting the Boers.

Even *Il Mattino*'s wonder-worn hacks were taken aback by what they found when they got there: 'a reign of terror, a kind of martial law'. The territory around Nola displayed all the telltale symptoms of a well-rooted criminal organisation: large numbers of crimes unsolved and unreported (meaning that witnesses and victims were being intimidated); vines and fruit trees cut down (meaning that extortion demands had been made). Mayors who tried to do something about the growing power of the bosses had been beaten up. An uncooperative priest had had his arms broken. Any man who protested to the authorities was liable to have his wife or daughter kidnapped, or his house or business dynamited. Bandits openly patrolled the roads, their rifles slung over their shoulders. And according to the police there was an organisation of only 100-150 men behind it all; they formed a federation of gangs, and divided the booty from their crimes equally.

For all these terrifying details, *Il Mattino*'s exposé barely skimmed the surface. Mobsters infiltrated the fields, market towns and supply routes that enveloped and nourished Naples. *Camorristi* were active down the coast in Castellammare and Salerno and in Nocera, Sarno and Palma Campania just beyond Mount Vesuvius. But the problem was at its worst to the city's north, in a vast expanse of hyper-productive land that catered for virtually every item on the Neapolitan menu. From the livestock centre of Nola in the east; to Acerra, which was particularly known for its cannellini beans and for the eel that flourished in its water courses; to the peach orchards around Giugliano; on to Marano, with its peas; and then up the coast to Mondragone, which was known for its onions, endive and chicory. All around Naples a population of farmers, guards, butchers, cart-drivers, brokers and speculators doubled as extortionists, vandals, fraudsters, smugglers, armed robbers and murderers. Out here, the line between legitimate and illegitimate business scarcely had a meaning: theft and racketeering were as valid a source of income as squeezing a profit from the peasantry.

But of all the agricultural bounty that issued from the Neapolitan hinterland, one product was more tightly controlled by hoods than any other.

South of the Garigliano river, north-west of Naples, there lay a malaria-cursed wilderness called the Mazzoni. Lush, flat, interminable and oppressively quiet, the Mazzoni were pocked by quagmires. The land's other features were few and strange. An isolated water channel threaded through lines of poplar trees; or a dust road, white as a scar, tracing a bullet-straight path to the horizon. Solitary herders were the only travellers: they galloped with their bellies flat to their ponies' bare backs, as if they had fled a stable fire and forgotten to stop. Once in a while the dust they kicked up would settle upon a bridge over a reed-choked ditch, with a gate propped between two posts. These marked the entrance to a *difesa*, in the local parlance – literally a 'defence' – which was a kind of boggy farm. Inside, beyond holm oak and cane thicket, were the buffalo: black, short-haired and massive, they stood in filthy water and glowered at nothing through the shimmering air. At the centre of each compound there was a thatched, whitewashed single-storey shed. Inside, where the air was gamey with the reek of buffalo milk, the herders thumbed mozzarella cheese into balls and dropped them into brine tuns ready for the journey to market in Santa Maria Capua Vetere.

Sallow and sullen with fever, the herdsmen worked the *difese* in teams, living little better than their animals, not seeing their womenfolk for weeks or months on end. Their boss, known as a *minorente*, was a rough and ready entrepreneur. Naples and Caserta paid good money for the creamily fragrant cheeses that miraculously issued from the muck and stench of the Mazzoni. The boss rented his *difesa* from a landowner who was probably too scared to go anywhere near his property. For the Mazzoni were among the most lawless areas in the whole of Italy, and the herdsmen who made the mozzarella also made much of the trouble. In 1909, a government inquiry into agriculture evoked the teams of buffalo herdsmen in the Mazzoni in the language of folk terror. 'For centuries these local tribes have hated one another and fought one another like prehistoric peoples.'

Yet as so often in Italy, lazy talk of 'primitives' served only to mask a far-from-primitive criminal logic. Violence was integral to the buffalo dairy economy. Bosses intimidated their competitors so they could negotiate a lower rent with the landowner. The herders set up protection rackets: if their threatening letters were not understood, they slaughtered buffalo, cut down trees, and burned buildings until they had made their position clear. Highway robbery was a constant risk for the men taking the cheese to market, and bringing the money back. In other words, mozzarella was for the Mazzoni what lemons were for Palermo's Conca d'Oro.

During the Cuocolo trial, *Il Mattino* reporters visited the Mazzoni to be cursorily horrified by the 'crass ignorance' and 'bloodthirsty instincts' of the buffalo herdsmen. What they failed to mention was that the camorra in the Mazzoni, and in the Aversa area between the Mazzoni and Naples, was integral to a political and business machine whose handles were cranked by the local Member of Parliament, Giuseppe Romano, known as

Peppuccio ('Little Joey'). It just so happened that Little Joey was a friend of *Il Mattino* editor, Edoardo Scarfoglio.

Despite the obliging reserve of Scarfoglio's journalists, Little Joey's career was doomed. Partly as a result of the fuss around the Cuocolo trial, he became too notorious to be tolerated even by Prime Minister Giovanni Giolitti (the 'Minister of the Underworld') who had been happy to accept his support in the past. During the 1913 national elections, there was an anti-camorra campaign in Little Joey's constituency (the cavalry were sent into the Mazzoni), and he was unseated. But with Little Joey out of the way, gangster life in the Neapolitan hinterland returned to normal.

From the Mazzoni to Nola, and down beyond Mount Vesuvius, *camorristi* were as at home in the towns and villages around Naples as they were in the prisons and alleys of the city itself. Indeed, there were close ties between the rural and urban organisations. The tomatoes, lettuces, salami and mozzarella that *camorristi* cornered in the countryside went first to the criminal cartels who controlled little portions of the city's wholesale distribution. It was all staggeringly inefficient, a system designed only to fatten the cut taken by middlemen. Poor Naples paid cruelly high food prices as a result. But official Italy hardly took any notice.

Until Fascism, that is.

During his Ascension Day speech in 1927, Mussolini introduced parliament to the Mazzoni. He assumed, naturally enough, that his audience would not have heard of them before: who in his right mind would bother leaving the city to find out where the delicious mozzarella actually came from?

> The Mazzoni are a land that lies between the provinces of Rome and Naples: they are a marshy terrain, a malarial steppe.

The inhabitants, the Duce continued, had a terrible reputation even in ancient times: *latrones*, they were called in Latin

303

– 'highwaymen' or 'brigands'. As was his wont, Mussolini then hurled statistics: between 1922 and 1926, the Mazzoni had seen 169 murders and 404 instances of extortion-related vandalism. But the Fascist scalpel was already cutting away at this millennial legacy of lawlessness. The Duce's orders had been abrupt: 'Free me from this delinquency with iron and fire!' Now, with yet another salvo of statistics, the Duce could announce the triumph of state authority: 1,699 underworld figures had been arrested in the Mazzoni; just to the south, among the vines and fruit trees of Aversa, another 1,278 had been brought to book. In rural Campania, just as in Sicily, Fascism was on the verge of victory.

The press called it Fascism's campaign of 'moral drainage' in the bogs of the Mazzoni. The man charged with conducting the campaign was Major Vincenzo Anceschi, a fifty-year-old *Carabiniere*. Anceschi was the son of a *Carabiniere*, and his own son would become one too: a lineage that testifies to the devotion that the *Arma*, as Italians call this military police force, can inspire in its members. Anceschi's anti-camorra operation was huge, entirely comparable to what Mori was doing in Sicily: between December 1926 and May 1928, 9,143 people were arrested and two suspects died in gunfights with the *Carabinieri*.

Anceschi's men patrolled the countryside in mounted squads, disarming notoriously dangerous families, arresting renegades and breaking up corrupt factions in local government. Although the toughest assignments were in the Mazzoni, their roundups also included the countryside as far east as Nola.

Anceschi could hardly have known this territory better: he was born in Giugliano, right on the edge of the Mazzoni. And on New Year's Eve 1926 he deployed that local knowledge in his most spectacular strike, at a gangland funeral that was intended to be a show of force, just like the Honoured Society funerals of the 1890s in Naples.

Vincenzo Serra was the most notorious *camorrista* in the Aversa countryside. An elegant figure with a lordly bearing, he had spent thirty-six of his seventy years in prison, and was particularly well known for shooting two *Carabinieri* in a tea house. Serra died in Aversa hospital following a mysterious accident. His open coffin was set up in a ground-floor mortuary, surrounded by black drapes, exotic plants and fat candles. Hoods from all around came to pay their respects. They then assembled in the hospital atrium, where (according to the press) the acting boss decided their positions according to rank: first the older *camorristi*; then the *picciotti*; and finally the 'honoured youths' lugging large wreaths. Vincenzo Serra's funeral procession was to be a solemn collective tableau of a structured criminal organisation.

But it never even began. The *Carabinieri* simply bolted the door of the hospital, locking the mobsters in the atrium until they could be herded onto a truck and taken to prison.

Major Anceschi made something of a speciality of raiding camorra funerals. This was a dangerous tactic: officers received frequent death threats. *Carabinieri* dressed in mufti would mingle with the crowds, while Anceschi supervised operations from an unmarked car parked nearby. He had the car wired so that anyone who tried to get in uninvited would receive an electric shock. But the rewards made the risks of this kind of operation worthwhile. The arrests were important, of course. Perhaps more important still was the chance to transform a show of force for the camorra into a show of force for the law.

What these reports suggest is that, even after the Honoured Society died out in the city of Naples as a result of the Cuocolo trial, its structures and traditions lived on in the countryside fifteen years later. Anceschi reported to Mussolini that, in the Mazzoni, the camorra had 'a rigid system based on hierarchy and *omertà*'. 'The country around Aversa and Nola', he went on, 'very close to Naples, was a daily destination for the members of the city's underworld, which was intimately linked to the rural criminals'. The countryside had become a kind of life-support system for urban organised crime.

Anceschi and his men discovered no less than twenty criminal associations and sent 494 men for judgement in eighteen separate trials, but historians have so far managed to locate only a few pages of the resulting documentation. Until more research is done and the archives surrender more of their secrets, we cannot know exactly what kind of criminal organisations dominated the Mazzoni, or indeed the successes and failures of Fascism's 'moral drainage'. What seems certain is that there were no further traces of an Honoured Society in the Neapolitan countryside after the 1920s.

To his credit, Major Anceschi gave a proud but sober assessment of his own work in a report to *Carabinieri* High Command in May 1928. The roads were now safe, the fields were once again filled with peasants, and the barrels of mozzarella cheese could make their way to market without being stolen or 'taxed' by the camorra. Public order was normal, all the way from Mondragone to Nola – for now. But Anceschi detailed a number of things that would need to happen before peace could settle definitively over this troubled territory. Extraordinary policing would need to continue. In the 'malign and fearful moorland' of the Mazzoni, there would have to be education, land reclamation, and road building. Above all – and here lay the most uncomfortable message for the Fascist state – there would have to be much more careful supervision of the personnel within both the government bureaucracy and the Fascist Party. Anceschi's operation had courageously exposed a number of corrupt functionaries who tried to influence the magistrature on behalf of *camorristi*, and who were involved in obscure dealings with the Freemasonry. The report ended with a brusque imperative: 'Prevent political infiltration in favour of organised crime.'

Despite Major Anceschi's caution, Mussolini decided by the late 1920s that the camorra, like the mafia, had been beaten. He also decided that he had solved the whole Southern Question – the persistent scandal of the backwardness, poverty and corruption of Italy's south. Further public discussion of these issues was therefore pointless. So pointless that it was banned. Between

Christ and the thieves overlook an 'ndrangheta heartland. Palmi, one of the centres from which the 'ndrangheta first emerged in the 1880s, can be seen in the middle distance. Beyond and below it lies the notorious plain of Gioia Tauro.

The Sanctuary of the Madonna of Polsi, on Aspromonte. Since at least 1894, the 'ndrangheta's annual gathering has coincided with the Festival of the Madonna of the Mountain held here.

Giuseppe Musolino, the 'King of Aspromonte'.

Musolino's sister Ippolita. According to police, she had also been oathed into the Calabrian mafia.

Musolino's weapons displayed for an avid press.

A scene from the Musolino trial in Lucca, 1902. Despite his ferocious deeds, he aroused much public sympathy. 'Poor Musolino!' wrote one leading man of letters. 'I'd like to write a poem that shows how every one of us has a Musolino inside.'

Emanuele Notarbartolo, the honest Sicilian banker stabbed to death by the mafia in 1893.

Giuseppe Fontana, citrus fruit entrepreneur, *mafioso* and alleged assassin of Emanuele Notarbartolo.

Raffaele Palizzolo, the mafia politician strongly suspected of ordering the Notarbartolo murder. He was photographed only reluctantly, complaining, 'We have become the object of public curiosity'.

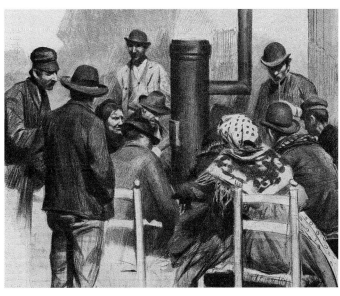

Poor Sicilians summoned to chilly Milan to give evidence in the first Notarbartolo murder trial. Fourteen of them were hospitalised with bronchitis, and one died. A local newspaper took pity on them and arranged a collection.

The accused arrive in Viterbo for the most sensational camorra trial in history, 1911. Following the brutal slaying of a former *camorrista* and his wife, the Cuocolo case generated worldwide interest. The man in the bowler hat is Luigi Fucci, 'the fizzy drink man', and nominally the supreme boss of the Honoured Society.

The stool-pigeon who destroyed the camorra: a dapper Gennaro Abbatemaggio gives evidence from the cage built to protect him from his former comrades, 1911.

Captain Carlo Fabbroni, who turned the Cuocolo murder case into an assault on the whole Honoured Society.

Enrico Alfano, or 'Erricone' ('Big 'Enry'). The camorra's dominant boss, and the principal defendant in Viterbo.

A CONTRAST TO THE DECORUM OF A BRITISH CRIMINAL TRIAL: TURBULENCE IN THE CAMORRA CASE.

...order in court. The chaotic scenes at the Cuocolo trial baffle and repulse observers across the world. From *The Illustrated London News*.

The many faces of 'Iron Prefect' Cesare Mori, who spearheaded Mussolini's attack on the Sicilian mafia in the 1920s.

Man of action, and scourge of the mafia.

Fascist role model.

Wannabe socialite . . .

. . . and friend to the Sicilian aristocracy.

'Master Joe' (seated). The *Carabiniere* who fought the Calabrian mafia under Mussolini.

Don 'Ntoni Macrì (inset), the most powerful of post-war *'ndranghetisti*, and Master Joe's dance partner at Polsi.

'The Fascist Vito Genovese' (right), the New York boss who enjoyed a profitable homecoming in Campania in the 1930s and 1940s.

fter the mafia's defeat 1937: Mussolini pays a triumphal visit to Sicily to open a new aqueduct. By this time the land's criminal Families had returned to full operation under the leadership of Ernesto 'the *generalissimo*' arasà.

Salvatore Lo Piccolo (above), arrested in November 2007, in possession of a mafia rulebook (see p.121). Lo Piccolo's territory included the Piana dei Colli, where many of the earliest dramas of the Sicilian mafia's history took place.

Francesco Schiavone, arrested in 1998, was boss of the camorra's *casalesi* clan. Known as 'Sandokan', because he looked like a heroic pirate from a 1970 TV series, Schiavone modelled his villa (above) on the house from the final scene of *Scarface*. But in Italy, the interplay between gangster fiction and gangster reality is nothing new.

1931 and 1933, the head of the Duce's press corps wrote frequently to newspaper editors exhorting them not to print the words 'southern Italy' and '*Mezzogiorno*' (another term for the south). From now on, Fascism would have other concerns: building a cult of the Duce, for example, and militarising the Italian people in preparation for imperial war. From this point on, whatever surprises mafia history might have in store were to be stifled by a subservient media.

Calabria: **The flying boss of Antonimina**

Domenico Noto had a lovely time in the Great War. Not for him the lice and shrapnel that millions of his fellow countrymen endured in the trenches scoured into the Alpine foothills between 1915 and 1918. Most of the Italians recruited to fight Austria were country folk, barely literate, whose mental horizon simply could not encompass the reasons for this mechanised slaughter. Noto had a loftier perspective. He had a good secondary school education, and used it to become a non-commissioned aviator. His duty was to patrol the breathtaking skies between Calabria and Sicily on the look out for Austrian mines in the Straits below. On one occasion he even overflew his home village of Antonimina, which clings to an Aspromonte outcrop above Calabria's Ionian coast. Noto's gesture won him the lasting reverence of the herdsmen who had shaded their eyes to see the local prodigy soar by. Aviators were the very epitome of a dashing, virile modernity. Domenico Noto seemed like the harbinger of a heroic Italian future. And he even had a good disciplinary record during the war.

Which is why it is striking that, on 19 December 1922 (that is, just after Mussolini became Prime Minister) Noto was convicted of being the boss of the local mafia. If the judges in the case are to be believed, Noto drew on his prestige as a wartime flyer to assume leadership of Antonimina's underworld.

Noto's gang had methods, rituals and a structure that were identical to those of the picciotteria discovered three decades or so earlier around Aspromonte. Thus, despite everything that had

308

happened since then – a communications and transport revolution, mass emigration, the destruction of the Honoured Society in Naples, and the titanic military slogging match with Austria – the 'ndrangheta's forefathers remained obstinately themselves.

Like their predecessors of the 1880s and 1890s, Noto's men took a blood oath and were ranked into two sub-groups: the *picciotti* and the *camorristi*. They had specific job titles, like the boss and the *contaiuolo*. They stole a great many farm animals: some of which they sent to connected livestock traders and butchers in distant towns; some they roasted and ate in banquets designed to nourish the gang's *esprit de corps*; some they miraculously 'found' and returned to the rightful owners – in return for cash and a solemn promise to say nothing to the *Carabinieri*.

Whole passages of the judges' ruling against Noto's *'ndrina* could have been copied from documents dating from thirty years before. The gang contained a few quite wealthy members, and some who had relatives in local government: a former mayor, called Monteleone, counted at least two nephews among the affiliates. The sect had strict rules: wrongdoers were punished with fines, acts of vandalism, or a deft flick of the blade.

Noto's men were also part of a great network of Calabrian mafia gangs. That much was clear from the occasion when he heard from his friends in Palmi, on Calabria's other coast, that one of their brethren had been imprisoned for attempting to murder a *Carabiniere*. Noto ordered his men to make a welfare contribution, and one member who refused was heavily fined. Boasting far-lying contacts like these, the Antonimina mob could demand, and get, 'resignation and respect', from the people at home, as the judge put it. Thefts and beatings were not reported to the police.

So the flying *capo* of Antonimina was a throwback, not a harbinger. Or rather, the future his example heralded was a depressingly familiar one: it was a future in which even educated young men from the mafia heartlands of Calabria, those who had seen the world and taken the chances offered by the national institutions that were supposed to turn them into good Italians, would prefer the career routes afforded by mafia violence.

Domenico Noto's group also betrayed many of the same weaknesses as the Lads with Attitude of the late nineteenth century. There was an admission fee for new members (which had now gone up to 25 or 50 *Lire*). Like the first *picciotti*, Noto and his men browbeat the vulnerable into paying the fee. One victim of this kind of extortion was a sixteen-year-old chicken thief. If the traditional rules of the Honoured Society had been respected, this boy would never have been allowed to join at all because both his sisters were prostitutes. But he was initiated, and exploited, all the same. Aggrieved by the treatment he received, he subsequently gave a vital testimony to the authorities. Nobody in the police and judicial system was remotely surprised by this kind of egregious breach in the code of silence. As a judge in another trial wearily opined, 'as judicial psychology teaches us, members of criminal associations always betray one another, and the solidarity between them is only superficial'. Clearly the Calabrian mafia was still a long way from becoming the byword for *omertà* that it is today.

Across the picciotteria's home territory the courts were encountering similar cases, similar gangs that mixed former soldiers with veteran mobsters, similar infractions of the law of silence. In Rosarno, on the plain of Gioia Tauro, 'the population was terrorised': in broad daylight there were knife fights, acts of sabotage, robberies, attacks on the *Carabinieri*. The picture was very similar in and around Africo, where a judge noted that there was 'a very marked and sudden resurgence in crimes against property' when the troops came home. In the mayhem of demobilisation and the accompanying economic crisis, the *picciotti* were resurgent.

After 1925, just as it did in Sicily and Campania, Fascism mounted an anti-mafia drive in Calabria. Once again, there were hundreds and hundreds of arrests, and some very big trials, especially in the years from 1928 to 1930. But compared to the Mori Operation in Sicily and to Major Anceschi's roundups in the Mazzoni, Fascism's crackdown in Calabria barely rated more than a few lines in the local press, let alone nationally – and that even before the media blackout on the 'Southern Question' from the early 1930s. Fighting organised crime in Italy's most neglected region provided no more political kudos under Fascism than it had done before.

In his 1927 Ascension Day speech, Benito Mussolini gave Italy a monumentally simple picture of his anti-mafia campaign: Fascism set against organised crime – two great blocks facing one another in mutual antagonism. Yet he did not mention the picciotteria at all. The silence is telling, not least because in Calabria the reality on the ground shattered Mussolini's marmoreal rhetoric into fragments. In some times and places, the state manifested its power in brave policework and shrewd investigation. But in others, it showed its weakness through gross naivety, cowardly brutality, idiotic posturing, and lazy collusion.

The archives from the Fascist era allow historians to identify a pattern in the fragments of Fascist anti-mafia policy. Continuity is undoubtedly part of that pattern: in some areas of southern Calabria the *picciotti* were still behaving like the flying boss of Antonimina and his men did after the First World War, and they would continue to do so after Fascism fell. But elsewhere the picciotteria was growing, transforming itself into something altogether more formidable than the sect of ex-cons and tavern rats of the 1880s and 1890s.

Calabrian hoodlums were not new to the mass arrests and major trials that came with Fascism. Comparatively unprotected from the state's wrath, they had always been vulnerable to the kind of repression that the Sicilian mafia eluded as a matter of course. Italy cut them back, but never managed to eliminate them. Under Fascism, the *picciotti* began to show that they were learning from this long and harsh experience. Wherever they could avoid the capricious swing of the Fascist axe, they infiltrated the institutions and bent justice to their own ends. If they had first emerged as a provincial version of the prison camorra of Naples, by the end of Fascism the most powerful Calabrian gangsters looked rather more like Sicilian *mafiosi*.

Looking back at the Lads with Attitude during the Fascist era is like watching ants. With an energy that at first seems utterly myopic, each indistinguishable insect scuttles, explores, fights and dies. Yet somehow, from their multiplied frenzy, the colony as a whole grows stronger and more numerous. Somewhere in the DNA of all Italy's mafias is the ability to think strategically and not just tactically, to evolve over time. A form of natural selection – namely the constant and ferocious competition for predominance within the ranks of each criminal organisation – partly explains this ability. But collective adversity can play a part too: it seems to me that the 'ndrangheta's long-term success was in good part the result of what it endured early in its history at the hands of the state. If 'ndranghetisti had a motto, it would be one drawn from the philosophy of Friedrich Nietzsche. Ironically, it was a maxim of which the Duce himself approved: *what does not destroy me, makes me stronger.*

Calabria: **What does not kill me, makes me stronger**

Fascist repression hit home across the various mob nurseries of Calabria. For example, in 1931 the Chief of Police of Catanzaro felt able to report that the mafia had 'almost been crushed' in his area, although he did add that the 'impetuous and primitive character' of the locals meant that there was still a very high level of bloodshed. Another notable success came in 1932 when the police in Reggio Calabria dismantled a whole criminal system: the bosses of five *'ndrine* were convicted.

But Fascism's early operations against the picciotteria were temporary successes at best. In fact in some places, ironically, they merely created a power vacuum in which other criminals could wreak havoc. Take the particularly nasty gang who ran riot on the plain of Gioia Tauro in the mid 1930s. As well as committing many robberies and acts of violence, their boss, a certain Michele Barone, was also convicted of smothering an old lady in her bed and throwing a prostitute off a bridge for giving him syphilis. Nasty this crew may have been, but it was *not* a cell of the picciotteria.

Michele Barone was a former member of the tax and customs branch of the police – a CV that would automatically have debarred him from membership of the picciotteria. Yet Barone and his friends operated unmolested for three years in the traditional mafia towns of Polistena and Taurianova. In other words, for a while, in this highly significant corner of Calabria, Fascist repression took away the mafia's monopoly of thuggery.

The picciotteria would not accept defeat. The crackdown had

to continue throughout the Fascist era: there was another peak in the number of trials in 1937 and 1938. During the mid and late 1930s, the police and *Carabinieri* were sending suspects into internal exile in greater numbers than almost anywhere else in Italy.

Fascism's drive against the Calabrian mob all too often lost its momentum where it really counted: in court. Already in 1923, one judge remarked that the *picciotti* relied on the 'acquiescence of the wealthiest classes who often use the criminals to further their own goals of personal supremacy and to guard their estates'. Just as in Sicily, the Lads with Attitude had used the subtle art of the protection racket to win friends among the upper echelons – friends who, as witnesses, could swing trials in the gangsters' favour. But as time went on, an increasing number of strange rulings were handed down by judges themselves, suggesting strongly that the picciotteria was beginning to subvert the workings of justice from the inside. One example comes from Villa San Giovanni, a port township that lies just north of Reggio Calabria. In 1927 a group of local *mafiosi* were acquitted of forming a criminal association, despite the fact that some of the mobsters had had themselves photographed, pistols pointed and palms raised, as they took an oath.

Among the big gangster trials of 1928 was the prosecution of fifty-two men from Africo. Some of them were almost certainly the sons and nephews of the *picciotti* whose killing crew took a razor to Pietro Maviglia's oesophagus in 1894. Africo was still, as one Fascist official admitted, 'real barbarian country, isolated from the world'; there were few places in Calabria with such a notorious history of mafia activity. Yet the judge's ruling in the 1928 case shows absolutely no memory of the criminal association's deep roots in the town. He even handed out reduced sentences on the grounds that

> The criminal association was partly the result of social causes such as the poverty of the Great War's aftermath and the moral upheaval that resulted from the war itself.

Obligingly, the judge went on to declare that the defendants were now 'changed men, morally and socially'. No Fascist iron and fire in Africo then, because society was to blame.

Two cases from the notorious Locri area on the Ionian coast also betray a suspicious degree of judicial leniency. In 1928 copious testimony from an insider who had gone through the picciotteria initiation ritual was not enough to convince the judge that a mafia gang was actually a criminal organisation. Yes, they were an association, the judge conceded. But they could have just got together, as they claimed, 'to defend one another from other people's violent attacks'. Acquittal on the grounds of insufficient evidence was the decision.

In 1929 two prosperous citizens were among forty-eight suspected *mafiosi* charged with 'associating for delinquency' and extortion in Ardore: one was an entrepreneur, the other a former cobbler who had become politically powerful. Both were freed on no more solid grounds than that 'it was implausible that they would have shady dealings with what was essentially a bunch of beggars'. The chief 'beggar', as it happens, was caught with a mafia rule book in his house.

Some of these rulings may be down to ignorant judges, or to displays of class prejudice. More likely, they are the end product of the Calabrian mafia's increasing power to infiltrate the judicial system through the state administration. For since Fascism's earliest months in power, when Blackshirts in the region had gone down with 'acute factionitis', the *Partito Nazionale Fascista* in Calabria had proved exasperatingly prone to the local vices of corruption, cronyism, and in-fighting. In Calabria, Fascism not only struggled to govern society, it struggled to govern its own ranks.

Predictably, the malaise was worst around Aspromonte, where cliques still squabbled over the funds allocated to repair the damage caused by the catastrophic 1908 earthquake a *generation* earlier. Mussolini dispatched a rapid succession of special commissioners from Rome to put an end to jobbery and mud-slinging. But what passed for 'Fascism' in the toe of the peninsula remained obstinately unruly throughout the twenty-year regime.

So the single most important weakness in Fascism's campaign against the Calabrian mafia was that it could not cut the tendrils that organised crime had wound around the hollow branches of the state. As early as 1933 the national Fascist Party Secretary in Rome was told that the local Party Secretary in Reggio was 'notoriously affiliated to the organised crime that still infects the province'; the man in question had a strong influence within the Prefect's office and police headquarters. In 1940 a special commissioner reported that a 'high number' of citizens were members of criminal associations, or had relatives who were members. Even his predecessor as special commissioner had several men in his circle who were suspected of involvement in organised crime.

The *picciotti* were growing stronger by sucking energy from the Fascist state. But their increasing vigour also came from within, from bonds that made the *'ndrine* even tougher to prise from the mountain crags and coastal plains where they had first marked out their territory. The Lads with Attitude were learning how to make crime a family business.

Calabria: **A clever, forceful and wary woman**

Italy's underworld networks have always been woven from many different strands, all of them stolen from other parts of the social fabric: Masonic rituals, male bonding, patronage, godparenthood, the language and rituals of a religion hollowed of any spiritual meaning, feasting, the glamour reflected back from literature . . . Anything will do, as long as it knits the organisation together. But the strongest criminal ties of all have been those braided from the purloined threads of kinship. Families lend gangs the kind of loyalty that more impersonal forms of organisation can rarely match. It is one thing to betray a comrade to the police: it is quite another when that comrade is also your cousin, your uncle, or your father-in-law.

Among Sicilian *mafiosi*, births, marriages and baptisms have never been *private*; that is, they are not purely domestic affairs that a gangland leader only turns his mind to once the day's extorting and smuggling are done. Rather, family is at the heart of quotidian underworld scheming: a wedding can seal a pact ready for war or end a season of bloodshed and signal the birth of a new alliance. Dynastic politics have always been integral to what the mafia is about. The *mafiosi* that Inspector Sangiorgi encountered during the 'fratricide' affair already cultivated the arts required to sire their own criminal bloodlines, to make their surnames echo fear down through the generations. Sangiorgi also discovered the first known occasion on which a Man of Honour was offered the distinctively Sicilian choice between murdering a relative and being killed himself: it was in 1883, when an uncle was made to take part in the murder of his own nephew, who was also a *mafioso*. In the Brotherhood of Favara, the mafia of the sulphur mines, those were the rules.

In Calabria, back in the 1880s and 1890s, family matters were handled very differently. The 'ndrangheta was originally a sect in which prisoner enlisted prisoner, rather than father enlisting son. Once they emerged from jail, *picciotti* did begin to spread along the pathways of kinship. The earliest picciotteria trial papers list brothers, cousins and other relatives among the members – it could hardly be otherwise given the tangle of intermarriage in some of the isolated Calabrian communities. Before long, a first generation of sons were joining their fathers in the criminal ranks. For example, if the police were right about the King of Aspromonte, Giuseppe Musolino, then his father founded the picciotteria in Santo Stefano. So family and gang crime were interlaced very quickly. But in the early days there seems to have been little strategic and legislative thought behind that interlacing: the *picciotti* did not call meetings about family matters; they did not make rules about who could marry whom; they did not cut faces for breaches of dynastic etiquette.

Today the 'ndrangheta is more resistant to repression than the Sicilian mafia or the Neapolitan camorra; its secrets are more closely guarded, because fewer of its members turn state's evidence. Ask any magistrate or policeman in Calabria why that should be, and they will reply with one word: family. These days, the 'ndrangheta is even more family-oriented than the Sicilian mafia: each *'ndrina* is deliberately *built* around one clan, often a single boss and his numerous male offspring. In bugged conversations from 2010, *'ndranghetisti* can be heard discussing what they call the principle of 'the line', meaning the hereditary principle, when it comes to deciding who will become the boss (of Roghudi, in this case). The rule that a son should inherit from his father is not inviolable but it is a rule all the same. No such statute exists in the Sicilian mafia, although the sons of bosses often follow their fathers into leadership positions.

So although the Lads with Attitude had very similar rituals and a similar structure to the 'ndrangheta as it is known and feared today, they lacked the strong basis in kinship for which the 'ndrangheta is most renowned. In fact the picciotteria was slow to take on board the full criminal potential of blood relationships. From the beginning, deaths were part of the Calabrian mafia's collective business; but it was only during the two decades of Fascism that births and marriages really entered the ledger too. The transformation was slow and patchy, but absolutely fundamental to the growing strength of the picciotteria.

By the time the Fascist dictatorship had asserted itself in Rome, judges were beginning to hear new kinds of family story among the hoodlums of Calabria. In Vibo Valentia, to the north of the Plain of Gioia Tauro, a *Carabiniere* was murdered in 1927 for trying to stop a marriage alliance between two criminal kinship groups, one of which had colonised the local Fascist state.

Three years later, in Nicotera just to the south, one boy was initiated into the Honoured Society at only eleven years old.

Across the mountains to the south-east, in Grotteria in 1933, the local boss heard rumours that his fiancée was pregnant by another *picciotto*. So the gang met to discuss this smear on their *capo*'s honour, and decided to put a contract out. Contrary to what one might expect, the target was not the woman's alleged lover, but the man thought to be spreading the rumours. Hearsay, after all, has always been the most dangerous of weapons in dynastic struggle. The chosen killer, a sixteen-year-old boy, took six goes before he managed to cut his victim's throat properly.

Such stories are undoubtedly significant. Yet an even clearer way to trace the evolution of the early 'ndrangheta's sexual politics is by following the changing role of women. Italy's criminal organisations were from their inception overwhelmingly masculine and inherently sexist. Mafia honour has always been a men-only quality. Nevertheless, as we have already seen, women had important uses to *mafiosi* and *camorristi*, and there was significant variety in the ways they were used.

Whores were the women most frequently found in the company of the early *'ndranghetisti*. Whereas Sicilian *mafiosi* have never had anything to do with prostitution, the first Calabrian *picciotti* tended to be ponces. As ponces do, they partied with the girls whose earnings they creamed off. (They raped and sometimes even married them too.) So unlike their contemporaries in the Sicilian mafia, and unlike *'ndranghetisti* of today, the Calabrian gangsters of the late 1800s and early 1900s did not view profiting from sex as dishonourable.

In this respect, the picciotteria was exactly like the Honoured Society of Naples had been in the nineteenth century. Neapolitan camorra slang bristled with derogatory synonyms for 'prostitute': *bagascia, bambuglia, bardascia, drusiana, risgraziata, schiavuttella* ('little slave'), *vaiassa*, and *zoccola* ('sewer rat'). There was also a whole nomenclature for different kinds of streetwalker. A new girl was a *colomba* ('dove'); one from the provinces was a *cafona* ('yokel'). A *gallinella* ('young hen') was a woman with kids; whereas a *pollanca* ('young turkey') was the term for a virgin set to be put on the market. In addition, there were several names for an old woman, like *carcassa* ('carcass') and *calascione* ('a battered old mandolin'). This was the jargon of an exploitative industry central to the camorra economy. We know little about the family lives of Neapolitan *camorristi* in the 1800s. But it seems unlikely that men so profoundly embroiled in the flesh trade could sire dynasties to compare with those of the Sicilian dons.

Like their Neapolitan peers, who had accorded *la Sangiovannara* exceptional honour in recognition of her vital role in the events of Italian unification, the *picciotti* of Calabria also sometimes hung around with strong women. A few women involved with the picciotteria in its early days directly participated in criminal actions. Female names leap out now and again from among the defendants listed in the trial documents. There were two 'Lasses with Attitude' found guilty in Palmi in 1892, for example: Concetta Muzzopapa, age 40, and Rosaria Testa, age 26.

Both were from Rosarno, at the opposite end of the Plain of Gioia Tauro from Palmi. Both had taken the oath to become members of the Calabrian mafia 'by making blood come out of the little finger of their right hand as they promised to maintain secrecy', the judges explained. Both also dressed up in men's clothing to take part in robberies and violent attacks. Rosaria Testa confessed her part in the organisation, and told prosecutors many of its secrets before she retracted after being threatened by the male members of the gang.

There were other oathed women too, such as in the King of Aspromonte's home town of Santo Stefano: investigations into the picciotteria during the brigand Musolino's rampage found that 12 of the 166 initiated members were women; they included Musolino's lover, Angela Surace, and his three sisters, Ippolita, Vincenza and Anna (who, it is worth recalling, were also the boss's daughters). 'Safe in the criminal association's moral and material support', the police wrote, 'women from the members' families are also able to issue threats and impose their will'. The oldest of the Musolino sisters, Ippolita, was particularly feared and it seems that she even advised her brother on who his targets should be. These are all fascinating cases, and we would know a lot more about the early 'ndrangheta if we had more documents on which to base a study of them. There is nothing quite like these Calabrian *mafiose* in the history of the other criminal organisations.

Some of the Calabrian hoodlums that came to trial in the 1920s and 1930s still displayed the same taste in women as the *picciotti* of the 1880s and 1890s. Like Domenico Noto, the flying boss of Antonimina: his gang pimped, forced whores to take part in robberies and regularly held meetings and parties in a hooker's house. But Noto was not content with 'wandering Venuses' (in the judge's delicate phrase). He arm-twisted his way into other beds, including those of an emigrant's wife, her fourteen-year-old daughter, and a vulnerable deaf-mute girl. But it was hard to keep the criminal brotherhood's secrets when you carried on like this. In court, the emigrant's wife gave crucial evidence against Domenico Noto and more than forty of his comrades. Other Calabrian mafia cells were undone on the say-so of streetwalkers. The habit of making money from prostitution, like the technique of browbeating young boys into being initiated, was a structural weakness in the picciotteria: both were bound to generate witnesses for the prosecution.

But elsewhere during the Fascist era there are clear signs of change in women's role. There are fewer prostitutes, and the gun-toting girl gangsters disappear. Instead, a cannier brand of gender politics begins to emerge. And with it, a new type of Calabrian mafia woman. Not a harlot. Or a cross-dressing brigandess. Instead a mother and wife whose nurturing energies are single-mindedly bent to building the honour of her menfolk, young and old.

It is often assumed that the 'ndrangheta's heavy reliance on family bonds grows from the culture of 'familism' in Calabrian society. The available evidence suggests this is wrong. The 'ndrangheta had to *learn* to base itself on kinship ties. The apparently traditional function of 'ndrangheta women – as the cult of honour's domestic priestesses – is actually a modern invention.

But even when this new model *mafiosa* first appears in the trial records during Fascism, she could wield real power and influence behind the scenes of picciotteria life. Maria Marvelli was one such woman. She was, to use a judge's words once again, a 'clever, forceful and wary woman', one well used to the ways of the Honoured Society. Not even these qualities stopped her husband meeting his gory end. But they did allow her to have her revenge. The following story comes from beneath Fascism's media blackout, and it draws heavily on Maria Marvelli's own evidence to dramatise the role women were playing in the evolution of the picciotteria. As it happens, Maria Marvelli's story also exposes the most savage face of Fascism's countermeasures.

Just south west of Antonimina, home of the flying boss, lies Cirella, yet another tiny settlement clinging to the flanks of

Aspromonte. Cirella was isolated in an inhospitable terrain; without roads fit for wheels, it was a village prey to the forces of nature and all but ignored by the forces of order.

The men of Cirella's Honoured Society did all of the things that might be expected of them: they robbed, vandalised, raped, mutilated and murdered. But they were also developing softer forms of power. Remarkably, they had elbowed the local priest aside: crooks, and not the cleric, ran Cirella's religious festivals. Anyone who wanted to do business with the local *picciotti* or marry one of their womenfolk had to join their ranks as a precondition.

Paolo Agostino was among the most influential men in Cirella's Honoured Society. Even among their number his ferocity stood out, as a judge would later note.

> He was one of those men who combines a robust and vigorous body with an audacious mind, a rare propensity for bullying, a strong tendency to commit all kinds of abuses, and the courage needed to make all these qualities count.

Paolo Agostino also had another quality that the judge did not identify, a quality that was becoming increasingly important for successful Calabrian bosses: he had a sharp eye for a smart woman. Those who went through the mafia initiation ritual in Cirella, as elsewhere in Calabria, had to swear to 'renounce family affections, putting the interests of the Society before their parents, siblings and children'. But Calabrian gangsters were also beginning to learn that families have advantages. Paolo Agostino made a particularly good choice of wife: the 'clever, forceful and wary' Maria Marvelli.

La Marvelli had been married before; she was a widow. (Like most Italian women then as now, she kept her maiden name.) Her son from her first marriage, Francesco Polito, joined her as part of the new family she made with the 'robust and vigorous'

Paolo Agostino. If the judge is to be believed, the marriage was not an equal one, at least within the walls of the Agostino home. Maria apparently 'exercised a commanding authority over her husband and son. And she was obeyed without debate.' Paolo Agostino's return on the union was a new heir, and a wealthy one too: Maria's son, Francesco Polito, had already inherited property worth one hundred thousand *Lire* from his late father.

The marriage seems to have been happy, and Maria had more children. Moreover her older boy, Francesco Polito, was initiated into the Honoured Society when he came of age, as befitted the stepson of a senior gangster. However his mother, smart and suspicious woman that she was, would not allow him to handle any money. So he had to steal twenty-four bottles of olive oil from his grandfather by way of a membership fee.

Francesco Polito, with his money and his powerful stepfather, was clearly a catch in the mafia marriage market. Before long, no less a felon than the boss of the Honoured Society in Cirella offered young Francesco his daughter's hand, along with a promotion from *picciotto* to *camorrista*. A marriage to the *capo*'s daughter and a promotion seemed like a very respectable offer. But young Francesco's stepfather, Paolo Agostino, put a stop to the alliance. It is not clear why, or whether Maria Marvelli had anything to do with the decision. The best guess is that he preferred to bind himself to another criminal lineage. But refusing such an offer would inevitably seem like a snub. If there were no divisions within the ranks of the Cirella Honoured Society before, they certainly appeared now.

At this point in the story, Mussolini intervened. The dire state of public order in Cirella came to the attention of the authorities in 1933. The local boss – and everyone knew he was the boss, for what need would he have had to be coy about his power? – was sent to enforced residence. His destination was the tiny island penal colony of Ustica, which lies some 80 kilometres north of Palermo. But as so often, this measure proved inadequate to stem the tide of violence. So the following year Paolo Agostino was also sent to Ustica to join his *capo* – the very man whose generous offer of a marriage alliance he had spurned. Rumours filtered back to Cirella that when the two had met, Paolo Agostino had smashed a bottle over the boss's head. Although the rumours were probably false, they were also a very real symptom of a potentially explosive power struggle: the issue of who Maria Marvelli's son was going to marry was an open sore in Cirella.

Soon other rumours began to fly in the opposite direction, from Cirella to the penal colony on Ustica, and this time sex was what generated the gossip. Before departing for Ustica, 'robust and vigorous' Paolo Agostino left his affairs in the hands of a trusted deputy, Nicola Pollifroni. Pollifroni very soon became very close to Agostino's wife, Maria Marvelli – close enough to set off some wry smiles: they were seen riding the same horse and he was seen sitting on her lap. The judge, rather primly, would later say that the gossip was 'not without plausibility'. When these reports reached Paolo Agostino on Ustica, he made his own inquiries as to how plausible they really were. Strangely, he was told by two separate witnesses, including his own brother, that nothing was wrong. Even more strangely, he believed them.

Paolo Agostino's relaxed attitude to his wife's infidelity contradicts all the stereotypes about the southern Italian male's violent possessiveness. It also transgresses the behavioural norms among gangsters. The picciotteria had already shown that mere rumours about marital infidelity could easily send a *mafioso* to a gruesome death. Yet in this case, Paolo Agostino was prepared to discount the rumours even when everyone else saw they were at the very least 'plausible'. One explanation of this failure to defend his own reputation is that Agostino realised that, as both a husband and a criminal, Maria Marvelli was just too valuable to him. With the tensions building within the *'ndrina*, he needed to keep his family compact, and had no choice but to overlook the affair. Mafia rules of honour, as always, were elastic.

While Paolo Agostino and his boss were in the penal colony on Ustica – the one pondering the subject of his wife's fidelity, and the other dwelling on how the offer of his daughter's hand had been rejected – back in Cirella the political terrain within the Honoured Society shifted. Three brothers, Bruno, Rocco and Francescantonio Romeo emerged as the new centre of power. The Romeo brothers decided they needed to hide their newly acquired authority behind a figurehead leader. So they began the search for a new boss, a dummy don who would not attract attention to himself, who would not be very *visible*, as the Romeo brothers stipulated.

Now, *visibility* is one of the great themes in the history of Italian organised crime. Absolute invisibility, absolute anonymity, is not an option for *mafiosi*, whose aim is to control their territory. However they do it, they have to let the local people know that it is *they* who must be feared, *they* who must be paid. But there are a thousand ways to carve out a profile, to cultivate respect. A gangster, like some colourful territorial animal, can save a lot of energy by being easy to identify: potential rivals quickly learn to spot the danger signs, and learn that flight rather than fight is the wisest reaction. So early *camorristi* advertised their power with quiffs, bell-bottom trousers, and tattoos. As did their cousins in the Calabrian picciotteria. But of course visibility brings risks – especially when the police are in the mood to repress the mafia rather than cohabit with it. It is one thing to flash your criminal rank and battle honours in a dungeon, where everyone is a felon, or in the police no-go areas of Naples' low city, or in some godforsaken Calabrian hill village. It is quite another to do so when the eyes of the *Carabinieri* are upon you, or when you want to pass through Ellis Island, or when your dealings with politicians and entrepreneurs demand a less showy façade. The 'middle-class villains' of Sicily have always tended to intimate their authority with little more than a stare, a stance or a stony silence. The other criminal associations, whose origins were humbler, took a while to master the visibility game's subtler stratagems. The learning process was already well under way by the dawn of the Fascist era. In Naples, the silly clothes and butterfly quiffs were gone by the time of the Cuocolo trial. The Calabria mafia abandoned them not long afterwards: there is little sign of them in the Fascist era.

Faced with more unwelcome police attention than they had ever known, the Romeo brothers looked for a new and less visible patsy, one without a criminal record whose wealth put him beyond suspicion. Their chosen candidate, a young man called Francesco Macrì, accepted without hesitation, despite not having even been a member of the gang before, and despite being rich enough to provide lawyers for his new co-conspirators. The judge later said that Macrì regarded being nominated boss as a 'special honour'. It is a telling testament to the prestige that this criminal association had now acquired that Macrì took on the job of *capo* so readily. As the judge explained, 'entry into the association was an essential condition if you wanted to win public esteem'. The picciotteria, less visible than it once had been, but more poisonous, was now seeping further still into the bloodstream of Calabrian life. The Romeo brothers formed a committee to 'advise' the enthusiastic but inexperienced appointee, while retaining the real power for themselves. And with that arrangement, the politics of organised crime in Cirella reached a new equilibrium.

Meanwhile, criminal business carried on as usual. And as usual, even the simplest criminal business could have lethal consequences. The local doctor had had a valuable yearling bull stolen a while earlier and he was still making strenuous and unsuccessful efforts to find out who had taken it. Eventually he approached Maria Marvelli, asking her to ask her exiled husband Paolo Agostino (a relative of the doctor's) to make inquiries among the inmates on Ustica. Prison, as ever, was the great junction box of mafia communications.

A letter soon came back from Ustica: Paolo Agostino wrote that the thieves were Bruno, Rocco, and Francescantonio Romeo – the men behind the 'invisible boss' who were now the most influential *picciotti* in Cirella.

Naively, the doctor passed Paolo Agostino's letter on to the

Carabinieri. Someone from inside the *Carabinieri* – whether a spy or an agent provocateur – told the three Romeo brothers that Paolo Agostino had tried to get them into trouble. Even before this tip-off arrived, the Romeos knew that Agostino would pose a threat to them once he was released from Ustica. So they swiftly issued a warning by burning down Maria Marvelli's house and stealing thirty of her goats.

As Agostino's return from Ustica neared, the Romeo brothers began to plan for more drastic action to defend their position. They tabled a motion with the Honoured Society to kill Maria Marvelli's husband; in support of it, they cited the impeccable legal logic that he had broken the code of *omertà* by telling the doctor who had stolen the yearling bull.

After two years away, Paolo Agostino finally arrived home on 2 March 1936. He was immediately summoned to a meeting of the Honoured Society: how could he justify his breach of the rules? His self-defence was a desperate show of chutzpah. He said that he no longer feared anyone in Cirella, because on Ustica he had found 'new and more powerful friendships by joining a mighty association that was represented there'.

What was this 'mighty association' on Ustica? A bluff? Or was Paolo Agostino hinting that he had become a member of the Sicilian mafia since last he saw Aspromonte? Ustica was more than usually full of Sicilian *mafiosi* at the time. Whether Agostino was bluffing or not, the Romeo brothers became even more determined to eliminate him. When Paolo Agostino flagrantly insulted the Honoured Society's protocols by failing to turn up for a second hearing into his case, the Romeos got their motion through, and a death sentence against Agostino was passed. The problem now for the Romeo brothers became a practical rather than a political one: how to carry out the hit – a task that would require both a carefully prepared trap and a narrative to bait it.

While waiting for their opportunity, the Romeo brothers had to content themselves with insults. They broke Paolo Agostino's gramophone at a gangland celebration to mark the engagement of his stepson, Francesco Polito. (After turning down the boss's daughter, Maria Marvelli's boy had finally found a suitable girl from a suitably delinquent family.) Only the presence of so many witnesses stopped the gramophone incident degenerating into a bloodbath.

If Paolo Agostino did not realise before that his time was running out, he certainly realised now. He became gloomy. Among friends he referred to himself wistfully as 'a bird just passing through life'. He refused to thrash his children, saying that he did not want to leave them with bad memories of him. His despondency was apparent to Maria Marvelli, who took charge of security at home, forcing her husband to sleep elsewhere when danger threatened.

The first attempt on Agostino's life involved the staged theft of his ox. The Romeo brothers sent men to steal the animal, making plenty of noise as they did, in the hope that Agostino would rush out of his house. If all went well, he could then be shot down, as if by anonymous robbers. But in the event it was the redoubtable Maria Marvelli who came out of the house, gun in hand, and chased off the would-be assassins.

A far more rigorously conceived plot would be needed to do away with Paolo Agostino. The Romeo brothers called a meeting of senior *mafiosi* in an abandoned shack on 30 April 1936. After much discussion their plan was agreed and a ten-man firing party picked to execute it. The dummy don, Francesco Macrì, volunteered to stand shoulder-to-shoulder with the Romeo brothers in the upcoming action; evidently he wanted to earn the lofty rank that he had so recently been given. But the crucial figure in the scheme, the man set up to betray Paolo Agostino to his enemies, was to be Nicola Pollifroni – the man who had a 'plausible' affair with Maria Marvelli. Pollifroni was made to kneel before his brethren, with his arms crossed flat on his chest, and swear to help kill his friend.

On 2 May Pollifroni invited Paolo Agostino along on an

expedition to raid some beehives, thereby insulting their owner with whom Pollifroni had an old beef. No member of the Honoured Society could refuse such an invitation. The raid was a success, and Pollifroni and Agostino returned along an isolated path, carrying pots of fragrant honey. The route took them through a narrow pass between two giant boulders covered in gorse. The judge would subsequently explain that the path reminded him of the ever-narrowing gulleys in an abattoir floor that isolate a single pig, forcing it to walk between two walls until it can no longer turn round or go back. By the time the butcher's knife comes into view, there is no longer any escape. The pass had a name locally: Agonia ('Agony').

Just as the two honey thieves were entering the pass, Pollifroni stopped. He had to take a pee. Agostino should walk on ahead, into the narrow walls of the pass.

The last thing Agostino ever heard came from somewhere on the boulder above him: a strangled cry of warning, both sudden and familiar. Agostino's stepson Francesco Polito was being forced to watch the murder, a dagger pressed to his throat. He had the courage and desperation to cry out a warning before a large hand was clamped over his mouth, and a shotgun chorus drowned out all other sound.

What gives an undeniably Fascist flavour to the story of the Cirella mafia was what happened to the Romeo brothers, the dummy don Francesco Macrì, and the others once they were arrested. Under interrogation, as their blood oaths dictated, they denied any knowledge of the criminal association they belonged to. So they were punched and whipped and beaten with anything that came to hand, like a heavy ruler and a blotter. They were forced to drink a clay pot full of piss. To muffle their screams, their own socks were stuffed in their mouths and secured with their own belts. Then they were pushed to the floor, and their legs chained up on chairs so that the soles of their feet could be beaten and their toenails pulled out. (Later, some would have amputations as a result.) Their wounds were doused in salt and vinegar. The most uncooperative among them were electrocuted: wires attached to a car battery were applied to their inner thighs, leaving them barely conscious. They were then hurled into damp, filthy cells in Locri jail with no food or water. All requests for medical visits were denied.

One by one, they confessed. Every time they were called on to confirm their confessions, the beatings began again. The men of Cirella's Honoured Society had found their own place called Agony.

Only in court could the allegation of police violence finally emerge. When the judge heard of the horrors he treated them as just that: mere allegation. Somehow, he deemed it no job of his to weigh up whether what the defendants alleged was true. Not even, it seems, by checking on their amputated toes. But the sheer detail of the judge's description, and the squirming of his logic, tell us he knew what had really happened: the accused before him had been brutally tortured by the *Carabinieri*.

Of course the judge had plenty of other evidence to draw on: the testimonies of Maria Marvelli and her son Francesco Polito; the suspects' utterly unconvincing alibis; and the jumble of patently false testimonies, mostly from their womenfolk, that the *mafiosi* had marshalled in their defence. The prosecution could also point out that the dummy don Francesco Macrì kept a list of the Honoured Society's members in a suitcase, and wrote down the names of the ten men chosen to kill Paolo Agostino.

The judge concluded that all of the evidence confirmed the confessions, 'without any regard to the way in which the suspects' initial statements were gathered'. So he felt able to 'put his conscience to rest', and take no further action about a blindingly clear case of police brutality. Torture or no torture, the verdict against the Lads with Attitude in Cirella was guilty.

Everything within the state. Nothing against the state. Nothing outside the state. Fascism's totalitarian ideology clearly gave the cops a licence to go far beyond any acceptable means of interrogation. No doubt the torture used here was also deployed elsewhere against *mafiosi* and *camorristi*. But it is rare to find such graphic and unambiguous evidence of it as there is in the trial papers from Cirella. More often, false claims about police brutality were made by mobsters. Fascism's battle with organised crime could be a very dirty fight indeed, but quite how frequently the authorities really abused their power is anyone's guess.

Maria Marvelli's story is but an isolated tableau of the piece-meal changes happening in Calabrian organised crime: the marriage politics that the *picciotti* were learning, and the new power behind the scenes that some women gained as a result. Marvelli was, without doubt, a loser: her house had been torched; her husband murdered. She lost her son too: despite his confession, the boy who had once been the most eligible criminal batchelor in Cirella was sentenced to six years and eight months under new, tougher Fascist laws against criminal associations. It is not known whether he was among the men who had their toenails extracted by the *Carabinieri*; it is not known what happened to him in prison.

But Maria Marvelli did at least have something to put in the scales to counterbalance her losses. The satisfaction of vendetta, for one thing. And even some money: she sued the defendants on her children's behalf, and won 26,000 *Lire* – roughly equal to the value of her house.

We do not know what happened to Maria Marvelli later. She is like thousands of other faceless mafia women in history, in that we can only wonder what became of her after the court records fall silent. If she did go back to Cirella, she would certainly have found a village still in the grip of the picciotteria. The same judge who was too timid to confront the *Carabinieri* about their repeated assaults on the prisoners was also too timid to pass a harsh verdict on the mafia: he acquitted 104 of the *picciotti* whose names appeared on the dummy don's list, on the less than convincing grounds that 'public rumour' was the only evidence against them. What this amounted to saying was that everyone in Cirella had seen these men strutting around the square; everyone knew at the very least that they were in cahoots and up to no good. They were visible, in other words. But even under Fascism, visibility alone was not enough to convict.

Campania: **The Fascist Vito Genovese**

On 8 July 1938 the Neapolitan daily *Il Mattino* published the following short notice.

> FASCIST NEWSBOARD
>
> The Fascist Vito Genovese, enlisted in the New York branch of the Fascist Party and currently resident in Naples, has donated 10,000 *Lire*. The Roccarainola branch received 5,000 *Lire* as a contribution to the cost of the land required to build the local party headquarters. The other 5,000 *Lire* is for building Nola's Heliotherapy Centre.

Vito Genovese would later reportedly subsidise the building of Nola's Fascist party HQ to the tune of $25,000. Visitors to Nola – and there are not many – can still see the building in piazza Giordano Bruno: a white block, long since stripped of its Mussolinian badges, it houses a local branch of the University of Naples, the Faculty of Law in fact.

Genovese was born in Risigliano, near Nola, on 21 November 1897. We do not know whether his family had any connections with the Campanian underworld before they emigrated to the United States in 1912. Nonetheless, New York offered bounteous opportunities for violent young immigrants. Vito rose rapidly through the ranks of gangland, alongside his friend, the Sicilian-born Charles 'Lucky' Luciano. A now famous mugshot of Genovese from this period shows a bug-eyed enforcer with a skewed crest of black hair.

In 1936, Lucky Luciano received a thirty-to-fifty year sentence on compulsory prostitution charges. (Which of course he would have avoided had he followed the conventions in force in the mafia's homeland.) Vito Genovese was scheduled to take over from Luciano at the apex of the New York mafia, an organisation still dominated by Sicilians. But he was also afraid that a pending murder charge might result in comparably harsh treatment. So in 1937 he fled to a gilded exile in the land of his birth.

In Italy, Vito Genovese's generosity, like his Fascism, were self-interested. Strong rumours suggest that he was busy shipping narcotics back to the United States. With the profits, Genovese made his contribution to the Fascist architectural legacy in Campania and lavishly entertained both Mussolini and Count Galeazzo Ciano, the Duce's son-in-law and Foreign Minister. It is only logical to assume that Genovese had excellent top-level contacts in Nola too.

Evidently, in Campania Fascism lacked the integrity and the attention span needed to follow up on Major Anceschi's recommendations following his operations in the Mazzoni in 1926–28. One way or another, in Campania Fascism lapsed from the crusading zeal of the Ascension Day speech into a quiet political accommodation with gangsters. As later events would prove, Vito Genovese was now part of a flourishing criminal landscape.

Sicily: **The slimy octopus**

We have known for a long time that Cesare Mori's boast that he had beaten the mafia would turn out hollow, and that the Mori Operation was a failure in the long-term. After all, once Fascism fell and democracy was restored, Sicily's notorious criminal fraternity began a new phase of its history that would prove more arrogant and bloodthirsty than any yet seen. A great deal of energy has been devoted to dishing out responsibility for the mafia's revival after the Second World War. Conspiracy theorists said it was all the Americans' fault: the mafia returned with the Allied invasion in 1943. Pessimists put the blame on Italian democracy: without a dictator in charge, the country was just not capable of staging a thoroughgoing repression of organised crime.

Whoever was to blame for the subsequent revival in the mafia's fortunes, most memories of the campaign to eradicate it were more or less in tune with Fascism's own trumpet calls. Even some *mafiosi* recalled the alarums of the late 1920s with a shudder. One Man of Honour, despite being too young to remember the Mori Operation, said in 1986 that

> The music changed [under Fascism]. Mafiosi had a hard life . . . After the war the mafia hardly existed any more. The Sicilian Families had all been broken up. The mafia was like a plant they don't grow any more.

So, until recently, the historical memory of the Iron Prefect's titanic campaign of repression in Sicily was fundamentally united: even if the mafia had not been destroyed, it had at least bowed its head before the thudding might of the Fascist state.

Until recently. Until 2007, that is, when Italy's leading historian of the mafia unearthed a startling report that had lain forgotten in the Palermo State Archive. Because of that report – many hundreds of pages long if one includes its 228 appendices – the story of Fascism's 'last struggle' with the mafia must now be completely rewritten. Some of the best young historians in Sicily are busy rewriting it. The Mori Operation, it turns out, involved the most elaborate lie in the history of organised crime.

The report dates from July 1938, and it addresses the state of law and order in Sicily since the last big mafia trial concluded late in 1932. It had no less than forty-eight authors, all of them members of a special combined force of *Carabinieri* and policemen known by the unwieldy title of the Royal General Inspectorate for Public Security for Sicily – the Inspectorate, for short. And the majority of its members were Sicilians, to judge by their surnames.

The report begins as follows.

> Despite repeated waves of vigorous measures taken by the police and judiciary [during the Mori Operation], the criminal organisation known in Sicily and elsewhere by the vague name of 'mafia' has endured; it has never really ceased to exist. All that happened is that there were a few pauses, creating the impression that everything was calm . . . It was believed – and people who were in bad faith endeavoured to make everyone believe – that the mafia had been totally eradicated. But all of that was nothing more than a cunning and sophisticated manoeuvre designed by the mafia's many managers – the ones who had succeeded in escaping or remaining above suspicion during the repression. Their main aim was to deceive the authorities and soften up so-called public opinion so that they could operate with ever greater freedom and perversity.

The mafia had sold Fascism an extravagant dummy, the Inspectorate claimed. Some bosses had used the very force and propagandistic *éclat* of the Mori Operation to make believe that they had gone away. The mafia had its own propaganda agenda – to appear beaten – and its message was broadcast by the Fascist regime's obliging megaphones. The Palermo *capi* may just as well have ghostwritten Cesare Mori's *The Last Struggle with the Mafia*.

The story of the 1938 report dates back to 1933, well within a year of the last Mori trial, when there was a crime wave so overwhelming as to make it obvious that the police structures put in place by the Iron Prefect were no longer fit for purpose. The police and *Carabinieri* were reorganised into an elite force to combat it: the Royal General Inspectorate for Public Security for Sicily. Thus the Facist state started the struggle with the mafia all over again. Only this time the national and international public that had lapped up reports of the Iron Prefect's heroics were not allowed to know anything about what was going on.

The men of the Inspectorate picked up again where Mori's police had left off in 1929. As they did, they slowly assembled proof that the mafia across western Sicily was more organised than anyone except perhaps Chief of Police Ermanno Sangiorgi would ever have dared imagine: the 'slimy octopus', they called it.

The chosen starting point was the province of Trapani, at the island's western tip, where the Mori Operation had made least impact and where criminal disorder was now at its worst: here the mafia 'reigned with all of its members in place', the Inspectorate found. When they arrested large numbers of Trapani *mafiosi*, the bosses still at liberty held a provincial meeting to decide on their tactical response. A letter was sent urging everyone in the organisation to keep violence to a minimum until this new wave of repression had crested and broken.

The Inspectorate's next round of investigations discovered a mafia livestock-smuggling network, 300 strong, that extended across the whole of the west of the island; *mafiosi* referred to it as the *Abigeataria* – something like 'The Cattle Rustling Department'. As they always had done, Sicilian *mafiosi* worked together to steal animals in one place and move them to market far away.

Then came the southern province of Agrigento. The Inspectorate's investigations into an armed attack on a motor coach gradually revealed that the mafia had a formal structure here too. *Mafiosi* interrogated by the Inspectorate used the term 'Families' for the structure's local cells. The Families often coordinated their activities. For example, the men who attacked the motor coach came from three different Families; they had never met one another before their bosses ordered them to participate in the raid, but they nonetheless carried it out in harmony. Even more alarmingly, the Inspectorate discovered that, just as the Mori Operation trials were coming to their conclusion in 1932, bosses in Agrigento received a circular letter from Palermo telling them 'to close ranks, and get ready for the resumption of large-scale crimes'.

Among the most revealing testimonies gathered by the Inspectorate was that of Dr Melchiorre Allegra, a GP, radiographer and lung specialist who ran a clinic in Castelvetrano, in the province of Trapani. Allegra was arrested in the summer of 1937, and dictated a dense twenty-six-page confession that shone the light of the Inspectorate's policework back into the past. Allegra was initiated in Palermo in 1916 so he could provide phoney medical certificates for Men of Honour who wanted to avoid serving in the First World War. The *mafiosi* who were formally presented to Dr Allegra as 'brothers' included men of all stations, from coach drivers, butchers and fishmongers, right up to Members of Parliament and landed aristocrats. After the Great War, the provincial and Family bosses would often come from across Sicily to meet in the Birreria Italia, a polished café, pastry shop and bar situated at the junction of via Cavour and via Maqueda, in the very centre of Palermo. For a few years, until the Fascist police became suspicious, the Birreria Italia was the centre of the mafia world, a social club for the island's gangster elite.

The Inspectorate were well aware that the men Dr Allegra called brothers were in a permanent state of war among themselves, whether open or declared. The mafia was prone to 'internecine struggles deriving from grudges which, whether they were recent and remote, nearly always revolved around who was to gain supremacy when it came to distributing the various positions within the organisation'. An 'internecine struggle' of just this kind would give the Inspectorate its route into the mafia's very nucleus, the lemon groves of the Conca d'Oro around Palermo.

When the Iron Prefect first came to Palermo in October 1925, his attention was immediately drawn to the Piana dei Colli, the northern part of the Conca d'Oro where Inspector Ermanno Sangiorgi first tussled with the mafia in the 1870s. Half a century later, the Piana dei Colli was the site of a particularly ferocious battle between two mafia factions. The conflict left cadavers in the streets of central Palermo, many of them belonging to senior bosses. Some of the mafia dynasties that had ruled the area since the 1860s did not survive the carnage. Those that did, and who didn't manage to escape to America, Tunisia or London, were rounded up by the Iron Prefect's cops. Then Mori left, and calm returned.

The Inspectorate discovered that the *mafiosi* from the Piana dei Colli who had been released, or returned from exile after the Mori Operation ended, could not reorganise their Families because of the residual tensions between them. The tit for tat killings resumed. In 1934, a boss named Rosario Napoli was slain; the culprits tried to frame Napoli's own nephew for the murder. This nephew was the first Palermitan *mafioso* to give information to the Inspectorate. His testimony slowly tipped into a cascade of confessions from other mobsters, some of whom described the initiation ritual they had undergone when they were first admitted. As so often, *omertà* had cracked. By bringing together these confessions, and patiently corroborating them, the Inspectorate then assembled a narrative of the war in the Conca d'Oro that shed an even more withering light on Mussolini's portentous Ascension Day claims.

The protagonists of this new narrative were the Marasà brothers, Francesco, Antonino, and above all Ernesto – the *generalissimo*, as the Inspectorate dubbed him. The Marasà brothers had their power base in the western section of the Conca d'Oro, between Monreale and Porta Nuova. That is, along the road travelled by Turi Miceli and his mafia squad when they launched the Palermo revolt back in September 1866. Like Turi Miceli, the Marasà brothers had money. In fact the Inspectorate estimated that they owned property, livestock and other assets worth 'quite a few million *Lire*'. One million *Lire* was worth some $52,000 at the time, and that amount in 1938 had the purchasing power of some $1.7 million today: so it is fair to conclude that the Marasàs were very rich criminals indeed.

What the men of the Inspectorate found most disturbing about the Marasà brothers was their ability to collect friendships among the island's ruling class, to place themselves above suspicion, to cloak the power they had won through violence, and to cover the bloody tracks that traced their ascent.

By poisoning the political system under the pre-Fascist governments, they carried out their shady criminal business on the agricultural estates, in the lemon groves, in the city, in the suburban townships, in the villages. They always managed to stay hidden in the shadows cast by baronial and princely coats of arms, by medals and titles. Thanks to the shameful complaisance shown by men who are supposed to be responsible for the fair and efficient administration of the law, they always slipped away from punishment. But behind the politician's mask, behind the honorific title, behind the all-pervasive hypocrisy and the imposing wealth, there lurked the coarsest kind of criminal, with evil, grasping instincts, whose warlike early years in the ranks of the underworld have left an indelible mark of infamy.

It is a testament to the Marasà brothers' success in shrouding their 'indelible mark of infamy' that, until the discovery of the Inspectorate's report in 2007, their names had hardly been mentioned in the chronicles of mafia history. No photographs, no police descriptions, hardly even any rumours: a criminal power all the more pervasive for being unseen and unnamed.

In the late 1920s, while the bosses of the Piana dei Colli were busy ambushing one another, and then falling victim to the Mori Operation, Ernesto Marasà and his brothers remained entirely untouched. Indeed, *generalissimo* Ernesto showed a breathtaking Machiavellian composure in the face of the Fascist onslaught: he actually fed incriminating information about his mafia rivals to the Iron Prefect's investigators. Mussolini's Fascist scalpel had been partially guided by a *mafioso*'s hand.

Ernesto Marasà's rise to power continued after the Mori Operation ended. While his enemies were held in jail, seething about being betrayed, Marasà constructed an alliance of supporters across the mafia Families of Palermo's entire hinterland, including the Piana dei Colli where he continued to undermine his enemies by passing information to the police. His plan was, quite simply, to become the mafia's boss of all bosses. The Inspectorate spied on the *generalissimo* as he ran his campaign from room 2 of the Hotel Vittoria just off via Maqueda, Palermo's main artery. Now and again, he and two or three of his heavies would clamber aboard a little red FIAT *Balilla* and set off to meet friends and arrange hits in one of Palermo's many mafia-dominated *borgate*.

After five years of work, the Inspectorate could conclude its 1938 report with a chillingly clear description of the mafia's structure that reads like a line-by-line demolition of the Iron Prefect's own views.

The mafia is not just a state of mind or a mental habit. It actually spreads this state of mind, this mental habit, from within what is a genuine organisation. It is divided into so-called 'Families', which are sub-divided into 'Tens', and it has 'bosses' or 'representatives' who are formally elected. The members, or 'brothers', have to go through an oath to prove their unquestioning fidelity and secretiveness.

The oath, no one will be surprised to learn, involved pricking the finger with a pin, dripping blood on a sacred image, and then burning the image in the hands while swearing loyalty until death.

The mafia was organised 'in the form of a sect, along the lines of the Freemasons'. Its Families in each province had an overall 'representative' whose responsibilities included contacts with the organisation's branches abroad, in the United States, France and Tunisia. The Families in the provinces of Trapani, Agrigento and Caltanissetta looked to Palermo for leadership at crucial times. The mafia, declared the Inspectorate, 'had an organic and harmonious structure, regulated by clearly defined norms, and managed by people who were utterly beyond suspicion'. At the centre of the mafia web, there was a 'boss of all bosses' or 'general president': *generalissimo* Ernesto Marasà.

The Inspectorate's 1938 report was sent in multiple copies to senior figures in the judiciary and law enforcement. The forty-eight brave men who put their names to the document were desperate for their sleuthing to make a real difference in Sicily. Their desperation was evident in an indignant, impassioned turn of phrase: in the lurid talk of a 'slimy octopus' (as if a beast as sophisticated as the mafia could ever have just one head); and also in the conclusion, which deliberately parroted the catch-phrases of Mussolini's Ascension Day speech. Somewhere, they hoped, their plea would meet the eyes of someone determined to make Fascism's results match up to its battle cries: there must be 'no holding back' against an evil that was 'dishonouring Sicily'; the state must once again wield the 'scalpel' against the mafia.

The passion and insight that went into the Inspectorate's 1938 report makes its every word chilling, for two reasons. First, because it provides the earliest absolutely indisputable evidence that the Sicilian mafia was a single highly structured organisation that extended right across western Sicily. Terms like 'Family', 'representative', and 'boss of all bosses' had never appeared before in the historical record. Second, because many years would pass, and the lives of many brave police, *Carabinieri* and magistrates would be sacrificed, before the moment in 1992 when a diagram of the Sicilian mafia that was *identical* to the one assembled by the Inspectorate would finally be accepted as the truth within the Italian legal system.

But in 1938 there was not the slightest hope that the Fascist state would return to a war footing against organised crime. In fact the signs that Fascism would fail to beat the mafia were there to be seen all along. In the Iron Prefect's refusal to believe that his enemy was an Honoured Society, for example. Or in his crass view of Sicilian psychology. Or in Fascism's preference for bundling suspects off into enforced residence on penal colonies: no noise, and no judicial process. For, as anyone with a historical memory for anti-mafia measures would have known, fighting organised crime in this way was like fighting weeds in your garden by transplanting them into your greenhouse.

The Mori Operation was only ever going to be a short-term measure. The aim was to draw a decisive line between the new regime and the corrupt democratic past; it was to show that Fascism was still vigorous even though the cudgels and the castor oil had been cast to one side. Fascist 'surgery' on Sicily was never intended to prepare the patient for a life of law and order. It was about putting on a propagandistic spectacle; it was about winning for Mussolini the support of the island's landed elite – the very aristocrats whose 'baronial and princely coats of arms' had shielded the Marasà brothers, like so many other *mafiosi* before them.

The Iron Prefect, the orphan boy from Pavia, was besotted with the sumptuous decadence of Palermo's *beau monde*. When

Mori socialised in the Sicilian capital, he went out in a luxurious carriage, its lustrous black bodywork bristling with gilt, intaglio, and all manner of baroque ornamentation. He was 'on heat for the nobility' – to use an enemy's crude phrase – as he swished from ball to ball, from salon to salon. The Iron Prefect believed, or chose to believe, that the landowners he played *baccarà* with were exactly what their lawyers had always said they were when, from time to time, their underworld connections were exposed: they were *victims* of the thugs, and not their strategic protectors.

The charges against the 'slimy octopus' that were meticulously assembled in the Inspectorate's 1938 report took until 1942 to come to court. By that time the Men of Honour who had told their secrets to the Inspectorate had retracted their confessions. Before the trial most of the *mafiosi* named in the 1938 report were released for lack of evidence – including the *generalissimo* Ernesto Marasà, with his brothers. And in the trial itself, most of the fifty-three men who were eventually convicted received only short sentences. The case set out in the 1938 report had slowly crumbled until it became a comparatively minor inconvenience for the Sicilian mob. As Ermanno Sangiorgi could have told the men of the Inspectorate, many earlier anti-mafia cases had fallen apart in the same way. What was different in 1942 was that the Fascist regime, which was busy crowing about dazzling feats of bravura by the Italian army in the Second World War, completely suppressed all mention of the Inspectorate's report and the resultant court proceedings. Once again, Italy had proved just how resourceful it could be when it came to denying the truth about the Sicilian mafia.

Master Joe dances a *tarantella*

If there is a servant of the state who encapsulates all the contradictions of Fascism's long fight against the Honoured Society in Calabria, but also elsewhere, then perhaps it is Giuseppe Delfino.

Delfino was a homespun hero of law enforcement. In August 1926, just as Fascism was first cranking up its clampdown, he took command of the *Carabiniere* station in Platì, overlooking the Ionian Coast. This was the territory where Delfino was born and he knew it as well as anyone. Both the picciotteria citadel of San Luca and the Sanctuary of the Madonna of Polsi were on his beat. Cussed and smart, Delfino would disguise himself as a shepherd to patrol the mountain unobserved, or slip into taverns so he could overhear the *picciotti* as they bragged. Among the peasants he earned the respectful nickname *Massaru Peppi* ('Master Joe') – *massaru* being the word for a farm overseer or factor. Master Joe dismantled a cattle-rustling network centred on San Luca in January 1927, and thereby – despite the murder of his key witness – brought seventy-six *mafiosi* to justice. Among them were men called Strangio, Pelle and Nirta: perhaps not coincidentally, families with these surnames would much later be caught up in the blood feud that led to the massacre at Duisberg on 15 August 2007.

The Calabrian press, which was generally sparing in its coverage of the anti-organised crime campaign, said that Delfino had 'brought honour on himself'.

> Meanwhile this resourceful station commander has not even allowed himself a day's rest, and is pressing on with his pursuit of the lawbreakers.

Shortly after the rustlers he had arrested had their convictions confirmed on appeal, 'Master Joe' Delfino even earned himself a walk-on part in the canon of Italian literature. Corrado Alvaro, the San Luca-born author who was our witness to the pilgrimage to the Sanctuary at Polsi, also wrote a vignette about Master Joe's relentless hunt for a small-time goat thief. Borrowing the peasants' own spare vocabulary, Alvaro evoked the holy terror that Delfino inspired on Aspromonte throughout Fascism's twenty-year rule.

> Delfino was the *Carabiniere* who couldn't hear a robber's name mentioned without setting off in pursuit as if he'd staked money on it . . . with his short cloak, his rifle, and his sparkly eyes, he rummaged everywhere: he knew all the hiding places, he knew every renegade's habits like he knew his own pocket – the hollow trunks, the grottoes that no one apart from the mountain folk could find, the perches high in ancient trees.

As publicity goes, this may not seem much. Indeed, compared to the Iron Prefect, the inveterate blowhard whose battle with the mafia in Sicily received glowing worldwide press, Master Joe's profile was positively meek. But the odd line in local newspapers and the hushed respect of the peasants amounted to about as much fame as anyone could possibly hope to accumulate by serving the law in far-off Calabria, even at the height of Fascism's short-lived enthusiasm for facing down the bosses.

Local legend and family memory are the only source we have to draw on to reconstruct much of Master Joe's long career on Aspromonte. But that memory, however much time may have embroidered it, gives us access to a truth that the newspapers and trial documents disguise. Even Master Joe's son, the current guardian of Delfino lore, portrays him as a man with very violent methods. This was a part of the world where there were two paths in life – 'Either you became a *Carabiniere*,

347

or you entered the 'ndrangheta' – and brutality lay along both of them.

The story goes that Master Joe once waited until Christmas for a runaway *picciotto* to return home, and did not swoop until his target had hunkered down over a plate of *maccheroni* with goat meat sauce. Master Joe then stood below the window, disguised as a shepherd, and played a wistful song on the bagpipes. The *picciotto* was so moved that he stopped eating and leaned out of the window to offer the minstrel a drink of wine, only to find a pistol pointed at his face. Recognising Master Joe, he said, 'Let me finish my *maccheroni*, at least'. The reply was blunt. 'That would be pointless, because back at the barracks we'd only make you vomit them all up again anyway'. Master Joe, it is said, was as good as his word: the thief spent a week on his back being punched and forced to drink salt water. When a doctor was finally allowed in, he saw the man's grotesquely swollen stomach, shook his head, and said, 'You don't need a GP here, you need an obstetrician'.

If this story sounds far-fetched then perhaps we should recall that Cirella, where the members of the picciotteria who killed Maria Marvelli's husband were tortured until they confessed, was also part of Master Joe's beat.

There is another family memory of Master Joe who shows us another side of his, and Fascism's, battle with the 'ndrangheta.

In the autumn of 1940 station commander 'Master Joe' Delfino was still on duty. With only one officer to help him maintain order during the annual pilgrimage to the Sanctuary of the Madonna of Polsi, it is said that he took a Chief Cudgel aside and made a deal so that there would be no trouble. If there were any murders decreed at Polsi that year, then they were performed at a polite distance in time and space from the Sanctuary. Indeed Delfino's son later recalled that, 'for all the years my father was in charge, nothing happened' at Polsi. The station commander would even join the celebrating crowds during the pilgrimage, taking his turn to dance a tarantella with the members of the

Honoured Society. The picture Delfino's son paints in our mind's eye is vivid. The sanctuary set amid the chestnut trees. The hectic trilling of a squeeze box. A circle of swarthy grins, some of them traversed by ghastly razorblade tracery. And there in the middle, the *Carabiniere*, kicking out the bold red stripes on his black uniform trousers.

Se non è vero, è molto ben trovato: if the picture isn't true, it's a very smart invention – one that historians should cherish. What official sources can scarcely ever record is just this kind of informal accord between the authorities and the mob. A cagey mutual respect. An improvised agreement to share power and territory. At Polsi, as in so many other parts of Sicily and southern Italy, after the roundups, and the beatings, and the trials, and the propagandistic speeches had passed, the Fascist state settled back into Italy's traditional dance with organised crime.

Liberation

The Second World War was the greatest collective tragedy ever endured by the Italian people. Between 1935 and 1942, Italian armies visited death and destruction on Ethiopia, Albania, France, Greece and Russia. In 1943, death and destruction came home to the peninsula with vengeful fury.

Italian territory was invaded for the first time on 10 July when seven Allied divisions launched a seaborne assault on Sicily. Up in Rome, in the early hours of 25 July, a meeting of the Fascist Grand Council voted to bring twenty years of Fascist rule to an end; Benito Mussolini was arrested the following evening. As news spread across the country, Italians tore down Fascist symbols; many people thought the war was over. But the catastrophe had only just begun.

On 17 August the last Axis troops completed their evacuation of Sicily. On 3 September the Allies crossed the Straits of Messina into Calabria, where they met only token resistance. On 8 September the Allied Supreme Commander, General Dwight D. Eisenhower, announced Italy's surrender. The very next day saw the beginning of Operation Avalanche – the landing at Salerno, just south of Naples. The Germans – no longer allies but invaders – rumbled down the peninsula to carry on their war. Italy's king fled. All semblance of his government's civil and military authority dissolved and the Italian people were left to find their own path to survival.

Naples was liberated on 1 October. But the Allied advance ground to a halt soon afterwards. For the next twenty months Italy was a battleground, as the *Reich* and the Allies slogged out a slow and bloody contest. Behind German lines in the north and centre, a civil war pitted recalcitrant Fascists against the Resistance. There were collective reprisals and atrocities, mass deportations of Italian workers and troops, and a campaign of racial extermination directed at Italy's Jews.

The south scarcely fared better under Allied Military Government in the Occupied Territories, known as AMGOT. In preparation for AMGOT, the War Office had drafted *Zone Handbooks* on the society and mores of Sicily, Calabria and Campania. Those *Handbooks* are revealing in two ways. First, they tell us what the world knew about organised crime after a century of history. Second, they allow us to measure how shocked the Allies were by the chaos that followed liberation and the rapid collapse of the Italian state. Score settling, hunger, contagion, corruption, black-marketeering and banditry: these were ideal conditions in which Italy's gangsters could shake off their Fascist-induced torpor.

War Office, London: Directorate of Civil Affairs.
Sicily Zone Handbook.
Secret.
The information contained herein is believed to be correct
as at May 1st, 1943.

*The head of the Palermo police has said that if a cross
were to be placed on every spot where a victim lies
buried in the plain of Palermo, the Conca d'Oro would
appear as a vast cemetery.*

*Mafia never was a compact criminal association, but
a complex social phenomenon, the consequence of
centuries of misgovernment. The Mafiuso is governed
by a sentiment akin to arrogance, which imposes a
special line of conduct upon him. A Mafiuso is thus
not a thief or a rascal in any simple sense. He desires*

351

> to be respected, and nearly always he respects others.
> *Mafia is the consciousness of one's individuality, the*
> *exaggerated conceit of one's strength.*
>
> All Italian governments have been anxious to
> *suppress this scourge of Sicilian life. The Fascist regime*
> *did its best to destroy Mafia, and the ruthless efforts of*
> *Mori, the Prefect of Palermo, resulted in many arrests.*
> *However, it is difficult to change the spirit of a people*
> *by mere police measures, and the Mafia may still exist*
> *in Sicily.*

Nicola (Nick) Gentile was born in 1885 in Siculiana, in the province of Agrigento, Sicily's notorious sulphur country. In 1906 he was initiated into the Honoured Society in Philadelphia, USA. An extortionist, murderer, bootlegger and drug dealer, he spent the next three decades of his life shuttling to and fro across the Atlantic as the demands of his criminal business, and the need to avoid his enemies in the police and mafia, dictated. Arrested on a narcotics charge in New Orleans in 1937, Gentile jumped bail and fled to Sicily.

Gentile was back in the province of Agrigento in the momentous month of July 1943, in his wife's hometown of Raffadali. When the American troops passed through, he smilingly offered them his services as a translator and guide to their commanding officer. Soon he and the officer had formed what he called 'an administration, a government' across many of the surrounding towns.

Thus began the Allies' crash course in the techniques for infiltrating state authority that the mafia had refined over the previous century. Nick Gentile's story is typical: across western Sicily *mafiosi* made friends with combat troops and then with the utterly bewildered military administrators who followed in behind. Amid an explosion of prison breakouts and armed robbery, AMGOT sought authority figures untainted by Mussolini's regime to help them deal with the anarchy. As 'middle-class

villains', Men of Honour are very good at creating the respectable façade that AMGOT was looking for. Nick Gentile could
even pose as a victim of Fascist oppression because he had spent
a couple of years on remand during the Iron Prefect's anti-mafia
drive of the late 1920s. Many of his brethren had similar tales
of woe to tell. So when AMGOT looked to replace Blackshirted
mayors with more friendly locals, there was often an obvious
candidate to hand. As Major General Lord James Rennell Rodd,
the British head of AMGOT, later admitted

> With the people clamouring to be rid of a Fascist *Podestà*
> [mayor], many of my officers fell into the trap of selecting
> the most forthcoming self-advertiser . . . The choices in
> more than one instance fell on the local 'Mafia' boss or
> his shadow, who in one or two cases had graduated in an
> American gangster environment.

Lord Rennell had a huge amount to cope with, in an uncertain
and fast-moving situation. But he was also being parsimonious
with the truth. The most insidious overtures to AMGOT were
those made by the members of the island's landowning elite. Lord
Rennell, the 2nd Baron Rennell, could hardly have been more
patrician: a multilingual former diplomat and banker who was
educated at Eton and Balliol College Oxford, he was also an
enthusiastic member of the Royal Geographical Society who had
travelled among the Touareg in the Sahara as a young man, and
was a devoted Italophile. To a man of Lord Rennell's breeding it
would scarcely have seemed credible that the suave noblemen who
invited him to dinner in their grand palazzi in Palermo could have
intimate connections with mafia thuggery.

One of those aristocrats was Lucio Tasca Bordonaro, Count
of Almerita, who emanated a distinct odour of mafia (as the
Italian phrase has it). Back in 1926–27, with the Mori Operation
rounding up hoodlums by the hundred, a mob war was raging
in the Conca d'Oro and threatening to bring the Fascist axe

crashing down on the very cradle of the Honoured Society. No less than three special commissions of *mafiosi* had come over from the United States, but failed to bring the warring factions together. The Inspectorate discovered that Count Tasca then approached the Iron Prefect on the mafia's behalf. He promised on his honour that the violence would soon end. So what need was there to go to all the trouble of arresting everyone involved?

In the summer of 1943, Lord Rennell, unaware of Count Tasca's record as a mafia mediator, appointed him Mayor of Palermo.

Seeing the mafia's intimacy with the Allies, Sicilians quickly lost faith in AMGOT's ability to impose law and order. And a state that has lost the faith of its citizens is just the kind the mafia likes.

Some American intelligence agents working for the Office of Strategic Services (or OSS, the forerunner of the CIA) came up with what they clearly thought was a smart and highly original scheme to address the crisis. Less than a week after Allied armies occupied the last corner of Sicily, in an enthusiastic bid to win more clout for his young and hitherto unimportant intelligence corps, the OSS's man in Palermo reported as follows.

> Only the Mafia is able to bring about suppression of black market practices and influence the 'contadini' [peasants] who constitute a majority of the population . . . We have had conferences with their [the mafia's] leaders and a bargain has been struck that they will be doing as we direct or suggest. A bargain once made here is not easily broken . . . We lent a sympathetic ear to their troubles and assured them, however feeble our cooperation, that it was theirs for the asking.

In other words, the OSS was suggesting, the Allies should use the mafia to co-manage crime. Throughout the AMGOT period in Sicily, as former agents have since confessed, the OSS continued to lend a 'sympathetic ear' to mafia bosses. The understanding between them, it seems, was based on an exchange of favours: the OSS received information in return for precious little tokens of trust – like tyres, which the *mafiosi* needed for the trucks they deployed in black market operations. In short, with the kind of naivety of which only those most determined to be cunning are capable, the OSS had fallen for the mafia's oldest trick. As had always been the case, robbery and smuggling did not just fill the mafia's coffers; they also had a handy political purpose from the bosses' point of view. A crime wave weakened the state and meant that the state had to seek help in ruling Sicily. Help from the mafia, that is.

Within weeks of the Allied landings in Sicily, much of what little Fascism had achieved against the mafia was obliterated. The AMGOT authorities had little time for the OSS's cynicism. Once Lord Rennell realised the terrifying speed with which the mafia had reasserted its grip, he took what countermeasures he could. But it was already too late. Where a mafia mayor was dismissed, other leading citizens were often afraid to take his place. Sicily's Men of Honour could now plot their course into a post-war world that would bring them greater power and wealth than even they had ever known before.

War Office, London: Directorate of Civil Affairs.
Calabria Zone Handbook.
Secret.
The information contained herein is believed to be correct
as at May 15th, 1943.

Physically, the Calabrian has his own look and build.
He is dark and whiskered, short and wiry; and in
Calabria it is the man who counts. The wife is a beast
of burden or a slave, the mother a nurse . . . Flirting
and courting in the English manner are not understood,

> *and may cost you your life . . . The tough natural*
> *conditions in which a Calabrian lives and works have*
> *made him hard and matter-of-fact . . . The Calabrian is*
> *a man of few words, and those straight to the point.*
> *He is scornful of comfort and luxury, which never*
> *enter his own life, and indifferent to pain and*
> *suffering . . . Public justice according to English ideals*
> *the Calabrian does not understand, never having*
> *experienced it . . . Thus no Calabrian, however well*
> *born and bred, can be expected to be on the side of*
> *the police as a matter of course.*
>
> *It is natural that in a country where feelings are apt*
> *to run high, crimes committed on a sudden violent*
> *impulse are far more numerous than those arising from*
> *cool deliberate malice. Indeed the latter class of crime*
> *is almost unknown in Calabria.*

The fighting between the Allies and the Germans in much of Calabria was brief. And after the fighting was over, AMGOT kept only a skeleton staff there. The *Calabria Zone Handbook* made no mention of a mafia in the region. No intelligence reports identified any organised criminal activity in 1943–44. Even Lord Rennell, who toured Calabria in early October 1943, failed to spot anything seriously amiss. If mayors linked to the picciotteria were appointed, which seems certain to have been the case, nobody noticed. The Honoured Society of Calabria entered the post-war era stronger than ever, and – as it had always been – far, far below the radar of public awareness.

The rise of one Calabrian Chief Cudgel gives us the measure of what the Allies could not see. Don Antonio ('Ntoni) Macrì was born in 1904 in Siderno, the economic heart of the notorious Locri region on the Ionian Coast. His career began in the late 1920s with repeated arrests for assault and carrying an illegal weapon – the classic profile of the enforcer. In 1933, with Fascism now claiming victory over the mafias, he was released from a five-year prison sentence on an amnesty. The obliging governor of his prison said that he had been 'well behaved and assiduously hard-working', and therefore deserved to be encouraged further along the path to complete rehabilitation. There was no rehabilitation: in 1937, he was categorised as a 'habitual delinquent', convicted of being the boss of a criminal association known by its members as the Honoured Society, and sent to an agricultural colony for three and a half years.

Once this 'habitual delinquent' was free again, the *Carabinieri* reports suddenly change their tone dramatically: 'irreproachable and hard-working', he was called. Don 'Ntoni was the boss that Master Joe danced the *tarantella* with in the last years of Fascism. So now we have an idea what he received in return for keeping control of his men during the pilgrimage to Polsi.

In August 1944, with the AMGOT period over and Calabria back under Italian control, don 'Ntoni was once more identified as the leader of a criminal organisation and recommended for enforced residence. The reports on him say that he was running protection rackets in the most valuable agricultural land of the Ionian Coast. A judge wrote that he 'dictated the price of oranges and lemons to suit his own whim and to serve his own interest as a dealer in the citrus fruit sector'.

Don 'Ntoni 'went on the run', but such was the control he exercised over his territory that he was able to stay exactly where he was. In April 1946 he was finally spotted and arrested in the centre of Locri, near to the Palace of Justice, with a revolver and a dagger in his pockets. In July of the same year magistrates dismissed the case against him because of 'insufficient evidence'. *Insufficient evidence*: since the 1870s, this had been the proud motto beneath many a Sicilian crime dynasty's family crest. Now don 'Ntoni Macrì had acquired the same degree of power and influence. Along with the same self-interested strain of family values. When don 'Ntoni's wife passed away not long after, his men forced large numbers of local people to attend her funeral. In a judge's words, the ceremony became 'the opportunity to stage a public demonstration of the Honoured Society's omnipotence'.

In this corner of Calabria at least, the humble picciotteria, the sect of brawlers, pimps and petty extortionists that had crawled out from the prisons in the 1880s, had completed its ascent.

By the 1960s don 'Ntoni had a criminal record – a shelf-bowing 900 pages long – that read like the bill for the decades since the 1880s in which Calabria's gangster emergency had been ignored. He was murdered in 1975, just after finishing a game of bowls in what was the most significant hit in 'ndrangheta history. For by that time, don 'Ntoni Macrì had become the most notorious *'ndranghetista* of them all – referred to by some Men of Honour as the boss of all bosses, and probably also an initiated member of Sicily's Cosa Nostra. But then that is a story for another era.

War Office, London: Directorate of Civil Affairs.
Campania Zone Handbook.
Secret.
The information contained herein is believed to be correct
as on July 1st, 1943.

Chapter VI, 'Folklore and Feasts'

*The real camorra, once a powerful secret society, does
in fact no longer exist, though there is much
underground life in Naples. One must beware of
pickpockets; if one is on the lookout for the singers
one can listen to the songs in the streets, 'o
bambeniello nasciuto' or 'l'amore non è più bagnato',
when many people cluster round, or, if one can
stomach it, one can even eat mussels and snails at a
'bancarella de maruzzaro' or 'purpetielli veraci'.*

The war brought horrors of all kinds on Italy, from the most viciously personal (mass rape), to the most terrifyingly impersonal (carpet bombing). In September 1943 Naples was a hungry city battered by air raids that left some 200,000 people homeless and destroyed much of the sewage system. The Germans then began a policy of deportation and summary executions. The Neapolitans rose in revolt, and freedom was already within their grasp when they greeted the first Allied tanks on 1 October.

But the traumas of war did not cease with the Wehrmacht's departure. Naples had always been a shambolic city, one that seemed to teeter on the edge of breakdown. Under AMGOT, it tipped headlong into squalor and degradation. To many in Naples at the time it felt as if all standards of human self-respect had been abandoned in the scramble to get a little food to eat, a little water to drink, and something to wear. The scenes of misery made a profound impression on the great movie director John Huston, who was in Naples making army newsreels. He later recalled that

> Naples was like a whore suffering from the beating of a brute – teeth knocked out, eyes blackened, nose broken, smelling of filth and vomit. There was an absence of soap, and even the bare legs of the girls were dirty. Cigarettes were the medium of exchange commonly employed, and anything could be had for a package. Little boys were offering their sisters and mothers for sale. At night, during the blackouts, rats appeared in packs outside the buildings and simply stood there, looking at you with red eyes, not moving. You walked around them. Fumes came out of the alleyways, down which there were establishments featuring 'flesh' acts between animals and children. The men and women of Naples were a bereft, starving, desperate people who would do absolutely anything to survive. The souls of the people had been raped. It was indeed an unholy city.

The facts from the archives back up Huston's memories. Prostitution was a very common survival tactic. The British Psychological Warfare Branch (PWB) which had responsibility for keeping tabs on civilian morale, estimated that there were around 40,000 prostitutes in Naples – about 10 per cent of the city's women. Nor was it just women. In the alleys, pimps were heard shouting 'Two dollars the boys, three dollars the girls!' to uniformed men who were openly eyeing and pawing the children lined up before them. Needless to say, venereal disease joined typhus among the scourges assailing liberated Naples.

Kleptomania gripped the city too. Anything of any conceivable value vanished: telegraph wires, manhole covers, railway tracks, even whole trams. It is said that a Papal Legate's car was found to be running on pilfered tyres.

Profiteers controlled much of the food supply from what the PWB called 'the almost miraculously fertile land in the low-lying ground around Naples'. The PWB referred to a 'fantastic gangland situation' between Nola and the coast north of the city. There were armed bands, many of them made up of deserters, but with widespread backing in this 'traditionally violent' area: 'they have the support of a whole organisation which includes prostitutes, receivers, Black Market specialists, etc.'

Among the worst offenders in Naples itself were rich industrialists, especially pasta manufacturers and millers. Spaghetti factories took to producing two varieties of product: a good one for the black market, and one that was 'almost black and of an unpleasant taste' for legal distribution. In March 1944 Antonio and Giuseppe Caputo, the owners of one of the city's biggest flour mills in the industrial quarter of San Giovanni a Teduccio, were sentenced to seven years for black market activities; investigators discovered machine guns and grenades in their house.

Floating comfortably on this tide of illegality, at least for a few months, was the Fascist Vito Genovese. 'Fascist', that is, only until the Allied armies reached Campania, at which point he shed his Mussolinian credentials like a worn-out suit, and stepped into a new disguise as a translator and guide to the US Army.

In May 1944 a sergeant from the US Army's Criminal Investigation Division received a tip-off and began looking hard at Genovese's interests. Before the war, the sergeant in question – Orange C. Dickey – had a job patrolling the leafy campus of Pennsylvania State College. His new assignment took him into the even leafier but rather more dangerous surroundings of Nola.

Sergeant Dickey's first breakthrough came when he found an elephants' graveyard of burned out military trucks in a vineyard outside Nola. He then heard two Canadian soldiers confess that they had delivered the trucks, with their priceless cargo of flour and sugar, with the transparent password 'Genovese sent us'.

By the end of August 1944 Sergeant Dickey had enough evidence to make an arrest: he picked Genovese up just after watching him collect a travel permit from the Mayor of Nola. A search of the gangster's wallet brought to light several enthusiastic letters of reference written by American officials in Nola on Genovese's behalf.

> Mr Genovese met me and acted as my interpreter for over a month. He would accept no pay; paid his own expenses; worked day and night and rendered most valuable assistance to the Allied Military Government.

Despite these letters, and a great deal more alarming evidence of Genovese's influence within the US Army, Sergeant Dickey's investigations would prove arduous and ultimately futile. After long months during which nobody seemed to want to take responsibility for the case, Genovese was eventually escorted back to the United States to face the murder charge that had originally provoked his flight to Italy. But one poisoned witness later, he was freed to resume his stellar career in American gangsterdom.

The intriguing thing about the Genovese story, from the Italian point of view, is the glimpse it affords of re-emergent criminal organisations in the Neapolitan hinterland. Sergeant Dickey's evidence showed that Genovese's black market network ran in many directions. The branches that most concerned Dickey were in AMGOT, of course. But Genovese also sheltered local thieves and smugglers from prosecution, assiduously cultivated friends in the Neapolitan judiciary, and even found protection from the Chief of Police of Rome. Sergeant Dickey also believed that Genovese partly controlled the electricity supply in the Nola area, giving him a stranglehold on manufacturing.

But if Genovese had links with existing criminal gangs in Nola, the signs are that things were not always friendly between them. Among the letters of recommendation written by Allied military officials for Genovese was one, dated June 1944, that contained the following curious phrase.

> [Vito Genovese] has been invaluable to me – is absolutely honest, and as a matter of fact, exposed several cases of bribery and blackmarket operations among so-called trusted civil personnel.

In traditional mafia fashion, Genovese was using his contacts with the authorities to eliminate his rivals.

Then there also is the mysterious informer whose tip-off first put Sergeant Dickey onto Genovese's black market empire. The man in question is likely to remain anonymous – his name was removed from the documentation for his own protection. Whoever he was, he spun Sergeant Dickey a particularly intriguing story. He said he was 'a former member of the Camorra' who had bought himself out of the organisation after marrying an American girl. The Camorra, he went on to explain, was 'the Italian counterpart of the Mafia Sicilian Union of the United States', and Vito Genovese was now its supreme boss.

At least two things about this story are odd. First, in 1944 there was almost certainly no such thing as the camorra, in the traditional sense of an Honoured Society. Second, the camorra

– even if it did exist – was nothing like Italy's equivalent of the mafia in the United States. It sounds to me as if the informer cooked his story to suit the tastes of his American interlocutor. If so, we can only guess at his motives. But it would be no surprise if he turned out to be an emissary of one of Genovese's local competitors. Perhaps the valiant Sergeant Dickey was lured into action by hoods from Nola or the Mazzoni who were eager to expel the American cuckoo from their Campanian nest. With the Fascist repression a fading memory, and Vito Genovese out of the way, the gangs of the Neapolitan hinterland could begin their history anew.

Meanwhile, in the hovels of the city centre, a contraband bonanza was changing the urban ground rules. In each tiny quarter, the street-corner boss or *guappo* was at the hub of the black market. Anyone who had under-the-counter goods to sell would turn to the *guappo* whose assistants would dart out into the alleys to find the right outlet at the right price. The profits to be made were enormous. PWB reported that the illiterate lumpen proletarians of the low city who made it rich in profiteering were too ignorant to count the bags of money they collected, so they weighed them instead. 'I have 3 kilos of thousand *Lire* notes'. On one occasion a passing bank clerk was stopped by an old crone and asked to help her count a great wicker basket of cash; when he had finished, she gave him a tip of 2,000 *Lire*. The story is poignant because it was so typical: bank clerks, factory workers, pensioners and bureaucrats – people on fixed incomes that is – suffered worst in the wild black market inflation of the Liberation period. In Naples, the PWB noted, 'class distinctions are disappearing'. Crime paid.

For much of the war in Italy Naples was the most important port of arrival for the colossal volume of provisions consumed by the advancing Allied armies. That deluge was simultaneously the city's deliverance and its damnation. By April 1944 an astonishing 45 per cent of Allied military cargo was being stolen. Only systemic corruption within Allied Military Government and among the Anglo-American forces can account for the industrial scale of the robbery. In September 1944 the PWB reported that Allied troops were openly ferrying packages of goods to market, and that the Military Police were doing nothing to stop them. The Italian police and *Carabinieri* who served under AMGOT at least had the defence of being as hungry as the rest of the local population. But they were just as likely to be venal as their British and American superiors. In May 1944 the PWB said that policemen were taking a cut of 20-30,000 *Lire* on every lorry load of goods that disappeared from the port. Everyone in Naples acquired a wily expertise on the relative merits of American and Canadian blankets, or British and French army boots. There was such a big racket in penicillin that the soldiers at the front went short.

The most visible retail outlets for stolen Allied goods were in via Forcella, near an American military depot. The street became a multinational, open-air, army surplus bazaar where anything intended for the Allied forces could be bought. And 'anything' included weaponry, it was said, as long as you knew who to ask.

Via Forcella runs through the cramped heart of the city; it lies only a few metres from the old Palazzo della Vicaria, the former prison and court house where, on 3 October 1862, Salvatore De Crescenzo, the gangland chieftain 'redeemed' at the time of Italian unification, had his rival stabbed to death and became the supreme boss of the Honoured Society of Naples. Eighty-one years later, at the time of AMGOT, the *guappi* in charge of via Forcella were the Giuliano boys, Pio Vittorio, Guglielmo and Salvatore. Today the Giuliano family name means only one thing: camorra.

In the ensuing decades new clans like the Giulianos, drawing on their experiences during the chaos of Liberation, would find different answers to the challenges that had ultimately defeated the old Honoured Society of Salvatore De Crescenzo, of Ciccio 'Little Lord Frankie' Cappuccio, of Enrico 'Big 'Enry' Alfano. How to organise tightly and network widely. How to infiltrate the economy and the political apparatus of the state. How to tame the police and courts. How to control and exploit women, and with them breed sons, and even daughters, able to perpetuate the system's power. How, by all these means, to turn mere delinquency into enduring territorial authority. 1943 was year zero for the rule of law in Naples. The Allied Liberation re-started the clock of camorra history.

Organised crime is Italy's congenital disease. The Honoured Societies of Naples and Sicily were born from the prison system in the middle decades of the nineteenth century. The violence and conspiratorial politics of Italian unification gave the hoodlums their passage out of the dungeons and into history.

The legacy of the *Risorgimento* in parts of the South and Sicily was a sophisticated and powerful model of criminal organisation. The members of these brotherhoods deployed violence for three strategic purposes. First: to control other felons, to farm them for money, information and talent. Second: to leech the legal economy. And third: to create contacts among the upper echelons – the landowners, politicians, and magistrates. In the environs of Palermo the mafia, boosted by the island's recent history of revolution, did not just have contacts with the upper class, it formed an integral facet of the upper class.

The new Kingdom of Italy failed to address that legacy. Worse, it lapsed into sharing its sovereignty with the local bosses. Italy allowed a criminal ecosystem to develop. It tried to live out the dream of being a modern state; but it did so with few of the resources that its wealthier neighbours could draw on, and with many more innate disadvantages. The result was political fragmentation and instability: an institutional life driven less by policies designed to address collective problems than by haggling for tactical advantage and short-term favours. This was a political system that frequently gave leverage to the worst pressure groups in the country – the ones sheltering men of violence. At election time the government sometimes used gangsters to make sure the right candidates won. Parliament produced bad legislation, which was then selectively enforced: the practice of dealing with *mafiosi* and *camorristi* by sending them into 'enforced residence' is one prime instance. Urgently needed reforms never materialised: an example being the utter legislative void around the likes of Calogero Gambino (from the 'fratricide' case of the 1870s) and Gennaro Abbatemaggio (from the Cuocolo trial of the early 1900s) – *mafiosi* and *camorristi* who abandoned the ranks of their brotherhoods and sought refuge with the state. Italy also had enough lazy and cynical journalists, wrong-headed intellectuals and morally obtuse writers to mask the real nature of the emergency, give resonance and credibility to the underworld's own twisted ideology, and allow gangsters to gaze at flattering reflections of themselves in print.

The criminal ecosystem spawned a new Honoured Society, the picciotteria, to retrace the evolutionary path of its older cousins: in the 1880s, it quickly progressed from prison to achieve territorial dominance in the outside world.

Yet to say that Italy harboured a criminal ecosystem is not to say that the country was run by gangsters. Italy has never been a failed state, a mafia regime. The reason why the mafias of Southern Italy and Sicily have such a long history is *not* because they were and are all-powerful, even in their heartlands. The rule of law was not a dead letter in the peninsula, and Italy *did* fight the mafias. *Omertà* broke frequently. Sometimes the mafias' territorial control broke too, leading to a reawakening in what good police like Ermanno Sangiorgi called the *spirito pubblico* – the 'public spirit': in other words, the belief that people could trust the state to enforce its own rules. Such moments offered a glimpse of an underlying public hunger for legality, and showed what could have been achieved had there been a more consistent anti-mafia effort.

But alas, Italy fought the Honoured Societies only for so long as their overt violence kept them at the top of the political agenda. It fought them only until the mafias' wealthy and powerful protectors could exert an influence. It fought them only enough to sharpen the gangster domain's internal process of natural selection. Over the years, weaker bosses and dysfunctional criminal methodologies were weeded out. Hoodlums were obliged to change and develop. The Sicilian mafia had the least to learn. In Naples, the Honoured Society failed to learn enough. Perhaps against the odds, the Calabrian picciotteria, that working museum of the oldest traditions of the prison camorras, proved itself capable of adapting to survive and grow.

In the underworld competition not just to dominate, but to endure, the mafias found perhaps their most important resource in family. Through their kin, *mafiosi, camorristi* and *picciotti* gained their strongest foothold in society, the first vehicle for their pernicious influence. Thus the lethal damage that the mafias caused to so many families – their own and their victims' – is the most poignant measure of the evil they did.

From 1925 Benito Mussolini styled his regime as the antithesis of the squalid politicking of the past, the cure for Italy's weak-willed concessions to the gangs. But Fascism ended up repeating many of the mistakes committed during earlier waves of repression. The same short attention span. The same reliance on 'enforced residence'. The same reluctance to prosecute the mafias' protectors among the elite. The same failure to tackle the endemic mafia presence in the prisons. Political internees in the 1920s and 1930s told *exactly* the same stories of mob influence behind bars as poor Duke Sigismondo Castromediano and the other patriotic prisoners of the *Risorgimento* had done three generations earlier.

The only thing that Mussolini did markedly better than his liberal predecessors was to pump up the publicity and smother the news. With a little help from the Sicilian mafia, he created the lasting illusion that Fascism had, at the very least, suppressed the mob.

So when it came to organised crime, Fascism's most harmful

legacy was forgetfulness. The *Zone Handbooks* with which the Allied forces arrived in Sicily, Calabria and Campania accurately reflect the desperately limited state of public knowledge that Fascism bequeathed. (They were based on Italian sources after all.)

When the Second World War ended, Italy would quickly become a democratic republic and, not long afterwards, a major industrial power. Here was a very different country from the *Italietta* – the 'mini Italy' – that had first confronted the mafias after 1860, or from the deluded, strutting Italy of the Blackshirt decades. But a forgetful democracy would prove that the country was as badly prepared to face the mafia threat as it had ever been. If there is one overriding lesson that the history of the mafias has to impart, it is that these organisations are *modern* – no less modern than the Italian state. Yet after the Second World War, just as it had done repeatedly over the previous century, official Italy tried all over again to convince itself that organised crime in the south was a residue of backwardness that would vanish of its own accord as the country progressed.

Perhaps the simplest and most telling symptom of post-war Italy's forgetfulness is how often public opinion would be *surprised*. Surprised, for example, in April 1955, when a mysterious homicidal rampage by a lone peasant from a mountain village in Calabria generated rumours of a strange criminal brotherhood in the region. Surprised, in October of the same year, when a young mother, the widow of a fruit and vegetable wholesaler from Nola, shot dead her husband's assassin near the main market in Naples, leading to a debate about the 'new camorra'. Or surprised yet again, late in 1962, when an outbreak of car bombs and city-centre slayings in Palermo showed that, whatever Sicily's mafia really was, it had greedily embraced the age of motorways and jet planes. But then these, and the many other 'surprises' of the post-war era, deserve deeper analysis, and a book of their own.

Acknowledgements

Much of the time spent researching and writing *Blood Brotherhoods* was awarded to me by the Leverhulme Trust: without a generous Research Fellowship, the book may never have been written, and so I am deeply grateful to everyone associated with the Trust. My academic home, the Italian Department at UCL, provides a wonderful environment for research and teaching, so my thanks must go to my colleagues on the academic and administrative staff there.

It was a pleasure and a privilege to meet a number of people in the front line of trying to understand and combat the 'ndrangheta in Reggio Calabria. The magistrates Nicola Gratteri and Michele Prestipino both impressed me with their courage, energy and rigour – and sent me away laden with fascinating documents. Peppe Baldessarro knows as much about the 'ndrangheta as any journalist, and has paid the price for his expertise with a death threat.

It is rare to find a historian who is as open-handed with his time and knowledge as Enzo Ciconte. Enzo sent me some documentation I had had trouble finding, and scrutinised an important chunk of the manuscript, making valuable suggestions. I discussed some of the ideas in *Blood Brotherhoods* at length with both Marcella Marmo and Gabriella Gribaudi. The book is much better as a result of their consideration and their profound understanding of the camorra. Since the very earliest stages of my research into the 'ndrangheta, I have been having exceptionally useful exchanges with Antonio Nicaso. Antonio also read a section of the manuscript, patiently and insightfully.

My friend Fabio Cuzzola was also my go-to guy in Reggio.

His generosity extended far beyond the intellectual, and even involved his developing an appreciation of Rory Delap's throw-ins and Ricardo Fuller's footwork. The great Nino Sapone was invaluable to me in many different ways. He knows his way around the Archivio di Stato di Reggio Calabria like few others, and he has a documented feeling for Aspromonte, its people and history; I will never forget our visits to Amendolea, S. Stefano, Montalto, and the Sanctuary at Polsi. Joseph Condello was an extremely helpful and friendly guide when we toured the Plain of Gioia Tauro together.

Several intrepid and shrewd researchers have helped me locate the archival and other sources on which *Blood Brotherhoods* is based; some of them also chipped in with precious ideas: Nick Dines, Nicola Crinniti, Manoela Patti, Vittorio Coco, Joe Figliulo, Salvo Bottari, Azzurra Fibbia. Fabio Truzzolillo not only hunted down some important material for me, but contributed positively to the content of the book: I hope by now that he has found the right home for his passion for research. Fabio Caffarena and Tenente Colonnello Massimiliano Barlattani of the Ufficio Storico dell'Aeronautica Militare helped me find the flying boss of Antonimina's war record. For certain localised but important aspects of my research I relied on the help of David Critchley, Tim Newark, and Eleanor Chiari. Christian De Vito was particularly insightful on the history of the prison system. Roger Parker found out what Silvio Spaventa went to see at the opera. Peter Y. Herchenroether generously sent me the results of his research into early Calabrian *mafiosi* in the United States. Alex Sansom, UCL's resident expert on early modern Spain, helped me find out more about Cervantes and the Garduña. Jonathan Dunnage was the source of some very useful prompts on the history of policing. My friend and colleague Florian Mussgnug generously surfed the German press on my behalf. A number of people in Australia offered tips on studying Calabrian organised crime in their country. David Brown was remarkably generous in letting me see his collection of material on the same subject: I regret only that

I was not able to analyse that area properly in *Blood Brother-hoods*. In Sicily, Attilio Bolzoni, Salvo Palazzolo, Dino Paternostro and Marcello Saija also offered advice and/or material. Pietro Comito passed on a rare copy of Serafino Castagna's autobiography. He is one of all too many courageous and professional Calabrian journalists who has had to face a death threat from the clans.

I owe a special debt to Lesley Lewis for allowing me to consult her late husband Norman's diaries – the notes he drew on while writing his profoundly compassionate and yet disillusioned observations in *Naples '44*.

Laura and Giulio Lepschy were for me, as for so many Italianists in the UK, an endless source of linguistic wisdom. Maria Novella Mercuri helped me work out some of the trickier, ungrammatical passages in some manuscripts.

Very many archivists and librarians have assisted me during the course of my work, but some of them were especially kind: Maria Pia Mazzitelli and the staff at the Archivio di Stato di Reggio Calabria; Salvatore Maffei at the marvellous Emeroteca Vincenzo Tucci in Naples; Maresciallo Capo Salerno and Col. Giancarlo Barbonetti at the Carabinieri Archive; and, once again, the staff in Humanities 2 at the British Library.

Several people read the manuscript of *Blood Brotherhoods* at various stages of its development. Theirs is a contribution to the cogency and readability of my work that I particularly appreciate: Laura Mason, Caz Carrick, Robert Gordon, Prue James, Vittorio Mete, Federico Varese, John Foot, Nino Blando.

I am lucky enough to have no fewer than four editors who were happy to listen to my ruminations about the project as it developed, and even to give sharp feedback on early drafts: Rupert Lancaster, Giuseppe Laterza and Peter Sillem. Marc Parent was particularly patient and incisive, and was excellent running company on the beach at St-Malo. Copy editor Helen Coyle had a much greater influence on the development of the typescript than her official responsibilities imply. My alchemical agent

Catherine Clarke has been a terrific source of support and insight, as always.

Yet again my biggest thank you goes to my wife, Sarah Penny. I am constantly astonished by her ability to juggle work, family and my seemingly endless demands for time. She has my gratitude and my love, always. The book is dedicated to her and to our two children, Elliot and Charlotte.

Every reasonable effort has been made to acknowledge the owner-ship of the copyrighted material included in this volume. Any errors that may have occurred are inadvertent, and will be corrected in subsequent editions provided notification is sent to the author.

I would like to thank the following:

Aliberti Editore, for permission to quote from Antonio Zagari, *Ammazzare stanca*, Aliberti editore, 2008; the Society of Authors as the Literary Representative of the Estate of Norman Douglas, for permission to quote from Norman Douglas, *Old Calabria*, M. Secuer, 1915; Edizioni Reno Sandron for permission to quote from Alfredo Niceforo, *L'Italia barbara contemporanea: studi e appunti*, R. Sandron, 1898.

Picture Acknowledgements

Reproduced by kind permission of Archivio dello Stato di Reggio Calabria: text page 201 above left.

Carlo Del Balzo, *Napoli e i napoletani*, Milan, 1885: 7 above.

Biblioteca Nazionale 'Vittorio Emanuele III', Naples, reproduced by kind permission of the Ministero per i Beni e le Attività Culturali, Italy: 8 below

Abele de Blasio, *Usi e Costumi dei Camorristi*, 1897: 7 below, text pages 36, 270.

Ablel de Blasio, *Il Tatuaggio*, 1905: text page 141.

© The British Library: 2 (from Francesco de Bourcard, *Usi e costumi de Napoli e contorni descritti e dipinti*, Volume II, 1858).

© The British Library Newspapers, Colindale: 5 above left and right and below right (from *Il Mondo Illustrato, 1860*), 8 above (from *Le Monde Illustré*, 1893).

Alfredo Comandini, *L'Italia nei centro anni del secolo XIX* (1801-1900) Volume 3: 3 below, text page 53.

© Corbis: 1 above/photo Ina Fassbender, 1 below/photo Armin Thiemer, 16 left.

Reproduced by kind permission of *Gazzetta del Sud*, 1986: 15 above left.

© Getty Images: 15 centre right, 16 above right.

Il Mattino, 1911: 13 above right.

Illustrated London News: 3 above left (1859), 4 below (1860), 5 below left (1859), 6 above (1860), 10 centre left and below (1902), 13 below (1911).

© John Dickie: 9.

La Scintilla, 1911: 12 above, 13 above left.

Library of Congress, Prints and Photographs Division, Washington DC: 12 below.

L'Illustration, 1860: 3 above right, 4 above.

L'Ilustrazione Italiana: 11 above right and left centre (1901), below (1899).

Reproduced by kind permission of Istituto Luce, Rome/Archivio Fotografico: 15 below.

Enrico Morselli, *Biografia di un bandito*, 1903: 10 above left and right, text page 201 centre and below.

Museo Pitré, Palermo, reproduced by kind permission of the Comune di Palermo: 6 below.

Private Collections: 11 above left, 14 above left and right and below left, 15 centre left, 16 centre right and below right, text pages 13, 121, 229.

TopFoto Topham Picturepoint: 14 below right.

NOTES ON SOURCES

The following notes take a slightly unusual form. In the absence of footnotes, which would be little more than clutter for most readers, I have opted to list my sources and include a few brief and eclectic observations on some of them. I hope that these observations will be helpful for specialists and interesting for the non-historian, and that they will go some way to recognising my many academic debts. I have erred on the side of inclusiveness. Some of the sources cited are not referred to or quoted from explicitly in the text. But I have included them here all the same, generally for one of two reasons: first, because they make points that I did not have the space to explore and illustrate in the text; second, because they add evidential weight. *Blood Brotherhoods*, as a comparative history, can have no pretentions to being an encyclopedic account of the camorra, the Sicilian mafia and the 'ndrangheta. My approach has been to choose stories that I consider to be exemplary. By including the full range of my archival sources on the picciotteria, for example, I hope to show that my choice of exemplary stories has a broad foundation in first-hand research, whether by me or by other people.

I have used the following abbreviations:

ACS = Archivio Centrale dello Stato
ASC = Archivio di Stato di Catanzaro
ASRC = Archivio di Stato di Reggio Calabria
ASN = Archivio di Stato di Napoli
ASPA = Archivio di Stato di Palermo

The following account of my sources begins with a short paragraph on the state of historical research on each of the three main criminal organisations. The texts cited are intended to be a guide for further reading, and a recognition of where I have drawn most heavily from other scholars.

CAMORRA

In the 1980s Marcella Marmo was among the pioneers of the new history of organised crime in Italy, and she is still *the* authority on the camorra from its origins to the Cuocolo trial. Her many essays should be the first items on any reading list about the camorra. Accordingly, I have drawn on them heavily and cited them in the appropriate chapters below. For now it is worth highlighting three essays that offer a broad survey of the Neapolitan Honoured Society: M. Marmo, 'Tra le carceri e il mercato. Spazi e modelli storici del fenomeno camorrista', in P. Macry and P. Villani (eds), *La Campania*, part of *Storia d'Italia. Le regioni dall'Unità a oggi*, Turin, 1990; M. Marmo, 'La camorra dell'Ottocento: il fenomeno e i suoi confini', in A. Musi (ed.), *Dimenticare Croce? Studi e orientamenti di storia del Mezzo-giorno*, Naples, 1991; M. Marmo, 'La città camorrista e i suoi confini: dall'Unità al processo Cuocolo', in G. Gribaudi (ed.), *Traffici criminali. Camorra, mafie e reti internazionali dell'illegalità*, Turin, 2009. This third essay makes some important observations about women in the camorra.

Marmo's essay on honour is also essential on one of the key themes that run through organised crime history: M. Marmo, 'L'onore dei violenti, l'onore delle vittime. Un'estorsione camor-rista del 1862 a Napoli', in G. Fiume (ed.), *Onore e storia nelle società mediterranee*, Palermo, 1989.

Francesco Barbagallo is best known for his work on the post-war camorra, but he has recently published a much needed summary of the entire history of organised crime in Campania: F. Barbagallo, *Storia della camorra*, Rome-Bari, 2010. As well as this excellent new book, I have also drawn on other books by Barbagallo that are cited in the appropriate places below.

Before Barbagallo's book, the only available single volume overview was Isaia Sales's collection of essays, *La camorra, le camorre*, Rome, 1988 (republished in a revised edition in 1993). Although Sales has been criticised (by Marmo among others) for his suggestion that the camorra was an expression of plebeian discontent that could find no political outlet, his book remains an important reference point in historical writing about the camorra and I have drawn on it in various passages.

MAFIA

Several scholars contributed to the foundation of a new school of history-writing on the Sicilian mafia in the 1980s – they are the people I cited in the bibliography to my *Cosa Nostra*. *Blood Brotherhoods* tries to apply the many lessons I absorbed from those historians to new material, and to the other criminal organisations. So if space prevents me from citing them and their works all over again here, my debt to them is nonetheless profound. One name does stand out among historians of organised crime in Sicily to an extent that demands explicit recognition once more: with his *Storia della mafia* (Rome, 1993) Salvatore Lupo confirmed his pre-eminence in the field. It is an indicator of the quality of Lupo's research that newly discovered material – like the documentation from Ermanno Sangiorgi's career that I found in the Archivio Centrale dello Stato – all too often confirms Lupo's fundamental insights. Lupo's recent *Quando la mafia trovò l'America. Storia di un intreccio intercontinentale, 1888–2008* (Turin, 2008) has brought a new analytical rigour to the study of the 'transatlantic mafia'. His book-length interview with Gaetano Savatteri, *Potere criminale. Intervista sulla storia della mafia* (Rome-Bari, 2010) is, among many other things, a persuasive argument for the importance of studying the mafia with the tools of the historian.

Salvatore Lupo it was who unearthed the 1938 report by the Royal General Inspectorate for Public Security for Sicily that I have used here. Two researchers working with Lupo, Manoela Patti and Vittorio Coco have analysed the report thoroughly and gone on to make huge advances in the understanding of the mafia under Fascism. Important essays by them, and by other scholars, are collected in a special issue of the journal *Meridiana. Rivista di storia e scienze sociali*, 'Mafia e fascismo' (63, 2008). The Inspectorate's report will have been published by the time *Blood Brotherhoods* appears: V. Coco and M. Patti, *Relazioni mafiose. La mafia ai tempi del fascismo*, Rome, 2010.

Chief of Police Ermanno Sangiorgi's extraordinarily insightful report into the mafia at the turn of the twentieth century – another discovery of Lupo's – is also due out in print: S. Lupo, *Il tenebroso sodalizio. La mafia d'inizio novecento nel rapporto Sangiorgi*, Rome, 2010. If all goes to plan, the book will also include my short biography of Sangiorgi.

'NDRANGHETA

The 'ndrangheta is the least known and least studied of the three major criminal organisations. And although there has been a recent wave of new publications on the 'ndrangheta today, historical research remains very rare indeed. For a long time, Gaetano Cingari was the only professional historian who took an interest in the Calabrian mafia. I have drawn on the precious pages in his *Storia della Calabria dall'Unità a oggi* (Rome-Bari, 1983), *Reggio Calabria* (Rome-Bari, 1988), and of course on his essay on the 'brigand' Musolino: 'Tra brigantaggio e "picciotteria": Giuseppe Musolino', in G. Cingari, *Brigantaggio, proprietari e contadini nel Sud*, Reggio Calabria, 1976. Enzo Ciconte's pioneering book *'Ndrangheta dall'Unità a oggi* (Rome-Bari, 1992) was the first systematic overview. Anyone who wants to find out about the history of organised crime in Calabria must start with Ciconte. As well as drawing the main outlines of 'ndrangheta history, Ciconte also brought together for the first time a vast quantity of evidence from the Archivio di Stato di Catanzaro. My approach has been to return to the same documentation, but to add a great deal of previously unstudied or understudied material from the Archivio di Stato di Reggio Calabria and the press that I think allows us to reach firmer and clearer conclusions on the early 'ndrangheta than either Ciconte or Cingari felt able to.

Ciconte also wrote the first comparative history of the three mafias: *Storia criminale. La resistibile ascesa di mafia, 'ndrangheta e camorra dall'Ottocento ai giorni nostri*, Soveria Mannelli, 2008. His approach is very distinctive – it is thematic rather than chronological – but it has given me a great many leads in preparing *Blood Brotherhoods*.

Two other important contributions to the early history of the 'ndrangheta deserve mention. The first is by a magistrate, Saverio Mannino: 'Criminalità nuova in una società in trasformazione: il Novecento e i tempi attuali', in A. Placanica (ed.), *La Calabria moderna e contemporanea*, Rome, 1997. Mannino's richly documented essay is particularly insightful on the Fascist era. The second contribution, just as richly documented, but with a focus on the pre-Fascist period, is by journalist and campaigner, Antonio Nicaso: *Alle origini della 'ndrangheta. La picciotteria*, Soveria Mannelli, 1990.

WOMEN IN ITALIAN ORGANISED CRIME

There is now a good body of scholarly work on the role that women and family relations play in mafia life, although it is all about the contemporary period. I hope that my study, whether the conclusions it draws are correct or not, at least shows that the comparative historical study of women and the mafia can yield insights about what Alessandra Dino has called the 'submerged centrality' of women in the underworld. The following four studies are recommended as essential starting points:

A. Dino and T. Principato, *Mafia donna. Le vestali del sacro e dell'onore*, Palermo, 1997.

A. Dino, *Mutazioni. Etnografia del mondo di Cosa Nostra*,

Palermo, 2002. Remarkable, amongst many other reasons, because it shows how much strategic thinking goes into the management of families within the Sicilian mafia.

O. Ingrascì, *Donne d'onore, Storie di mafia al femminile*, Milan, 2007.

R. Siebert, *Le donne. La mafia*, Milan, 1994.

SOURCES CONSULTED

Preface

S. Lupo, *Quando la mafia trovò l'America. Storia di un intreccio inter-continentale, 1888–2008*, Turin, 2008. Explains how the name 'Cosa Nostra' took hold among *mafiosi* both in Sicily and the United States following Joe Valachi's testimony to the McClellan committee in 1963.

L. Malafarina, *Il codice della 'ndrangheta*, Reggio Calabria, 1978. There is no canonical form of the legend of the three Spanish knights: it seems never to be reproduced in the same form twice in 'ndrangheta mythology. References to it in 'ndrangheta rituals are reproduced in many sources including Malafarina.

P. Natella, *La parola 'mafia'*, Florence, 2002. Suggests the derivation of *Carcagnosso* from *calcagna*.

'Books of The Times; Journey to a Strange Land That Seems Like Home', *New York Times*, 18/7/2003. On the 'unpronounceable name' of the 'ndrangheta.

To my knowledge the name 'ndrangheta or 'ndranghita does not make a consistent public appearance before press coverage of the so-called 'Marzano operation' in the autumn of 1955. One can see it surfacing, in tentative inverted commas, in 'Il Ministro Tambroni e il sottosegretario Capua in disaccordo nel valutare la situazione esistente nelle province calabresi', *L'Unità*, 10/9/1955; or 'Latitanti che si costituiscono e altri che vengono arrestati', *Il Mattino*, 14/9/1955. The man who seems likely to have been responsible for giving the name a broad currency was Corrado Alvaro, with his article 'La fibbia', *Corriere della Sera*, 17/9/1955.

Introduction: Blood brothers

Relazione annuale della Commissione parlamentare d'inchiesta sul fenomeno della criminalità organizzata mafiosa o similare. 'ndrangheta. Relatore On. Francesco Forgione, 2008. On the Duisburg massacre and the 'ndrangheta's international reach. Can be downloaded from: http://www.camera.it/_dati/leg15/lavori/documenti parlamentari/indiceetesti/023/005/intero.pdf

Procura della Repubblica Presso il Tribunale di Reggio Calabria, Direzione Distrettuale Antimafia, Decreto di Fermo di indiziato di delitto – artt. 384 e segg. c.p.p. Agostino Anna Maria + 155. I have drawn on this document, which is better known as '*Operazione Crimine*', for an up-to-date insight into the 'ndrangheta's structure based on the most recent investigations.

F. Barbagallo, *Storia della camorra*, Rome-Bari, 2010. Another very good source on the contemporary situation.

G. Gribaudi, 'Guappi, camorristi, killer. Interpretazioni letterarie, immagini sociali, e storie giudiziarie', in *Donne, uomini, famiglie*, Naples, 1999. Also the source for my remarks on the *guappi* after the demise of the Neapolitan Honoured Society.

G. Gribaudi, 'Clan camorristi a Napoli: radicamento locale e traffici internazionali', in G. Gribaudi (ed.), *Traffici criminali. Camorra, mafie e reti internazionali dell'illegalità*, Turin, 2009. An excellent short summary of the camorra today based on judicial sources. Here I owe the observation about the Honda 'Dominator', along with many other points, to Gribaudi's essay.

P. Martino, *Per la storia della 'ndranghita*, Rome, 1988. Suggests the most plausible derivation of 'ndrina.

L. Paoli, *Fratelli di mafia. Cosa Nostra e 'ndrangheta*, Bologna, 2000. A fine comparative study of the Sicilian and Calabrian organisations.

R. Saviano, *Gomorra. Viaggio nell'impero economico e nel sogno di dominio della camorra*, Milan, 2006. Saviano's powerful, impassioned and enormously successful book is a shocking denunciation of camorra power today. Compared to Gribaudi and Barbagallo, however, it has the disadvantage for historians of not citing its sources. Readers who do not know Italian will be hampered by the book's dreadful English translation.

A. Zagari, *Ammazzare stanca. Autobiografia di uno 'ndranghetista pentito*, Cosenza 1992.

1: *VIVA LA PATRIA!* THE CAMORRA, 1851–61

ASN, Ministero della Polizia, Gabinetto, f. 1702, incart. 38. Ministero e Real segreteria di Stato della polizia generale, Affari di conferenze con S.M. il Re Nostro Padrone D.G. Undated report, but c. 20/10/1853. On the links between liberals and *camorristi*.

ASN, Ministero della Polizia, Gabinetto, f. 1648, incart. 295. Corrispondenza tra il Prefetto di polizia Farina e il Ministro Romano. On the setting up of a new police force in the summer of 1860.

ASN, Dicastero di polizia e delle luogotenenze, f. 202, inc. 4. Letter from Prefettura di Polizia signed by Filippo De Blasio to Luogotenente del Re Luigi Carlo Farini dated 22/11/1860. On the 'perniciosissima peste della Camorra' and on Romano's policy of co-opting *camorristi* into the police.

ASN, Dicastero dell'Interno e Polizia della Luogotenenza, f. 202, incart. 112. Componimento dello stato dei camorristi in questa città . . . Trasmesso il 21/6/1861 dal questore Tajani al Dicastero di Polizia. A list of '*gamorristi*', by city quarter, drawn up under Spaventa.

ASN, Questura di Napoli. Archivio Generale 1a serie. Archivio dei pregiudicati. Fascicoli personali (1860–1887). B. 1581, numerazione autonoma 53. Salvatore De Crescenzo. Contains De Crescenzo's lengthy criminal record.

Foreign press sources (UK unless stated): *The Times*; *London Daily News*; *Morning Chronicle*.

Other sources drawn on throughout this section:

G. Machetti, 'Cultura liberale e prassi repressiva verso la camorra a Napoli degli anni 1860–70', in M. Marmo (ed.), *Mafia e camorra: storici a confronto, Quaderni del Dipartimento di Scienze Sociali dell'Istituto Universitario Orientale*, 2, 1988.

G. Machetti, 'Camorra e criminalità popolare a Napoli (1860–1880)', *Società e Storia*, 51, 1991.

G. Machetti, 'L'impossibile ordine. Camorra e ordine pubblico a Napoli nella congiuntura unitaria', *ParoleChiave*, 7–8, 1995.

M. Marmo and O. Casarino, '"Le invincibili loro relazioni": identificazione e controllo della Camorra napoletana nelle fonti giudiziarie di età postunitaria', *Studi Storici*, 2, 1988.

M. Marmo, 'Camorra anno zero', *Contemporanea. Rivista di storia dell'800 e del '900*, 1999/3. Reproduces and comments on the two reports on the camorra compiled under Spaventa from ASN, Alta polizia, f. 202, f. lo 4, *Luogotenenza generale del Re* (Carignano), *Gabinetto del Segretario Generale di Stato* (Nigra) *a Dicastero di Polizia*, 5/4/1861.

M. Marmo, 'I disordini della capitale', *Bollettino del Diciannovesimo Secolo*, 6, 2000.

M. Marmo, 'Quale ordine pubblico? Notizie e opinioni da Napoli tra il luglio '60 e la legge Pica', in Macry, P. (ed), *Quando crolla lo Stato. Studi sull'Italia preunitaria*, Naples, 2003. Among Marmo's essays (already cited above), this one is crucial for its narrative of the events of 1860-63, which I have substantially followed here.

M. Monnier, *La camorra. Notizie storiche raccolte e documentate*, Lecce, 1994 (1862). This edition has a useful introduction by Gabriella Gribaudi.

A. Scirocco, *Governo e paese nel Mezzogiorno nella crisi dell'unificazione (1860–61)*, Milan, 1963.

How to extract gold from fleas

L. Agnello, 'Castromediano, Sigismondo', in *Dizionario biografico degli Italiani*, vol. 22, Rome, 1979.

P. Bourget, *Sensations d'Italie. (Toscane – Ombrie – Grande-Grèce)*, Paris, 1891.

R. Canosa and I. Colonnello, *Storia del carcere in Italia dalla fine del '500 all'Unità*, Rome, 1984. This remarkable study traces some of the traditions of prison extortionists back to the early modern era.

S. Castromediano, *Carceri e galere politiche*, 2 vols, Lecce, 1895.

W.E. Gladstone, 'First Letter to the Earl of Aberdeen, on the state prosecutions of the Neapolitan government' (1851), in *Gleanings of Past Years, 1843–78*, vol. IV, London, 1879.

E. Martinengo Cesaresco, 'Sigismondo Castromediano', in *Italian Characters in the Epoch of Unification*, London, 1901 (2nd edn).

F. Montuori, *Lessico e camorra. Storia della parola, proposte etimologiche e termini del gergo ottocentesco*, Napoli, 2008. This is the best source on the etymology of 'camorra' and the history of Neapolitan underworld slang more generally. Montuori argues that camorra meant 'extortion' or 'extortion payment' for many decades before we hear of the existence of a secret society called the camorra.

R. Shannon, *Gladstone*, vol. 1, *1809–1865*, London 1982.

S. Zazzera, *Procida. Storia, tradizioni e immagini*, Naples, 1984.

G. Neppi Modona, 'Carcere e società civile' in *Storia d'Italia*, v. 5, *I documenti*, t. 2, Turin, 1973. Still the best starting-point for the history of the prison system in Italy.

There are many sources on the prison camorra in the nineteenth century, and on the continuing influence of organised crime behind bars into the twentieth century:

M. Beltrani Scalia, *Sul governo e sulla riforma delle carceri in Italia*, Turin, 1867.

A. Gramsci, *Lettere dal carcere*, Turin, 1947. Especially the letter of 11/4/1927.

I. Invernizzi, *Il carcere come scuola di rivoluzione*, Turin, 1973.

J.W. Mario, 'Il sistema penitenziario e il domicilio coatto in Italia', I, *Nuova Antologia*, 1/7/1896.

L. Settembrini, *Lettere dall'ergastolo*, Milan, 1962.

L. Settembrini, *Ricordanze della mia vita*, vol. II, Bari, 1934.

V. Susca, *Le isole Tremiti. Ricordi*, Bari, 1876.

Co-managing crime

G. Alessi, 'Polizia e spirito pubblico tra il 1848 ed il 1860. Un'ipotesi di ricerca', *Bollettino del Diciannovesimo Secolo*, 6, 2000.

C.T. Dalbono, 'Il camorrista e la camorra', in F. De Bourcard (ed.), *Usi e costumi di Napoli e contorni descritti e dipinti*, vol. II, Naples, 1858. Interesting on how widespread knowledge of the camorra was before 1860. Blames the Spanish for the camorra's origins. The essay also reproduces the camorra's 'national anthem' (see chapter 5).

A. De Blasio, *Nel paese della camorra. L'Imbrecciata*, Naples, 1973 (1901).

S. De Renzi, *Topografia e Statistica medica della città di Napoli . . . ossia Guida medica per la città di Napoli e pel Regno*, 4th edn, Naples, 1845.

C.A. Mayer, *Vita popolare a Napoli nell'età romantica*, Bari, 1948.

J. Murray, *Southern Italy*, London, 1853. Describes via Toledo as the busiest street in the world, and gives sound advice to wary travellers.

C. Petraccone, *Napoli dal Cinquecento all'Ottocento. Problemi di storia demografica e sociale*, Naples, 1974.

A. Scialoja, *I bilanci del Regno di Napoli e degli Stati Sardi con note e confronti*, Turin, 1857.

C. Spadaccini, *Pensieri sulla polizia detta pubblica sicurezza*, Naples, 1820. An early discussion of the *feroci* and their role in policing Naples.

The redemption of the camorra /
Uncle Peppe's stuff: The camorra cashes in

K. Baedeker, *Italie. Manuel du voyageur*, III, *Italie du Sud et la Sicile*, Coblenz, 1872. Gives an authoritative assessment of Marc Monnier's hotel.

S. Baridon, *Marc Monnier e l'Italia*, Turin, 1942.

'I camorristi', in *Giornale Universale*, 15/9/1860.

C. Cavour, *La liberazione del Mezzogiorno e la formazione del Regno d'Italia, Carteggi di Camillo Cavour con Villamarina, Scialoja, Cordova, Farini, ecc.* 5 vols, Bologna, 1949–54. Vol. 3. Contains Scialoja's letter to Cavour on the *camorristi* being received by ministers under Garibaldi's dictatorship. Vol. 4 contains much material on Spaventa. '*Memorie di* Giuseppe Ricciardi' in vol. 5 explains the role of Monnier's hotel for the *Comitato d'Ordine*.

P. De Riccardis, 'Una guardia nazionale inquinata: primo esame delle fonti archivistiche per Napoli e provincia, 1861–1870', in M. Marmo (ed.), *Mafia e camorra: storici a confronto, Quaderni del Dipartimento di Scienze Sociali dell'Istituto Universitario Orientale*, 2, 1988.

R. De Cesare, *La fine di un regno*, I, *Regno di Ferdinando II*, 3rd edn, Città di Castello, 1908.

R. De Cesare, *La fine di un regno*, II, *Regno di Francesco II*, 3rd edn, Città di Castello, 1909.

G. De' Sivo, *Storia delle Due Sicilie dal 1847 al 1861*, vol. 2, Naples, 1964. De Cesare and De' Sivo, two chroniclers from opposite political points of view, are among the richest contemporary sources on the fall of the Bourbons in Naples. Naturally enough they have very different takes on Liborio Romano.

G. Ghezzi, *Saggio storico sull'attività politica di Liborio Romano*, Florence, 1936.

G. Lazzaro, *Liborio Romano*, Turin, 1863.

M. Monnier, *Garibaldi. Rivoluzione delle Due Sicilie*, Naples, 1861.

M. Monnier, *Garibaldi. Histoire de la conquête des Deux Siciles*, Paris, 1861.

L. Romano, *Il mio rendiconto politico*, Locorotondo, 1960.

L. Romano, *Memorie politiche*, Milan, 1992.

XX (i.e. anon), 'Corrispondenza di Napoli', Al Direttore della Rivista Contemporanea, *Napoli* 20/8/1860, in *Rivista Contemporanea*, September 1860. On *la Sangiovannara*.

Spanishry: The first battle against the camorra

L. Arsenal and H. Sanchiz Álvarez de Toledo, *Una historia de las sociedades secretas españolas*, Barcelona, 2006. On the myth of the Garduña.

F. Barbagallo, *Il Mattino degli Scarfoglio, 1892–1928*, Milan, 1979. On San Donato's political career.

P. Bevilacqua, 'La camorra e la Spagna', *Meridiana*, 9, 1992. Praiseworthy for its scepticism about the story of the camorra's Spanish origins.

M. de Cervantes, 'Rinconete and Cortadillo' (1613), in *Exemplary Stories*, Oxford, 2008.

P. Costantini, *Silvio Spaventa e la repressione del brigantaggio*, Pescara, 1960.

Il Carteggio Cavour-Nigra dal 1858 al 1861, vol. IV, *La liberazione del Mezzogiorno*, Bologna, 1929.

E. Croce, *Silvio Spaventa*, Milan, 1969.

J. Davis, *Naples and Napoleon. Southern Italy and the European Revolutions (1780-1860)*, Oxford, 2006. For a good summary of the role of the *Carbonari* (Charcoal Burners) in early nineteenth-century politics in Southern Italy.

V. de Féréal (pseud. of Madame Suberwick), *Mystères de l'inquisition et autres sociétés secrètes d'Espagne, par V. de F., avec notes historiques et une introduction de M. de Cuendias*, Paris, 1845. The origin of the supposedly medieval sect of the Garduña.

D. Fozzi, 'Una "specialità italiana": le colonie coatte nel Regno d'Italia', in M. Da Passano (ed.), *Le colonie penali nell'Europa dell'Ottocento*, Rome, 2004. A good study of *domicilio coatto*.

G. Machetti, 'Le leggi eccezionali post-unitarie e la repressione della camorra: un problema di ordine pubblico?', in F. Barbagallo (ed.), *Camorra e criminalità organizzata in Campania*, Naples, 1988.

C. Magni, *Vita parlamentare del Duca di San Donato patriota e difensore di Napoli*, Padova, 1968.

L. Musella, *Individui, amici, clienti. Relazioni personali e circuiti politici in Italia meridionale tra Otto e Novecento*, Bologna, 1994. On Spaventa.

E. Peters, 'The Inquisition in Literature and Art' in *idem, Inquisition*, Berkeley, 1989. On Mme Suberwick's novel's place in anti-Catholic polemic.

S. Ricci, 'La difesa della rivoluzione unitaria, 1860–64', in S. Ricci and C. Scarano (eds), *Silvio Spaventa. Politico e statista dell'Italia unita nei documenti della biblioteca civica "A. Mai"'*, special issue of *Bergomum*, 2–3, 1990.

P. Romano, *Silvio Spaventa. Biografia Politica*, Bari, 1942.

S. Spaventa, *Dal 1848 al 1861. Lettere, scritti, documenti*, Naples, 1898.

2: GETTING TO KNOW THE MAFIA, 1865–1877

Sources cited throughout this section:

S. Carbone and R. Grispo (eds), *L'inchiesta sulle condizioni sociali ed economiche della Sicilia, 1875–1876*, 2 vols, Bologna, 1968–69. The papers of the 1875–76 inquiry into Sicily. Contains the material on the Uditore *cosca* and Antonino Giammona; Carlo Morena's testimony on the state of justice in Sicily; Rudinì's testimony about the 'benign mafia'; and much information on prominent early *mafiosi* mentioned here.

S. Lupo, *Storia della mafia*, Rome, 1996 edn.

Rebels in corduroy

P. Alatri, *Lotte politiche in Sicilia sotto il governo della Destra (1866–74)*, Turin, 1954.

O. Cancila, *Palermo*, Bari, 2000. Also includes much interesting information on the figure of Rudinì.

P. Catalanotto, 'Dal carcere della Vicaria all'Ucciardone. Una riforma europea nella Palermo borbonica', *Nuovi Quaderni del Meridione*, 79, 1982. I have referred to the Palermo prison as the Ucciardone here to avoid confusion with the Vicaria in Naples.

G. Ciotti, *I casi di Palermo. Cenni storici sugli avvenimenti di settembre 1866*, Palermo, 1866.

G. Pagano, *Sette giorni d'insurrezione a Palermo. Cause – fatti – rimedî*, Palermo, 1867.

M. Da Passano (ed.), *I moti di Palermo del 1866. Verbali della Commissione parlamentare di inchiesta*, Rome, 1981. Includes both Rudinì's testimony and Chief of Police Albanese's notorious statements about 'getting the mafia interested' in helping maintain order.

W. Dickinson, 'Diario della rivoluzione siciliana dalla notte del 9 al 10 gennaio 1848 sino al 2 giugno 1849', in vol. 1 of *Memorie della rivoluzione siciliana dell'anno MDCCCXLVIII pubblicate nel cinquantesimo anniversario del XII gennaio di esso anno*, 2 vols, Palermo, 1898. On Turi Miceli in the revolution of 1848.

G. Fiume, *Le bande armate in Sicilia (1819–1849). Violenza e organizzazione del potere*, Palermo, 1984.

Gazzetta Ufficiale del Regno d'Italia, 18/10/1866, 'Relazione del marchese Rudinì, Sindaco di Palermo, sugli ultimi avvenimenti di quella città'.

Gazzetta Ufficiale del Regno d'Italia, Supplemento al n. 302, 3/11/1866, 'Relazione del Sindaco di Palermo, marchese Di Rudinì, sui fatti avvenuti in quella città nel settembre scorso.'

Gazzetta Ufficiale del Regno d'Italia, 20/11/1866, 'Relazione al Ministro dell'Interno del questore della città e circondario di Palermo sui fatti del settembre 1866'.

N. Giordano, 'Turi Miceli. Il brigante-eroe monrealese nei moti del 1848, 1860 e 1866', *Il Risorgimento in Sicilia*, 1, 1, 1965.

S. Lupo, *Il giardino degli aranci: il mondo degli agrumi nella storia del Mezzogiorno*, Venice, 1990. On organised crime and the citrus fruit business.

A. Maurici, *La genesi storica della rivolta del 1866 in Palermo*, Palermo, 1916.

G. Moncalvo, *Alessandra Di Rudinì. Dall'amore per D'Annunzio al Carmelo*, Milan, 1994.

'The Week's Republic in Palermo, 1866', *Quarterly Review*, vol. 122, no. 243, January 1867.

L. Riall, *Sicily and the Unification of Italy. Liberal Policy and Local Power, 1859–1866*, Oxford, 1998. Also includes the quotation about *camorristi* in Turi Miceli's entourage.

U. Santino, *La cosa e il nome. Materiali per lo studio dei fenomeni premafiosi*, Catanzaro, 2000. One of the many places that cites the 1838 report from Trapani on the 'Unions or brotherhoods, sects of a kind'.

The benign mafia / A sect with a life of its own: The mafia's rituals discovered

ACS, Ministero dell'Interno, Direzione Generale Affari Generale e del Personale, Fascicoli del personale del Ministero, Ia e IIa Serie, B. 542. Albanese, Giuseppe. Personal papers on the shady figure of Chief of Police Albanese showing how Rudinì was responsible for appointing him.

ACS, Ministero di Grazia e Giustizia, Direzione generale degli affari penali. Miscellanea B. 44, Fasc. 558, 1877 Sicilia. Associazioni di malfattori. Including the files on the various associations discovered across Sicily, and Carlo Morena's letter denying any link between them.

ACS, Ministero di Grazia e Giustizia, Ufficio superiore personale e affari generali, Ufficio secondo, Magistrati, fascicoli personali, primo versamento 1860-1905, Morena, Carlo.

ASPA, Gabinetto Prefettura serie I (1860-1905), b. 35, fasc. 10, 1876, Denuncia Galati – Malfattori all'Uditore. Il Questore Rastelli al Procuratore del Re, Palermo 29/2 (1876). The first document reproducing the mafia's initiation ritual.

A. Crisantino, *Della segreta e operosa associazione. Una setta all'origine della mafia*, Palermo, 2000. Contains a great deal that is useful about policing and the mafia between the Right and the Left.

P. Pezzino, 'Stato violenza società. Nascita e sviluppo del paradigma mafioso', in idem, *Una certa reciprocità di favori. Mafia e modernizzazione violenta nella Sicilia postunitaria*, Milan, 1990.

D. Tajani, *Mafia e potere. Requisitoria (1871)*, P. Pezzino (ed.), Pisa, 1993. On the Albanese affair.

Double vendetta

ACS, Ministero dell'Interno, Direzione Generale Affari Generale e del Personale, Fascicoli del personale del Ministero (1861–1952) IIa Serie, B. 256. Sangiorgi Ermanno, Questore. Sangiorgi's career file, containing the documentation on the 'fratricide' case and much else besides. Most of what I have written about Sangiorgi is from this source.

ACS, Ministero di Grazia e Giustizia, Dir. Gen. Aff. Penali, Miscellanea, b. 46, fasc. 589. The correspondence concerning Carlo Morena's defence of Pietro De Michele, including Sangiorgi's evidence against the latter.

A. Cutrera, *I ricottari. La mala vita di Palermo*, Palermo, 1979 (1896). On the differences between *ricottari* and *mafiosi*.

J. A. Davis, *Conflict and Control*, London, 1988. Good for contextual information on policing in Liberal Italy.

J. Dunnage, *The Italian Police and the Rise of Fascism*, London, 1997. Contains a good brief summary of policing history in Italy before Fascism.

I. Fazio, 'The family, honour and gender in Sicily: models and new research', *Modern Italy*, 9 (2), 2004. An exceptionally useful survey of the vast literature on the Sicilian family.

C. Guerrieri, 'L'azione repressiva di Giovanni Nicotera contro mafia e camorra', in A. Bagnato, G. Masi and V. Villella (eds), *Giovanni Nicotera nella storia italiana dell'Ottocento*, Soveria Mannelli, 1999. For the background to the whole Sangiorgi-Morena-De Michele story told here.

P. Pezzino, '"La Fratellanza" di Favara', in idem, *Una certa reciprocità di favori. Mafia e modernizzazione violenta nella Sicilia postunitaria*, Milan, 1990.

'Processo Amoroso e compagni', in *Giornale di Sicilia*. Series of articles covering the trial begins on 29/8/1883 and ends on 20/10/1883. The trial is a classic instance of the way only the mafia's losers were successfully prosecuted. The trial is, among other things, an unexplored source on the role of women in the mafia.

G. Vaccaro, *Notizie su Burgio*, Palermo, 1921. One of the few published sources of information on the history of this Sicilian agrotown. Suspiciously, it portrays De Michele as a victim of the 1848 rebellion.

3: THE NEW CRIMINAL NORMALITY, 1877–1900

Born delinquents: Science and the mob

G. Alongi, 'Polizia e criminalità in Italia', *Nuova Antologia*, 1/1/1897. Summarises police accommodation with organised crime after the crucial years of 1876–77.

G. Alongi, *La camorra. Studio di sociologia criminale*, Turin, 1890.

G. Alongi, *La maffia nei suoi fattori e nelle sue manifestazioni: studio sulle classi pericolose della Sicilia*, Rome, 1886.

A. Cutrera, *La mafia e i mafiosi. Origini e manifestazioni*, Palermo, 1900. The best of the policemen writing in the era of positivism.

C. D'Addosio, *Il duello dei camorristi*, Naples, 1893.

A. De Blasio, *Usi e costumi dei camorristi*, 2nd edn, Naples, 1897.

A. De Blasio, *Nel paese della camorra. (L'Imbrecciata)*, Naples, 1901.

A. De Blasio, *Il tatuaggio*, Naples, 1905.

A. De Blasio, *Il tatuaggio ereditario e psichico dei camorristi napoletani*, Naples, 1898.

F. Manduca, *Studii sociologici*, Naples, 1888. An interesting and contradictory text by a leading former magistrate with experience in both Sicily and Naples. In positivist style he blames ethnic factors for the mafia and camorra, but runs against the consensus of the time by believing that the mafia, like the camorra, is an organisation with a hierarchy.

C. Fiore, 'Il controllo della criminalità organizzata nello Stato liberale: strumenti legislativi e atteggiamenti della cultura giuridica', *Studi Storici*, 2, 1988.

C. Lombroso, *L'uomo delinquente in rapporto all'antropologia, alla giurisprudenza ed alle discipline carcerarie*, 4th edn, 2 vols, Turin, 1889.

A. Niceforo, *L'Italia barbara contemporanea*, Milan, 1898.

An audience of hoods

La fondazione della camorra is covered in *Il Mattino, Roma* and *Corriere di Napoli*, October-November, 1899.

The photograph of a scene from *La fondazione della camorra* can be viewed at:
http://archiviteatro.napolibeniculturali.it/atn/foto/dettagli_foto?oid =127417&descrizione=stella&query_start=10
The letter from the Ispettorato Vicaria to the Questura (Police HQ) in Naples on the *Fondazione della camorra*, dated 4/11/1899 was available on the same site, but now seems to have been taken down.

V. Bianco, *La mala vita* ovvero *I camorristi nella Vicaria*, manuscript play held in Biblioteca Lucchesi Palli, Biblioteca Nazionale, Naples.

V. Bianco, *La mala vita o 'E carcere 'a Vicaria*, manuscript play held in Biblioteca Lucchesi Palli, Biblioteca Nazionale, Naples.

V. Bianco, *La mala vita o 'O zelluso d' 'o Mercato* (1923) manuscript play held in Biblioteca Lucchesi Palli, Biblioteca Nazionale, Naples.

G. Castellano, *'E guappe 'a Vicaria*, manuscript play held in Biblioteca Lucchesi Palli, Biblioteca Nazionale, Naples.

F.P. Castiglione, *Il segreto cinquecentesco dei Beati Paoli*, Palermo, 1999.

E. De Mura (ed.), *Enciclopedia della canzone napoletana*, Naples, 1969, vol. III. See the entries on the San Ferdinando and on Eduardo Minichini.

S. Di Giacomo and G. Cognetti, *Mala vita*, Naples, 1889. A camorra play by one of the best known Neapolitan authors of the era.

S. Di Giacomo in (various authors), *Napoli d'oggi*, Naples, 1900. On the camorra in the theatre, the San Ferdinando, Stella, etc.

S. Di Giacomo, 'Il "San Ferdinando"', in *idem, Napoli. Figure e paesi*, Naples, 1909.

V. Linares, 'I Beati Paoli', in *idem, Racconti popolari*, Palermo, 1886.

F. Mancini, 'I teatri minori' in F. Mancini and S. Ragni (eds), *Donizetti e i teatri napoletani nell'Ottocento*, Naples, 1997. On the San Ferdinando.

G. Montemagno, *Luigi Natoli e i Beati Paoli*, Palermo, 2002.

F. Renda, *I Beati Paoli. Storia, letteratura e leggenda*, Palermo, 1988.

G. Tessitore, *Il nome e la cosa. Quando la mafia non si chiamava mafia*, Milan, 1997. On modern-day *mafiosi* – men of the criminal calibre of Totuccio Contorno, Gaetano Badalamenti, Totò Riina and Gaspare Mutolo – who believe, or profess to believe, that their organisation is the modern form of the *Beati Paoli*.

G. Trevisani (ed.), *Teatro napoletano. Dalle origini a Edoardo Scarpetta*, 2 vols, Bologna, 1957.

V. Viviani, *Storia del teatro napoletano*, Naples, 1969.

The slack society

ACS, Archivio di Francesco Crispi, Crispi Roma, fasc. (79) 320, Relazioni e promemoria relativi alla organizzazione della PS e dei CC specie in Sicilia, 1888.

ACS, Archivio di Francesco Crispi, Crispi Roma, fasc. (222) 321, Relazione d'inchiesta sul personale e sull'organizzazione delle guardie a cavallo di Pubblica Sicurezza nelle provincie di Palermo, Trapani, Girgenti e Caltanissetta, 1887. Contains Sangiorgi's report dated 25/10/1888. There is also material on Sangiorgi's mission to Sicily at this time in his career file (see above). Davis, *Conflict and Control*, also covers the mission.

Il Mattino. For coverage of Ciccio Cappuccio's funeral, 7–8/12/1892; and 9–10/12/1892 for Ferdinando Russo's poem about the *camorrista*.

La Gazzetta Piemontese is a very useful press source on the disturbances of August 1893. The profile of Sangiorgi when he was appointed Police Chief in Milan is in the issue of 14/2/1889.

A.G. Bianchi (ed.), *Il romanzo di un delinquente nato. Autobiografia di Antonino M.*, Milan, 1893.

G. Fortunato, *Corrispondenze napoletane*, Cosenza, 1990. A collection of classic writings on the Southern Question originally published 1878–80. See particularly, 'La camorra'.

M. Marmo, *Il proletariato industriale a Napoli in età liberale*, Naples, 1978. On the camorra-backed cab drivers' strike. Davis, *Conflict and Control* is also useful on this.

S. Pucci, 'Schizzo monografico della camorra carceraria', in *Allegazioni e discorsi in materia penale*, Florence, 1881. Article by a magistrate involved in prosecuting the prison camorra.

F.M. Snowden, *Naples in the time of cholera, 1884–1911*, Cambridge, 1995.

P. Turiello, *Governo e governati in Italia*, P. Bevilacqua (ed.), Turin, 1980 (1882).

P. Villari, 'La camorra', in *idem., Le lettere meridionali ed altri scritti sulla questione sociale in Italia*, Florence, 1878.

4: THE 'NDRANGHETA EMERGES, 1880–1902

Court rulings on the emergence of the 'ndrangheta:
ASRC:

Tribunale Reggio Calabria, Sentenze, 16/7/1890, n. 301, Arnone Alessandro + 36. Based in Reggio. One of several cases where prostitutes testify against the *picciotti*.

Ditto, 12/3/1896, Triveri Giacomo + 4. A group tried for petty thefts in Gherio. The criminal association element of the prosecution is not proven.

Ditto, 16/11/1896, n. 1028, Attinà Domenico + 18. A group based in Condofuri, Casalnuovo and Roccaforte. One witness blames the railways for the spread of the picciotteria. Several local notables testify against the *picciotti*, despite having relatives in the gang, whose members have 'trying it on with women' among their aims.

Ditto, 7/9/1897, Arena Michele + 57. A large group based in Reggio.

Ditto, 7/10/1899, n. 22. A case based in Melito, which sees *picciotto* Beniamino Capri sentenced to six months for rape and membership of a criminal association.

ASC:

Corte di Appello delle Calabrie, Guzzi Giovanni + 2, 4/9/1877. A case in Nicastro involving ex-cons.

Sezione accusa, Zema Demetrio + 5, 23/10/1878. A case in Gallina (just outside Reggio Calabria) where a man imprisoned for assault in 1872 was released in 1876 and formed a criminal association. The gang, who practised extortion, are accused of shooting a man in the head for offending Zema's 'concubine'.

Sezione accusa, Serraino Giuseppe + 7, 23/12/1879. Here the 'criminal association' charge is dismissed.

Sezione accusa, Battista Antonino + 16, 17/12/1879. A group of thieves, one of whom had a record as a prison *camorrista*, but who do not create a formal criminal association; based in the Palmi area.

Sezione accusa, Voce Vincenzo + 2, 30/06/1882. A classic tale of factional rivalry between wealthy families rather than an organised crime episode. Three brothers in Bruzzano are accused of hiring a killer to eliminate one of the opposing clan; one of the brothers is a judge.

Sezione accusa, Barbaro Felice + 6, 23/4/1883. Municipal corruption in the Locride. As yet no criminal association element, it would seem. This case and the previous one show the Calabria that would prove vulnerable to the emergence of the picciotteria.

Sezione accusa, Anania Giuseppe + 27, 21/4/1884. The first signs of the picciotteria in Nicastro, dating back to 1883. All of the accused are ex-cons, and they have links with Ciccio Cappuccio, the 'Little Lord Frankie' of the Neapolitan camorra. Pimping is their primary source of income.

Corte di Appello delle Calabrie, Crocè Paolo + 3, 22/3/1884. Four *picciotti* from Reggio Calabria appeal against their convictions.

Sezione accusa, Romeo Bruno + 27, 7/12/1899. *Picciotti* from S. Cristina.

Sezione accusa, Auteri Felice + 316, 7/12/1899. The picciotteria centred in Iatrinoli, Radicena and Cittanova in the Plain of Gioia Tauro. A vast prosecution based on the evidence of a killer from the gang who was not offered help by his comrades once he had been arrested.

The leader is a 39-year-old shepherd. He and his men stole cattle and forced landowners to take *picciotti* on as guards.

Corte di Appello delle Calabrie, Auteri Felice + 229, 25/2/1901. A later stage in the same trial – the document is particularly insightful on the *picciotti*'s attitude to women. Ciconte reads this trial as an example of dynastic marriages in the picciotteria. But while there are two marriages mentioned, it seems to me that we are still clearly in a milieu dominated by face-slashings and petty conflicts of 'honour' over prostitutes, of a kind familiar from the world of the Neapolitan camorra. The bosses, nonetheless, are said to have 'risen from squalor' and 'accumulated a fortune'.

Sources consulted throughout this section:

Cronaca di Calabria. This weekly has occasionally good coverage of the picciotteria emergency. For the quotation from the initiation ritual ('Are you comfortable? Very comfortable!), see 'La mala vita a Palmi', 30/09/1896. The Trimboli testimony on the myth of the Spanish knights is in 'La mala vita a Palmi' 11/03/97. On the 'innately wicked' well-to-do *africoti*, see 12/03/96.

G. Cingari, *Storia della Calabria dall'Unità a oggi*, Rome-Bari, 1983.

G. Cingari, *Reggio Calabria*, Rome-Bari, 1988.

G. Cingari, 'Tra brigantaggio e "picciotteria": Giuseppe Musolino', in *idem, Brigantaggio, proprietari e contadini nel Sud*, Reggio Calabria, 1976.

E. Ciconte, *'Ndrangheta dall'Unità a oggi*, Rome-Bari, 1992. Ciconte in particular identifies evidence of what he believes is a mafia presence in Calabria before the 1880s. My interpretation of that evidence, broadly speaking, is that it represents localised instances where the prison camorra established a temporary bridgehead in the outside world – a bridgehead that would turn into a full-scale colonisation in the 1880s and 1890s. The quotation about the 'the wails of the wounded and dying' being audible before the Angelus is cited from Ciconte, p. 211.

F. Piselli and G. Arrighi, 'Parentela, clientela e comunità', in P. Bevilacqua and A. Placanica, *Storia d'Italia. Le regioni dall'Unità a oggi. La Calabria*, Turin, 1985. Important on society and the economy in the Plain of Gioia Tauro, but does not square that socio-economic profile with the available evidence on the nature of the early picciotteria.

P. Bevilacqua, 'Uomini, terre, economie' in P. Bevilacqua and A. Placanica, *Storia d'Italia. Le regioni dall'Unità a oggi, La Calabria*, Turin, 1985. Another fundamental study, which is particularly good on the vulnerability of the peasantry. Again it would be interesting to match this account of the family's role in the peasant economy with what we know about the nature of the picciotteria. For the moment, it is the *contrast* between the peasant family and the gangs that is most striking.

V. Cappelli, 'Politica e politici', in P. Bevilacqua and A. Placanica, *Storia d'Italia. Le regioni dall'Unità a oggi, La Calabria*, Turin, 1985. Particularly important for the effects of the electoral reforms of the 1880s.

Harsh mountain

K. Baedeker, *Italy. Handbook for Travellers*. Third Part: *Southern Italy and Sicily*, London, 1869.

P. Borzomati, *La Calabria dal 1882 al 1892 nei rapporti dei prefetti*, Reggio Calabria, 2001. Contains the first reports on a substantial mafia presence in Reggio.

L. Costanzo, *Storia delle ferrovie in Calabria*, Cosenza, 2005.

L. Franchetti, *Condizioni economiche ed amministrative delle province napoletane*, Florence, 1875. Franchetti does use the m-word on one occasion, on p. 155. 'I hear tell that quite a few big landowners who live in the big cities are, as it were, excluded from their estates by a kind of maffia of middle-class people who rent those estates. But this phenomenon is not as generalised as some people seem to believe'. Franchetti does not give enough information for us to be able to interpret this observation. We know of course that he would go on to write a famous study of the 'middle-class villains' of Sicily (his term), so we can be sure that the Tuscan intellectual had no qualms about denouncing the mafia when he saw it. The best we can do, perhaps, is to add this isolated note to the list of fragmentary sightings of Calabrian *mafiosi* before the 1880s.

F. Manduca, *Studii sociologici*, Naples, 1888. Manduca, a magistrate, tells us that as chief prosecuting magistrate (*procuratore del Re*) in Reggio Calabria he was friends with some politicians who had been imprisoned under the Bourbons who, they alleged, put *mafiosi* and *camorristi* in their cells to provoke them and cause trouble; they had to defend themselves with knives. We can add this reference to the list of early mentions of organised crime in Calabria.

G. Verga, 'Fantasticheria', in *idem, Vita dei campi*, Milan, 1880.

U. Zanotti-Bianco, 'Tra la perduta gente – Africo', in *idem, Tra la perduta gente*, Milan, 1959.

The following maps allow one to trace the progress of railway construction through the areas of 'high mafia density' (to use an Italian phrase) in Calabria:

Corpo di Stato Maggiore, *Carta delle strade ferrate del Regno d'Italia in esercizio nell'Aprile del 1869*.

Comando del Corpo di Stato Maggiore (Direzione Trasporti), *Carta delle ferrovie e delle linee di navigazione del Regno d'Italia*, Istituto Topografico Militare, gennaio 1877.

Ditta Artaria, *Carta speciale delle ferrovie e della navigazione in Europa*, Milan, 1878.

Comando del Corpo di Stato Maggiore (Direzione Trasporti), *Carta della ferrovie e della linee di navigazione del Regno d'Italia*, Istituto Geografico Militare, 1883.

Carta delle ferrovie, telegrafi, tramways a vapore e corsi d'acqua navigabili del Regno, Milan, 1886.

Cesare Ramoni, *Ferrovie italiane nel 1890. Carta completa delle reti ferroviarie*, Milan, 1890.

Istituto Geografico Militare, *Carta delle ferrovie e delle linee di navigazione del Regno d'Italia*, Edizione giugno 1891.

Carta della ferrovie e delle linee di navigazione del Regno d'Italia, Istituto Geografico Militare, gennaio 1894.

The figure of 1,854 people successfully prosecuted for membership of the picciotteria between 1885 and 1902 comes from a speech by the prosecutor Sansone in the Musolino trial, as reported in *Giornale d'Italia,* 1/5/1902.

The tree of knowledge

I have used the following documents to try and reconstruct the emergence of the 'ndrangheta in the Plain of Gioia Tauro chronologically:

ASC, Sezione Accusa. Corte d'appello di Catanzaro, Lisciotto Francesco + 23, v. 133, 18/1/1889.

ASC, Sezione Accusa. Corte d'appello di Catanzaro, Sciarrone Giovanbattista + 95, v. 137, 21/2/1890.

ASC, Corte d'appello delle Calabrie. Tripodi Carmine, v. 323, 27/8/1890.

ASC, Corte d'appello delle Calabrie. Calia Michelangelo + 65, v. 324, 14/10/1890.

ASC, Corte d'appello delle Calabrie. Marino Francesco + 147, v. 336, 9/9/1892. The trial that mentions the two oathed women members of the picciotteria.

ASC, Corte d'appello delle Calabrie. Saccà Rocco + 45, v. 364, 31/5/1897. This is the trial based on the testimony of Pasquale Trimboli, who gives us our first evidence of the myth of the three Spanish knights.

La Ragione. This local paper was threatened by the *picciotti* and covered its emergence in Palmi in 1888 closely. The paper was also concerned about the relationship between the police and the gangs: 'the police should not trust anyone they pay for information, because such people perhaps belong to the gangs themselves: instead of uncovering the criminal cabals, these informers help cover them up' (1/4/1888).

Zivì. A radical paper that on 16/6/1895 complains about the overly friendly relations between the police and *picciotti* in Palmi.

F. Arcà, *Calabria vera. Appunti statistici ed economici sulla provincia di Reggio*, Reggio Calabria, 1907.

G. A. Carbone, 'Cenni sull'agricoltura ed industrie agrarie del circondario di Palmi', *L'Agricoltura e le Industrie Agrarie*, 15/4/1893. The first of a series of articles running until 15/10/1893 that are essential on the economic background to the emergence of the picciotteria.

N. Marcone, *Un viaggio in Calabria. Impressioni e ricordi*, Roma, 1885.

Darkest Africo

The following court documents from the ASRC constitute the most concentrated documentation from any early 'ndrangheta trial. They include the voluminous court papers, including witness statements, and the judges' rulings from the four trials of the Africo picciotteria: three groups of defendants prosecuted separately as part of the same criminal association and a smaller group accused of murdering the main witness in the case, Pietro Maviglia.

ASRC, Tribunale penale di Reggio, b. 750, inv. 68, vol. 1, 2. Associazione a delinquere 1887–1894.

ASRC, Tribunale penale di Reggio, b. 154, inv. 68, fasc. 4. Assise RC. Procedimento contro Callea Domenico +10 per l'omicidio di Maviglia Pietro 1894.

ASRC, Tribunale penale di Reggio, b. 543, inv. 68, no. 3069. Procedimento contro Ioffrida Domenico di Roghudi + 39 associazione a delinquere 1896.

ASRC, Tribunale Reggio Calabria, Sentenza 25/3/1896, Velonà Filippo + 29.

ASRC, Tribunale Reggio Calabria, Sentenza 27/4/1896, n. 210, Ioffrida Domenico + 39.

ASRC, Tribunale Reggio Calabria, Sentenza 26/5/1896, n. 444, Favasuli Bartolo + 29.

C. Alvaro, *Polsi nell'arte, nella leggenda, nella storia*, Reggio Calabria, 2005 (1912).

G. Chirico, *Una vicenda giudiziaria di associazione per delinquere di tipo mafioso nella provincia di Reggio Calabria (1890–1900)*, Tesi di Laurea, Facoltà di Scienze Politiche, Università degli Studi di Messina, 1989–90. A precocious analysis of part of the above material.

P. Martino, 'Per la storia della 'ndrànghita', *Biblioteca di Ricerche Linguistiche e Filologiche*, vol. 25, no. 1, 1988. Very useful on the jargon of the picciotteria and its derivation.

G. Postiglione, *Relazione statistica dei lavori compiuti nel circondario del tribunale civile e penale di Palmi nell'anno 1890*, Palmi, 1891.

J. Steinberg, *The Number. One man's search for identity in the Cape underworld and prison gangs*, Johannesburg, 2004.

F. Varese, *The Russian Mafia. Private Protection in a New Market Economy*, Oxford, 2001. An excellent account of the Russian mafia.

The King of Aspromonte

Archival sources:

ASRC, Gabinetto di Prefettura, n. 1089, Associazione a delinquere in S. Stefano, b. 27, inv. 34. Mangione's reports on the picciotteria in Musolino's hometown. Includes remarkable material on Musolino's sisters.

ASRC, Gabinetto di Prefettura, Serie prima, affari riservati. Bandito Musolino. The vast collection of documents on the Musolino case. See for example:

Ditto, b. 2, fasc. 11. Delegati di PS impegnati nella cattura di Musolino, sottofasc. Mangione. On the policeman who investigated the picciotteria in Santo Stefano.

Ditto, b. 2, fasc. 23. Stampa. Notizie sul brigante Musolino. Press clippings on Musolino that show how worried the authorities were about the growth of his mythical status as an innocent avenger.

Ditto, b. 2, fasc. 13. Favoreggiatori. A collection of false leads from all over Italy and the USA.

Press: I have followed the Musolino trial in *Giornale d'Italia* and *Avanti!* (April-June, 1902).

G. Cingari, 'Tra brigantaggio e "picciotteria": Giuseppe Musolino', in *idem*, *Brigantaggio, proprietari e contadini nel Sud*, Reggio Calabria, 1976. Fundamental for all aspects of the Musolino case. The brigand's open letter to *La Tribuna*, dated 28/3/1900, is quoted from Cingari.

N. Douglas, *Old Calabria*, London, 1983 (1915).

E. Morselli and S. De Sanctis, *Biografia di un bandito. Giuseppe Musolino di fronte alla psichiatria ed alla sociologia*, Milan, 1903.

M. Pascoli, *Lungo la vita di Giovanni Pascoli*, Milan, 1961.

A. Rossi, 'Alla ricerca di Musolino', *L'Adriatico*, 11/2/1901. The first of a brilliant series of twenty articles (most published under the title 'Nel regno di Musolino') running until 6/4/1901.

5: MEDIA DONS, 1899–1915

Bankers and Men of Honour / Floriopolis / Four trials and a funeral

ACS, DGPS, aa.gg.rr. Atti speciali (1898–1940), b. 1, fasc. 1, 'The Sangiorgi Report'. It is worth noting that there were some links between Palizzolo and the *mafiosi* detailed in Sangiorgi's report. The MP provided character references for some of the Men of Honour whose gun licences the Chief of Police confiscated. Palizzolo's favourite Villabate *cosca* sold stolen cattle through the same Palermo butcher who hosted summits attended by Antonino Giammona, Francesco Siino, *et al*.

There is information on Sangiorgi's activities as Chief of Police of Palermo in the Sangiorgi career files, including the transfer notification telegram I quote.

The best accounts of the Notarbartolo affair are in:

S. Lupo, *Storia della mafia*, Rome, 1996. The quote from the police on Palizzolo as 'the mafia's patron' is quoted on p. 115. Lupo also describes Ignazio Florio's free ride during the trial as 'miraculous'.

G. Barone, 'Egemonie urbane e potere locale (1882–1913)', in M.

Aymard and G. Giarrizzo (eds), *Storia d'Italia. Le regioni dall'Unità a oggi. La Sicilia*, Turin, 1987. Florio on the mafia as 'an invention created to calumny Sicily' is quoted on p. 317. The quotation about the fear among honest journalists is from p. 314. Cosenza quoted on the 'priests of Themis' is on p. 325.

There are also useful points in:
F. Renda, *Socialisti e cattolici in Sicilia (1900-1904)*, Caltanissetta, 1972.
F. Renda, *Storia della mafia*, Palermo, 1997. The quotation on 'the high mafia planned the murder long in advance' is on p. 147.

N. Colajanni, *La Sicilia dai borboni ai sabaudi (1860-1900)*, Milan, 1951.
L. Notarbartolo, *Memorie della vita di mio padre*, Pistoia, 1949. On the *Tribuna Giudiziaria* being close to Cosenza, see p. 365.
R. Poma, *Onorevole alzatevi!*, Florence, 1976. Quotes the lines on the Florence verdict hailed as a sign of national unity.
S. Sonnino, *Diario 1866–1912*, vol. 1, Bari, 1972. On the possibility of an early election due to the first Notarbartolo trial.

I followed the various trials in a number of newspapers:
Avanti! On Palizzolo's convulsive laughter at the verdict 1/8/1902.
Corriere della Sera. On Palizzolo 'accessible to the voters', 1–2/10/1901 (quoted in Lupo, *Storia della mafia*, p. 111).
Daily Express. On the Florence verdict, 25/7/1904.
Giornale di Sicilia. 'La questione Avellone', 2–3/4/1892 (quoted in O. Cancila, *Palermo*, Bari, 2000, pp. 234–5). For the new prefect's proclamation of a campaign against extortion, see 14–15/9/1898. On how well respected the Giammona family were, 13–14/5/1901. On the Giammonas' generosity: 20-21/5/1901. On the mafia as a 'hypertrophy of individualism', 24–25/5/1901. Interestingly the full quote comes word-for-word from Cosenza's 1900 speech opening the judicial year (see Renda, *Socialisti e cattolici*, p. 408). Cosenza also quotes Giuseppe Falcone, a lawyer of Palizzolo's and the man responsible for trying to smear Sangiorgi at the end of the story. On Sangiorgi's death, 4–5/11/1908.

Il Mattino. On Sangiorgi's death, 4–5/11/1908.

Morning Post. On the hypocrisy at the pro-Notarbartolo demonstration, see 22/12/1899.

L'Ora. On the mafia as 'rustic chivalry' 5–6/6/1901. For the letter slandering Sangiorgi, 19–20/11/1903. On Sangiorgi's death, 4/11/1908.

Resto del Carlino. Sangiorgi on 'the mafia is powerful', 30-31/10/1901.

The St Louis Republic. 'The bandit-king's levee' (anon), 14/1/1900. For the scene at Palizzolo's bedroom receptions.

The Times. On Leopoldo Notarbartolo's 'sobriety, scrupulous attention to fact', 18/10/1901.

Tribuna Giudiziaria. See 29/11/1903 and the article 'Commedia poliziesca' for Sangiorgi's 'slanderous' testimony.

The criminal Atlantic

C. Alvaro, 'La fibbia', *Corriere della Sera*, 17/9/1955. For the anecdote about the 'association' in San Luca.

G. Cingari, *Storia della Calabria dall'Unità a oggi*, Rome-Bari, 1983.

G. Cingari, *Reggio Calabria*, Rome-Bari, 1988. On the picciotteria in the aftermath of the earthquake of 1908.

D. Critchley, *The Origin of Organised Crime in America. The New York City Mafia, 1891–1931*, London, 2009. Marshalls a vast amount of excellent documentation but is marred by its lack of knowledge of the best Italian studies on the mafia, which leads, for example, to his taking the Sicilians like Joe Bonanno at their word on 'honour' and such like. All the same, Critchley's book is important in that it is the first to assemble an overview involving both Campanian and Calabrian gangs as well as Sicilians. I have drawn on Critchley for Erricone's time in New York, among other things.

P.Y. Herchenroether, *Helltown. The Story of the Hillsville Black Hand*, unpublished typescript, kindly provided by the author. On picciotteria-style gangs among miners in Pennsylvania.

S. Lupo, *Quando la mafia trovò l'America. Storia di un intreccio intercontinentale, 1888–2008*, Turin, 2008. Among many other things, Lupo quotes Antonio Musolino's statement to the police.

New York Times. 'By order of the mafia', 22/10/1888. Salvatore Lupo identifies this first mafia murder in the USA. Walter Little-field, 'Criminal band that murdered Petrosino in police coils', 11/9/1910.

The ASRC contains some interesting files on the re-importation of the Black Hand into Calabria and on links between Calabrian gangs and the mining communities of the USA:

Tribunale penale Reggio Calabria, 1906, b. 981, fasc. 11156, Leone Antonino +63, Associazione a delinquere mano nera.

Ditto, b. 993, fasc. 11732. Ignoti: minacce.

Ditto, b. 1028, fasc. 12896. Romeo Francesco e altri (11/1907).

The 'high' camorra / The camorra in straw-yellow gloves / Gennaro Abbatemaggio: Genialoid / The strange death of the Honoured Society

F. Barbagallo, *Il Mattino degli Scarfoglio, 1892–1928*, Milan, 1979.

F. Barbagallo, *Stato, parlamento e lotte politico-sociali nel Mezzogiorno (1900-1914)*, Naples, 1980. On Peppuccio Romano, among other things.

F. Barbagallo, *Storia della camorra*, Rome-Bari, 2010.

R. Canosa, *Storia della criminalità in Italia, 1845–1945*, Turin, 1991. The request from the *carabinieri* for more money to pay witnesses is quoted on p. 291.

E. Ciccotti, *Come divenni e come cessai di essere deputato di Vicaria*, Naples, 1909. On the election and the camorra in tricolour cockades once more.

E. De Cosa, *Camorra e malavita a Napoli agli inizi del Novecento*, Cerchio, 1989 (1908).

G. Garofalo, *La seconda guerra napoletana*, Naples, 1984.

G. Machetti, 'La lobby di piazza Municipio: gli impiegati comunali nella Napoli di fine Ottocento', *Meridiana*, 38–39, 2000.

M. Marmo, '"Processi indiziari non se ne dovrebbero mai fare". Le manipolazioni del processo Cuocolo (1906–1930)', in M. Marmo and L. Musella (eds), *La costruzione della verità giudiziaria*, Naples, 2003.

M. Marmo, 'Il reato associativo tra costruzione normativa e prassi giudiziaria', in G. Civile and G. Machetti (eds), *La città e il tribunale. Diritto, pratica giudiziaria e società napoletana tra Ottocento e Novecento*, Naples, 2004.

M. Marmo, 'L'opinione pubblica nel processo penale: Giano bifronte, ovvero la verità giudiziaria contesa', *Meridiana*, 63, 2008.

F. Russo and E. Serao, *La camorra. Origini, usi, costumi e riti dell' 'annorata soggietà'*, Naples, 1907. The source of the quote on absinthe and debt.

R. Salomone, *Il processo Cuocolo*, Arpino, 1930. Contains Abbatemaggio's recantation and information on his life; also Erricone's speech at the verdict, p. 102.

F. Snowden, *The fascist revolution in Tuscany, 1919–1922*, Cambridge, 1989. On Abbatemaggio's life under Fascism.

F.M. Snowden, *Naples in the time of cholera, 1884–1911*, Cambridge, 1995.

A. Train, *Courts, Criminals and the Camorra*, London, 1912. The 'bear garden' quote is from p. 184. The 'best dressed' *camorristi* from p. 211. The 'excitability' of Italians, p. 202.

The press on the Cuocolo trial:

The Advertiser (Australia). Abbatemaggio as 'a rascal of almost inconceivably deep dye' 13/7/1912.

Bulawayo Chronicle. For the damning verdict on the Cuocolo trial, 8/9/1912.

Il Mattino. Unless otherwise stated, I have quoted from *Il Mattino*'s copious coverage. For example: Abbatemaggio's initial testimony begins on 25–6/3/1911; Abbatemaggio questioned on his theatre-going, 3–4/5/1911; Abbatemaggio's 'mnemonic and intuitive capacities', testimony of Prof Polidori 14–15/3/1911; Erricone on 'the gramophone', 29–30/3/1911; Erricone on the 'sons of Vesuvius', 1–2/4/1911; on the pederast / spitting episode, 3–4/5/1911; Fabroni's testimony, with its accusations against Abbatemaggio, begins on

13–14/7/1911; Simonetti testimony, 9–10/6/1911; Catalano testimony, 22–23/6/1911; Ametta testimony and Erricone's outburst, 23–24/6/1911; on the *camorrista*'s printed defence and 'rustic chivalry', 20-21/3/1911.

New York Times. 'The greatest criminal trial of the age', 11/9/1910; 'Camorrist told all to win his bride', 6/3/1911; 'the black vitals of the criminal hydra', 11/9/1910; 'one of the most remarkable feats of detection', 15/1/1912.

Otautau Standard and Wallace County Chronicle (New Zealand). One of many papers across the world to use the Sherlock Holmes parallel.

La Stampa. Curiously, Gennaro Abbatemaggio kept himself in the headlines by claiming to know important inside details of the Matteotti murder; he gave evidence at the trial. See 'Le rivelazioni di Abbatemaggio sulla premeditazione dell'assassinio Matteotti', *La Stampa*, 7/9/1924. After the war, Abbatemaggio tried and failed to get a film of the Cuocolo trial made, and was also prosecuted in 1954 for falsely claiming to have crucial information on the notorious Montesi murder case. See 'Gennaro Abbatemaggio arrestato per le sue false dichiarazioni', *La Stampa*, 24/8/1954.

Washington Times, 12/9/1910.

6: MUSSOLINI'S SCALPEL, 1922–1943

Sicily: The last struggle with the mafia / Sicily: The slimy octopus

ASPA, Questura, Affari generali, 1935, b. 2196. Questura di Palermo. Archivio Generale b. 2196 Anno 1935. R. Ispettorato generale di PS per la Sicilia – Nucleo centrale Carabinieri reali, Processo verbale di denunzia di 175 individui responsabili di associazione per delinquere (16 luglio 1938).

Manchester Guardian. Ascension Day speech, 27/5/1927.

New York Times. 27/5/1927; 'signs of increasing megalomania', 29/5/1927.

M. Allegra, 'Come io, medico, diventai un mafioso', *Giornale di Sicilia*, 22–23/1/1962.

M. Allegra, 'La mafia mi ordinò di entrare in politica', *Giornale di Sicilia*, 23–24/1/1962.

M. Allegra, 'Tutti gli uomini della "cosca"', *Giornale di Sicilia*, 24–25/1/1962. Intriguingly, Allegra mentions Ernesto Marasà, says he has more to say about him, and then does not return to the subject.

M. Andretta, 'I corleonesi e la storia della mafia. Successo, radicamento e continuità', *Meridiana*, 54, 2005.

A. Blando, 'L'avvocato del diavolo', *Meridiana*, 63, 2008.

A. Calderone, *Gli uomini del disonore*, (ed. P. Arlacchi), Milan, 1992.

V. Coco, 'Dal passato al futuro: uno sguardo dagli anni trenta', *Meridiana*, 63, 2008.

V. Coco and M. Patti, 'Appendice', *Meridiana*, 63, 2008. A breakdown of trials following the Mori operation.

V. Coco, 'La mafia dell'agro palermitano nei processi del periodo fascista', in G. Gribaudi (ed.), *Traffici criminali. Camorra, mafie e reti internazionali dell'illegalità*, Turin, 2009.

F. Di Bartolo, 'Imbrigliare il conflitto sociale. Mafiosi, contadini, latifondisti', *Meridiana*, 63, 2008.

M. Di Figlia, 'Mafia e nuova politica fascista', *Meridiana*, 63, 2008.

C. Duggan, *Fascism and the Mafia*, New Haven, 1989. Duggan's study remains important for the context to the Mori Operation. But the book is best known for the thesis that the mafia-as-organisation was invented by Fascism as a pretext to exert political control over Sicily. That thesis was controversial at the time of publication, and it is now contradicted by a crushing weight of evidence.

S. Lupo, *Storia della mafia*, Rome, 1996. Mori 'on heat' for the nobility, quoted p. 182.

C. Mori, *The Last Struggle with the Mafia*, London, 1933.

C. Mori, *Con la mafia ai ferri corti*, Naples, 1993 (1932).

B. Mussolini, 'Discorso dell'Ascensione', 26/5/1927, in *idem*, *Opera Omnia*, ed. E. Susmel and D. Susmel, 44 vols, Florence, 1951–80, vol. 22.

M. Patti, 'Sotto processo. Le cosche palermitane', *Meridiana*, 63, 2008.

V. Scalia, 'Identità sociali e conflitti politici nell'area dell'interno', *Meridiana*, 63, 2008.

A. Spanò, *Faccia a faccia con la mafia*, Milan, 1978. For Mori's lifestyle in Palermo, p. 38.

I have estimated the extent of Marasà's wealth using www.measuringworth.com (the unskilled wage index) 1938–2009.

Campania: Buffalo soldiers / Campania: The Fascist Vito Genovese

Comando Generale dell'Arma dei Carabinieri. Ufficio Storico, various reports from the career of Vincenzo Anceschi, including *Bollettino Ufficiale dei Carabinieri Reali* 1919 (p. 214), 1927 (p. 109), 1929 (pp. 330, 461, 585, 871), 1930 (p. 882).

E. Anceschi, *I Carabinieri reali contro la camorra*, Rome, 2003. Includes the article from *Il Mezzogiorno*, 2–3/6/27 on which I base my description of the Mazzoni.

L. Avella, *Cronaca nolana. Dalla Monarchia alla Repubblica*, vol. 7, *1926–1943*, Naples, 2002. For the quote on Vito Genovese's donation.

F. Barbagallo, *Storia della camorra*, Rome-Bari, 2010. On 'Little Joey', pp. 86–88.

O. Bordiga, *Inchiesta parlamentare sulle condizioni dei contadini nelle provincie meridionali e nella Sicilia*, vol. IV, *Campania*, tomo I, *Relazione*, Rome 1909. On the 'tribes' of the Mazzoni.

P. Frascani, 'Mercato e commercio a Napoli dopo l'Unità', in P. Macry, and P. Villani, (eds.), *Storia d'Italia. Le regioni dall'Unità a oggi. La Campania*, Turin, 1990.

G. Gribaudi, 'Guappi, camorristi, killer. Interpretazioni letterarie, immagini sociali, e storie giudiziarie', in *Donne, uomini, famiglie*, Naples, 1999. On the *guappo*.

M. Marmo, 'Tra le carceri e il mercato. Spazi e modelli storici del fenomeno camorrista', in P. Macry and P. Villani (eds), *La Campania*, part of *Storia d'Italia. Le regioni dall'Unità a oggi*, Turin, 1990. The best starting point for the history of the camorra outside Naples itself.

P. Monzini, *Gruppi criminali a Napoli e a Marsiglia. La delinquenza organizzata nella storia di due città (1820-1990)*, Rome, 1999. On the obscure fate of the camorra after the Honoured Society, pp. 53–.

H.S. Nelli, *The Business of Crime. Italians and Syndicate Crime in the United States*, New York, 1976. On Genovese and Fascism.

C. Petraccone, *Le «due Italie». La questione meridionale tra realtà e rappresentazione*, Rome-Bari, 2005. On Fascism's ban on 'Mezzogiorno', p. 190.

Il Mattino. The articles triggered by the Nola murders run through August and September, 1911. See esp., 9–10/8/1911 'Il brigantaggio nell'Agro nolano'; and on the 'crass ignorance' and 'bloodthirsty instincts' in the Mazzoni, 'Brigantaggio nei Mazzoni di Capua', 18–19/9/1911. I have followed Anceschi's operation in *Il Mattino* (November 1926 to May 1927).

Roma. Also contains extensive coverage of Anceschi's operation (November 1926 to June 1927). On the funeral interrupted by Anceschi's men, 1/1/1927, 'I maggiori maladrini avversani tratti in arresto mentre accompagnano in camposanto la salma del loro "capintesta"'.

Calabria: The flying boss of Antonimina /
Calabria: What does not kill me, makes me stronger /
Calabria: A clever, forceful and wary woman/
Master Joe dances a *tarantella*

Overview of archival sources on the 'ndrangheta under Fascism:

ASRC:
Tribunale di Reggio Calabria, Sentenze, 6/6/1923 n. 15, Battaglia Giuseppe + 46, vol. 206.
Ditto, 1/12/1924, Callea Giovanni + 8, vol. 210.

Ditto, 18/2/1924, Calù Clemente + 25, vol. 208.

Ditto, 23/9/1924, Palamara Francesco + 6, vol. 210. A Casalnuovo-based group that decide to punish anyone who voted Fascist in the local elections. They are acquitted on the grounds of insufficient evidence.

Ditto, 15/4/1926, n. 192, Minniti Antonio, vol. 215.

Ditto, 2/8/1926 n. 395, Mafrici Stefano + 13, vol. 216.

Ditto, 7/5/1927 n. 153, De Gaetano Andrea + 28, vol. 218. Three of the accused get themselves photographed with pistols pointing at a sheet of paper and raising hands as if to take an oath. They are all acquitted.

Ditto, 29/3/1927, Schimizzi Giacomo + 64, vol. 217. In Melito the gang initiation oath emerges from insider evidence: 'before us there is a tomb covered in flowers, and he who breaches secrecy will receive five dagger blows to the chest'. The judge explains why such insider evidence often emerges: 'judicial psychology teaches us, members of criminal associations always betray one another'.

Ditto, 13/7/1928 n. 395, Bruzzaniti Giovanni + 51, vol. 224. A case in Africo where there was an upsurge in picciotteria violence after the First World War. The judge lamely blames 'social causes' and reduces the sentences on the grounds that the culprits are reformed characters.

Ditto, 19/6/1928, Putortì Vittorio +5, vol. 223.

Ditto, 14/8/1930, Passalacqua Giuseppe + 19, vol. 234. A nasty case involving the rape of a retarded prostitute.

Ditto, 26/5/1930 n. 341, Curatola Francesco, vol. 232.

Ditto, 12/6/1931 n. 524, Altomonte Carmelo + 8, vol. 238.

Ditto, 16/7/1931 n. 752, De Gaetano Domenico + 20, vol. 239. Describes a battle for territory in San Roberto (nr Villa San Giovanni) between Fascists and *picciotti*. The latter have a close web of kinship and marriage ties between them.

Ditto, 6 *aprile* 1933 n. 174, Spanò Demetrio + 106, vol. senza numero *Anno* 1933 – *dal* 15 *gennaio al* 30 *aprile*. Trial of a whole network of picciotteria groups in Reggio Calabria. The leaders pimp and extort money from junior members. A detailed picture of the organisation emerges. There is, as always, a *Società minore* and a *Società maggiore*, but the latter is further divided between the *Società in testa* a.k.a. *Gran criminale* grouped around the boss, and the *Società indrina* of which there are several based in different quarters of the city.

ASC:

Corte di Appello di Catanzaro, Sentenze, 7/6/1922, De Paola Gregorio + 11, vol. 486.

Ditto, 8/8/1923, Noto Domenico + 46, vol. 489. The flying boss.

Ditto, 14/11/1923, Alfinito Donato + 36, vol. 489. Prosecution of a group in Petronà. Two women accused of being in the *cosca* are acquitted for insufficient evidence. The boss was unseated because his wife betrayed him, ostensibly.

Ditto, 16/4/1923, Costa Salvatore + 6 , vol. 488.

Ditto, 19/7/1924, Bruzzi Camillo + 18, vol. 491. From Radicena and Gioia Tauro. The gang's practice of forced initiation produces a witness for the prosecution.

Ditto, 11/3/1925, Cotela Giuseppe + 14, vol. 492. Some members admit the existence of the association, based in Serrata. Forcible enlisting of members still practised, at least according to some witnesses.

Ditto, 19/12/1925, Barbara Antonio + 35, vol. 494.

Ditto, 26/1/1925, Panucci Gesuele + 17, vol. 492.

Ditto, 22/5/1926, Fabrizio Giuseppe + 26, v. 495. Like many rulings, this one shows an organisation divided between *picciotti* and *camorristi*. Once again the evidence is from turncoats inside the group.

Ditto, 6/2/1926, Pandurri Pietro + 14, vol. 495.

Ditto, 10/2/1926, Facchineri Giuseppe + 18, vol. 495.

Ditto, 12/4/1926, Notarianni Vincenzo + 34, vol. 495. Dagger duels.

Ditto, 13/2/1926, Mascaro Camillo + 3, vol. 495.

Ditto, 17/3/1926, De Caro Vincenzo, vol. 495. A group in the ethnically Albanian village of Santa Sofia d'Epiro. The group kept women's clothes for disguise purposes.

Ditto, 26/4/1926, Albanese Domenico + 26, vol. 495. The ruling describes the disorder following demobilisation in Rosarno.

Ditto, 28/6/1926, Gullà Francesco, v. 496. Gullà, from Celico in the province of Cosenza, has ties with the Black Hand in the USA.

Ditto, 10/10/1927, Biancamaro Arturo + 6, vol. 500.

Ditto, 4/12/1928, Bumbaca Vincenzo + 45, vol. 505. One of several cases where the prosecution case fails to stand up.

Ditto, 8/6/1928, De Santis Giuseppe + 21, vol. 503.

Ditto, 9/7/1928, Lucà Luigi + 38, vol. 504. In Gioiosa Jonica the picciotteria calls itself the 'Montalbano family'.

Ditto, 12/11/1928, Speranza Stefano + 26, vol. 505.

Ditto, 17/12/1928, Cristiano Giuseppe + 13, vol. 505. The *Carabinieri* fail to produce enough evidence against this group from Staiti.

Ditto, 18/8/1928, Saccomanno Antonio + 11, vol. 504. The defendants are acquitted because, in the judge's view, the prosecution has not proved that this society was a *criminal* association, despite several confessions.

Ditto, 2/5/1929, Palermo Rinaldo + 48, vol. 507. Interesting case from Gerace in which the picciotteria extort bribes on marriages. Two wealthy members were acquitted on the flimsy grounds that 'it was implausible that they would have shady dealings with what was essentially a bunch of beggars'.

Ditto, 17/5/1929, Napoli Pasquale + 7, vol. 507. A spike in thefts follows the return of a *picciotto* from the United States.

Ditto, 25/11/1929, Gareri Domenico + 13, vol. 509.

Ditto, 26/9/1929, Romeo Stefano + 75, vol. 508. Important trial of the picciotteria in San Luca. Giuseppe Delfino uses the evidence of an informer (subsequently murdered) to dismantle the local cattle rustling operation.

Ditto, 1/4/1930, Gullace Domenico + 20, vol. 512.

Ditto, 6/12/1930, Spanò Vincenzo + 33, vol. 517.

Ditto, 11/7/1930, Vallone Giuseppe + 6, vol. 514.

Ditto, 13/6/1930, Carioti Francesco, vol. 513.

Ditto, 15/11/1930, Corio Santo + 144, vol. 516. Several women are involved in this clan from Palmi, Gioia Tauro and Rosarno.

Ditto, 20/10/1930, Sorace Salvatore + 9, vol. 515.

Ditto, 25/11/1930, Annacorato Vincenzo + 93, vol. 516. A 'Montalbano family' in Nicotera, Polistena and Gioia Tauro. One boy is initiated at age eleven. The judge is unsurprised that most of the evidence comes from turncoats inside the picciotteria: 'It is natural that underworld trials grow from the revelations of gangsters who betray the secrets of the sect that they were affiliated to'.

Ditto, 29/11/1930, Mollica Vincenzo + 41, vol. 516.

Ditto, 29/8/1931, Ponzano Gaetano+ 10, vol. 521.

Ditto, 1/3/1932, Lupino Giovanni + 16, vol. 525.

Ditto, 25/11/1932, Argentano Menotti + 12, vol. 529.

Ditto, 12/5/1933, Piccione Francesco + 10, vol. 531.

Ditto, 21/9/1934, Pollifrone Rocco + 22, vol. 536. The picciotteria in the Locride smuggles its stolen animals to market in the Plain of Gioia Tauro.

ASC:

Corte di Assise di Catanzaro, Sentenze, 2/11/1931, Pugliese Francesco + 4, vol. 62.

Ditto, 21/5/1932, Rosello Francesco + 2, vol. 63. A *Carabiniere* is murdered for trying to prevent an underworld marriage alliance. He may have got too close to one of the factions involved.

ASC:

Corte di Assise di Locri, Sentenze, 2/2/1933, Andrianò Vincenzo+ 8, b. 1.

Ditto, 19/7/1937, Commisso Francescantonio + 56, b. 3. The boss rules that a man spreading rumours about his wife must die, and orders a sixteen-year-old boy to perform the deed.

Ditto, 8/2/1938, Oppedisano Francesco + 5, b. 3.

Ditto, 6/9/1939, Macrì Francesco + 141, b. 4. The case involving Maria Marvelli.

Ditto, 9/2/1939, Canario Vincenzo + 26, b. 4.

ASC:

Corte di Assise di Palmi, Sentenze, 11/6/1937, Vicari Francesco, b. 3.

Ditto, 18/3/1937 Romeo Procopio +2, b. 3. A butcher in a *frazione* of Oppido Mamertina is hit by shotgun pellets in the thighs, genitals, scrotum, penis and left hand while excreting in an olive grove. There follows a chain of attacks that the judge puts down to family rivalries.

Ditto, 6/12/1938 Vinci Alfonso + 10, b. 3. Acquittals despite an outbreak of razor slashes to the face in Cittanova.

Ditto, 8/4/1938 Corso Rocco + 1, b. 3.

Ditto, 7/3/1940 Barone Michele + 37, b. 4. The gang, under the leadership of Michele Barone convicted of smothering an old lady in her bed and throwing a prostitute off a bridge, seems not to have been part of the picciotteria, despite operating in the classic 'ndrangheta territories of Polistena and Taurianova.

ASC:

Gabinetto di prefettura, Affari gen. e disposizioni riguardanti la P.S. – b. 14. On the picciotteria that has 'almost been crushed', see letter from Chief of Police to the Prefect, 21/11/1931.

Gabinetto di prefettura, Ordine Pubblico – b. 609.

Ufficio Storico Stato Maggiore Aeronautica (USSMA), Fondo aviatori Grande Guerra, b. 132, fasc. 14. Noto Domenico. The flying boss's war record.

Comando Generale dell'Arma dei Carabinieri. Ufficio Storico, various documents on the career of Giuseppe Delfino including: *Bollettino Ufficiale dei Carabinieri Reali* 1911 (p. 289), 1919 (p. 285), 1927 (p. 104); Comune di San Luca, 'Deliberazione del consiglio comunale', 4/12/1915 and another dated 14/7/1921; Partito Nazionale Fascista, Sezione de Platì, 'Deliberazione' 20/12/1926; letter from the Procuratore del Re, Gerace Marina, 3/6/1929.

Cronaca di Calabria. Has low-key coverage of the picciotteria during the early Fascist years, 1922–28. On the actions of Giuseppe Delfino, see 'Vasta associazione a delinquere', 8/12/1927.

Gazzetta di Messina e delle Calabrie, 1924–27. On Giuseppe Delfino's tireless work, see, 'Da Platì. Un maresciallo dei carabinieri che si fa onore', 3/4/1927.

Il Popolo di Calabria, 1927–30. More low-key coverage.

G. Buccini, 'I due Delfino, carabinieri, e i boss Nirta: un'epopea a Platì', *Corriere della Sera*, 16/10/1993. Delfino family lore.

L. Malafarina, 'La leggenda di Massaro Peppe', *Gazzetta del Sud*, 9/9/1986. An interview with Delfino's son.

P. Bevilacqua, *Le campagne del Mezzogiorno tra Fascismo e dopoguerra. Il caso della Calabria*, Turin, 1980.

V. Cappelli, *Il fascismo in periferia. La Calabria durante il Ventennio*, Lungro di Cosenza, 1998.

F. Cordova, *Il fascismo nel Mezzogiorno: le Calabrie*, Soveria Mannelli, 2003.

L. Izzo, *Agricoltura e classi rurali in Calabria dall'Unità al Fascismo*, Geneva, 1974.

E. Miséfari, *L'avvento del fascismo in Calabria*, Cosenza, 1980. On 'acute factionitis', p. 116.

A. Placanica, *Storia della Calabria*, Rome, 1999 (1993).

J. Steinberg, 'Fascism in the Italian South: the case of Calabria', in D. Forgacs (ed.), *Rethinking Italian Fascism. Capitalism, Populism and Culture*, London, 1986.

33. Liberation

ASRC, Tribunale di Locri, Sentenza 20/3/1937, Macrì Antonio + 12, vol. 286. Don 'Ntoni has one of his early brushes with the law.

La mafia a Montalto. Sentenza 2 ottobre 1970 del Tribunale di Locri, Reggio Calabria, 1971. Includes a detailed criminal profile of don 'Ntoni Macrì.

National Archive, London

Italy. Zone Handbook Sicily. WO 220/277.

Italy. Zone Handbook no. 3. Calabria. WO 220/278.

Italy. Zone Handbook no. 6. Campania. WO 252/804.

WO 204/9719, Sicily and Southern Italy: reports on social, economic and political aspects of provincial living conditions. 1943 Oct.-1944

Jan. Includes Lord Rennell's report from Calabria.

WO 204/11462, Psychological Warfare Branch. PWB and OSS activities reports. 1944 Dec–1945 May. Includes accounts of food riots in traditional picciotteria areas but no mention of gang activity.

WO 204/12625, Italy. Political situation. Naples and Campania. For figures on prostitution in Naples see the report reviewing the situation since Liberation, dated 19/4/1945. On the food supply from the hinterland see report dated 2/5/1945.

WO 204/12627, Italy. Political situation. Naples and Campania. On the 'fantastic gangland situation' in the hinterland north of the city see report of 21/2/1946 .

WO 204/6313, Psychological Warfare Branch. Naples: weekly reports on economic and political conditions. 1944 Apr.-Aug. Report dated 3/5/1944 on the police cut on goods coming out of the port, and on the main black market sales points in the city. Report of 23/6/1944 on the problems of those on fixed incomes. Report of 30/6/1944 on class distinctions disappearing.

WO 204/6314, Psychological Warfare Branch. Naples: weekly reports on economic and political conditions. 1944 Aug.-Oct. Report of 16/8/1944 on two kinds of spaghetti. Report of 28/9/1944 on the inactivity of the Military Police. Report of 5/10/1944 on the old crone tipping a bank clerk for counting her money. Report of 26/10/1944 (interview with woman) for the role of street-corner bosses.

WO 204/6315, Psychological Warfare Branch. Naples: weekly reports on economic and political conditions. 1944 Nov.-1945 Jan. Report of 23/11/1944 on a Casoria gang that stages train robberies between Rome and Naples.

WO 204/6277, Psychological Warfare Branch. Italy: reports on conditions in liberated areas. 1944 Jan.-Mar. Report of 28/3/1944 on the Caputos sentenced to seven years.

C. Alvaro, 'Il canto di Cosima', in *idem*, *L'amata alla finestra*, Milan, 1994.

F. Barbagallo, *Storia della camorra*, Rome-Bari, 2010. On the Giuliano boys in Forcella, p. 103.

E. Ciconte, *'Ndrangheta dall'Unità a oggi*, Rome-Bari, 1992. On mafia mayors and what little we know about this under-researched period of 'ndrangheta history, pp. 239–44.

E. Ciconte, *Storia criminale. La resistibile ascesa di mafia, 'ndrangheta e camorra dall'Ottocento ai giorni nostri*, Soveria Mannelli, 2008. On Delfino pp. 283–4.

D. Ellwood, *Italy 1943–1945*, Leicester, 1985. Also quotes Lord Rennell on mayors from an 'American gangster environment', p. 59.

N. Gentile, *Vita di capomafia*, Rome, 1993.

A. Gramsci, *Lettere dal carcere*, Turin, 1947. For an example of the prison gangs as viewed by a political prisoner under Fascism. When Antonio Gramsci, the founding member and leader of the Italian Communist Party, was jailed by Mussolini, he witnessed a camorra initiation in a Naples prison. He also saw a 'fencing academy' and a friendly duelling tournament conducted according to the rules of what he termed the 'four realms of the southern Italian underworld (the Sicilian realm, the Calabrian realm, the Puglian realm, and the Neapolitan realm)'. The weapons, in this case, were harmless: spoons rubbed against the wall so that whitewash marked hits on the duellers' clothing. But even so, the rivalry between Sicilians and Calabrians was so intense that they did not even fight with spoons in case the battle escalated. See particularly the letter dated 11/4/1927.

J. Huston, *An Open Book*, London, 1988 (1980).

N. Lewis, *Naples '44*, London, 2002 (1978). I have used Lewis's classic work of reportage here, but sparingly. After reading the manuscript notes upon which the text is based, I felt that the references to the '*zona di camorra*' in *Naples '44* were not sufficiently reliable to be used as historical evidence, and that they may well have been a product of literary licence based on Lewis's later visits to Naples and his encounters with films such as *La sfida*.

C. Malaparte, *La pelle*, Rome-Milan, 1950. 'Two dollars the boys, three dollars the girls!' p. 19.

T. Newark, *The Mafia at War: Allied collusion with the mob*, London, 2007. Quotes the OSS report ('theirs for the asking', dated 13/8/1943), pp. 209–10. On 45 per cent of Allied military cargo stolen, Newark quotes the report from Allied Civil Affairs to the War Cabinet in London 19/4/1944 (National Archive, MAF 83/1338), p. 217.

V. Paliotti, *Forcella. La Casbah di Napoli*, Naples, 2005.

E. Reid, *Mafia*, revised edn, New York, 1964. Reproduces Dickey's testimony, pp. 163–89.

C. Stajano, *Africo*, 1979. On Delfino's dancing.

'Lord Rennell', obituary in *The Geographical Journal*, vol. 144, No. 2 (July 1978).

Index